'I recommend Gary Sheffield's iconoclastic *tour de force, Forgotten Victory: The First World War — Myths and Realities*. Sheffield is one of the new generation of military historians determined to demolish the old cliché of "lions led by donkeys"' Niall Ferguson, *Sunday Telegraph*

'The second chapter, on the origins of the war, is succinct and brilliantly written, as good as AJP Taylor on form' John Keegan, *Daily Telegraph*

'Gary Sheffield, one of a new generation of World War I historians looking afresh at the hard evidence, rightly sets about redressing the balance and exploding the myth' Correlli Barnett, *Daily Mail*

'a clear and sensibly judged synthesis' Hew Strachan, *Sunday Times*

'Sheffield ... sets out the arguments for an interpretation not based exclusively on the war poets, Alan Clark and Blackadder ... One can only hope that his compassionate, clearly argued book will displace the [mythical] version' David Horspool, *Guardian*

'Anyone content with smug *Blackadder* stereotypes of generals as butchers and bunglers will find his thesis uncomfortable. But they should study this as a lively and accessible survey of half a century of revisionist research' Matthew Bennett, *BBC History Magazine*

'Sheffield['s] ... overall grasp of the problems of combat on the Western Front make this book outstanding ... The real guts of the book consists of a description of the "learning curve" of the British Army ... a topic on which Gary Sheffield is now the acknowledged expert ... for any student of the First World War, particularly beginners, this is essential reading' Sir Michael Howard, *Royal United Services Institute Journal*

'This is revisionist history at its best — thought provoking and original' Trevor Royle, *Sunday Herald*

'In *Forgotten Victory*, Gary Sheffield mounts one of the most compelling defences of the British war effort ever made; it is likely to be recommended in university courses on the First World War for years to come' William D. Rubenstein, *History Today*

'[*Forgotten Victory*] must be the first serious study of the Great War to begin with ... an analysis, not of the assassination of Archduke Franz Ferdinand or the Schlieffen Plan, but of the impact of Rowan Atkinson, Hugh Laurie and company in *Blackadder Goes Forth*' *Oxford Times*

'This devastating reappraisal of WWI reveals how Britain lost its nerve in trying to forget its greatest-ever triumph of arms. The victories of 1918 were soon forgotten as a wave of war weariness swept the country. It has been forgotten for too long just how much we owe to our grandfathers' generation' John Hughes-Wilson, *The Week*

'[Sheffield is] one of Britain's leading authorities on land warfare of the twentieth century ... [He] has been one of the leading figures who have attempted to bring a greater clarity to bear on the history of the First World War' Jon Cooksey, *Battlefields Review*

'the picture we have of the war ... is of a meaningless mud and bloodbath ... That slanted picture, Sheffield shows, wasn't how it was for the vast majority of men who fought and won the war' *Daily Express*

'For Gary Sheffield, the war, far from being some monstrous mistake, was justified to crush rampant German militarism. The British generals were not blimpish buffoons who sent thousands of men to certain death ... I trust the fruit of Dr Sheffield's decade of patient research ...' Nigel Jones, *Sunday Express*

'All in all, this is a remarkable and masterful book that is well overdue, giving a far more balanced view of the Great War which may well, at last, break through into the consciousness of our guilt-ridden nation and remind us of a truly forgotten victory' Tim Newark, *Military Illustrated*

'Gary Sheffield's *Forgotten Victory* ... is essential reading for anyone with an interest in that war, and an essential corrective to the way it is "taught" in many schools. Tragic – yes, but futile – no; wasteful – yes, but unnecessary – no' Alan Judd, *Sunday Telegraph*

FORGOTTEN
VICTORY

The First World War:
Myths and Realities

Gary Sheffield

review

First published in 2001
by HEADLINE BOOK PUBLISHING

First published in paperback in 2002
by REVIEW

An imprint of Headline Book Publishing

10 9 8 7 6 5 4 3

Maps: pages xxviii–xxix, 106, 160, 192, 193, 222, 238 adapted from Cyril Falls,
The First World War (Longman, 1960); page 76 adapted from J.M. Bourne,
Britain and the Great War (Arnold, 1989)

ISBN 0 7472 6460 0

Typeset by Palimpsest Book Production Limited,
Polmont, Stirlingshire
Printed and bound in Great Britain by
Mackays of Chatham plc, Chatham, Kent

HEADLINE BOOK PUBLISHING
A division of Hodder Headline
338 Euston Road
London NW1 3BH

www.reviewbooks.co.uk
www.hodderheadline.com

To Viv, as always

Dr Gary Sheffield is Land Warfare Historian on the Higher Command and Staff Course, Defence Studies Department, Joint Services Command and Staff College, Shrivenham, and Senior Lecturer at King's College London (War Studies Group). He is also Adjunct Professor at the University of Southern Mississippi, USA. From 1985 to 1999 he taught in the Department of War Studies, Royal Military Academy Sandhurst. A former Secretary General of the British Commission for Military History, he is a council member of the Army Records Society and was the 2000 Douglas Haig Fellow. Educated at the University of Leeds and King's College London, he has published widely on twentieth-century military history.

CONTENTS

PREFACE

At 11.00 a.m. on 11 November 2001, Armistice Day, I happened to find myself on London's Paddington Station, on my way to give a lecture at the National Army Museum. I joined a small crowd of people, clearly drawn from a wide spread of backgrounds, that had gathered around the fine war memorial. Jagger's figure of a Great War soldier, dressed for a winter's day in the trenches and reading a letter from home, is one of the most evocative and poignant memorials I know, bringing home as it does one of the commonest hardships of war − separation from loved ones. Perhaps, I thought, some of the silent and respectful crowd were remembering the pictures that had appeared in the press earlier in the year, photographs of a newly discovered mass grave of British soldiers. Victims of the 1917 Battle of Arras, their skeletal remains had been lost for eighty-four years. After a short service and the sounding of the Last Post, the crowd quietly dispersed and one of London's busiest railway stations continued about its business. Similar scenes have occurred at myriad memorials since 1918. On this occasion, the events of exactly two months earlier in New York and Washington gave the ceremony an added edge. As some commentators pointed out, many of the themes debated in the aftermath of 11 September 2001 – sacrifice, the vulnerability of populations, the demands a liberal state can place on its people – have stark parallels with the situation faced by the generation who went through the First World War. For the British public, the Great War is not mere history. It is a living reality.

For all that, the 1914–18 war is also commonly misunderstood. I wrote *Forgotten Victory* with the intention of bringing some of the new 'revisionist' thinking to a wider audience. The book seems to have achieved this ambition, judging by the coverage in the media and the number of letters and invitations to speak that I have received. Perhaps the time had come for a book of this type, an accessible text that reflected current scholarship. *Forgotten Victory* was widely reviewed – a welcome novelty for this author – and much to my surprise the reaction was mostly favourable. There were a few bad and mixed reviews, but generally speaking, those who had more than a superficial knowledge of the subject took a positive view of the book, even if they might disagree with some of my interpretations. The bad reviews demonstrated the tenacious grip of the 'lions led by donkeys' version of the war, espoused even by some who write history books for a living. Emotionally driven criticism and personal abuse are, however, no substitute for analysis based on a firm grasp of the facts.

I have been much encouraged by those readers who have written to me along the lines of 'my father/grandfather who served in the Great War would have approved of your book'. It seems clear that many who fought in that war did not hold the view that it was futile, and maintained their pride in their achievements to the end of their days.

The health and vitality of the debate on the 1914–18 war is demonstrated by the recent publication of a number of important books. I would like to mention just four. *To Arms*, the first volume of Hew Strachan's *The First World War* (Oxford University Press, 2001) is a magisterial work that sets the standard for the rest of us to follow. Also impressive in its breadth of scholarship is Ian Beckett's *The Great War 1914–1918* (Longman, London, 2001). In *Seeking Victory on the Western Front* (University of Nebraska, Lincoln and London, 2000) Albert Palazzo demonstrates, by means of a study of chemical warfare, the effectiveness of the BEF's style of war, and the extent to which it outfought the Germans. Finally, Cathryn Corns and John Hughes-Wilson in their *Blindfold and Alone: British Military Executions in the Great War* (Cassell, London, 2001) bring some much needed perspective and cool analysis to this most emotive of subjects.

However, the traditional view of the British army is far from dead. It took particularly vigorous form in John Mosier's *The Myth of the Great War* (Profile Books, London, 2001). Like Paul Fussell, John Mosier is an American professor of English, rather than an historian by background. He argues that the Germans were militarily superior in every way, the British army being particularly inept, and the war was won only by the intervention of tactically excellent American forces. This interpretation is diametrically opposed to the one presented in this book, and indeed to much other recent scholarly work on the British and US armies in the Great War. Thus eighty-eight years on from the first shots being fired, the First World War retains its ability to shock and cause public controversy. If *Forgotten Victory* contributes in a small way to inform the debate, it will have served its purpose.

I would like to thank a number of people who have helped in all manner of ways since the publication of the hardback edition of *Forgotten Victory*. At Headline, Lucy Ramsey handled the publicity in an exemplary fashion. Colonel John Hughes-Wilson has enthusiastically championed the book and its author. Annie Maddison and Sarah Landa-Font of the JSCSC Library organised book signings. Two friends of very long standing, Adrian Chamberlain and Pam Cooper, have been immensely supportive and have provided extremely wise counsel. Above all, I would like to reiterate my thanks to my wife Viv, to whom the book is dedicated. I thank God for her love and support during what has been a memorable but demanding year.

GDS
JSCSC, Shrivenham

FOREWORD

by Professor Richard Holmes

The Western Front smoulders darkly in the middle of Britain's national consciousness, like some exhausted volcano whose once-deadly lava still marks our landscape. Its overall losses were exceeded by the Second World War, which was far and away history's most bloody conflict, and there were aspects of that struggle – like the battles in the mountains around Cassino, the freezing ruins of Stalingrad or the jungles of Burma – which must rival the Western Front for human suffering. But as far as Britain and her dominions were concerned the Western Front was the most costly event of modern history, and we remain touched by its long cold shadow.

I admitted, at the beginning of a recent book, that I was haunted by the Western Front, and the scale of the public response to the BBC television series the book accompanied – I am still answering letters almost two years on – suggested that I was not alone. The subject arouses a mixture of emotions, amongst them horror, regret, anger, pride and curiosity, experienced by thousands of people whose own contact with the war often comes from the discovery of photographs, medals, discharge papers or, all too frequently, notification of death in action, amongst family papers. There are few brands burned deeper into our collective memory, and no historical topics more likely to provoke a response than the Western Front.

Often the vehemence of this response, while scarcely surprising in view of the sheer scale of suffering experienced on the Western Front, has actually impeded balanced assessment, establishing myths which have solidified into 'facts'. For years, if one was to point out that it was more dangerous to be a British general in the First World War than in the Second; to observe that, during the war's last hundred days, the British army captured almost as many prisoners as the French, Americans and Belgians put together; or to suggest that the overwhelming majority of the British soldiers sentenced to death were justly condemned by the law as it stood at that time, then reactions ranged from gentle disbelief to blind fury.

The usual suspects were arraigned for conviction. Politicians first blundered into the war and then either meddled foolishly in its conduct, or supinely failed to intervene to prevent fresh acts of military folly. Generals, the lion-leading donkeys of that quote which continues to defy reputable attribution, were stupid and conservative, and, in their elegant châteaux, remote and comfort-loving to boot. And the British, mysteriously on the winning side, were consistently less astute than the Germans, who somehow managed to lose. Class, that all-purpose explanation for national misfortune, helped depict empty-headed young Bertie leading trusting Tommy to certain death, overlooking the fact that for most of the war the British army – alone amongst its allies or opponents – had an ex-ranker as its professional head, and commissioned 500 warrant officers and NCOs in the first month of the war as part of creating an officer corps that was far less socially restrictive than the German.

I went on to suggest that we had at last reached a time when it was possible to make balanced judgements on a struggle which had polarised opinion for so long. It is a particular pleasure, therefore, to write this Foreword to Gary Sheffield's timely and well-balanced contribution to the widening stream of new scholarship which sees the Western Front not in terms of yesterday's conditioned responses but today's measured analysis of evidence too often disregarded. Such is the popular and media perception of the war, as the author trenchantly observes early on, that any revisionist scholar must press forward, as it were, against uncut barbed wire and well-guarded trenches.

I have no doubt that he scores at least four notable victories. First, by emphasising that Britain had little real prospect of standing on the sidelines in 1914; second, by demonstrating that there was no real alternative to the Western Front; third, by examining the BEF's painful but successful ascent of the learning curve at a time of profound military change; and finally, by giving the British army due credit for its stunning achievement in the late summer and autumn of 1918. By the end of the book the Western Front looks no less malign, but we can, I think, peer into its smoking crater not only with a much greater measure of understanding, but even with pride for the not inconsiderable achievements of fathers, grandfathers and great-grandfathers.

INTRODUCTION

The First World War was a tragic conflict, but it was neither futile nor meaningless. Just as in the struggles against Napoleon and, later, Hitler, it was a war that Britain had to fight and had to win. This achievement has become obscured by myths. For instance, the image of the British army of 1914–18 as being inept, 'lions led by donkeys', is highly misleading. In fact, against a background of revolutionary changes in the nature of war, the British army underwent a bloody learning curve and emerged as a formidable force. In 1918 this much-maligned army won the greatest series of victories in British military history.

To many people, these views will appear bizarre, shocking or even offensive. This was forcibly brought home to me in 1996 when I appeared as a 'talking head' on a BBC *Timewatch* television documentary on the British commander in chief on the Western Front, Field Marshal Sir Douglas Haig. Provocatively entitled 'Douglas Haig: The Unknown Soldier', it was broadcast on 3 July 1996, two days after the saturation media coverage of the eightieth anniversary of the first day of the Battle of the Somme. In Britain the First of July 1916 is a day, more than any other, associated in the popular mind with the stupidity and futility of the Great War, and Haig is indelibly fixed as 'the Butcher of the Somme'. The programme juxtaposed these traditional views of the war, eloquently put by the prolific Australian writer, John Laffin, author of *British Butchers and Bunglers of World War One*,[1] with revisionist historians such as Professor Trevor Wilson of Adelaide University and myself.

My argument was that Haig was not a military genius (few commanders are), but nonetheless deserved to be taken seriously as the commander of the victorious army of 1918. The subtlety of my argument was the victim of the cutting room floor. Such is television; it is extremely difficult to convey complex academic arguments that in the seminar room would be qualified with a plethora of 'howevers', 'buts' and 'maybes', within the confines of a fifty-minute television documentary. On the following day, the programme was reviewed in virtually every national newspaper. To put it mildly, the television critics seemed unconvinced by the case put forward by the revisionist historians. Indeed, some expressed anger that anyone could say anything at all in mitigation of Haig's conduct: 'It seems that for eighty years we've had it all wrong ... Haig ... just learned a lot from the horror of the Somme. Some learning curve. All those crosses making points on his graph,' commented one reviewer.[2]

I received letters from angry viewers forcefully denouncing Haig and accusing me of misleading my military students (at the time, I taught in the Department of War Studies at the Royal Military Academy Sandhurst). Interestingly, relatively few of my correspondents were of the variety familiar to most authors, the users of block capitals and red ink.

It is not difficult to understand the roots of my correspondents' anger. The losses on the Western Front were the greatest ever sustained by a British army. The enormous casualties, the 'One Million Dead', left the people of the British Empire in a profound state of shock that has shaped perceptions of the war ever since. What was the point, it is asked, of the bloody battles of 1915–17? Why could the generals not fight 'decisive' battles in the manner of Waterloo in 1815 or Alamein in 1942? The generals, it is commonly believed, were inept and made terrible mistakes, resulting in huge loss of life. Furthermore, in hindsight we know that the First World War was not the 'war to end all wars', that an even greater struggle against the same enemy was to break out only twenty years later. All that effort, all that suffering, all those deaths – for what?

I am well aware that by advancing a contrary view, I am not merely engaging in academic debate: I am picking at a scar on the British national psyche that is still raw. This book is not an attempt to whitewash the generals or politicians of 1914–18. It is certainly not intended to glorify war. What it is is an attempt to shed the emotional baggage of the last eighty years and treat the First World War as an historical topic like any other.

Once I shared the common view of the First World War as a futile tragedy conducted by a gang of incompetents. Although I was born sixteen years after Germany and Japan surrendered, I was very much a child of the Second World War, which was usually referred to simply as 'The War'. No one was in any doubt that the 1939–45 conflict had been a good war. Not only had it been just and righteous, it had also been won without an unduly heavy cost in lives (at least, Anglo-American ones). But from an early age I was dimly aware that before the good war there had been an appalling national catastrophe. The Second World War was all about tanks, aircraft and victories. The First World War was about infantrymen and machine guns and massacres of British soldiers. The generals had been unbelievably incompetent, I learned, and millions had died as a consequence of their folly. One had only to look at the war memorials that stand in every British city, town and village and compare the list of dead from the First World War with the much shorter list of dead from the Second. And for what purpose did they die? For nothing, it seemed, an impression strengthened by the first book I can remember reading on the war, A.J.P. Taylor's *The First World War*. Viewed through the lens of the 'Good War' of 1939–45 the struggle of 1914–18 seemed to be a very bad war indeed.

My simplistic views on both world wars did not long survive contact with the world of academic history. As a history undergraduate, I was soon exposed to arguments that undermined some of my cherished beliefs. In particular, I began to understand that there was a reason for fighting the war, and British strategy did make some sense, even if it did not always work. When I began postgraduate research, which involved extensive work in archives reading primary documents, even more scales dropped from my eyes. As I came into contact with other historians at institutions such as the War Studies departments at Sandhurst and King's College London, the Imperial War Museum, and others in Australia, Canada and the USA, I discovered that there was an informal school of historians doing the hard work of archival research into the British army of the First World

War. Although some influential writers such as John Keegan continue to take a very traditional, that is unfavourable, view of the British army on the Western Front and have little time for the revisionist school of historians,[3] the composite picture that has emerged is of an army very different from the incompetent shambles of popular myth. Likewise, the work of many diplomatic and political historians points firmly away from the popular view that the war was a ghastly accident and instead underlines that the war was fought over substantive issues.

For the last decade and a half I have sat in academic seminars in which historians have complained about the difficulty of shifting public opinion on these issues. It seems that every time an important new book comes out, another popular book or television programme appears repeating the same old tired myths. Clearly, a large part of the blame for the failure of revisionist history to become accepted by a wider audience lies with the historians themselves. Articles published in obscure learned journals or vastly expensive academic tomes are never likely to be widely read. Furthermore, until very recently, the study of battles and generals was not a popular or respectable field in most universities. Such frustration is not merely a matter of wounded professional pride, or jealousy at the sales of popular books on the subject. At the grand strategic level, the 'futility' view has had an impact on national self-perception, and there is always the danger of decision-makers drawing flawed 'lessons' from history. Second, at the personal level there is the fate of the widow or orphan of a soldier, sailor or airman killed during the First World War. The loss of a loved one is bad enough. To be constantly told, quite erroneously, that he died for nothing must be even worse.

That is not to argue that all academic writers on the First World War have failed to find a mass audience: far from it. In the words of Dr Stephen Badsey, one of the world's leading authorities on war and the media, a school of scholars of literature, media and culture have come to view the First World War as

> *such* a uniquely terrible experience that it cannot be understood
> as part of any historical process or analysis. Instead, it can only
> be understood through the emotional response of individuals,

and in particular the works of literature and art produced by participants ... a modern cultural meaning of the war ... is first derived from a close reading of such texts, and then this meaning is used retroactively to colour and interpret the events of the war itself.[4]

This approach, based on empathy and emotion, collides head on with the archive-based 'scientific' approach to the writing of history.[5] Thus far, the cultural view of history, epitomised by the writings of scholars such as Paul Fussell, has had a huge influence on the media. The result is that there are now two distinct perceptions of the First World War. The majority of people view it as a unique cultural event, essentially 'outside' history. In contrast, a small group of historians see the war in the context of political and military history.

This book is not a complete history of the conflict, consisting as it does of a number of essays on a linked theme. The first chapter addresses the question of why, in Britain and the USA, the First World War has such an evil reputation. The second chapter deals with the nature of the origins of the war, and the third addresses the question of why the war lasted as long as it did, examining domestic factors and the war aims of the belligerents. In chapter 4, I analyse the nature of British strategy in the First World War, dealing with such matters as the viability or otherwise of an alternative to fighting on the Western Front, the role of the Royal Navy, and the constraints imposed by operating within a coalition of allies. In chapter 5 the focus shifts to the battlefield, examining the emergence of trench warfare in 1914–15 and the British Expeditionary Force in the early years of the war. Chapter 6 acts as a bridge to the second part of the book, by examining the BEF and Haig as a commander, and placing both in the context of the war on the Western Front. In chapters 7 to 9 the BEF's operations from 1916 to 1918 are examined in some detail, a chapter being devoted to each year. Given the importance of the operations in 1918, the chapter on this year is a little longer than its fellows. Finally, in chapter 10, I consider the nature of the post-war peace settlement, place the First World War in the context of warfare and assess its place in history.

This book contains some original research but I have drawn heavily upon the work of other scholars in the field. I have striven and I hope succeeded in avoiding misrepresenting their views. Inevitably, my interpretations differ from those of other historians. I greatly admire the stimulating works of scholars such as Tim Travers, Niall Ferguson, Robin Prior and Trevor Wilson, but take issue with them on some key points. That is the nature of history, well described by one historian as 'an argument without end'.

In this book, I use the terms 'strategy', 'operations' and 'tactics' to refer to the various levels of war. The strategic level refers to the big picture, the fighting of wars. It is usually divided into 'grand strategy', the concern of politicians and commanders at the highest echelons, and the slightly lower level of 'military strategy'. The tactical level refers to the conduct of battles. The operational level refers to the conduct of campaigns, and serves as a link between strategy and tactics, the highest and lowest levels of war.

'War makes rattling good history; but Peace is poor reading.' Such a view, expressed in Thomas Hardy's novel *The Dynasts*, glosses over the fact that war is ultimately about human beings killing and maiming each other to achieve a political objective. The human cost of the First World War has never been far from my mind while writing this book, yet in a conflict fought on a scale as vast as that of 1914–18, it is easy to lose sight of the individual soldier. The brutal reality was that battles, successful or otherwise, invariably took a heavy toll of human life. The capture of Vimy Ridge in April 1917 is a case in point. It was a highly effective operation that gained terrain of great strategic value, but was only achieved at the cost of 11,000 Canadian and British casualties, in addition to the losses suffered by the defenders. A French commander of the Great War, General Mangin, hit upon an essential truth when he observed 'whatever you do, you lose a lot of men'.

Today, Western governments and peoples are not prepared to countenance heavy casualties in the pursuit of political goals. Indeed, in an age of weapons of mass destruction it may be that total war is a redundant response to even the gravest of threats. Governments and peoples in the second decade of the twentieth century had a very different view, and one should avoid the temptation to impose modern values upon an earlier era.

ACKNOWLEDGEMENTS

I would like to thank Madame de Roary for permission to quote from the correspondence of her grandfather, Sir Henry Horne, held in the Imperial War Museum. Quotations from materials held in the USMC archives appear by kind permission of the United States Marine Corps. The National Archives of Canada kindly granted permission to quote extracts from Crown Copyright material in the F.R. Phelan papers. Otherwise, Crown Copyright material appears with the kind permission of Her Majesty's Stationery Office.

Some material in chapter 1 appeared in a slightly different form in Ian Stewart and Susan L. Carruthers (eds.), *War, Culture and the Media*, published by Flicks Books in 1996. I am grateful to the publishers for permission to reproduce this material. Similarly, a somewhat longer version of my piece in the same chapter on *Oh! What a Lovely War* first appeared in *The English Review*. I am grateful to Dr Christine Gerrard for permission to use this material. Part of chapter 9 previously appeared in *Military Illustrated*, and I am grateful to the editor, Tim Newark, for permission to reproduce this material. To anyone whose copyright I have unwittingly infringed I offer my sincere apologies.

The views expressed in the book are my own and do not represent those of the Joint Services Command and Staff College or any other organisation or body.

Personal thanks

Many people gave me advice and read portions of the manuscript. Professor Peter Simkins and Dr Stephen Badsey read almost all of it. My sincere thanks are due to everyone who gave me all manner of help and advice in the writing of this book, and indeed over two decades of researching the history of the Great War. Any blemishes that remain are solely my responsibility. I would especially like to acknowledge the assistance of Professor Richard Holmes, for kindly writing the Foreword. Also, at the Joint Services Command and Staff College: Dr Niall Barr, Major Tim Blackmore, Dr Bob Foley, Dr Andrew Gordon (who gave some excellent advice on naval matters), Dr Christina Goulter, Wing Commander Paul Haines, Dr David Jordan (who freely gave of his expertise on air warfare), Dr Helen McCartney, Brigadier Mungo Melvin, Dr Kate Morris, Mrs Susie Oldnall, Brigadier Nick Parker, Mrs Sarah Somers, Mrs Barbara Taylor, Professor Geoffrey Till, Captain Keith Winstanley RN; at the Royal Military Academy Sandhurst: Dr Duncan Anderson, Mrs Pam Bendall, Lloyd Clark, Andrew Orgill (who compiled the index), Michael Orr; at the Imperial War Museum: Chris McCarthy and Nigel Steel; and elsewhere, Dr Kathy Barbier, Professor Brian Bond, Nigel Cave, Dr Hugh Cecil, Dr Paddy Griffith, Tony Cowan, Dr Tony and Mrs Mary Heathcote, George Karger, John Lee, Matthew Parker, Nick Perry, Michael Piercy, Kathy Stevenson, John Terraine, David Trim, Dr Andy Wiest. If I have missed anyone out, I hope they will forgive me.

I have been very lucky to be able to draw upon the resources of two excellent libraries, at Sandhurst and the JSCSC. I am very grateful to the staffs of both for all their assistance. Likewise, I would like to thank Dr Jim Ginther and Dr Tim Dubé for facilitating research in the United States Marine Corps Archives and the National Archives of Canada respectively. It is with great pleasure that I again thank my friends at the Imperial War Museum and the Australian War Memorial for their help in my archival research.

A huge vote of thanks is due to my agent, Simon Trewin, and to my editors at Headline, Heather Holden-Brown and Lorraine Jerram. An even bigger one goes to my children, Jennie and James, and to my wife, Viv, who had to live with me while I was writing this book.

LIST OF ABBREVIATIONS

ADC	*Aide de Camp* — junior assistant to a senior officer
AEF	American Expeditionary Force
AWM	Australian War Memorial
BBC	British Broadcasting Corporation
BEF	British Expeditionary Force
CID	Committee of Imperial Defence
CIGS	Chief of the Imperial General Staff
CinC	Commander in Chief
CND	Campaign for Nuclear Disarmament
GHQ	General Headquarters
HQ	Headquarters
IWM	Imperial War Museum
JRUSI	*Journal of the Royal United Services Institution*
KGB	The Soviet intelligence service
LC	Liddell Collection, University of Leeds
LHCMA	Liddell Hart Centre for Military Archives, King's College London
MP	Member of Parliament
NAC	National Archives of Canada
NCO	Noncommissioned Officer
nd	not dated
OODA	Observe, Orientate, Decide, Act
Pdr	Pounder
POW	Prisoner[s] of War
PPU	Peace Pledge Union
PRO	Public Record Office
RAF	Royal Air Force
RFC	Royal Flying Corps
RHS	Royal Historical Society
RKP	Routledge & Kegan Paul
RMA	Revolution in Military Affairs
RNAS	Royal Naval Air Service
SLOCs	Sea Lines of Communications

SMLE	Short Magazine Lee Enfield (rifle)
SCL	Staff College Library
SWC	Supreme War Council
TF	Territorial Force
UBC	University of British Columbia
UDC	Union of Democratic Control
UP	University Press

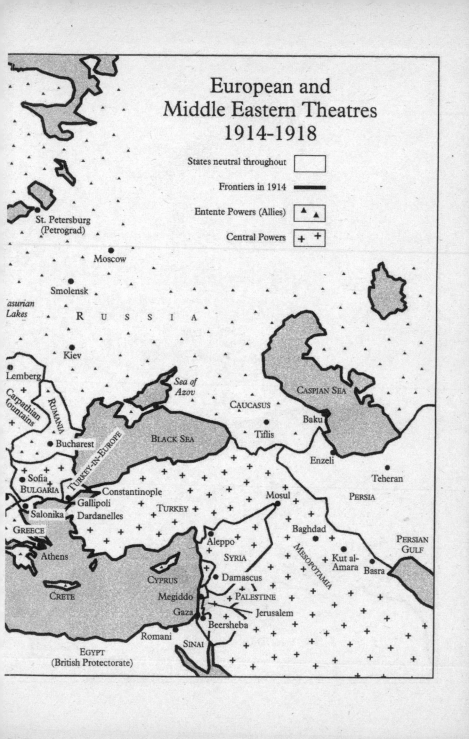

European and Middle Eastern Theatres 1914-1918

States neutral throughout

Frontiers in 1914

Entente Powers (Allies)

Central Powers

St. Petersburg (Petrograd)

Moscow

Smolensk

asurian Lakes

R U S S I A

Kiev

Lemberg

Carpathian Mountains

RUMANIA

Sea of Azov

CASPIAN SEA

CAUCASUS

Baku

Bucharest

TURKEY-IN-EUROPE

BLACK SEA

Tiflis

Enzeli

Sofia

BULGARIA

Constantinople

Mosul

Teheran

PERSIA

Gallipoli

Dardanelles

TURKEY

Salonika

GREECE

Baghdad

PERSIAN GULF

Athens

Aleppo

SYRIA

MESOPOTAMIA

Kut al-Amara

Basra

CYPRUS

Damascus

CRETE

Megiddo

PALESTINE

Gaza

Jerusalem

Beersheba

Romani

SINAI

EGYPT (British Protectorate)

CHAPTER 1

OH WHAT A FUTILE WAR?
THE FIRST WORLD WAR
IN BRITISH AND
AMERICAN MEMORY

Blackadder and the First World War

Captain Edmund Blackadder, Private S. Baldrick and Lieutenant The Hon. George Colthurst St. Barleigh first marched onto British television screens in 1989, accompanied by a military band crashing out the *British Grenadiers*. Played by Rowan Atkinson, Tony Robinson and Hugh Laurie respectively, these three characters were first seen on the parade ground, passing a saluting base manned by General Sir Anthony Hogmany Melchett (Stephen Fry), and, squinting around his general's elbow, his ADC, Captain Kevin Darling (Tim McInnerny). These five were the principal characters of *Blackadder Goes Forth*, a highly successful BBC television comedy set on the Western Front during 1917. The popularity of the series is attributable in large part to the sheer quality of the scripts, which blend perfectly with the sparkling performances of the actors. The element of conflict, which lies at the heart of much great comedy, is provided by Blackadder's clashes with his real enemies, who are not the Germans but the brainless, braying Melchett and the cowardly, column-dodging Darling. But there is another reason for the success of *Blackadder Goes Forth*. It reflected and reinforced the majority of the public's views and emotions about the Great War.

All four series of *Blackadder* (the others were set in the middle ages, the Elizabethan era and in the eighteenth century) drew upon a half-remembered folk memory of the *1066 and All That* variety. As the British national perception of the First World War is of an unmitigated disaster, *Blackadder Goes Forth* has a dark side largely absent from the three previous series, in the last episodes of which the principal characters had met violent but comic deaths. But when Blackadder, Baldrick, George and Darling finally go 'over the top' into German machine gun fire, the mood is deadly serious. Only a minimum of scene setting was needed to make *Blackadder Goes Forth* intelligible. Nothing more than a shot of a trench was needed to establish the context, nor was any explanation needed of the conflict between Captain Darling, living in a luxurious château, and Captain Blackadder in his rat-infested frontline trench. The portrayal of British strategy and tactics – in one memorable scene Field Marshal Sir Douglas Haig, played by Geoffrey Palmer, casually brushes toy soldiers off a model battlefield and sweeps them up in a dustpan – is funny because everybody 'knows' that British generals were incompetent and their battles were invariably bloody failures. Even the modern British army, which one might have thought had a vested interest in putting forward a more positive view of the First World War, gave the series tacit endorsement by allowing the band of the Royal Anglian Regiment to appear on screen. *Blackadder* builds on a shared interpretation of history, but also on a common cultural heritage. The series contains echoes of works as diverse as the 'War Poets' of 1914–18, R.C. Sherriff's play *Journey's End*, and W.E. Johns' juvenile *Biggles* novels.

Blackadder simply would not work in the absence of a British national perception of the First World War. My conviction that such a thing exists is based on observation of the media, and discussions with a large number of people over a period of nearly twenty years. I do not know of a properly conducted study of public opinion on the matter, but the preliminary findings of the Sandhurst historian Lloyd

Clark suggest that there is a general awareness of the First World War as a uniquely terrible experience, and that perceptions of this war tend to colour perceptions of conflict in general.

In classic Christian 'just war' theory, conflicts have to be judged on two criteria, by the reason for going to war *(jus ad bellum)*, and the conduct of the fighting *(jus in bello)*. The First World War, according to the national perception, failed to measure up on both counts. It began, it is commonly believed, over a trivial incident in the Balkans, which triggered off a series of actions that resulted in the Great Powers slithering into war. It was a futile, pointless conflict that was fought about nothing and solved nothing. At the end, the brutally harsh Treaty of Versailles imposed by the victors laid the foundations for Hitler's rise to power and more or less ensured that a Second World War would break out, sooner rather than later, as the Germans sought redress. In the same way, it is believed that war was conducted by bone-headed British generals who, faced with trench deadlock, could think of nothing more imaginative than to hurl long lines of troops against German trenches and barbed wire, where time after time they were cut down in swathes. The great battles of the First World War, 'Gallipoli', 'The Somme', 'Passchendaele', were, in the popular conception, colossal blood baths, utter disasters. The ordinary soldiers, this version of events continues, who had enlisted almost in a holiday mood, became deeply disillusioned with the war, and expressed their disenchantment by writing bitter poetry.

So deep has this image of the First World War been driven into the national psyche that modern Britons constantly invoke 'The Trenches'. A reference to the First World War is often used as shorthand for stupidity, blind obedience, failures of leadership, appalling physical conditions and deadlock. In 1999, a sports journalist reached deep into his vocabulary of insults and emerged with 'the England football team showed all the tactical acumen of a First World War general'.[1]

However, it is in the arena of politics that the richest harvest of Western Front references is to be found. The view of the Great War as a national tragedy, with the ordinary soldier, however courageous and tough, the victim of his leaders' incompetence, is held across the political spectrum. In 1990 a prominent Labour politician, John Prescott, wrote in a foreword to a book on the Hull 'Pals':

> Senior officers well behind the enemy lines [sic] seldom felt the conditions of horror, or the bitter consequences of their own orders, ignored the growing list of casualties and enforced a barbaric discipline which saw the shooting of shell-shocked soldiers.[2]

Despite the presumably unintentional suggestion that Haig and co. defected to the Germans, the message of futility is clear enough. Journalists and politicians habitually reach for Western Front metaphors. In July 1999 William Hague, the leader of the Conservative opposition, in a memorably confused comparison, likened the Prime Minister to 'a First World War general who had sent out for new infantry while he went off to his château for the holidays'.[3]

Very occasionally, though, 'the trenches' is used as a more positive metaphor. Tony Adams, the Arsenal captain, scored the winning goal in the quarterfinals of the 1994 European Cup-Winners' Cup. He was praised as a 'hero' in a middle-brow newspaper in terms that mixed sport and the First World War, throwing a typical bit of British social class consciousness into the equation: 'Tony Adams may not be Sandhurst material but when the bullets are flying and the call is for courage he constantly proves to be the man you would want in the trenches.'[4] Adams, a Londoner of humble origins, is here seen as a lineal descendant of the tough, bloody-minded and courageous British working class 'Tommy' celebrated in literature by Kipling and in epic war movies such as *Zulu*. Given the rich heritage of historical examples upon which the journalist, Steve Curry, could have drawn, it is nonetheless interesting that he chose to evoke folk memories of the Western Front. In referring to Arsenal's 'patience and discipline' Curry, wittingly or not, also highlighted two of the characteristics of the British army on the Western Front.

For British audiences in the late twentieth century these references did not need to be placed in context. No one had to explain what happened on the Western Front. As the popular success of *Blackadder Goes Forth* indicates, it is not only readers of the quality press who can be relied upon to recognise and understand references to the First World War. During the Falklands War of 1982, the *Sun*, a populist tabloid newspaper, ran an aggressively jingoistic campaign. At one stage it juxtaposed photographs of Royal Marines surrendering to the Argentine invaders with a headline of LEST WE FORGET. This spread was intended to remind readers of the gravity of the issues at stake, the surrender being described as 'a black moment in our history' with the Task Force being dispatched to 'wipe out the memory and free our loyal friends'.[5] In order to reinforce its ultra-patriotic message the *Sun* dug deep into the British collective memory, for 'Lest we forget' is a phrase soaked in associations with the sacrifices of 1914–18. Taken from Rudyard Kipling's 1897 poem 'Recessional', after 1918 these words became an 'emblematic text for remembrance',[6] synonymous with commemoration of the First World War. By linking the Falklands War with 1914–18 the *Sun* risked reminding its readers not only of heroic, self-denying sacrifice, but also of the 'futility' of war, which was precisely the opposite message to the one that the newspaper wished to convey.

Disillusionment – Reality or Myth?

The First World War was not always viewed like this. In this book I argue that the Great War was seen by the vast majority of British people as a just and worthwhile war – while it was still going on. There is evidence, too, that such attitudes continued to hold sway in the immediate aftermath of the war. War novels based on wartime experiences that 'appeared shortly after the war tended to be patriotic and romantic'. There were, of course, exceptions, but 'in much of this war fiction [published in the 1920s as a whole] the message was ambiguous: it was the reader or playgoer who decided whether or not a work was "anti-war"'.[7] The same is true of many war memoirs. Even a book with the apparently unequivocal title of *Torment* reveals, on careful reading, ambiguous attitudes towards the author's wartime experience.[8]

Why, then, did popular opinion undergo such a dramatic change? One explanation is that for the decade after the end of the war Britain was an emotional dam about to burst. If there is one word that sums up why the First World War came to be viewed as a futile tragedy, that word is 'casualties'. The defeat of Imperial Germany cost the British Empire 947,023 military dead of which 744,702 were from the British Isles. This was more than any previous war had cost Great Britain, and indeed would dwarf the 264,000 military dead of the Second World War. Britain in 1919 was a nation in a state of profound shock. The hysterical celebrations at the news of the Armistice gave way to numbness, as the full horror of the scale of the deaths sank in. In 1924 an author commented that:

> The European War, with its serried ranks of graves counted in millions, each marking a life cut off, has entirely altered our conceptions of mass death. What trifles seem the few tens of thousands of the Great Plague [of London in 1665]![9]

The massacre of young men left a generation of parents without sons, wives without husbands, children without fathers. Even at a distance of over eighty years, the grief is palpable.

During the war, the British population had for the most part accepted the heavy loss of life as the cost of fighting a necessary war. Attitudes did not alter overnight, but as early as 1920 there is evidence that times were changing. In that year a book co-authored by an officer close to Haig adopted a distinctly defensive tone when referring to critics of British operations.[10] But mourning and commemoration rather than blame and recrimination were the major themes of the immediate post-war period. One important result was a rash of memorials that permanently changed the British landscape.

Perhaps such a heavy loss of life would have been more bearable if the post-war world had been obviously 'better' than that which had perished between 1914 and 1918. A story that appears in the memoirs of the broadcaster Robert Robinson reveals a profound truth about the reason why the Great War came to be seen as a disaster. As a child in the 1930s, living in suburban Surrey, he encountered a 'respectable man' who was reduced to hawking goods from a cheap suitcase. Before he went to serve in the Great War, the man had been a commercial traveller working for an established firm. He was wounded and lamed, and after the war failed to get his old job back. When Robinson with childish candour commented 'And now you're only a pedlar', the man began to weep.[11]

As a tragedy, this man's story hardly bears comparison with the fate of maimed men rotting in veterans' hospitals, an experience captured in *Johnny Got his Gun* (1938) a novel by an American author, Dalton Trumbo, that has still not lost its power to shock. Yet it was a tragedy all the same. Ex-servicemen re-entering civilian life did not return to a 'land fit for heroes'. Instead, they found a country troubled by declining industries, unemployment and labour unrest.

The end of the war with Germany had not brought prosperity; neither had it brought security to Europe. Russia was in revolution, and posing a threat to western stability. Superficially, Britain's position in the world had been enhanced. In reality, Britain had slipped from her apparently pre-eminent place in the world. By agreeing to naval parity with the USA in 1921, Britain was admitting the extent of her decline. The Chanak incident of 1922, when Britain came close to war with Turkey, showed that Britain could not even count upon the automatic support of the white Dominions in times of crisis. Above all, the spirit of optimism that had characterised, despite everything, the Edwardian period had vanished. Against this background it is not surprising that some people began to question whether the enormous sacrifices had been worthwhile.

The dam finally burst in 1929. One trigger appears to have been the publication of a German war novel, Erich Maria Remarque's *All Quiet on the Western Front*. In this book, which was turned into a highly successful Hollywood film in 1930, the theme is the destruction of youthful idealism. The other trigger was the first staging of *Journey's End*, a play by a British wartime officer, R.C. Sherriff. Set in a dugout on the eve of the German offensive in March 1918, *Journey's End* is a claustrophobic picture of the strain of modern war on ordinary men. Such works gave exposure to views expressed by one Western Front veteran-turned-pacifist that war had 'passed from the heroic to the blackguardly ... obscene in its ruthlessness and sub-human in its mechanisation'.[12] These literary events coincided with the Wall Street Crash, which began a world-wide depression, the gravest international crisis since 1918.[13] A stream of British 'disillusioned' novels and memoirs followed. Many of the classics of the genre date from this period, such as Siegfried Sassoon's *Memoirs of a Fox Hunting Man* (1928), Robert Graves's *Goodbye to All That* and Richard Aldington's *Death of a Hero* (both 1929). Polemical attacks on the conduct of the war by military historians Captain B.H. Liddell Hart and Major General J.F.C. Fuller belong to the same literary genre. So do the memoirs of the wartime prime minister, David Lloyd George, which featured a series of scathing attacks on British high command, particularly Douglas Haig.

Thus British public opinion moved towards pacifism between the wars. Founded soon after the outbreak of war in 1914, the Union of Democratic Control (UDC) acted as a pressure group, its members believing that the war was caused by the pursuit of 'balance of power' politics and secret diplomacy – the organisation's title referred to the democratic control of foreign policy.[14] After the war, the UDC won the intellectual battle.[15] While not strictly pacifist, that is completely rejecting the use of war, the UDC has aptly been described as 'pacific-ist'.[16] This word sums up much public feeling in the late interwar years – the period in which the UDC's views on the causes, conduct and consequences of the war became highly influential.

Neo-pacifist influences can be detected behind the widespread belief that the terms of the Versailles peace settlement were iniquitous and injurious to the prospects of future peace. Such views also underpinned the decision in 1933 of the socially elite youths of the Oxford Union to support the motion that 'This House will in no circumstances fight for its King and Country'. In 1935 11.5 million people voted in the 'Peace Ballot', organised by the League of Nations Union, which affirmed support for the League and the reduction of armaments. By 1936 the Peace Pledge Union (PPU), founded two years earlier by Canon 'Dick' Sheppard, had 100,000 members who declared: 'I renounce War and never again will I support or sanction another, and I will do all in my power to persuade others to do the same.'[17] Intellectuals on the Left, and even some on the Right, now viewed the Great War as a disaster, albeit for different reasons.[18]

The political consequences of such widely held views are demonstrated by comments made in January 1936 by Anthony Eden, Foreign Secretary and a Western Front veteran. He said he feared that 'public opinion . . . would rise up in anger' at the thought of the part-time soldiers of the Territorial Army 'being sent to "another Passchendaele"'.[19] I have argued elsewhere that many of the generation of young men who fought in the Second World War came to hold as an article of faith that no matter how terrible the experiences which they endured, the men of 1914–18 had had it worse. '[As] a result, they sometimes failed to recognise just how terrible "their" war was.'[20]

Thus far we have a tidy structure to our story. Britain suffers enormous casualties during the First World War. For over ten years after the war the nation is numb. Literary events and the onset of the Depression at the end of the 1920s trigger an outpouring of grief and disillusionment as Britons are forced to admit that their land is far from fit for heroes. An age of cynicism and disillusionment commences.

Inevitably, it is not quite that simple. For a start, we should be careful before assuming that Sassoon and the like accurately reflected the views of war veterans. Moreover, the influence of some of the war poets now regarded as spokesmen for the soldiers on the Western Front – Wilfred Owen is the obvious example – was minuscule in the 1930s. Professor Brian Bond has argued that 'disenchantment with the First World War was mainly literary in character . . . and, above all, limited in its impact on the general public'.[21] Ironically, Sherriff, who remained proud of his service in the East Surrey Regiment until the end of his life, did not intend *Journey's End* to be an anti-war play. The producer of the first version, however, was a pacifist, and the resulting production (and indeed most subsequent ones) conveyed the message that the war was squalid and futile.[22] The cultural historian Modris Eksteins has argued that 'the sentiments on war' articulated in the film of *All Quiet* 'were not representative of the prevailing sentiments of soldiers during the war'.[23] I would go further: neither were they representative of the way that most British and US veterans viewed the First World War in the early 1930s.

Certainly, the publication of 'disillusioned' novels and memoirs did not halt the flow of works that had an ambiguous or even positive view of the war. As literary historian Hugh Cecil reminds us, even when the disenchanted school seemed to reign supreme 'there were enough successful novels with a contrary message for the public to receive a fairly balanced picture'. Indeed, judged by sales, the British public seems to have preferred patriotic to disillusioned fiction, not least because much of the former offered consolation for loss.[24]

Also to be set against the idea of widespread disillusionment from 1929 onwards is the fact that British national unity survived the 'devil's decade' of the 1930s more or less intact. In spite of unemployment, hunger marches and appeasement, the vast bulk of the British population entered the Second World War in 1939 prepared to 'do their bit' – in other words to go through the experience of total war for the second time in twenty-five years. This was truly astonishing. There is much evidence that it was widely believed that a new European war would be worse than that of 1914–18, and would include devastating air raids, when enemy bombers would rain high explosive and poison gas onto British cities.[25] Yet the generation that had grown to adulthood during the apparent 'disillusionment' boom proved themselves ready to fight. Some put aside their youthful pacifism, while some had been educated, at home or school, to believe that the First World War had been a righteous, even glorious conflict, or that it was simply part of the long British military tradition. Even young men whose relatives had been killed or wounded during 1914–18 were ready, even eager, to fight in the Second World War.[26] Moreover, millions of greying veterans of the Western and other fronts offered themselves for service in a new war, in bodies such as the Home Guard and Air Raid Precautions.

Thus we have a paradox. Clearly, the intellectual and literary climate of the late twenties and early thirties was largely one of disenchantment with the First World War. Equally clearly, for large numbers of Britons, disenchantment was at best skin deep, and some did not share this view at all. This schizophrenic view of the war was mirrored in the interwar British cinema. 'Going to the pictures' was a principal source of entertainment in the 1930s. From 1919 to 1927 British Instructional Films produced a series of movies that re-enacted 1914–18 battles. In one, General Sir Horace Smith-Dorrien recreated his role as the victor of Mons and Le Cateau. The films treated these battles as heroic events to be celebrated, depicting them as fitting neatly into the tradition of Blenheim and Waterloo.[27]

In the 1930s British films displayed a more complex attitude to the First World War. Only twenty-six British war films appeared from the start of the decade up to the beginning of the Second World War. This can be seen as a consequence of the neo-pacifist mood of the earlier part of the decade, or, conversely, a lack of intent on the part of filmmakers to spread pacifist propaganda. Several important British war films appeared during the height of the War Books boom, and to some extent they reflected the 'disillusioned' themes of the ghastliness of war. Yet both *Journey's End* and *Tell England* (both 1930) were based on original sources which had an ambiguous (or even positive) view of the war. Moreover, both can be viewed as having an ultimately positive message: the nobility of sacrifice of upper class officers and – explicitly in *Tell England* – that the survival of England was worth the sacrifice and suffering.

Thus the jump from these apparently 'pacifist' films to contemporary 'establishment' films celebrating the monarchy and class consensus – *Victoria the Great* (1937), *Royal Cavalcade* (1935) – is not as great as it might at first seem. Much the same could be said of a film like *Fire over England* (1937), which advocated national alertness in the face of the growing power of Nazi Germany by invoking a previous threat (that of Philip II's Spain).[28] Yet, as Jeffery Richards has commented, 'the overall impression one gets from films about the Great War is that causes and principles become unimportant and that the war itself is the monstrous central fact of life and getting through it decently is the main thing.'[29] Perhaps the very ambiguity of the apparently anti-war films helps to explain the relative ease with which the pacifist mood of films of the early 1930s was changed into a reluctant acceptance of the necessity of war in 1939.

America, the First World War and Vietnam

American responses to the First World War were even more complex. To a far greater extent than in Britain, the war divided the US population. Unlike in Britain, the part of the country where one lived and one's ethnic background could play a significant role in one's attitude to the war.[30] The East Coast was the home of pro-Allied, interventionist sentiment, while the Mid West was more isolationist. German-Americans were posed with obvious dilemmas in contemplating a war against their ancestral home, and many Irish-Americans were cool about the idea of aiding the British.

The soldiers of the American Expeditionary Force (AEF) that fought in France were spared the full gamut of trench warfare. One and a third million American soldiers out of the two million present with the AEF had combat experience, but 'few saw sustained or repeated battle'.[31] Instead, the AEF fought its major battles, bloody though they were, when the trench deadlock had been broken, and when the German army was clearly on the back foot. The American experience, then, was of military success, of driving the enemy before them. The first major American battle was the attack at St. Mihiel on 12 September 1918, and the armistice that ended the war came into force only two months later.

As an important recent study has argued, the combat experience of the AEF 'could not shake American optimism'.[32] Judging from the responses to surveys completed in the 1970s, Great War veterans continued to hold broadly positive views about the war.[33] During the war there was a tendency amongst the public to follow President Woodrow Wilson's rhetoric that the New World entered the war to save the Old.[34] In the early 1920s, a number of popular books were published that had ambiguous or positive attitudes to the war, such as Edith Wharton's *A Son at the Front* (1933). Wartime books with similar themes, such as Alan Seeger's *Poems* and Arthur Guy Empey's *Over the Top* (both published in 1917) enjoyed continued popularity.[35] But it was the writings of John Dos Passos (*Three Soldiers*, 1921), e.e. cummings (*The Enormous Room*, 1922), William Faulkner (*Soldier's Pay*, 1926) and Ernest Hemingway (*A Farewell to Arms*, 1929) that took centre stage. Like many books that are seen as their European equivalents, it is often too simplistic to describe such works as 'disenchanted'. Instead they fit into a tradition of American writing that long predates 1917; they are protesting against authority, and conservative interpretations of the war.[36]

The events of the mid-1920s onwards provided a context for intellectual cynicism about the war to reach a wider audience. The Wall Street Crash and the subsequent Great Depression impoverished many Americans and created the conditions for the rise of Nazism in Germany. President Woodrow Wilson's idealistic vision of a benevolent New World Order seemed to be a distant memory. As in Britain, the belief grew that the beginning of the war had been a terrible mistake and that the treaty of Versailles had been monstrously harsh. In addition, many Americans came to think that the US had been tricked into entering the war by British propaganda and/or the machinations of arms manufacturers and bankers.[37] Moreover, there was a widely held belief that the USA had been cheated out of the fruits of victory. Apparently working on the principle of 'once bitten, twice shy', a prominent Mississippian argued in the Second World War that Britain should hand over Canada and parts of the West Indies in return for support.[38]

Added to this home-grown cynicism about the war were imports from Europe. In 1931 William Faulkner declared: 'America has been conquered not by the German soldiers that died in French and Flemish trenches, but by the German soldiers that died in German books.' Faulkner might well have added 'and in the movies'.[39] High culture had a relatively modest impact on the American popular imagination. Hollywood's influence, by contrast, was huge. For most of the 1920s, war films such as *The Big Parade* (1925) did not harp on disillusioned themes. *All Quiet on the Western Front* changed all that. Others followed this seminal film with similar anti-war messages.

Films did not have to be explicitly 'about' war in order to carry a 'disillusioned' message. One of the most graphic scenes that hammered home the 'disenchantment' message came not in a war film but in a musical, *The Gold Diggers of 1933*. Only the year before, in the depths of the Depression, Great War veterans had marched on Washington demanding the early payment of pensions. General Douglas MacArthur, himself a Western Front veteran, had used troops to disperse the 'Bonus Marchers'. Against this background, the musical climax of the film, the song 'Forgotten Man', packed a powerful emotional punch:

> Remember my forgotten man
> You put a rifle in his hand
> You sent him far away
> You shouted – Hip Hooray!
> But look at him today!

The scene was choreographed by Busby Berkeley, with lavish use of 'doughboys' in the uniforms of 1918.[40]

In the late 1930s Hollywood, with its large colony of European émigrés, many of them Jewish, was an island of concern about the rise of Nazism in a sea of American apathy and isolationism. One consequence was that, somewhat late in the day, Hollywood began to take a far more positive view of the Great War. *Sergeant York* (1941) with the title role played by Gary Cooper, is a masterful piece of propaganda. York, a citizen soldier from Pall Mall, Tennessee, won the Medal of Honor three weeks before the end of the war in 1918.[41] In the film York stands for America. Overcoming his hesitations, York decides it is right to fight.[42]

As far as there is an American popular perception of the Great War, it tends to follow the erroneous British pattern. In fact, many Americans have very little impression of it at all.[43] In America it is overshadowed by the Civil War and the Second World War, two conflicts that had a major impact on the USA and which still have a firm grip on the American imagination, not least in the media. Had sizeable American forces fought at Passchendaele, or for that matter had the war dragged on into 1919, when US forces would have undoubtedly borne the brunt of the fighting, no doubt the Great War would have a much greater hold on the American imagination. There are, of course, American historians who have stressed the importance of the First World War to the USA; but they seem to have made little impact on popular awareness of the conflict.[44]

America does in fact have a 'First World War' of its own in the shape of Vietnam. Both wars were, without any doubt, the most traumatic conflicts of the twentieth century for Britain and the US respectively. American optimism died in the paddy fields, just as surely as the First World War changed Britain forever. The number of American dead in Vietnam was, in comparison with the British losses of 1914–18, small – approximately 59,000 to 750,000. But the attrition and frustration that comprised much of the experience of the American front-line soldier in Vietnam can be compared, not entirely fancifully, to the trenches of France and Flanders from 1915–17 – without the compensation of a 1918-style victory. Even when the US forces achieved a substantial military success, as they did in destroying the Tet Offensive in 1968, the victory was Pyrrhic. The initial Viet Cong surprise attacks of 30 January 1968 grabbed the headlines and did more than anything else to undermine American will to continue with the war. The beginning of the campaign is naturally remembered at the expense of the subsequent and successful US response, just as 1918 is remembered largely for the initial German successes rather than the crushing Allied riposte.

In the USA Vietnam is still regarded by many as a bad war. Even some of those who took the decisions to commit America to Vietnam have now admitted that it was a mistake. Arthur M. Schlesinger Jr, historian and special assistant to President John F. Kennedy, described America's war as a 'tragedy without villains'.[45] A scholarly textbook, widely used in American colleges, concludes by speculating on the emotions of visitors to the Vietnam War memorial in Washington DC in language that could have been used to describe British visitors to a cemetery at Passchendaele. Even though visitors may have no personal connection with the men who are commemorated there, 'They too are filled with grief and sadness at the loss, and perhaps rage at the waste and futility of an unnecessary and pointless war.'[46] Unlike London's Cenotaph, the Vietnam War Memorial proved controversial on its unveiling. Yet both memorials serve the same purpose: they are empty tombs, places to mourn and remember, to try to comprehend a tragic event.

If the image of the Vietnam War as an avoidable tragedy is dominant in the USA, there are other interpretations. One school points to imperialism as a root cause of American intervention in Indochina. Another school holds the view that the Vietnam War was worthwhile and was far from futile. For the student of British history, there are clear echoes of debates over the Great War: liberal thinkers aghast at the casualties, radical thinkers blaming imperialism and secret diplomacy, conservatives pursuing a patriotic line and historians trying to maintain objectivity. Eighty years after the event, when almost all participants in the Great War have passed away, it remains Britain's most controversial war. There is every sign that Vietnam will continue to fulfil a similar function for the United States.

Parallels between Vietnam and the Great War do not end there. The 1970s in the United States, like the 1920s in Britain, saw a period of numbness followed by an explosion of books and films. The traumatic experiences on the Western Front and in South East Asia demanded that individuals and nations made sense of the conflicts, a procedure entailing a painful period of reassessment and mental adjustment. This stands in sharp contrast with the Second World War, a good war for both Americans and Britons, where individuals underwent this process but nations did not see the need. Not surprisingly, post-Vietnam books and films had much in common with their counterparts of the 1920s and 1930s. Many memoirs, novels and films of Vietnam have an ambiguous attitude to the war reminiscent of much writing by Western Front veterans; Francis Ford Coppola's movie *Apocalypse Now* (1979) is a case in point. It is perhaps unsurprising that *All Quiet* was remade in

1979, at the time when the Vietnam War movie industry was hitting its stride.

The 1960s and the Birth of the British National Perception

British popular interest in the 1914—18 war, dormant during the 1939—45 conflict, began to reawaken in the mid- to late-1950s. It was during the 1960s, however, that the British national perception of the First World War as futile and incompetent became firmly established: to borrow a Marxist phrase, it had become a 'dominant ideology', constantly reinforced by the media. Horror and revulsion at the human cost of the war was given a spur by the relatively small loss of British life in the recently concluded Second World War.

In the 1950s and 60s a series of popular histories powerfully reinforced the British national perception of the war and helped to redefine it in the wake of the 1939—45 conflict. None of these books stand up well in the light of modern scholarship. Alan Clark's *The Donkeys* is the worst, and was heavily criticised by other historians when it was published. Leon Wolff's *In Flanders Fields* was perhaps the best, and the most influential was probably A.J.P. Taylor's brilliant, but unreliable *The First World War*.[47] Taylor was a prominent CND supporter and the book is coloured by contemporary concerns about the Cold War. But these books are still influential and many later additions to the genre have continued their basic theme.[48] The opening of the British official archives for 1914—18 in the late 1960s revolutionised academic study of the war, but as noted in the introduction, the popular impact of such archival-based works has been severely limited. In sharp contrast, popular works of military history sell well, are widely read and are reviewed in the general press.

While there is often a delay in academic ideas becoming accepted, or even noticed by the general public, the difference between academic and popular perceptions of the First World War is still especially marked. Key Stage 3 of the national curriculum which operated in British schools in the mid-1990s dictated that the First World

the innocence that seems to have been present in Britain before the 1914 war'.[56] The Great War, which destroyed this innocence and security, was thus an obvious target of the radical writers of the 1950s and 1960s. The most influential treatment was probably Joan Littlewood's 1963 Theatre Workshop production of *Oh! What a Lovely War*. This was a seminal work whose influence stretches far beyond the comparatively few people who have actually seen it on the stage. Richard Attenborough's 1969 film version, although inferior as art, was seen by a much wider audience, both at the cinema and in subsequent showings on television. For whatever reason, *Oh! What a Lovely War* came to symbolise for many people the essential 'truth' about the First World War, and was much quoted, alluded to and parodied.[57]

The play has a seductive message: the war was pointless and the soldiers died for nothing. The Allied military victories of July to November 1918 are literally written out of the script. Instead, in the film version, the fighting just stops, the front lines apparently in place. For the original play, Joan Littlewood chose as the finale not the victory of the Allies (which might appear logical) but a scene from Henri Barbusse's novel *Under Fire* in which French soldiers follow an officer in a hopeless attack 'baa-ing like sheep till they were all mown down'.[58]

Theatre Workshop's 'Military Advisor' was Raymond Fletcher, a future Labour MP. His perspective on 1914–18 can be judged by his own description of the content of a lecture he gave the Theatre Workshop company on the War; 'one part me, one part Liddell Hart [a military historian fiercely critical of British high command] the rest Lenin!' Only six months before the play was first performed, the Cuban Missile Crisis brought the USA and the USSR close to nuclear war. Parallels with the way Europe had apparently slipped into war in August 1914 seemed all too obvious. Fletcher's 'Lenin' remark is especially interesting in view of the fact that in 1999 it was revealed that the KGB recruited him in 1962, the year *before Oh! What a Lovely War* was first performed.[59]

Writing in the late 1960s, the writer A.P. Herbert, who served with the Royal Naval Division during the Great War, accurately noted that 'Its message ... is that young men like ... myself were duped into the forces by damsels singing patriotic songs or bullied in by peremptory posters.' Such posters and songs were certainly used in 1914. However, Herbert firmly denied that he had been duped into joining up. Instead, he 'was calmly persuaded that we had gone to war for a just cause'. The experience of Gallipoli and the Western Front did not cause him to change his mind. *Oh! What a Lovely War* tells us very little about the First World War. It tells us a great deal about the 1960s, and how the First World War was perceived in Britain during those years.

It was through the medium of television, however, that images of the First World War were to have the greatest impact on a mass audience in Britain. Especially significant was the 1964 BBC series *The Great War*.[60] This was a 17-hour, 26-part series made in co-operation with the Imperial War Museum and the BBC's counterparts in Australia and Canada. Each episode of the series attracted on average eight million viewers. *The Great War* was a landmark not just in popular military history, but in television as a whole. Some 845,000 feet of archive film was used, and actors of the calibre of Sir Ralph Richardson, Marius Goring and Sir Michael Redgrave (the narrator) were enlisted to provide voice-overs.

On the scriptwriting team were the two leading military historical iconoclasts of the 1960s, Correlli Barnett and John Terraine. Both held views on the First World War that were sharply at odds with prevailing wisdom. Haig, according to Terraine, pursued a strategy of attrition – the only possible strategy, he argued, given the circumstances – which wore down the German army, and prepared it for the *coup de grâce* delivered by the Allies in 1918. His fundamental thesis, although frequently assailed over the last forty years, has yet to be demolished.[61]

The BBC television series seemed to have matched the man with the hour; here, at last, was a golden opportunity to present an alternative viewpoint to a mass audience. John Terraine wrote the scripts for the all-important programmes covering the battles of the Somme and Third Ypres. Yet his viewpoint was ignored, or at least not understood, by the audience; instead, the series ended up reinforcing the existing perception of the war as a futile waste of life. In the case of the Passchendaele episode, entitled 'Surely We Have Perished', it seems that Terraine's revisionism was overwhelmed by extracts from the poetry of Sassoon and Owen. The public reaction to the *Great War* series suggests that programmes do not have to carry an explicitly anti-war message to build up negative images in viewers' minds: all they need to do is to show scenes of carnage. In the case of *The Great War*, it was probably the case that the viewers' response simply reflected their existing impression of the war. In contrast, the showing of documentaries on the Second World War, which often feature gory footage, does not seem to have changed the public perception of this conflict as a 'good' war, in which men died to achieve a discernible and laudable end. The 1939–45 war has also been the subject of some revisionism, but it does not appear to have affected popular views on the conflict. The public controversy that surrounded the publication of John Charmley's critical biography of Winston Churchill in 1993, fuelled by Alan Clark's suggestion that Britain should have made a compromise peace with Hitler, is a case in point.[62]

The First World War continues to be a favourite subject for television documentaries and dramas, most of which hammer away at the theme of 'futility'. More than twenty such programmes were made in the UK between 1970 and 1995. An ambitious series, entitled in the USA *The Great War and the Shaping of the 20th Century*, and in Britain the pithier *1914–1918*, was screened in 1996. An international co-production between Public Broadcasting System (PBS), the Corporation for Public Broadcasting and the BBC, it had a literary/cultural focus. The series' academic prime mover (and co-author of the subsequent book) was Jay Winter. A Cambridge-based American academic, Winter is one of the world's leading cultural historians of the First World War. The driving concept behind the series seems to have been to demonstrate the importance of the past in terms of its impact on the present. This is indicated by the title of the American version. Fussell's *Great War and Modern Memory* is explicitly stated to be the starting point of the process that led to the making of the series.[63] One result was that military history was given short shrift. In the US version, the episode on the Somme deals almost entirely with the atypical first day of the battle. Correlli Barnett, in a scathing review entitled 'Oh! What a Whinging War' denounced it as 'Britannocentric' and a 'turkey', criticising the cultural bias of the series, its treatment of military operations and its failure to describe the war's 'political and strategic dynamics'.[64] The BBC was so dissatisfied that several episodes were re-shot for a British audience. A British historian on the advisory board, Peter Simkins, helped to ensure that these episodes were rather more balanced. In that it undoubtedly served to bring the conflict of 1914–18 to a wider audience in the United States, *The Great War and the Shaping of the 20th Century* was an important series. However, it reinforced many existing stereotypes rather than challenged them.

The 1996 BBC *Timewatch* programme on Douglas Haig, already discussed in the Introduction, was apparently intended in part to act as something of a counterweight to *The Great War and the Shaping of the 20th Century*. It was a seminal programme, in which for the first time a mass audience (3.5 million viewers) was brought face to face with revisionist history, and the shock, as we have seen, was considerable.[65] In 1999 this was followed by *Western Front*, a series written and presented by a military historian with an engaging screen presence, Professor Richard Holmes, whose cautious revisionism does not seem to have caused the same degree of outrage as the more confrontational, and much shorter, *Timewatch*.[66]

The eleventh of November 1998 marked the eightieth anniversary of the end of the fighting on the Western Front. Earlier that year, in July, the distinguished historian Professor Sir Michael Howard wrote to *The Times* suggesting that in view of the approach of the eightieth anniversary of the beginning of the 'Hundred Days' of Allied victories that ended the war, the media should devote as much attention as it had done to the eightieth anniversary of the first day of the Battle of the Somme two years earlier. Needless to say, that did not happen. Instead, a middle-brow tabloid newspaper, the *Daily Express*, devoted its front page to the suggestion that the statue of Field Marshal Sir Douglas Haig in Whitehall represented an insult to the memory of those who died through his ineptitude, and should be torn down from its plinth.[67]

Thus, at the end of the twentieth century, Britons almost unanimously regarded the First World War as a disaster, the significance of the war and the victories that won it all but forgotten. In the United States the war has largely dropped from public memory altogether. This book is intended to address these cases of historical amnesia.

CHAPTER 2

A WAR FOUGHT ABOUT NOTHING? THE ORIGINS OF THE FIRST WORLD WAR

The Treaty of Versailles was signed on 28 June 1919. The signature of this document marked the formal end of the First World War.[1] In his diary, a British diplomat recorded the scene in the Hall of Mirrors, the very room where the King of Prussia was proclaimed as German Emperor in 1871. Clemenceau, the French Prime Minister, ordered the German delegates to be brought in:

> They do not appear as representatives of a brutal militarism. The one is thin and pink-eyelidded: the second fiddle in a Brunswick orchestra. The other is moon-faced and suffering ... They sign ... We kept our seats while the Germans were conducted like prisoners from the dock, their eyes still fixed upon some distant point of the horizon.[2]

When the draft treaty had been presented to the German cabinet in May, its terms had caused outrage. The Chancellor, Philipp Scheidemann, had resigned rather than sign it. The bitterest pill of all was article 231 of the treaty. It read:

> The Allied and Associated Governments affirm and Germany

accepts the responsibility of Germany and her allies for causing all the damage to which the Allied and Associated Governments and their nationals have been subjected as a consequence of the war imposed upon them by the aggression of Germany and her allies.[3]

This 'war guilt clause' came to symbolise to Germans all that they believed was unfair about the 'Diktat' of Versailles. In the 1930s, many Britons and Americans, including the wartime Prime Minister, David Lloyd George, came to share the German viewpoint[4] and today it is popularly believed that Versailles made Hitler and the Second World War inevitable. Our examination of the justice of the charges in article 231 begins with the creation of the German Empire.

Bismarck and the German Question

The emergence of a united Germany in 1871 was a seismic shift in international relations comparable to the end of the Cold War 120 years later. Germany emerged as the most powerful state in Europe, pushing France and Austria to one side. Under the political leadership of the Chancellor, Otto von Bismarck, and the military leadership of Helmuth von Moltke, between 1864 and 1871 the heterogeneous collection of states that comprised 'Germany' was united under the Prussian crown. In the process Bismarck disposed of Prussia's rival for the leadership of Germany when in 1866 Austria was defeated in a brief but decisive war. Four years later Prussia went to war with and defeated France, the major military power of the time, and the Prussian King became *Kaiser* (Emperor) of Germany. That Bismarck had achieved his goal was remarkable enough. Perhaps just as extraordinary was that, having destroyed the existing international system, Bismarck was instrumental in creating and sustaining a new one. The position of Germany in the European balance was the cause of two world wars in the twentieth century and could easily have sparked a third. However, under Bismarck Germany was a power essentially satisfied with the status quo.[5]

Through deft diplomatic footwork, Bismarck established a series of alliances that safeguarded Germany's position. Thanks in no small measure to the moderate peace of 1866, by 1879 Austria-Hungary was sufficiently conciliated to sign an alliance with Berlin. Bismarck recognised that the two greatest threats to German security were Russia and France; the French were never reconciled to Germany's seizure of the provinces of Alsace and Lorraine in 1871. By treaties with both Austria-Hungary and Russia, Bismarck sought to prevent Paris from finding an ally who might aid the French in a war of revenge. Britain, eagle-eyed for powers that threatened to upset the European equilibrium, generally regarded Germany as a satisfied state and was thus prepared to side with her on various issues. Britain was far more concerned about France and Russia, rival imperial powers.[6]

Bismarck's European system had been in existence for less than twenty years when a series of events occurred that would eventually lead to its collapse. The old Kaiser died in 1888 at the age of 91. The pro-British heir died after only three months on the throne, and was succeeded by his son, Wilhelm II, who proceeded to pension off Bismarck in 1890. With both Kaiser and Chancellor new in post, German policy took a different path.

Kaiser Wilhelm II was physically damaged at birth and may also have suffered brain damage. Certainly, some of his contemporaries doubted his sanity; in 1891 Lord Salisbury, the British Prime Minister, in a fine piece of understatement wondered whether Wilhelm was 'all there'. Wilhelm never matured, loved dressing up in uniforms, and may have been a repressed homosexual. His character had an unpleasant streak which revealed itself in his love of jokes that humiliated and caused pain to others. As we shall see, the Kaiser's erratic behaviour was to have a destabilising effect on European security.

A Clash of Ideologies?

The war was perceived, and was presented during the conflict, as a struggle of liberty against authoritarianism. But some historians have disputed the idea that in 1914 Britain was substantially more democratic than Germany. If they are correct, the case that Britain had to respond to German aggression in 1914 is substantially undermined. Avner Offner, for instance, has argued that 'British and German societies differed in detail, not in substance, and the details were too minor to justify unlimited human sacrifice.'[7]

Edwardian Britain has been described as 'An Imperial Democracy' and this phrase nicely captures some of the ambiguities inherent in the political system.[8] Substantial portions of the population did not have the vote, and political leaders were overwhelmingly drawn from a small social elite. As one Edwardian expressed it, Britain enjoyed 'government of the people, for the people, by the best of the people'.[9] Edwardian Britain might have been an imperfect democracy, but it was a democracy nonetheless. Governments did not have untrammelled power, being answerable to parliament. Elections were held regularly and were, on the whole, free and fair. The armed forces were firmly under the control of the politicians, and foreign policy was also subject to the disciplines of parliamentary and cabinet government.

Perhaps more important than the precise details of the Edwardian electorate was Britain's espousal of liberal values such as respect for the rule of law, freedom of speech and of association, and the emphasis placed on individual liberty. While democracy was not available to the non-white subjects of Britain's vast empire, liberal values to some extent underpinned the way in which the colonies were governed. At home, free market capitalism went hand-in-hand with liberal democracy, which contributed to the fact that Britain in 1914 was a country of vast inequalities, of extremes of wealth and poverty. Paradoxically, Imperial Germany, which was much less democratic than Britain, had a superior welfare system.

The state Bismarck created in 1871 was a mixture of ancient and modern.[10] It was a monarchy, closer in spirit to the autocratic Russian than to the constitutional British model, but it also had some of the trappings of a parliamentary and even democratic state. The Kaiser remained King of Prussia, but other states within the empire such as Bavaria retained their monarchs and governmental organisations. On the surface, the Reichstag appeared to compare favourably with the House of Commons as a democratic institution. It 'was elected by the most progressive franchise in Europe: universal, secret, equal, direct manhood suffrage'. This enfranchisement of the working classes produced a large number of left-wing Social Democrat deputies, to the alarm of the Imperial authorities. But in reality, the Reichstag's powers were few. It could reject money bills but could not initiate legislation.[11] Although in some respects the Reichstag's influence grew during the new century, it 'remained ultimately impotent'.[12] There were few effective checks on the power of the Kaiser, unlike on his relative the British monarch. The Kaiser and his court remained at the centre of German political life. He was not an autocrat in its most literal sense, but certainly exercised a great deal of influence and real power. He was commander in chief of the armed forces, and could hire and fire the Chancellor, the rough equivalent to the British Prime Minister. The Chancellor himself was not answerable to the Reichstag. Neither were the German equivalent of 'ministers', who were actually state secretaries working within the Chancellor's department.

Under Wilhelm II, the weaknesses in the German political system became more pronounced. The atmosphere around the court − of flattery, favourites and seeking to catch the 'All Highest's' eye − would have been familiar to a courtier of a Tudor monarch. Wilhelm appointed officials to do his bidding and could and did dismiss them. There was no Reich cabinet in which foreign policy could be debated. This had disastrous results in the face of a diplomatic service characterised by 'obsequiousness' towards the Kaiser. In short, the Second Reich was a monarchy, 'on which the very highest officials of the Reich and state bureaucracy (as well as the leaders of the army and the navy) were psychologically and politically dependent'.[13]

Some historians have argued that Germany pursued a 'special path', a *Sonderweg*, instead of developing on the same lines as other 'normal' Western industrialised states such as France, Britain and the United States.[14] It is not necessary to accept the full implications of this theory to recognise that the German political system was different from that of its Western neighbours, and that this difference did matter. John Röhl, one of the leading historians of Wilhelm and his court, has painted the dreadful consequences of Germany's archaic political system. Germany's decision to go to war was taken by a small clique with disregard for the consequences of such an awesome step: 'a constitutional monarchy with a collective cabinet responsible to parliament and the public would not have acted in such isolation and ignorance and, for this reason alone, would have decided differently.'[15]

The Kaiser's Foreign Policy

Historians have at different times fixed the blame for 'causing' the First World War on a variety of states and factors.[16] A by no means complete short list would include Austria-Hungary, Germany, Russia, militarism, economic rivalry, colonial rivalry, naval rivalry, social-Darwinism, nationalism, capitalism, the development of rival alliances, railway timetables, inflexible military plans, the balance of power, the decline of the Ottoman Empire, and the 'short war illusion'. The truth is that there is no simple answer to the question 'what caused the First World War?' All of these factors, and others, need to be considered for a balanced judgement. However, German foreign and military policy from the mid-1890s onwards runs like a thread through any account of the origins of the Great War.

The first indication that German foreign policy was going to be different in the post-Bismarck era came when Wilhelm declined to renew the three year 'Reinsurance Treaty' that Bismarck had signed in 1887 with Russia. This was a secret deal negotiated as a back-up to the 1879 'Dual Alliance' with Austria-Hungary. The motives for this decision are complex, and involved a decisive tilt towards

Austria-Hungary. The end result was increased Russian suspicion of Germany. In 1892–3 Russia concluded an alliance with France. The very thing that Bismarck had striven to avoid had come about within three years of his dismissal: Germany, situated squarely in the heart of Europe, now had a potentially hostile alliance on both her western and eastern frontiers.

Over the next two decades the German strategic position was to worsen, thanks largely to the Wilhelmine 'New Course' in foreign policy. At the centre was a bid for what Chancellor Bülow described in 1897 as *Weltpolitik* (world policy). This was an attempt to gain colonies, to expand German power and economic influence. The spread of German economic interests in the Balkans and Turkey, and support for Austria-Hungary, a Balkan rival, further entrenched Russia's suspicion and fear of Berlin. In one respect, this might have played to Germany's advantage. In the 1890s Wilhelm believed that an alliance with Britain was achievable, if only on the basis of 'my enemy's enemy is my friend' given British fears of Russian expansionism in Asia.

Britain's refusal, for the moment, to abandon Splendid Isolation was a factor in the ambitious German naval plans unveiled in 1898. The architect of the new German fleet was Admiral Alfred von Tirpitz.[17] As Tirpitz assured Wilhelm, a sufficiently powerful navy would bring about a situation in which 'England will have lost every inclination to attack us and as a result concede to Your Majesty such a measure of naval mastery and enable Your Majesty to carry out a great overseas policy.'[18] The Royal Navy would be haunted by the prospect that even a victory over Tirpitz's newly powerful navy would be a Pyrrhic one, as a loss of ships could weaken it sufficiently to leave Britain in a poor position to face a challenge from French and Russian naval power. A powerful navy would give Germany leverage to get Britain to abandon its non-aligned stance. It is possible that Tirpitz really believed that Germany could take on Britain in a naval arms race, and actually win it, at least to the extent that the German navy could concentrate its warships in the North Sea. The Royal Navy, with its global responsibilities and fear of French and Russian threats to the empire, would have to spread its assets thinly. Like the leaders of the

German army, Tirpitz became obsessed with the idea of the single, decisive battle. The Royal Navy, its strength worn down by guerrilla action from mines and torpedoes, would be destroyed in a climactic contest. The British Empire would then be there for the taking.

Such a strategy rested on the least stable of foundations: wishful thinking. Tirpitz and Wilhelm assumed that the British would do nothing during the period when this new German navy was being built, that they would just sit back and watch their margin of superiority be whittled away. As the building programme began, British suspicions of Germany increased. The German foreign office was supposed to ensure that relations between London and Berlin remained harmonious, but their job was complicated by the Kaiser's habit of shooting from the mouth, which helped create a climate of fear and distrust. In an interview with the *Daily Telegraph*, for instance, Wilhelm declared that while he was pro-British, the same could not be said of the rest of his fellow Germans.

Even as German naval power increased, Britain did not seriously contemplate a preventive war, despite the fears of some leading Germans. Instead, she managed something that Tirpitz assumed was impossible and reached agreements with her colonial rivals, France and Russia, in 1904 and 1907 respectively. This allowed the Royal Navy to concentrate the bulk of its fleet in the North Sea, something else that Tirpitz had discounted as a possibility. The final flaw in Tirpitz's strategy was its reliance on the British coming out to fight. In early 1914, a senior German naval officer asked Tirpitz a simple question: 'What will you do if they do not come?' Tirpitz had no answer.[19] This policy backfired spectacularly. It led directly to the growth of antipathy between Britain and Germany, and was among the worst of a long list of foreign policy errors committed by Wilhelm's government. Some scholars have argued that the German navy was a symbol behind which a deeply divided society could unite.[20] If so, it failed, instead exacerbating the fault-lines in German society as the true cost became apparent.[21]

Judged by the standards of the era, Germany's *Weltpolitik* seems less unreasonable. Germany, after all, was only seeking to do what Britain had done in previous years, and the USA and Japan were doing at exactly that time. Whether Germany's bid for world power was wise was a different matter. Germany's economic and political advances to the east of her borders clashed directly with Russia's interests. France, still bitter over the loss of her provinces in 1871, remained unreconciled to German power. Worse still was the souring of relations with Britain. Although economic rivalry with Britain was bound to cause tensions, this need not have led to hostility, let alone war. Britain, after all, resigned itself to being surpassed in economic terms by the United States while simultaneously improving relations with Washington at the very time *Weltpolitik* was getting underway. As late as 1901 Britain had been considering an alliance with Germany, while the idea of an entente with France and Russia had appeared remote.

Several factors drove Britain and Germany into conflict.[22] The first was proximity. Unlike the USA, Germany was a near neighbour of the British. Moreover, unlike the American navy, the German fleet posed an obvious threat to the fundamental security of the British Isles and the sea lines of communication with the Empire. Britain took a conscious decision not to enter a naval arms race with the USA. The US Navy was not directed at Britain, while the German fleet self-evidently was. The second factor was that geography placed the Royal Navy's bases squarely across the routes which German ships would need to take to gain access to the Atlantic Ocean. To fulfil its *Weltpolitik*, Germany needed to remove the Royal Navy from these areas, either by agreement or conflict. Whatever Tirpitz may have imagined, wielding a fleet like a club in a crude attempt to intimidate the British was never likely to succeed.

Was it the case, as a British journal stated in 1911, that 'There is an inevitable conflict of ideals between Germany and Great Britain, between the satisfied nation and the unsatisfied nation, between the nation which desires to maintain the *status quo* and the nation that desires to alter it?'[23] The British could perhaps have been more generous in their response to the emergence of German power. The Germans could certainly have been less confrontational. A conciliatory policy towards Britain that served to sugar the pill of the economic challenge might have kept rivalry within bounds. An Anglo-German clash was not preordained; but a German decision to launch a naval arms race was the one thing most likely to bring one about.

There is a darker interpretation of *Weltpolitik*. In the aftermath of the Second World War, democratic West Germany was readmitted to the family of Western states. West German historians were understandably anxious to stress the discontinuities of German history, to argue that Hitler and the Nazis had been a uniquely evil phenomenon. It is easy to understand the fury that exploded in the 1960s when the Hamburg historian Fritz Fischer published books arguing that Germany deliberately planned and executed a war of aggression in 1914. Perhaps worse, Fischer drew attention to the similarities between the German war aims under the Kaiser and those of the Third Reich. Fischer's writings caused more than a spat between historians; they were of national consequence. By implying continuities between some aspects of the policy of Wilhelmine and Nazi Germany, he caused Germans to question the comfortable notion that Nazism had been an aberration. Forty years later, Fischer's thesis is still at the centre of the debate of the origins of the First World War. His ideas have been vigorously rebutted, but never debunked.

One factor common to both Imperial and Nazi Germany was militarism, here defined both as 'a veneration of military values and appearances in excess of what is strictly necessary for effective defence'[24] and as a situation where the armed forces have a strong degree of political influence and even power within the state. Eighteenth-century Prussia was famously described as an army with a state, rather than a state with an army, and Wilhelmine Germany inherited some of the characteristics of its ancestor. The peculiar constitutional arrangements meant that the army was effectively outside civilian control, with senior officers being responsible directly to the Kaiser, who had his own military cabinet. This gave them considerable political influence which they did not hesitate to use, even on subjects outside the military sphere. In turn, the German military and political leadership viewed the army as an instrument of social control. The deference shown to the military by civil society was highlighted in a ludicrous fashion in 1906, when a cobbler masquerading as an officer succeeded in arresting the mayor of a town and stealing some money. Dazzled by the uniform, no one thought to question his actions. A rather less amusing example of the power of the military came in 1913 when in the 'Zabern case' soldiers mistreated civilians in a town in Alsace. This affair brought out the extent to which the army, supported by senior figures including the war minister and the Crown Prince, was immune from political control. Militarism was by no means a purely German phenomenon. It was rife in Europe in the decade before the outbreak of war, but in Germany it was particularly virulent.[25]

The German army's planning for war was also 'militarist' in the sense that it stressed the purely military and organisational aspects at the expense of the political. By 1905 the Schlieffen Plan had been devised by the eponymous general and it was modified by his successor as Chief of the General Staff, the younger Moltke. A response to the reality of strategic encirclement, it called for a swift knockout blow against France, followed by a rapid redeployment via strategic railways to face the Russian 'steamroller' advancing from the east.[26] This plan was to be launched no matter the actual form of the crisis. The Schlieffen Plan has been criticised for its rigidity, logistic weaknesses, and over-optimistic assumptions about what could be achieved. Perhaps the most serious weakness of the plan was that the invasion of Belgium was likely to bring Britain into the war. Schlieffen was certainly aware of this possibility, but he and his successor underestimated its importance. If the Schlieffen Plan had worked and France and Russia had been defeated in short order, the ability of Britain to tip the balance in a protracted war of attrition would have been immaterial. Small wonder that historians have caught their breath at the sheer irresponsible scale of the gamble that the Schlieffen Plan represented.[27] The position of the army in Imperial Germany was such that politicians deferred to it, but in this case it was not simply a matter of abdication of political responsibility. In fact civilian leaders 'knew and approved of the Schlieffen Plan and of its political implications'.[28]

A Deliberate Plan for War?

On 8 December 1912 Kaiser Wilhelm summoned a meeting of some of his senior military advisers, including Tirpitz and General von Moltke. This meeting occupies a central place in the debate over the origins of the Great War. The 'Fischer school' of historians have interpreted this meeting as a 'War Council' at which the German elite took a deliberate decision for war in about eighteen months hence – when, in fact, war did break out.[29] Others have seen this meeting in less apocalyptic terms.[30] The jury is out over the real meaning of the 'War Council'. One problem is that the timings and circumstances for war sketched out by the Kaiser and Moltke in December 1912 coincide too closely with what actually happened in the summer of 1914 – real life is not usually like that. The idea of calculated planning for war goes against the long-established view that the outbreak of the war was accidental, or at worst the result of calculated risks going wrong. Yet the contrary case cannot lightly be discounted. There is other evidence of the Kaiser's bellicose state of mind in December 1912, his desire for Germany to achieve 'absolute hegemony'. At the very least, the meeting reveals that the eccentric and quite possibly deranged Kaiser was not alone among the highest levels of the German military elite in being willing to contemplate aggressive war. Many of the same men were still in place in July 1914.[31]

In the last decade or so, the role of Austria-Hungary in bringing about the war has once again been emphasised by historians. One of the few questions on which historians of the origins of the war are agreed is that the assassination of Archduke Franz Ferdinand, heir apparent to the Dual Monarchy, on 28 June 1914 acted as a catalyst for the war. When he was fatally shot in Sarajevo, capital of Bosnia-Herzegovina, which had only been formally annexed by Austria-Hungary in 1908, the finger of suspicion pointed at Serbia. Vienna felt that Serbia's challenge could not go unanswered if the ramshackle multi-ethnic empire, which included many Slavs, was to hold together. It was a matter, they believed, of the empire's credibility. The 'hawks' in Vienna – including General Franz Conrad von Hötzendorf, the Chief of Staff of the army and Berchtold, the foreign minister – eventually won the day. Fully understanding the possible repercussions, that Russia might react and thus bring about a much larger conflict, the Austrian leadership launched a local war against Serbia on 28 July.[32]

But without German approval, the Austrians are highly unlikely to have acted as they did. On 5–6 July Berlin had issued the so-called 'blank cheque', giving the Austrians the promise of unconditional support in a showdown with Serbia. Why the Germans took this step is crucial to an understanding of the events that led to general war in Europe.

The stakes were high. Germany, by supporting Austria-Hungary against Serbia, might drive a wedge between the Entente partners. Before, in the Bosnian crisis of 1908–9 and in the Balkan Wars of 1912–13, Britain and France had been very reluctant to support Russia in the Balkans. This might happen again. On 8 July 1914, Kurt Riezler, the Chancellor's secretary, recorded in his diary that 'if war does not come, if the Tsar does not want it or if an alarmed France advises peace, then we still have the prospect of manoeuvring the Entente apart over this move'.[33] If this happened, and in July 1914 German leaders believed it would, Germany would have broken her diplomatic encirclement without war.[34] But German leaders were fully prepared to risk war to achieve their objectives – the war they anticipated of course being short and victorious.

One view sees Germany's willingness to contemplate war as an 'escape forward', a way out of the domestic crisis: many a beleaguered regime has begun a foreign war to unite the nation behind the government.[35] An Argentine junta was to attempt something similar with its invasion of the Falkland Islands in 1982. Another view is that *Weltpolitik* had effectively painted Germany into a corner by July 1914. The Triple Entente of France, Russia and Britain had Germany encircled. Relations with Russia were poor. A decade after their defeat by the Japanese the Russians were busily rebuilding their armed forces, a process that would be complete by about 1916–17.

At the War Council in 1912 Moltke clearly had this in mind when arguing for war. Moreover, Britain's naval discussions with Russia in the summer of 1914 had exercised the mind of Bethmann-Hollweg, the German Chancellor since 1909, and his colleagues.[36] If Germany did not strike soon, the argument went, her international position would deteriorate further. Better war in 1914 than several years down the line under worse conditions. Germany's decision for war was thus, in this view, basically defensive.

None of these explanations for German bellicosity is mutually exclusive. That domestic factors played a part is shown by the eagerness with which the German leadership pinned the blame on Russia, which did help to unite the German people, including the Social Democrats, behind a 'defensive' war. Yet the state of domestic turmoil in 1914 should not be exaggerated. Neither should German fears about its future strategic situation. They existed, although they were probably exaggerated by the military to gain political capital.

In May 1914, even before the assassinations at Sarajevo but almost exactly eighteen months after the December 1912 War Council, Moltke again called for a 'preventative war'. Whatever his attitude a year and a half earlier, in July 1914 Chancellor Bethmann-Hollweg took a more hawkish position, being at the least ready to run the risk of conflict. In fact, there is strong evidence that the German leadership was prepared to go much further. A senior Austrian foreign office official, visiting Berlin in July 1914, discovered that Germany planned 'to fight an imperialist war of conquest against the Western Powers via us and Serbia'. The attitudes of many senior figures, including the Kaiser, Moltke, Jagow (the foreign secretary), the Crown Prince and Bethmann-Hollweg, support this contention. Certainly the Chancellor was no pawn, carried into war against his wishes by the generals, but, in his secretary's words, he 'calculated the risk very carefully'.[37]

Germany thus needed Austria-Hungary to take strong action against Serbia; indeed, German policy would have been in severe difficulties if it had not. Fortunately for the German plan, the terms of the ultimatum delivered to Belgrade on 23 July were so severe that they could only have been intended to cause the Serbs to reject them and thus bring about a pretext for war. The Serbs capitulated, which was not in the German script, but on 28 July the Austrians declared war anyway.

The Russians had begun to carry out partial mobilisation of their forces on 24–5 July. In contrast to the actions of Germany and Austria-Hungary, this was essentially a defensive move, but it gave the Germans a pretext to get further involved. As the initial Russian show of strength had not caused Austria to back down, on 30 July the Czar ordered full mobilisation, which was a propaganda gift to the Germans, who mobilised on the following day and declared war on Russia on 1 August.

General war was not inevitable in July–August 1914, in the sense that Germany and Austria, having embarked upon their high-risk strategy, might have got their way without fighting. The system of treaties has often been blamed for automatically dragging Europe into war, but this is to misunderstand the reality of 1914. Italy reneged on her treaty with Germany and Austria-Hungary, and remained neutral, only to join the war on the side of the Entente powers in 1915. The French might have similarly failed to honour their commitment to Russia, although France would probably have been invaded anyway, courtesy of the Schlieffen Plan. In the event, the French decided that the threat to Russia was so serious that France had no choice but to back her. To do otherwise would have been to stand by and watch the almost certain humiliation of her ally. This might well have broken the alliance and even led to Russia aligning herself with Germany, a foreign policy disaster of the first magnitude for France. Thus it was not solely to honour the Franco-Russian alliance that France went to war, but also because it was not willing 'to live again in the shadow of an almighty Germany'.[38]

Aided and abetted by Austria-Hungary, Germany's behaviour in July 1914 was the most important single factor in bringing about the First World War. The German leadership wanted hegemony in Europe and was prepared to go to war to achieve it. Article 231 of the Treaty of Versailles, the 'war guilt clause', which declared that the Great War was 'imposed upon' the Allies 'by the aggression of Germany and her allies' was, therefore, fundamentally correct.

Was it a Mistake for Britain to Enter the War?

Britain's *casus belli* in 1914 was the fate of Belgium. Concern over the fate of the Low Countries was nothing new. In the early 1580s the England of Queen Elizabeth I was faced with a threat that was to become all too familiar over the next 400 years. The most powerful state in Europe, Philip II's Spain, was seeking to dominate the continent by force of arms. In a memorandum the Queen's principal minister, Lord Burghley, emphasised the importance of preventing Spain from 'overthrow[ing] the Low Countries, which hitherto have been as a counterscarp to your Majesty's kingdom'.[39] A counterscarp was literally an outer part of the defences of a fortress. Burghley's insight, that denying modern-day Netherlands and Belgium to a hostile power was essential to English security, remains valid to the present day.

As a group of islands, historically Great Britain has been invulnerable to attack as long as her navy has been powerful enough to prevent an enemy from conveying an invading army across the English Channel or North Sea. If, however, a would-be invader could weaken or even destroy the power of the Royal Navy, Britain's security would vanish in an instant. This is what Winston Churchill meant when he described Admiral Jellicoe, the commander of the Grand Fleet at the Battle of Jutland in May 1916, as 'the only man on either side who could lose the war in an afternoon'.[40] Possession of the Low Countries handed an enemy a powerful weapon against the Royal Navy and the seaborne trade on which Britain's prosperity depended by opening up another front and giving a rival navy facilities in continental Channel ports. 'Keep your attention upon Antwerp', British Foreign Secretary Lord Castlereagh urged an assistant in 1813:

> The destruction of its arsenal is essential to our safety. To leave
> it in the hands of France is little short of imposing upon Great
> Britain the charge of a perpetual war establishment.[41]

For the word 'France' one could substitute that of any other hostile power over the last four centuries: British security interests have remained essentially the same.

'He that commands the sea is at great liberty, and may take as much and as little of the war as he will.' This seductive view was penned by the philosopher Francis Bacon (1561–1626) and has influenced many strategists since.[42] Back in the 1580s Elizabeth I demolished the strategic logic behind this way of thinking with her remark that 'If the nation of Spain should make a conquest of those [Low] Countries ... in that danger ourself, our countries and people might shortly be'.[43] In short, England had to prevent an enemy gaining possession of the Low Countries. With the outer ramparts in the enemy's possession, fortress England would become much more difficult to defend, as was to be frequently demonstrated over the next four centuries. Successive governments shared Elizabeth and Burghley's view of British security interests. A search for security led Britain to go to war over the Low Countries in 1793, to guarantee Belgian neutrality by a treaty of 1839 and to go to war in defence of that treaty in 1914, to fight to defend Belgium in 1940, and to include the Benelux states in a system of defensive alliances during the Cold War.

Belgium has been cursed by a geo-strategic position which has ensured that it has been sucked into many wars, willingly or not. A meeting of the British Committee of Imperial Defence (CID) in 1912 concluded that Belgian and Dutch neutrality in a future war would hinder a British blockade of Germany. Therefore the Royal Navy considered blockade operations against the Low Countries. This would have involved a clear breach of the non-aligned status of the Belgians and Dutch, and would certainly have undermined Britain's 'moral superiority' in claiming to go to war for 'Belgian neutrality' in 1914.[44] Winston Churchill was faced with a not dissimilar situation in December 1939 over whether to lay mines in the territorial waters of neutral Norway. He robustly advocated such a course on the grounds that Britain was at war 'to re-establish the reign of law and to protect the liberties of small countries. Our defeat ... would be fatal, not only to ourselves, but to the independent life of every small country in Europe ... Small nations must not tie our hands when we are fighting for their rights and freedom ...' Churchill argued not so much that necessity knew no law, but that there was a higher law than the strict and selfish observance of neutrality by small nations.[45] Underpinning Churchill's argument was the whole question of intent. The Western powers in both world wars were faced by the dilemma that in order to survive they needed to adopt some of the ruthless measures used by their ideological foes. Before the Great War, the Low Countries represented an even more fundamental British interest than did Norway in 1939.

The Balance of Power

The concept of the Balance of Power lay at the heart of British foreign policy. This has meant different things at different times to different people, but a classic statement of one of the principles underlying it was made by the Victorian statesman Lord Palmerston to parliament in 1848:

> It is a narrow policy to suppose that this country or that is marked out as the eternal ally or the perpetual enemy of England. We have no eternal allies, and we have no perpetual enemies. Our interests are eternal and perpetual.[46]

Essentially, Britain's 'eternal and perpetual' interests have lain in preventing any one state from becoming too powerful, especially if that state has sought to flex its muscles by way of military conquest in Western Europe. Palmerston once commented privately that Britain acted as 'impartial mediators' between France and the eastern Powers: ' ... as long as both parties remain quiet, we shall be friends with both; but ... whichever side breaks the peace, that side will find us against them'.[47] If one state should succeed in dominating Europe, Britain's economic interests would be threatened. On some occasions, Britain has been faced by the unwelcome prospect of the triumph of an ideological enemy. Above all, if a hostile power did succeed in achieving a dominating position in Europe, with no powerful continental allies Britain would be very vulnerable to attack – particularly with major ports in enemy hands. Given Britain's strategic weaknesses and strengths, she has almost invariably fought as part of a coalition with other threatened powers.

Over the years Britain's allies and enemies have been interchangeable. When Spain was the threat, Elizabeth I supported France. A century later, Louis XIV of France sought to gain hegemony and Britain allied with Austria and a host of smaller states to resist him. From 1793 to 1815, with one brief break, Britain fought Napoleonic France in a series of coalitions with at various times Russia, Prussia, Spain and Austria. In the twentieth century France and Russia became allies against Germany, and for forty years West Germany became an ally against the USSR. Since 1688 there has been only one major war, the American War of Independence or Revolutionary War (1776–83), in which Britain has faced a hostile Europe without a major ally. It is no coincidence that this was the only one in which the British were defeated.

Britain and the End of Splendid Isolation

Amidst the military parades and self-congratulation that surrounded Queen Victoria's Diamond Jubilee in 1897, Rudyard Kipling struck a discordant note. His poem, 'Recessional', warned against smugness and complacency. Britain might have 'Dominion over palm and pine' but 'Far-called, our navies melt away/On dune and headland sinks the fire/Lo, all our pomp of yesterday/Is one with Nineveh and Tyre!'[48] Kipling's gloom was shared by a number of Britain's elite at the end of the nineteenth century. Britain's position in the world no longer looked as secure as it had twenty or thirty years earlier. The United States and Germany were challenging British economic dominance. The rise of new powers, Germany, the USA and Japan, threatened to overturn the international status quo in which Britain had the pre-eminent position. Britain, in the arch-Imperialist Joseph Chamberlain's striking phrase, was a 'weary titan', bowed down under a vast burden of responsibilities.[49] This sense of weakness led to the gradual reshaping of British foreign policy and strategy.

Things changed first in North America. By the turn of the century Britain had recognised the growing strength of the USA and in 1901 she abandoned the attempt to compete with the US as a naval power. Anglo-American relations were good, which was just as well because Britain tacitly admitted that Canada was indefensible. An alliance with Japan in 1902 came next. This was the first substantial breach of 'Splendid Isolation', the policy of holding aloof from alliances. By doing so Britain relieved the pressure in the Far East.

Far more dramatic was the rapprochement with the French. This brought together two long-standing colonial rivals who had come close to war as recently as 1898, but whose fears about the changes in the international scene proved stronger than their mutual antipathies. The accumulated historical baggage of hundreds of years, of battles fought and won and struggles for empire, could not be simply forgotten overnight, and was to re-emerge with a vengeance in 1940. Yet the two states had much in common. When President Poincaré proclaimed that Britain and France were 'equally attached to peace, equally passionately devoted to progress, equally accustomed to the ways of liberty' he was not simply engaging in 'platitudes'. Their common liberal democratic heritage was important when faced by an autocratic, militaristic enemy. France and Britain fought a war of national survival between 1914 and 1918. Strategic realities mean that Britain would have probably fought alongside France whatever the nature of the French regime in 1914. Nonetheless, during the First World War 'a sense of common values was a vital cement for Anglo-French relations, as well as a first-class theme for propaganda to the rest of the world'.[50]

This is to anticipate events. The 1904 *entente cordiale* was not an alliance, still less one aimed at Germany. Rather, it involved the settling of colonial disputes between the two states, setting the scene for better relations. Ultimately, it was German behaviour which drove the two states closer together. This process began in 1905, when the Kaiser made a typically ham-fisted intervention in the affairs of Morocco, an independent state in which the French had strong interests. Britain offered France limited diplomatic support. These first, tentative steps towards transforming the *entente cordiale* into something more concrete became firmer during the Second Moroccan Crisis.[51] On 1 July 1911 the German gunboat *Panther* sailed into Agadir harbour in the midst of an international dispute over the imposition of a *de facto* French protectorate over Morocco. War between Britain and Germany briefly seemed a possibility. Britain was less concerned with the details of colonial arrangements in Africa than with fears that Germany was seeking to undermine the entente and rearrange the European balance of power. British fears were exaggerated, fuelled by 'insecurity'.[52] The German foreign minister, Kiderlen, had intended the dispatch of the *Panther* to be a bit of opportunistic gunboat diplomacy of the most literal kind, to secure colonial gains that would have played well with opinion at home.[53] Instead, the Agadir crisis resulted in Britain swinging behind France more firmly than ever before. Germany, and specifically the Kaiser, paid the price of frightening the British with its blustering belligerence and Tirpitz's naval programme.

One major reason why Britain had been able to pursue a policy of Splendid Isolation was the absence of a state seeking to overturn the balance of power in Europe. With the emergence of Germany in this role Britain began, with a certain reluctance, to return to her traditional policy of constructing coalitions to uphold the status quo. Thanks to India, Britain was a Great Power in Asia with a long land frontier to defend, and for much of the nineteenth century Britain had feared that Russia posed a threat to her Indian empire. The defeat of Russia at the hands of Britain's new ally Japan in 1904–5 allowed the British to breathe somewhat more easily. By concluding the 1907 Anglo-Russian agreement (a step even more radical than the rapprochement with France) the British could now concentrate on the main threat from Germany. In the ten years since Kipling wrote 'Recessional', Britain, recognising her increased weakness, had come to terms with three out of four of her potential rivals. France, the United States and Russia had challenged British imperial interests. The fourth, Germany, imperilled

British security in her backyard. There was a huge difference between the two categories of threat.

The Doctrine of the Free Hand

Despite the new strategic reality, some old habits died extremely hard. One that was exceptionally difficult to eradicate was the notion that Britain had 'a free hand' in international relations. One politician defined this in 1896 as 'the freedom to act as we choose in any circumstances that may arise'.[54] There is little doubt that some British leaders continued to believe in this doctrine down to August 1914, and technically they were correct to do so. The pre-war Anglo-French naval and military discussions did not commit Britain to going to war in support of France. The British made this crystal clear on a number of occasions, and the French understood this. General Joffre, the French army commander in chief, chose to exclude the British from his calculations when drawing up war plans; after all, he could not be certain that the British army would show up, and if they did, in what strength. In November 1912 Sir Edward Grey, the Foreign Secretary, and Paul Cambon, the French Ambassador, carried out an exchange of notes which reaffirmed that neither party was committed to supporting the other militarily. The only definite commitment was for the two sides to consult with each other in time of crisis, to decide 'whether both Governments should act together to prevent aggression and preserve peace, and if so what measures they would be prepared to take in common'. This was a document sanctioned not just by Grey and other interventionists, but by the entire Liberal cabinet, which included some members with a heritage of anti-militarism, anti-imperialism and suspicion of Great Power politics.

Thus in theory, Britain was in the happy position of both having its cake and eating it: the understanding with France gave her a measure of security while leaving the government free to decide whether the circumstances of a European war really warranted British involvement. In reality, though, Britain was becoming increasingly committed to supporting France, morally if not legally. In July 1912, the two powers had agreed to an arrangement by which the Royal Navy reduced its forces in the Mediterranean, while the French navy did the same in the Channel. Both navies would thus look after the interests of the other. This was a good deal for Britain as it allowed her to maintain the strength of the fleet in the North Sea without exorbitant cost.[55] Morally, the defence of the French Channel coast thus passed to Britain. In the crisis of July–August 1914 the inherent contradictions in British policy became clear for all to see, weakened Britain's response, caused trouble with France without doing anything to deter Germany and brought Asquith's government to the verge of collapse.

On the outbreak of war the Liberal cabinet was divided over whether German forces passing through a narrow corridor of Belgian territory would constitute a *casus belli*, or whether the whole country had to be invaded. Certainly, nine years before, the Foreign Office had taken the view that the 1839 treaty did not oblige Britain to come to the aid of Belgium 'in any circumstances and at whatever risk'.[56] There are several issues here, but *Realpolitik* was at the heart of them. That Foreign Office officials (of any state, at any time) might seek to find loopholes in existing commitments which might prove inconvenient is not surprising. This is particularly true given the British notion of the 'free hand'. Still less surprising was the initial response of Asquith's cabinet, given the type of men of which it was composed, and that they had to answer to their constituencies, both narrowly and broadly defined. Even Lloyd George, who was to become an advocate and practitioner of total war, had a heritage as a Radical and had been a prominent opponent of the Boer War and had to be argued round to supporting British intervention.

However, *Realpolitik* intervened. Asquith set out his thinking in a letter to Venetia Stanley, a younger woman with whom he was having a (possibly platonic and one-sided) affair. Asquith noted that Britain was not *formally* obliged to help Russia and France, and sending the BEF to support the French 'at this moment is out of the question & would serve no object'. On the other hand, Asquith pointed out that Britain had 'ties' with France born of 'long standing & intimate friendship'; that it was not to the advantage of Britain to see France 'wiped out as a Great Power'; that Britain 'cannot allow Germany to use the Channel as a hostile base'; and that Britain had 'obligations to Belgium to prevent her being utilised & absorbed by Germany'.[57] Asquith thus identified the need to maintain the balance of power, a moral commitment to France and legal obligations to Belgium, and a direct threat to British security. Substituting the names of the appropriate states, this summary of the situation on 2 August 1914 would have been instantly recognisable to Palmerston, Castlereagh and even Elizabeth I.

In the end the cabinet did decide for war, with only two resignations in protest. Undoubtedly the German attack on Belgium simplified matters. Going to war for 'poor little Belgium', in defence of a treaty, was easier to 'sell' to the public than going to war for the sake of the balance of power. It was certainly easier to sell than going to war for the sake of good relations with Russia, which was also a factor.[58] Entering the war on the side of France and Russia was the right decision. If Britain had done otherwise it would have turned its back on the strategy that had provided security for four centuries, betraying a fellow democracy in the process. Russia and France would probably have been defeated, leaving Britain 'deservedly friendless'[59] and forced to gamble on the goodwill of an ideological enemy with apparently limitless ambitions. For the first time in a century, a powerful enemy would have been on Britain's counterscarp. For Britain, the alternatives in August 1914 were not war or peace, for peace involves more than the mere absence of conflict. If Britain had stood aside from the war, her reward would have been massive insecurity, and the likelihood of facing a war at a later date, without allies, against a Germany with naval bases in the Low Countries or even northern France. Taking the long view, then, the First World War appears not as an aberration in British history but simply as one round in a long struggle to prevent one continental state from dominating the rest. The German invasion of Belgium made British entry into the war virtually inevitable, for Britain was no more willing to countenance hostile occupation of the Low Countries in 1914 than in previous centuries. To have failed to stand up to the German attack in the west would have been an abdication of responsibility that would have courted national disaster.

CHAPTER 3

TOTAL WAR

To many it is a source of amazement that the First World War lasted so long, that the armies of Europe were prepared to continue fighting, despite the fact that the Western Front had solidified into a bloody deadlock. Why did the states of Europe endure such appalling casualties without coming to a compromise peace?

The short answer is that the war went on because the peoples of Europe willed it so. In the first years of the war the home fronts of all the belligerents provided a steadfast level of support for their national governments and armed forces. Not until 1917 was there substantial wavering of resolve, and even then only Russia was forced out of the war. Until 1917, there was little pressure from below for a compromise peace. This fact allowed governments on both sides to pursue far-reaching war aims that made a compromise peace impossible. This was the reality of total war, an all-out struggle that involved the mobilisation of entire economies and societies.

The Emergence of Total War, 1914–16

By 1914 popular nationalism was more than a century old. In the last decade of the eighteenth century the modern 'Nation in Arms' was born. The nineteenth-century Prussian soldier and military philosopher Karl von Clausewitz described the new partnership as a 'remarkable trinity': alongside the government and the armed forces, the people now had a key role to play. Although popular nationalism was a creation of the French Revolution, conservative governments using such means as education, the press, military service and the popularity of monarchs, had very largely tamed and diverted it into approved channels. Some states, notably Britain and France, had become democracies. Although there was widespread apprehension among Europe's elite about how reliable the working classes would prove in time of war, truly revolutionary socialism had made little headway in Western states. In 1914, to the deep disappointment of those socialists who believed that a concerted series of strikes could prevent Europe going to war, the majority of socialists across Europe supported the national war effort, although some dissented from this consensus. In Britain, opposition was fairly low-key. Ramsay Macdonald resigned as the leader of the Labour Party, and anti-war groups held meetings – many, like that sponsored by North London Herald League in Finsbury Park, facing violent opposition from 'patriots'.[1]

As far back as the 1830s, Alexis de Tocqueville had pointed out that, once roused, democracies could fight wars with the same fervour as they had formerly clung to peace. One of the paradoxes of total war in the twentieth century is that, much as de Tocqueville predicted, liberal democratic states have had to adopt many of the trappings of authoritarian states in order to defend their values against ideological enemies.[2] This included the persecution of minorities such as aliens or pacifists believed (rightly or otherwise) to pose a threat to effective prosecution of the war effort. Campaigns such as that for 'One Hundred Per Cent Americanism' launched in the USA in 1917–18 attacked some of the basic freedoms that underpin democracy, such as the right of freedom of expression,[3] and in retrospect the brave individuals who stood out against the tide deserve our admiration.

But they remained a minority. At the beginning, the vast bulk of the British population was willing to participate in the war, as the figures for enlistment into the army indicate. Initially they did so in the belief that the war would be short. Lord Kitchener, the Secretary of State for War, announced on 7 August that the war would last for three years, but neither this, nor the later beginning of the trench stalemate, shook popular support for the struggle. That the public continued to back the war was vital. History suggests that a democracy cannot fight and win a total war without the consent and active involvement of the masses. There are, of course, plenty of examples of propaganda and coercion. Some British recruiting posters resorted to moral blackmail (on one, a child asked her father 'Daddy, what did YOU do in the Great War?'). Some men came under pressure from peers or employers to enlist. Following a strike in May 1915 a number of tram workers of military age were sacked by the London County Council, in part to get them to join the army.[4] But in 1914, 1915 and 1916 coercion was less important in gearing the British population for war than 'persuasion' and 'self-mobilization', that is, individuals and groups choosing to become involved, both emotionally and physically, in the war effort. The same was true of France and Germany.[5] Overall the level of genuinely voluntary activity in Britain was impressive. In addition to countless acts of sock-knitting and the like, a number of public-spirited voluntary bodies existed, the Volunteer Training Corps (a Great War version of 'Dad's Army') and the Women's Police Volunteers among others.[6]

The most remarkable example of mobilisation for total war was the creation of the New Armies.[7] On 7 August 1914 Kitchener issued an appeal for 100,000 volunteers for the army. Within five months 1,186,000 men had joined the colours. Kitchener's appeal to arms overturned pre-war planning, which had assumed that the British army would remain a small force. The vast influx of men swamped existing facilities, and in the autumn and winter of 1914–15 many men of 'Kitchener's Army' were billeted in private homes or in makeshift camps. At first they lacked uniforms, and drilled with wooden rifles. In addition, some units were raised by private individuals, organisations or by local authorities. Lord Derby, a political magnate with a power-base on Merseyside, recruited four battalions of Liverpool Pals, while the 15th, 16th and 17th Battalions of the Highland Light Infantry were respectively the 'Glasgow Tramways', 'Glasgow Boys' Brigade' and 'Glasgow Chamber of Commerce' battalions. The majority of units were, however, raised by the government, and simultaneously Britain's pre-war Territorial Force (TF) of part-time citizen soldiers was greatly expanded.

The raising of Kitchener's Army was only the beginning of the mobilisation of British society for war. Soon men had to be found to replace the huge casualties sustained by the British army on the Western Front and elsewhere, and the demands of the armed forces for manpower had to be weighed alongside those of the factory and farm.[8] Although 2,466,719 volunteers had joined the army by the end of 1915, in January 1916 conscription had to be introduced. In all, 5,704,000 men served in the British army during the First World War, split roughly equally between volunteers and conscripts.[9] The army of the First World War was larger by far than any other army raised by Britain, before or since.

Britain's mobilisation for total war was paralleled in the Empire. Out of a population of 8 million Canada sent 458,000 men overseas, of whom 57,000 became casualties. The 5 million Australians sent 332,00, resulting in 59,000 casualties; for New Zealand the figures were 1.1 million, 112,000 and 17,000. India found one and a half million volunteers. Moreover, in the last two years of the war about one third of the BEF's munitions were produced in Canada.[10]

The passing of the Defence of the Realm Act (DORA) in August 1914 gave the British government enormously enhanced powers. In the first few months of the war the government carried out some actions that demonstrated the increased grip of the state. On the day after war was declared, for example, temporary control was taken of the railways. However, for the most part the slogan of 'business as usual' was initially well deserved. The first major break with this came after the Battle of Neuve Chapelle in March 1915. Failure in the battle was blamed on the shortage of shells, which eventually resulted in Lloyd George taking control of the newly created Ministry of Munitions. This was 'an emergency Department of State, created to serve one purpose – the organization of productive resources for munitions manufacture' and it was an undoubted success in raising the production of guns and ammunition.[11] Lloyd George became the dominant figure in the Coalition government which itself came into being partly as a result of the 1915 'shell scandal'. In December 1916, trading on his reputation as a 'man of push and go', he replaced Asquith as Prime Minister. Under Lloyd George's administration the government's tentacles spread far and wide into the economy, eventually bringing munitions, transport, much of the labour force, imports, food supplies and prices under government control.[12]

As part of the consensus established to wage total war, business and organised labour were taken into partnership by government. Lloyd George championed Sir Eric Geddes, a railway entrepreneur who served successively at the Ministry of Munitions, reorganised the BEF's transportation, and finally became the political head of the Royal Navy.[13] Labour MPs, first Arthur Henderson and later George Barnes, were appointed to the cabinet and the government negotiated with trades unions to introduce into factories 'dilution' – the use of non-skilled workers, perhaps women, for jobs previously confined to skilled men. For their part, unions secured improvements in working conditions for their members. The creation of a total war economy was far from smooth. Strikes continued to be a problem throughout the war, much to the disgust of many soldiers in the trenches. The government tended to respond to individual problems with *ad hoc* solutions, rather than creating and then executing a grand plan.[14] The teething problems of the new war economy had ramifications on the battlefield. The massive expansion of the munitions industry in 1915–16 inevitably led to a fall in the quality of material. The large number of dud shells fired by British gunners before the Battle of the Somme was a symptom of this problem. But by 1917–18 factory workers had gone through a learning curve of their own, and were able to provide frontline soldiers with high quality munitions in vast quantities. The creation of a centrally directed war economy capable of supplying its huge armies with sufficient quantities of weapons, ammunition and all the other equipment it needed to fight a modern high-intensity attritional war was a considerable achievement of the British nation in arms. Without it, the victories of the BEF on the battlefields of France and Belgium would have been impossible.

The same is true of the vital contribution of the American economy. Britain and France had a huge advantage in being able to draw upon American economic power even before the USA entered the war. Simultaneously, the Royal Navy prevented the Central Powers from getting access to American resources. Between 1914 and 1916, American trade with Allied states grew from $824 million to in excess of $3 billion, while trade with Britain's enemies declined from $170 million to below $1 million. The US government also in 1915 made it easier to issue loans to belligerents, and on the eve of America's entry into the war, the Allied powers were benefiting from over $2.5 billion of loans, the Central Powers receiving only $127 million.[15] During the Somme campaign about 75 per cent of the British army's light field artillery shells was produced in the USA. Over the course of the entire conflict the bulk of the Allies' supply of high explosive came from American companies such as Du Pont and the Hercules Powder Company. Similarly, firms like New England Westinghouse provided $181 million worth of infantry weapons.[16]

The Allied demand for loans and war goods gave American industry an important boost and ensured that the USA had a significant stake in an Entente victory. It also helped enormously in preparing the United States itself for participation in a total war. Between 1914 and 1916 an industrial base was established that was capable of supplying a mass army with war goods. Moreover, the Council of National Defense, established in 1916, played a major role in beginning the process of mobilising the vast resources of the state. The advocates of 'preparedness' − prominent individuals allied to elements of the Wilson administration and the armed forces − had undertaken important planning and succeeded in preparing the way psychologically for America to fight an all-out war. Conscription was no longer unthinkable, and the US Army General Staff had planned how to train and officer a mass army. By 1917, the preparedness campaign had laid the foundations for the United States to wage total war.[17] Ironically, much of the equipment of the American Expeditionary Force (AEF) came from the USA's allies, because American industry was committed to producing materiel for Britain and France.[18]

War Weariness and Remobilisation, 1917–18

By 1917–18, the initial enthusiasm for war was wearing thin. The staggering casualty lists and the lack of any spectacular military success were taking their toll on morale. Added to that was the burden of the war on ordinary people: long hours; the greyness of everyday life; the dread of the arrival of the telegram from the War Office that would bring bad news about a husband, son or father; the fear of death from an air raid. A civilian noted in his diary on 20 January 1918 that:

> This week end has been a difficult one for the housewife. There is a great shortage of meat and many families have had to go without. Even in our own quiet village long queues wait outside the shops for hours to get small quantities of margarine, etc. ... It is reported from Chesterfield that horse-flesh is being sold for human food and that it is fetching 1/– per lb, at which price it is said to have found ready purchasers ... [A] man was fined yesterday £500, and sentenced to imprisonment for one month as well, for hoarding food.[19]

All the belligerent nations were suffering from the same war weariness and the idea of a compromise peace of some sort began at last to seem attractive. The response was what has been described as 'remobilisation' – a concerted effort by governments to galvanise support for the war amongst their populations.

These days, historians are inclined to emphasise the continuities between the policies of the Asquith and Lloyd George governments. Nevertheless, the change in personal style was important. The Welsh Wizard was a masterful exponent of democratic politics. Of humble birth and Radical credentials, he contrasted with the remote and patrician style of his predecessor. Lloyd George symbolised the move to reinforce the legitimacy of the British state in the eyes of its population. The campaign featured the announcement of 'democratic' war aims (see page 72), the reformation of the franchise by the introduction of near-universal suffrage, and propaganda to emphasise the ideological nature of the war. Judged by results, the campaign was a considerable success – as were similar efforts in France. Remarkably, in Britain civilian support for the war was probably as strong in November 1918 as it had ever been.[20] The regeneration of popular support for a war fought to a victorious conclusion was undoubtedly an important factor in maintaining civilian and military morale.[21]

A favourite debate among social historians is the extent to which war brings about social and political change. The example of Britain in the two world wars suggests that the greater the participation of a population in a war, the greater must be the reward (or bribe) offered.[22] The situation in Germany contrasted starkly with that in Britain and France. Initially, the German people were united behind the war effort, at least superficially. The next couple of years put national unity under strain. The 1916 'Hindenburg Programme' of mobilisation for total war made huge demands on the German economy and the people that worked in it. They had to do so without full stomachs; the winter of 1916–17 became notorious as the 'turnip winter'. The population did not starve, but it did go hungry, and the patent inequalities in the system of food distribution produced a high level of disgruntlement with the Kaiser's regime.

The German response to the onset of war weariness was rather different from that of the Western democracies. Efforts by the civilian politicians to remobilise the population in 1917–18 were sabotaged by the unwillingness of the German military dictatorship to countenance moves towards democracy. The German equivalent of the populist total warriors Lloyd George and his French counterpart, Georges Clemenceau, was Field Marshal Paul von Beneckendorff und von Hindenburg. While the British and French governments held out to their populations the enticements of civilian democracy and reform, all that the German leadership offered was military dictatorship and 'patriotic instruction'. The failure to offer a carrot in the form of political reform contributed to the German crisis in morale, which in 1918 played a significant role in determining the result of the war.[23] Substantial portions of the population came to believe that the regime had 'broken faith' with them by failing to provide the basic necessities of life; this 'undermin[ed] the legitimacy' of the regime.[24] This was bad enough, but the German leadership compounded the problem by failing to offer the ordinary German a genuine stake in the survival of the regime. The legitimacy of the Wilhelmine state crumbled, followed shortly after by the collapse of the army and then Imperial Germany itself.

War Aims, 1914–17

All wars have to end at some point. Most end with a compromise peace of one sort or another. It might be a peace of mutual exhaustion, or a situation in which one belligerent achieves some limited aims and then offers a moderate peace or simply decides not to fight on. It is rare for a war to continue until one side is utterly defeated. The First World War was unusual, although not unique, in that it was a total conflict with a strong ideological element. While in theory this should not have ruled out a negotiated settlement, in reality it made it almost impossible. Both sides believed that too much was at stake to allow a compromise; both sides, until almost the very end of the war, believed that they could win.

At bottom, the reason for the failure to negotiate an end to the fighting came down to utterly irreconcilable aims. Germany sought to achieve hegemony over Europe, while Britain, France and later the USA sought to prevent this from occurring. The impetus of the

Germans' initial assault brought them important gains in Belgium and eastern France, and allowed the German army to sit on the tactical defensive in the West while concentrating on knocking Russia out of the war. As long as the British and French were unable to force them out of their conquests by military means, the Germans saw no reason to compromise. For the Entente Powers to have agreed to peace on the basis of Germany holding on to her gains in the West would have been to concede defeat, and would have left both French and British security gravely weakened.

As Bethmann-Hollweg's 'September Programme' of 1914 demonstrates, even at this early stage Germany was not thinking in terms of a moderate peace. Rather, Belgium would become a 'vassal state', and French power would be crushed, although France would be allowed to exist as a third-class power which posed no threat to Germany. *Mitteleuropa*, a 'central European customs union' would, it was planned, 'stabilize Germany's economic dominance over Central Europe'.[25] German policy was by no means fully consistent over the question of *Mitteleuropa*, which caused some serious problems with Austria-Hungary. 'None the less,' as one of the leading historians of war aims has recently written, 'an imperialist settlement was desired by powerful forces in German society, including the right and centre in the Reichstag and much of heavy industry, agriculture, and the intellectual elite, as well as by Wilhelm II himself.'[26]

For the most part, Germany's war aims in Western Europe remained unchanged throughout the war, as did plans for a large empire in Africa and naval bases in the Atlantic and Indian Oceans, and, closer to home, the Mediterranean Sea. In the East, as military victory handed Germany control of huge swathes of the Czar's empire, Berlin's ambitions grew from the comparatively modest aim in the September 1914 Programme of pushing Russia's borders eastwards to, by 1917, the establishment of puppet states in Poland, the Baltic region and the Ukraine. Thereby Germany missed a strategic opportunity. The cohesion of a coalition is often a weak point. Germany might have detached Russia from the other Entente Powers in 1915 by making a firm offer to the Czar of an acceptable peace. However, the German version of a 'moderate' peace consisted of annexing a strip of land in Russian Poland that would be ethnically cleansed of Slavs and Jews and repopulated with Germans. But at this time the Russians had wide-ranging territorial aims of their own, and the tentative proposals were rejected.[27] Having failed to detach Russia from the enemy coalition, in 1916 the Germans tried to knock the French out of the war through a major offensive at Verdun. This attempt also failed. Germany's paradox was that it was unlikely to win the war unless a major adversary could be brought to conclude a separate peace, but the nature of German war aims meant that none of its enemies would take such a course unless it had already suffered a catastrophic defeat.

The record of the conflicts of the twentieth century demonstrates that if democracies are going to fight protracted and attritional wars they need the issues to be painted in bright, bold colours. This seems to be the lesson of the Korean and Vietnam Wars, which were protracted and attritional but also limited and thus difficult to 'sell' to electorates. In 1914 British war aims were fairly limited. Belgium was to be restored, and the power of the German military broken. This was not to be achieved by smashing the enemy state so thoroughly that Germany could be remoulded in the victors' image, as actually occurred in 1945. Rather, as Michael Howard has noted, a beaten Germany would 'be purged of "Prussianism", as a century earlier France had been purged of Bonapartism, and reformed once again as a co-operative member of the Concert of Europe'. As the juggernaut of total war gathered momentum, these relatively modest aims grew more ambitious. However, civilians 'had not flocked to the colours in 1914 to die for the balance of power'. British and American war aims were thus portrayed in terms of the defence and spreading of democracy, of destroying Prussian militarism, and of self determination for the peoples of the Austro-Hungarian empire.[28]

Such aims were not mere inventions of propagandists. There was a strong ideological element to the war. Neither is it the case that the masses were duped. British propaganda skilfully built on existing popular beliefs about the nature of the German threat. In this they were greatly assisted by the Germans themselves, who demonstrated an unerring ability to hand Allied propagandists gift-wrapped weapons. The German use of poison gas at Ypres in 1915 and the bombing of British cities were seen as examples of typical Hunnish 'frightfulness', as was the celebrated German execution of Nurse Cavell for aiding Allied prisoners. Another was the sinking of the liner *Lusitania* with the death of citizens of the then neutral United States. The democracies, too, were quite ready to take off the gloves, using economic blockade and strategic bombing, but their antennae were much more finely attuned to the importance of presenting themselves as being in the right, especially during the period when the USA was still neutral.

In so many ways the unpalatable behaviour of the German regime in the First World War has been overshadowed by the crimes committed by the Third Reich. Unlike the Nazis, Imperial Germany did not carry out conscious policies of genocide – at least not in Europe.[29] For all that, the sufferings of people in German-occupied territories were real enough, and placed another barrier in the way of achieving a 'civilised' compromise peace. While holding out the possibility of a negotiated settlement, Germany began to realise its war aims by exploiting its newly conquered territories. Some 100,000 Frenchmen were shipped to Germany for forced labour.[30] Other French civilians of both sexes were deported from the cities of Lille, Roubaix and Tourcoing to other parts of German-occupied France. Some women were sent to Germany to become prostitutes. Those left behind suffered from hunger, cold, and fear. As in Belgium, the German occupiers requisitioned everything from industrial machinery from factories to mattresses from civilian houses. As a French historian has recently observed, 'In occupied territory, war is total war' and in northern France, women and children were among its primary targets.[31]

The Germans overran all but a sliver of Belgium in 1914. Belgium was a small state but an economically important one. Faced by the resistance of Belgian workers and industrialists to working for the invader, the Germans effectively de-industrialised Belgium by destroying plant or shipping it back to Germany. Belgium was also viewed as a valuable source of labour. As many as 120,000 Belgians were deported to Germany to work in war factories in 1916–17.[32] The Germans used starvation as a weapon to force the Belgians to work. William Alexander Percy, an American volunteer with Herbert Hoover's Commission for Relief in Belgium, remembered seeing batches of Belgian workers returning from forced labour in Germany. 'They were creatures imagined by El Greco – skeletons, with blue flesh clinging to their bones, too weak to stand alone, too ill to be hungry any longer. This was only a miniature venture into slavery, a preliminary to the epic conquest and enslavement of whole peoples in 1940, but it seemed hideous and unprecedented to us in 1917.'[33] One major difference between German policy in the two world wars was that the deportations during the First World War were halted in the face of international condemnation.

Similarly, German policy in Poland during the First World War was harsh, but there were some attempts to gain support for a German-dominated Polish puppet state – by, for instance, promoting the use of the Polish language, forbidden under Czarist Russian rule. But, as in Belgium, the Germans ruthlessly engaged in economic plunder that undermined these faltering attempts to win Polish 'hearts and minds'. In June 1917 a German official noted Polish resentment of forced labour and

> requisitions and particularly the manner in which they had been implemented ... [also] the seizure of raw materials, factories, machines, the compulsory purchase of houses and the stripping of private forests ... All these measures have given rise to a sense of specific complaints, as have the generally rough handling of the population by German soldiers and officials and the imposition of unnecessary restrictions on movement.[34]

German imperialism in Poland has fairly been described as 'brutal and crude', and it had obvious and disturbing parallels with the German occupation of Poland during the Second World War. While German behaviour during the First World War fell well short of the Nazi treatment of Poland a generation later, when slavery and massacre was the lot of the Polish population, it was bad enough.

Neither Britain nor France entered the war in 1914 to expand their territory, but once war had begun politicians and officials began to think in those terms. Britain, almost from force of habit, picked up enemy colonies, as she had done in her eighteenth-century wars against France. She agreed to divide with France captured Ottoman territory in the Levant. France began to think not merely of regaining Alsace and Lorraine, but also of achieving security against future German aggression by breaking up the Rhineland into a number of mini-states that could be dominated by the French – in effect, reviving Napoleon's Confederation of the Rhine. French and British aims in Europe were basically defensive. Those of her ally, Russia, were expansionist. Against a background of dark hints of abandoning the Entente, the Russians persuaded the French and British to agree to let Russia take the Turkish capital, Constantinople. This decision reversed a long-standing British policy of preventing the Russians from dominating the Dardanelles, and if it had been implemented would have brought a new set of strategic problems for the British and French. It also precluded a separate peace with Turkey.[35] The coalition brought great strengths; but the diverse interests of the various partners also made it more difficult to bring about a compromise negotiated settlement.[36]

The Role of the United States

The longer the war remained deadlocked, the more important became the role of the United States. For much of the nineteenth century the United States seemed safe from attack and could turn its back on affairs in Europe. Only the Civil War of 1861–5 offered a serious threat to US security. Otherwise the vast size of the country, and the fact that two large oceans separated it from areas of conflict in Europe and Asia, appeared to provide the United States with more than adequate security – battles with Native Americans and the occasional war scare notwithstanding. It had not always been like this. The success of the American Revolution was only secured because it became caught up in a wider European war. The second Anglo-American conflict, the 'War of 1812', was in a large part a by-product of the titanic struggle in Europe. Peace in Europe and North America came about virtually simultaneously in 1814–15, and in the subsequent 99 years Europe was not troubled by a hegemonic power seeking to dominate the continent by force of arms. Against this background, the notion that American security was guaranteed purely by geography seemed plausible.

America's founding fathers had a clearer and more realistic vision of American security. Even in 1814, when Britain was fighting two wars, against Napoleon and against the United States, Thomas Jefferson clearly identified that 'It cannot be to our interest that all Europe should be reduced to a single monarchy'. Even if French failure in Europe were to lead to the 'longer continuance' of the conflict with Britain, 'I would rather meet them than see the whole force of Europe wielded by a single hand'. As the distinguished American historian Arthur M. Schlesinger, Jr has commented, 'In this last incisive phrase Jefferson defined the national interest that explains American intervention in the twentieth century's two world wars as well as in the subsequent Cold War'.[37]

Since the late nineteenth century the United States Navy had identified the German navy as its principal potential foe. As American relations with Britain improved, those with Germany worsened. The British, recognising their weakness, came to see that conflict with the USA had to be avoided at all costs and approved the Monroe Doctrine (which, by shutting out European rivals from the Americas, actually enhanced British security). Simultaneously, Germany's drive for world power brought it into conflict with the Doctrine. The Germans wanted colonies; the United States, acquiring an empire of its own, stood in the way. One would have thought that Germany's hands were full with its potential enemies in Europe. But true to the bizarre course of Wilhelmine foreign policy, Germany antagonised the United States, which led to a naval arms race – and, of course, helped nudge America further in the direction of Great Britain. The Royal Navy, still the world's greatest maritime force, stood as a bulwark between America and German aggression. A British defeat at the hands of Germany would amount to a defeat for America as well.[38]

At the peak of his triumphs in 1940 Adolf Hitler, allied with the Soviet Union, seemed to be able to wield the 'whole force of Europe', with incalculable potential consequences for American security. This fact brought about what has rightly been described as the greatest 'strategic crisis' in American history.[39] It was to avoid such a crisis that in 1917 President Woodrow Wilson took Jefferson's view to its logical conclusion and entered the war against Germany.

Thomas Woodrow Wilson was a controversial figure during his presidency and remains one among historians. Born in Virginia in 1856, he grew up in the defeated South, which undoubtedly had an influence on his subsequent dislike of war. Calvinistic Christianity, his father being a Presbyterian minister, also influenced him; he exuded a high moral tone that to some seemed arrogant. He became a lawyer and then a successful academic before entering politics comparatively late in life, being elected as the Democratic Governor of New Jersey in 1910, and President of the United States two years later. He, like many others of the United States elite, was instinctively sympathetic to Britain on cultural grounds, seeing Britain and the US as two branches of the same family. From the very beginning of the war his instincts were un-neutral and pro-Allied. In December 1914 he told a newspaperman that while it would be best 'if no nation gets the decision by arms', he did not think that 'it would hurt greatly the interests of the United States if either France or Russia or Great Britain should finally dictate the settlement'.[40] But well aware of the strains that the European war might place on America's ethnically diverse society, Wilson strove to keep out of the conflict.

As the war became increasingly total, both sides began to wield all the weapons in their arsenal. Britain employed its classic response to conflict with a continental opponent: a naval blockade. Germany responded with a counter-blockade of Britain.[41] In such circumstances the United States was bound to become involved, as her ships, and the lives of American citizens, would inevitably come under threat.

In 1909 the Declaration of London laid down a code of conduct on neutrality and belligerence that sought to regulate and minimise the impact of naval blockades. By 1914 it had yet to be ratified, and the British refused to abide by its provisions (although the Germans did). Instead, the British sowed mines in the Atlantic, which interfered with American trade, and confiscated goods from neutral ships. The Germans used their U-boats (submarines) to sink merchant shipping. According to the existing rules of war, warships should have given the crews of merchantmen a chance to escape before sinking the vessel. For U-boats to abide by these rules would have meant surfacing, which laid the submarine open to attack. Instead, the U-boats chose not to play by the rules of maritime law, thus increasing the problems of spotting whether a vessel was British or neutral.

Wilson, eager to avoid a confrontation with London, responded to British violations of American neutrality by downplaying them. By contrast, he was willing to run the risk of a serious breach with Berlin. The German declaration of the waters around the British Isles as a 'war zone' inevitably led to American losses, most famously the death of the 128 Americans on board the British liner *Lusitania*, sunk by a U-boat on 7 May 1915. Wilson responded with a protest to Germany that contained a veiled threat: 'The Imperial German Government will not expect the Government of the United States to omit any word or any act necessary to the performance of its sacred duty of maintaining the rights of the United States and its citizens ...'[42] The British responded to the German declaration of a war zone by introducing measures that were an attempt to force the Americans to trade only with the Allies. The US reply was much lower key, Wilson opting for negotiation rather than confrontation with the British. The US Ambassador in London was told to convey that Washington's mild protest 'is made in the most friendly spirit'.[43] The lack of an even-handed approach to the belligerents led to a dispute within Wilson's government, with William Jennings Bryan, his Secretary of State, resigning in June. For more than two years Wilson's policy of standing up to the Germans enjoyed success. Berlin suspended unrestricted submarine warfare in September 1915. The Germans again backed away from confrontation with the United

States after the sinking of the *Sussex* in March 1916, which prompted Wilson to issue a threat 'to sever diplomatic relations'.[44]

There were good reasons for Wilson's pro-British stance, ranging from sentiment to the fact that the war was good business for American factories making war goods for the Allies. Above all, Wilson's understanding of the nature of the German threat developed as the war went on. That is not to say that he was eager to lead the United States into war with Germany: quite the contrary. But Wilson remained sympathetic to the Allies, in spite of his increasing frustration that the British did not share his own views on ending the war short of victory. In February 1916 Colonel House, Wilson's confidant, made an agreement with Sir Edward Grey, the British Foreign Secretary, to hold a peace conference that would end the war on terms favourable to the Allies. If the Germans rejected them, the US would enter the war. Wilson heavily modified this proposal and it came to nothing, but the very fact that House was prepared to float it is highly suggestive.[45]

In the end, the Germans themselves decided the course of US policy. At a landmark meeting on 9 January 1917 the political and military elite of Imperial Germany took the decision to commence unrestricted submarine warfare. This, like so many other German strategic decisions of the twentieth century, was an enormous gamble. Battered on the Somme, the Germans staked everything on knocking the British out of the war by starving them into submission before the Americans could turn their enormous military potential into troops on the ground – if, as seemed almost inevitable, they entered the war. Wilson was still reluctant to do so. He had just fought and won the 1916 presidential election on the slogan 'he kept us out of the war'. But German provocation grew too strong. Not only were American ships being sunk, but also the Germans touched a raw nerve by showing a willingness to breach the Monroe Doctrine. The 'Zimmermann telegram', sent by the eponymous German foreign minister, revealed plans to offer Mexico land in Texas, New Mexico and Arizona if it joined an anti-American alliance. The British intercepted and decoded the telegram and passed it on to the US government, which published it. As Wilson said in his address to Congress on 2 April 1917, asking for a declaration of war:

'It is a fearful thing to lead this great peaceful people into war, into the most terrible and disastrous of all wars, civilization itself seeming to be in the balance.' Despite this, the President continued, 'the right is more precious than peace ...'[46]

Great Britain and France believed, correctly, that they were fighting a just war against autocratic German aggression. Wilson clearly saw the importance to European (and hence American) security of defeating Germany, but his concept of 'right' was altogether more elevated than that held by Westminster and Paris. Wilson struck a chord when he announced that 'The world must be made safe for democracy. Its peace must be planted upon the tested foundations of political liberty'. But his ambitions went much further than the defeat of an expansionist authoritarian power.[47] Wilson aimed at nothing less than a New World Order based on a set of rules for the conduct of international relations very different from those that prevailed prior to 1914. In entering the First World War with such a liberal internationalist agenda, Woodrow Wilson was carrying out a revolutionary act. He established an ideology that over the course of the twentieth century was to compete with two others, Marxist-Leninism and Fascism, for the soul of the Western world. By the last decade of the bloodiest century in history, after three world wars (two hot, one cold), Wilson's creed emerged victorious.

Two of the key planks of Wilson's creed were the encouragement of nationalism and democracy. Wilson's belief in the importance of the spread of 'democratic government, aside from its moral appeal, was that it was more stable and less predatory than autocratic government'. He saw the democratic nation state as a bulwark against war, as democracies do not usually fight each other, not least because in democracies 'governments derive their just powers from the consent of the governed'. Wilson believed, as an article of faith, that he was

speaking for the silent mass of mankind everywhere who have as yet had no place or opportunity to speak ... no nation should seek to extend its polity over any other nation or people, but every people should be left free to determine its own polity, its own way of development, unhindered, unthreatened, unafraid, the little along with the great and powerful.

The masses would help to keep their rulers in check, and Wilson believed that 'democracy's internal procedures for conflict resolution and compromise – for providing unity while respecting diversity – might be transferred to institutions governing world affairs'.[48] Democracy's partner was to be the liberal capitalism of open markets.

Wilson's historical timing was perfect. In 1862, when Abraham Lincoln had referred to 'the last, best hope of earth', republican, constitutional democracy was a rarity indeed.[49] There had been important converts to this form of government in succeeding years – Britain (albeit as a constitutional monarchy) in the late 1860s, France in the 1880s – but in 1914 much of the world was dominated by autocratic regimes. By April 1917 the latter were clearly under strain. In the following eighteen months the old empires of Austria-Hungary, Turkey, Russia and Germany shattered and new nations emerged from the wreckage, many espousing – at least initially – democratic principles. Wilson's vision coincided with the emergence of a rival, similarly universalist, ideology, that of V.I. Lenin. The Bolsheviks seized power in Russia in November 1917 and sought peace without annexations and, it soon became clear, aimed for global revolution against capitalism. 'Much of the subsequent history of the twentieth century grew out of the clash between these ideologies – Wilson's versus Lenin's, that appeared at almost precisely the same time.'[50]

For Britain and France, Wilson's America was an uneasy ally. Following his request to the belligerents in December 1916 to state their war aims, on 22 January 1917 Wilson had set out his aim of 'peace without victory'. On 4 December of that year he promised the German people a peace based 'on generosity and justice', if only they would free themselves from Kaiserism. The culmination of Wilson's 'new diplomacy' was his Fourteen Points, announced in January 1918. These were some of the most extraordinary proposals ever to be introduced in the arena of international relations. Point I called for 'open covenants of peace' and no secret diplomacy; point II for 'freedom of navigation upon the seas'; point IV for reductions of 'national armaments' to the 'lowest point consistent with domestic safety'. These proposals, together with others for collective security and self-determination of nationalities, were nothing short of revolutionary.[51]

The Fourteen Points induced a mixture of discomfort and hilarity in London and Paris. Britain was fundamentally opposed to point II, although at the time differences were fudged for the sake of coalition unity. Clemenceau, the French prime minister, commented that while Wilson had made 14 points, God had needed only ten.[52] France and the USA were fighting for broadly the same things, but Wilson's utopian vision was sufficiently different from that of the British and French to ensure that the USA remained an 'Associated Power' rather than a full ally in both name and substance. Yet Wilson's challenge – and also Lenin's – demanded a response from the Western powers.

The Response to Wilson: War Aims and Remobilisation

For the first three years of the war what might be called the 'In Flanders Fields' argument contributed to ruling out a compromise peace. The poem of that name, written in late 1915 by John McRae, a Canadian medical officer, gave voice to those killed on the battlefield. It retains its popularity today, one suspects, because some assume it to be a near-pacifist tract. In fact, the third verse makes a powerful case against a compromise peace:

> Take up our quarrel with the foe:
> To you from failing hands we throw
> The torch; be yours to hold it high.
> If ye break faith with us who die
> We shall not sleep, though poppies grow
> In Flanders fields.[53]

Anything less than victory, in short, would represent a betrayal of those who had died. But by 1917, as we have seen, commitment to fight on until final victory was beginning to waver. A Conservative former Foreign Secretary, Lord Landsdowne, horrified at the social implications of total war, privately advocated a compromise peace at the end of 1916 and went public with his views a year later. It 'came as a bombshell' a Tory MP noted in his diary, 'several men have told me they were really in agreement with the letter on the ground [sic] that we could not win and had better make the best terms possible'.[54] The Reichstag voted in July 1917 for a peace settlement without annexations, although this had little effect on German strategy. Karl, the new Austrian emperor who had succeeded Franz-Josef at the end of 1916, cautiously put out feelers for a separate peace. There was an attempt to bring together Socialists from all over Europe for a conference at Stockholm, which was largely still-born but nonetheless caused concern in London and Paris. In 1917 there were large-scale mutinies in the French army and industrial unrest in Britain and France. Above all, there were the two revolutions in Russia. As we have seen, governments, still committed to victory on their terms, responded with 'remobilisation' − making concerted efforts to galvanise support for the war amongst their respective populations.

Germany fired the first shot in a diplomatic offensive on 12 December 1916 when, on the back of its conquest of Rumania, it issued a 'Peace Note'. Couched in confrontational terms, it did not give specific war aims. Six days later, President Wilson issued a Peace Note of his own that asked the belligerents to state their war aims. The Entente rejected the German Note out of hand, but in reply to Wilson on 10 January 1917 set out some very specific war aims. Not only was Germany to evacuate all occupied territory, the Allies also placed question marks over the future of the multi-national Austro-Hungarian and Ottoman Empires, at least in their existing forms. 'It is in the interests of future peace,' Balfour, the Foreign Secretary noted, 'that territorial arrangements after the war should take account of the principle of nationality.' This response was aimed not only at the White House, but also at domestic opinion in Britain and France. The move was not taken lightly, and it further reduced the possibility of signing a separate peace with Germany's two main allies. But it did help to make the winning of protracted war possible. Such 'democratic' war aims demonstrated the ideological gulf between the Entente and the Central Powers (British and French attempts to expand their empires notwithstanding), played well with Washington, and helped with the remobilisation of public opinion in France and Britain. While the Entente reply of 10 January 1917 was a shrewd move politically, it should not be thought that it was an entirely cynical ploy. There was a genuine belief that 'a defeated Germany would become democratic and would lose its appetite for expansion and its hopes for world-power status'. 'If Germany had had a democracy,' Lloyd George mused, 'we should not have had this trouble.'[55]

By the end of 1917, with the military and political situation looking dark, Britain withdrew from some of the more ambitious of its aims. A series of abortive contacts failed to detach any of Germany's allies, but Lloyd George tried to make the prospect of negotiation with the Entente appear attractive. In his important war aims speech of 5 January 1918 at Caxton Hall, London, the Prime Minister tried to juggle the idea that 'government with the consent of the governed must be the basis of any territorial settlement' with a declaration that Britain was not 'fighting to destroy Austria-Hungary or to deprive Turkey of its capital, or of the rich and renowned lands of Asia Minor and Thrace, which are predominantly Turkish in race'. He also attempted to appeal directly to the German people, bypassing their government. Lloyd George claimed that 'We are not fighting a war of aggression against the German people'. Germany's 'military autocratic constitution' was 'a dangerous anachronism in the twentieth century' and 'the adoption of a really democratic constitution by Germany ... would make it much easier for us to conclude a broad democratic peace with her. But that is a question for the German people to decide'.[56]

The moderation of these aims was prompted by pessimism about the extent of a likely victory which would enable the Entente forcibly to democratise Germany. It also formed part of the attempt to remobilise Britain by stressing the 'reasonableness' of British war aims.[57] Inevitably, the Caxton Hall speech was too radical for some, not radical enough for others. In retrospect, it was a finely balanced speech. It held to basic war aims such as the German evacuation of occupied territory — which, of course, effectively ruled out negotiations with Germany — and its emphasis on democracy and self-determination ensured that the British government did not appear completely out of kilter with Wilson, who announced the Fourteen Points only three days later. Wilson's agenda was undoubtedly more radical than Lloyd George's, unacceptably so to the British in some areas, but on certain key questions they were singing in harmony. Their aims certainly contrasted sharply with the conditions that Germany forced on Russia barely two months after Caxton Hall.

Germany's Final Bid for Victory

Two German-initiated events coincided in March 1918. In that month the Germans announced the harsh terms of the Treaty of Brest-Litovsk, forced on the new Russian Bolshevik government. This coincided almost exactly with the opening of the German 1918 spring offensive, which brought the Allies face to face with defeat. British propagandists were able to point to what a German victory actually meant, that the Reichstag proposal for a peace without indemnities or annexations was an empty sham. The new Bolshevik government lost important territories including the Ukraine, the Baltic provinces, Finland, and Poland, and with them 50 million people, much of their best agricultural land, half their industry, and 90 per cent of their coal. British morale stiffened: bad as the war was, the prospect of defeat was even worse.[58] After the trough of 1917, civilian morale remained resolute until the end of the war.[59]

By the beginning of 1918 the Germans had won a stunning victory in the East. Out of the wreckage of the Czar's dominions they were busy creating a network of client states and spheres of influence that added up to a new German colonial empire with enormous economic potential. They also had the possibility of adding further territory such as the Caucasus. Senior British politicians and officials were acutely aware of the threat posed to British interests in the Middle East and even in India.[60] The new German empire menaced the existing British one, but by the end of the year it had collapsed. Instead of cutting her losses in the West, by making concessions, Germany's leaders chose to fight on. If Germany had offered to pull out of her conquests in the West it is entirely possible that the enemy coalition would have unravelled; and trading Belgium for the Ukraine would still have left Germany in a position of much greater power than before 1914.

In the event, the Germans staked everything on a huge gamble that they would be able to defeat the British and French in the field before the Americans arrived in sufficient numbers to turn the tide. This gamble failed, in part because 500,000 troops were tied up in the East. Hindenburg and Ludendorff made the same mistake that Napoleon had made a century earlier, and which Hitler was to repeat a generation later: none of them knew when to stick with the cards in their hand, rather than continually raising the stakes. Having played for everything, in 1918 the Germans lost everything.

CHAPTER 4

THE WESTERN FRONT: RIGHT OR WRONG? BRITISH STRATEGY IN THE FIRST WORLD WAR

For many Britons, the First World War seems so terrible because it is like nothing else in British history. Wars before and since have been fought without anything like the same cost in British blood. In the 1930s the enormously influential military writer Basil Liddell Hart argued that between 1914 and 1918 Britain had abandoned her traditional 'Way in Warfare'. According to Liddell Hart, this had eschewed sending large armies to fight on the continent. Instead, Britain had traditionally used her financial strength to pay allies to do her fighting for her, and her naval power to launch small military expeditions 'against the enemy's vulnerable extremities'. The consequences of opting instead for the strategy that led to a mass British army being committed to the Western Front were, in Liddell Hart's view, disastrous. 'Today,' he wrote in 1931, 'we are suffering not only from exhaustion of the body, political and economic, but exhaustion of the spirit.' Britain had paid a high price indeed for her abandonment of the British Way in Warfare.[1]

Liddell Hart's reputation, after a spell in the doldrums in the late 1980s, is once again riding high. By contrast C.R.M.F. Cruttwell is an almost forgotten figure. Cruttwell, an historian who had served

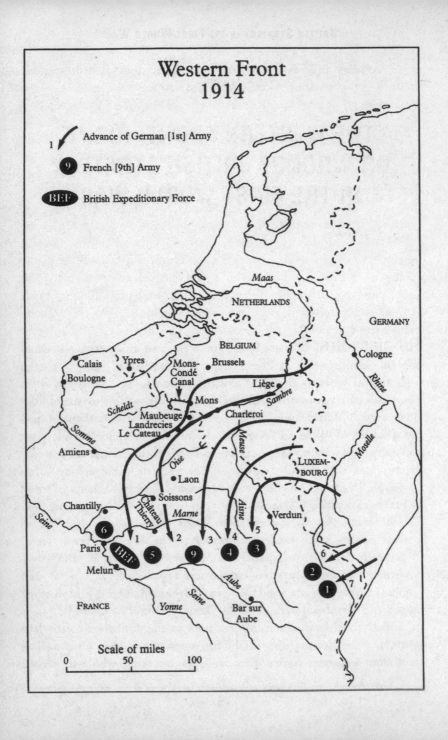

Western Front
1914

1 — Advance of German [1st] Army

9 — French [9th] Army

BEF — British Expeditionary Force

NETHERLANDS

Maas

GERMANY

BELGIUM

Calais Ypres Mons-Condé Canal Brussels Cologne

Boulogne Liège

Scheldt Mons *Sambre* *Rhine*

Maubeuge Charleroi

Landrecies *Meuse*

Le Cateau

Somme LUXEM-BOURG *Moselle*

Amiens *Oise* Laon

Chantilly Soissons Château Thierry *Marne* *Aisne* Verdun

Seine **6** **1** 2 3 4 5 6

Paris BEF **5** **9** **4** **3** **2**

Melun 7

Aube **1**

FRANCE *Yonne* *Seine* Bar sur Aube

Scale of miles

0   50   100

as an infantry officer on the Western Front, took British strategy in the war as his subject for the 1936 Lees Knowles lectures at the University of Cambridge. The beginning of the first lecture struck a very different note from Liddell Hart: 'The Great War, except for its unexampled magnitude, was a type with which British statesmen and soldiers were traditionally familiar.' At a time when the Great War was almost universally seen as a ghastly aberration from the norm, Cruttwell's theme was distinctly unfashionable. 'Once every century since the end of the sixteenth,' Cruttwell went on, Britain had gone to war 'to uphold what was idealistically called the freedom of Europe and more prosaically the balance of power.' Time after time, Britain fought for 'self-preservation' versus naval rivals, and against 'the threat of hostile dominion in the most precious outwork of her security, the Low Countries.' In war after war, he pointed out, Britain fought as part of a 'loose and often jarring continental coalition'. Britain's position within these groupings was 'peculiar, indeed unique'. Immune from invasion, she used her sea power to wage war in 'a semi-detached eclectic' fashion.

Cruttwell went on to argue that long drawn-out, attritional wars were actually the norm, not least because the main enemy, as the aggressor, was invariably better organised for war than Britain and her allies. This proved expensive in cash terms but cheap in lives: the armies of Britain's allies did the bulk of the fighting, killing and dying. Moreover, he continued:

> It is true that British influence over continental wars has not been to determine their strategy in the narrow sense, but rather their general course and character. And this is so just because in naval as opposed to military strategy we have maintained our choice and control practically unfettered ...

Cruttwell's lectures sought to prove that the latter 'generalisation in its broad terms holds good'. As he recognised, in 1914–18 Britain's commitment of troops, and therefore casualties, was on a much larger scale than in previous conflicts, of a similar order to those of her allies and enemies. '[Y]et our actual share in the determination of Allied strategy on land remained surprisingly small ... [but] it is profoundly true that our policy at sea alone enabled a great deal of that continental strategy to be put into force at all.'[2]

Cruttwell and Liddell Hart were by no means diametrically opposed in their theories, but Cruttwell emphasised the 'traditional' nature of Britain's conduct of the First World War. In framing his theory of the British Way in Warfare, Liddell Hart was writing as a polemicist, bending history to fit his theories. Contrary to his assertions, in the great struggles against France from the late seventeenth century to 1815, Britain usually deployed sizeable bodies of her own troops on the continent alongside foreign units paid for by the British and allies proper.[3] By contrast Cruttwell's thesis is essentially correct. Two factors indeed set the Great War aside from previous conflicts: its scale and the fact that Britain itself provided a larger army than normal to fight alongside its allies. Otherwise, the war of 1914–18 was a war of a very traditional type. It was a conflict fought as part of a coalition against a power seeking hegemony over continental Europe – a war, in short, to maintain the balance of power. Specifically, it was fought to prevent Flanders and northern France from falling into hostile hands. It was a long, attritional war in which British naval power played a key role, but one in which Britain's voice was far from a dominating one when it came to determining military strategy. If one can indeed deduce a 'British Way in Warfare' from the experience of the previous three centuries, British strategy in 1914–18 fell squarely within its parameters.

Pre-war Strategy

Five years to the day before the Battle of Mons, where the British army fought its first major action of the First World War, the Committee of Imperial Defence (CID) held a meeting to decide the shape of British strategy in the event of a major continental war. The Royal Navy's position was influenced by the ideas of Julian Corbett, a naval strategist whose views would later influence Liddell Hart. Corbett believed that as a maritime power Britain could apply Francis Bacon's approach to war and engage in an otherwise total war to a limited extent, alongside continental Allies who did not have this ability to take 'as much and as little of the war' as they desired. Corbett was fully aware of the importance of co-operation between the navy and the army, seeing the latter, in Admiral Sir John 'Jacky' Fisher's phrase, as 'a projectile to be fired by the navy'.[4] At the CID meeting on 23 August 1911 Sir Arthur Wilson, the First Sea Lord, put forward an incoherent case for an amphibious strategy of raids and littoral operations. This failed to receive approval, as did a strategy of blockade. The problems were palpable. France and Russia would probably have been beaten long before these strategies began to bite – if indeed they ever did.[5]

The views of Major General Henry Wilson, the Director of Military Operations, in favour of a continental strategy were much more persuasive. The British army had been holding secret talks with the French army since 1906. Since 1910 the Francophile Wilson had been preparing a plan for the British Expeditionary Force (BEF) to support the French army, and it was believed that the addition of six British divisions could give the French the decisive edge. The BEF was to be deployed to France and placed on the left of the French army. A military-political council of war on 5 August, the day after Britain entered the conflict, endorsed Henry Wilson's plan, although not without some debate.[6] Thus the First World War began, as had many previous conflicts, with Britain dispatching a small expeditionary force to the continent to fight alongside coalition partners. Meanwhile, the Royal Navy swung into operation, mounting a blockade of Germany. Whether or not the navy's plan for a Napoleonic-style war of attrition would be necessary was to be decided by the clash of arms in Belgium and France. In the meantime, a new factor was introduced into the British strategic calculations: the appointment of Lord Kitchener as Secretary of State for War.

By chance the War Office was without a permanent political head in 1914. There was a popular clamour for Herbert Horatio, Earl Kitchener of Khartoum, to be appointed Secretary of State for War.[7]

Asquith could discern several advantages. The Liberal government was light on military expertise and the appointment of a military and ostensibly non-party man would broaden the base of support. 'K of K' was a national hero, an Imperial warrior much of whose professional career had been spent with one eye on Britain's colonial rivals, which just happened to be Britain's allies in this war, Russia and France. Kitchener brought certain perspectives to the job. He had broad strategic vision, and set about raising a mass citizen force of volunteers — 'Kitchener's Army' — which gave Britain for the first time in history an army to match those of her continental allies and enemies. What, however, did he intend to do with this vast force?

Kitchener's habit of playing his cards extremely close to his chest was enormously frustrating to his cabinet colleagues, and is scarcely less so for historians. The Public Record Office contains no master plan for the use of Kitchener's Army. However, from hints and other fragmentary pieces of evidence, David French has constructed a satisfyingly plausible explanation of Kitchener's strategic plan.[8] He sees Kitchener playing a very long game indeed, hoping that after about three years the continental armies would be exhausted. At that stage, in 1917, his armies would take the field — persistent rumour had it that Kitchener himself would be at their head — and defeat the enemy. Not only would the Germans have been beaten, but Britain's allies would have been satisfyingly weakened. This would enable Britain to shape the subsequent peace process and make sure that the world that emerged after the war was in accordance with British interests. German militarism would have been broken, and a new balance of power constructed that would serve to keep the British Empire safe from the attentions of her erstwhile allies France and Russia, who might otherwise re-emerge as colonial rivals. There was no point, Kitchener seemed to have reasoned, in swapping the German threat to British security for one posed by another power.

Kitchener's strategy was a variant on the traditional British approach of committing troops to the continent only on British terms. This was a plan that promised huge rewards, if it could be made to work. In the event a large, fresh army did enter battle shortly before the end of the war, which allowed its government largely to dictate the nature of the peace – but it was the United States and not Britain that was the beneficiary.

Coalition Warfare

Britain fought the First World War as part of a coalition of states. This simple fact explains much about British strategy. Coalitions bring great strengths. They allow formidable concentrations of economic, political and military power to be directed against a common enemy. In an attritional war, they give depths of resources not available to individual states. The downside is that operating within a coalition curtails the ability of individual powers to pursue desirable policies and strategies. Inevitably, partners within a coalition will have differing interests. Sometimes the only thing binding a coalition together is fear of a common enemy. Strategy is decided, often painfully slowly, through a series of compromises, thrashed out in a succession of conferences and committees. The centre of gravity of a coalition, which is the thing that if successfully attacked will do maximum damage, is often its cohesion. In the twentieth century democracies fought large-scale wars in coalition. The same basic problems faced by the British, French and Americans in 1918 were still on the agenda of their NATO successors during the Kosovo crisis in 1999.

General Tasker H. Bliss, who served as the US Permanent Representative at the Supreme War Council in 1917–18, wrote in 1922 that the Allies in the Great War had suffered from 'absence of unity of purpose'; each power was fighting 'its own war against the enemy, and too largely for separate ends'.[9] Britain, Imperial Russia, France and the United States, while each desiring the defeat of Germany, sought to achieve different things from the war, and were not bereft of suspicions of their partners' motives. As Paul Kennedy has noted, 'military alliances were and are not the same as friendships'.[10] Russia, physically separated from her Western allies, was always a somewhat 'semi-detached' member of the coalition and eventually was defeated without Britain and France being able to do much to prevent it – or, it must be said, the coalition collapsing. Belgium was careful to keep her distance from France and Britain and was a potential 'weak link' in the coalition as she would have been happy with a compromise peace that would get German troops off Belgian soil.[11] At the same time, Britain and France were suspicious of each other's colonial ambitions. The United States remained serenely detached from the Entente as an 'Associated Power'. Such differences could not fail to have effects. There were some colossal arguments between the Allies, and on some occasions, notably during the German spring offensives of 1918, the coalition seemed on the verge of collapse.

When Sir John French took the BEF to France in 1914, Kitchener issued him with a set of instructions which emphasised that his 'command was an entirely independent one' but that 'every effort must be made to coincide most sympathetically with the plans and wishes' of his French allies.[12] These instructions – similar ones were given to Haig in 1915 – neatly captured the dilemma of British strategy. Britain, by virtue of numbers of soldiers on the ground, remained the junior partner in the alliance. Both commanders in chief had to strive to maintain some freedom of action but were denied the compensations of unity of command, not least because French and Haig resisted subordination to a French general. In order to satisfy the French, the British were forced to fight some battles at times and places not of their choosing.

The coalition was essentially an *ad hoc* creation, formed in August 1914. In spite of the pre-war discussions, Franco-British military co-operation was fairly rudimentary. In coalition warfare much always depends on the personal chemistry between individuals; in the absence for most of the war of the formal machinery for co-ordinating strategy and military operations, the personal element was more important than ever. There were indeed tensions and arguments – a particularly volcanic row erupted on 3 July 1916 between Haig and Joffre over British strategy on the Somme, for instance – but for the most part the unwieldy command relationships were made to work in spite of personal likes and dislikes and inter-Allied suspicions.

As the BEF grew from six to sixty divisions and, from mid-1916 onwards, took on a much greater share of the fighting, British influence and power increased. By early 1918, Britain and France held positions of rough equality within the coalition. A similar process occurred when the United States entered the war, its influence growing during 1918 as huge numbers of fresh American troops arrived on the Western Front. Newton D. Baker, the US Secretary of War, in May 1917 had issued Pershing with instructions similar to those given by the British government to French and Haig: to co-operate with allies but to maintain the 'identity' of the US forces as a 'separate and distinct component' of the coalition.[13] Like his British counterparts, Pershing was to learn just how difficult this balancing act really was. Had the war lasted into 1919, as many expected, Pershing would have assumed a dominating position within the military councils of the alliance, which would have given the coalition a very different complexion.

The worst crisis in alliance relations occurred in March 1918, when the German offensive threatened to divide the British army from the French. The danger was that the movements of the Allied armies would diverge, the BEF falling back to protect its lines of communication with the Channel ports and the French on Paris. The prospect of the Allied armies being defeated individually and separately was at last enough to sweep away objections to unity of command. At the end of 1917 a Supreme War Council (SWC) had been set up at Versailles to co-ordinate coalition strategy, but this new arrangement did not include a supreme commander. The March offensive brought about that innovation, and Ferdinand Foch was appointed Generalissimo. His powers were limited, and although they increased in time, he remained a co-ordinator rather than a true commander. Unlike Eisenhower in the next war, he lacked a large, integrated staff. Although a French general, Foch was not the commander of the French army, which remained under Pétain. Thus the BEF was not placed directly under the French army. Foch made an important contribution to Allied victory in 1918. He had wide strategic vision over the whole Western Front and indeed beyond, and behaved as a true coalition commander, placing himself above narrow national interests. Whereas the SWC was 'an organ of consultation and study', Foch saw his role as to act as 'a higher organ of command, which can at all times defend the general plan adopted as against personal inclinations and individual interests, and take rapid decisions and get them carried out without any loss of time'.[14] 'Thank goodness we have got a central authority to fight the battle as a whole,' a senior British officer commented in April 1918.[15]

The command system that emerged on the Western Front in 1918 was imperfect, but it worked effectively enough. Coalitions tend to be most effective when one partner is much more powerful than the others, and acts as a 'framework' for the alliance – the United States served this function during the 1990–1 Gulf War. The events of 1918 perhaps offer a model of how a future coalition might operate in the absence of an overwhelmingly powerful national force, where the partners are of approximately equal weight – by no means an impossible situation in the strategic environment of the early twenty-first century.

One almost entirely unexpected consequence of the massive expansion of Britain's armed forces was that by 1918 the BEF had itself become a coalition force. During 1916–17 the various Dominion contingents emerged as powerful and elite formations, with a consequent spur to nationalism. The Canadian and Australian Corps, the New Zealand Division and the South African Brigade were not true national armies in that they were not self-contained. They had a symbiotic relationship with the BEF as a whole, with the British supplying most of the logistic backup, much of the artillery and all of the tanks that supported the Dominion troops' actions in 1916–18.[16] However, by 1918 the Australians and Canadians, in particular, could and did demand to be treated as 'junior but sovereign allies'[17] by British high command and government. On the whole the British accepted the situation and adjusted to it. Whether they would have been as receptive if the Dominion troops and commanders had not so emphatically proved their worth on the battlefield is an unanswerable question.

It is easy to pick holes in the Entente coalition, perhaps by citing a juicy quote in which a senior politician or general expresses rude sentiments about an ally. Such comments are not difficult to find.[18] The coalition was never as harmonious or close-knit as the Anglo-American alliance of 1941–5, which itself had its fair share of dissension and infighting. It is true to say it fell apart shortly after the defeat of Germany, with momentous consequences for the future peace of Europe. Yet in comparison with the Anglo-French coalition of 1939–40, which collapsed in military defeat and mutual rancour, it was almost an example of sweetness and light. Most importantly, one should never lose sight of the fact that the coalition actually worked. The *ad hoc* alliances of 1914–18 deserve to be judged on results, and in accomplishing the military defeat of the Central Powers the coalition was undeniably effective, in spite of the disadvantages that may have accrued to individual members.

The Collapse of Kitchener's Strategy

One of the casualties of the pressures of coalition warfare was Kitchener's strategy of holding back his forces to enable them to make a grand entrance in 1917. The reality, as Kitchener admitted on 20 August 1915, just twelve months into the war, was that 'unfortunately we had to make war as we must, and not as we should like to'.[19] Contrary to some pre-war assumptions, Britain did not have a 'free hand' in devising its strategy.

By August 1915 France had suffered horrendous casualties and was, understandably, demanding more action from the British. The BEF was being asked to take over ever further stretches of trench, and to conduct offensives in support of the French troops' own efforts. At the same time, the Germans were having alarming success against Russia, whose armies were being driven out of Poland. The Allies had to attack in the West, if only to attempt (not entirely successfully) to pin German forces there and relieve the pressure on their eastern ally. The British had to commit their newly raised divisions to the Western

Front rather than keep them at home. Quite simply, France and Russia were unable to resist the Germans without substantial support from British forces actually on the ground. Thus in September the BEF was committed to fight the Battle of Loos, in which for the first time, divisions of Kitchener's Army fought in a major action on the Western Front.

The pressures were political as well as military. British forces also had to be sent to the Western Front to convey the right signals, to demonstrate to their allies that 'Perfidious Albion' was indeed committed to the war. Britain had to commit more than just ships and treasure to the war effort. She had to send troops, lots of them, and to take on her share of the burden of fighting. This was the inescapable reality of coalition warfare.

Just as in 1915 Kitchener was forced to change his strategy, so a wider transition was taking place as the nature of the British war effort moved from being essentially limited to essentially total. The fundamental divide during 1915 among the British decision-making elite has usually been depicted as being between the 'Westerners', those committed to fighting in France and Belgium, and the 'Easterners' who wished to use seapower to fight elsewhere. This perception has disguised the real fault-line, which was between proponents of 'business as usual' – that is, a limited commitment to the war – and the total warriors. The former included Reginald McKenna and Walter Runciman, respectively Chancellor of the Exchequer and President of the Board of Trade in Asquith's Coalition.[20] Both men, who had major responsibilities for the British economy, wanted to aid Britain's allies with sea power and financial and economic muscle, while keeping the BEF small. The latter included David Lloyd George, in August 1915 Secretary of State for War, and General Sir William Robertson, the Chief of the Imperial General Staff (CIGS). They were poles apart on many issues, but shared the belief that only by total mobilisation of Britain's population and economy, as well as the army and navy, could the war be won.

Events in 1915 and 1916 weakened the position of the 'business as usual' school. In August 1915, a particularly important month in the evolution of British strategy, the landings at Suvla Bay failed to reinvigorate the Gallipoli campaign, and the disappointment at the Dardanelles undermined the credibility of a maritime strategy as a real alternative to the Western Front. In the same summer month the Germans won a substantial victory over the Russians in Poland. It was clear that nothing but a total commitment by Britain to the war could save the coalition. This itself presented new problems for the British. In spite of massive economic mobilisation at home, the demands of the expanded war effort could only be satisfied by placing orders for munitions and other supplies in the USA, but in August 1915 bankers warned that Britain was running out of dollars to pay for them.[21]

The fears of fiscal conservatives like Runciman and McKenna that total war spelled economic ruin were exaggerated, but the consequences were nonetheless serious. The First World War weakened Britain's economy, and escalated the process by which the USA replaced Britain as a major economic power.[22] The likes of Lloyd George were aware of the risks that total war involved. Ultimately, they took the decision that the prospect of a German victory was even worse. In September 1940, another British cabinet was confronted with a similar dilemma: fight on and risk bankruptcy, or acquiesce in a German victory. In both world wars British leaders took the difficult decision to wage total war at any cost to Britain's position in the world.

The Legacy of Nelson: the Role of the Royal Navy in British Strategy

When the First World War began, many people confidently expected that the Royal Navy would quickly take on and destroy the German fleet in a decisive battle. Since 1843, a statue of Lord Nelson has towered 162 feet above central London. The very name of its location, Trafalgar Square, is a permanent reminder of Nelson's final and greatest victory, won over the combined French and

Spanish fleets on 21 October 1805. Just as Nelson's Column looms over one of London's most famous open spaces, so Nelson's legacy dominated both the British nation and the Royal Navy. Nelson had bequeathed a diet of victory. His navy had handed Britain more than a century of supremacy at sea, and ushered in the period of *Pax Britannica*, in which the British Empire had grown to unparalleled size and prosperity.

In the 1890s Nelson's methods found a new interpreter in the shape of Alfred Thayer Mahan, an officer of the United States Navy. Mahan's theories, or at least how they were interpreted by contemporaries, were founded upon 'the command of the sea', which could be achieved by the most powerful battlefleet. This bestowed, he wrote,

> possession of that overbearing power on the sea which drives the enemy's flag from it, or allows it to appear only as a fugitive; and by which, by controlling the great common, closes the highways by which commerce moves to and from the enemy shores.[23]

Mahan's influence reached far beyond a narrow circle of naval officers. His theories contributed to an explosion of popular interest in things naval, in his own country, in Germany, where the Kaiser was an admirer, and in Britain.

On the centenary of Nelson's final battle, a novel entitled *Trafalgar Refought* appeared in which Britain's greatest naval hero commanded a modern battlefleet.[24] But when the Great War broke out nine years later, the British public was to be sorely disappointed in its expectation of the Royal Navy winning a swift Nelsonic victory over the German fleet. Instead, there was a series of losses of ships to mine and torpedo, and outright failures such as the escape in 1914 of the German warships *Goeben* and *Breslau* through the Mediterranean to neutral Turkey (which played a significant role in bringing the Turks into the war against the Allies). The one occasion on which the major fleets of Britain and Germany came into contact, off Jutland on 31 May 1916, exposed the Royal Navy's tactical and doctrinal shortcomings. Sir David Beatty, the commander of the Royal Navy's battlecruisers, memorably commented as he saw British ships blowing up and sinking, 'There seems to be something wrong with our bloody ships today.'[25] Most serious of all, the German campaign of unrestricted submarine warfare, which concentrated on sinking merchant shipping bound for the British Isles, came close in early 1917 to starving Britain into submission, and the Royal Navy, the world's most powerful fleet, had seemed powerless to prevent it. The U-boat threat was only mastered by the use of convoys, a system that many naval officers associated with the long-gone days of sail and who therefore fought hard against its reintroduction in 1917.

Technology, and the use made of it, helps to explain why the Royal Navy's performance fell so far short of popular expectation. Between Trafalgar and Jutland warships underwent a change for which, for once, that overworked word 'revolution' is entirely appropriate. In place of the wooden-walled sailing vessels armed with muzzle-loading smoothbore cannon that conducted battles within boarding range, were armoured, steam-powered vessels equipped with modern guns. In 1906, only eight years before the beginning of the Great War, Admiral Jacky Fisher introduced a new type of battleship, named after the first of its class, HMS *Dreadnought*. Dreadnoughts were fast battleships armed entirely with big guns; the super-dreadnought HMS *Queen Elizabeth*, which saw service in the First World War, had eight 15-inch guns that fired 1,920-pound shells out to 23,000 yards. Dreadnoughts made battleships of the previous era, of which the Royal Navy had more than anyone else, obsolete. The resulting race to build dreadnoughts meant that each ship was more valuable than ever; Britain's naval security depended on a smaller number of ships.

The advance in naval technology was not confined to battleships. Soon after the outbreak of war in 1914 it was clear that warships were vulnerable to the relatively inexpensive shell, mine and torpedo, the latter forming a particularly potent combination with the submarine. The battlecruiser, effectively a battleship with additional speed provided by sacrificing armoured protection, proved especially vulnerable. Even worse, in small actions such as the Battle of Dogger

Bank (January 1915), the German navy showed worrying signs of tactical effectiveness, while on occasions the Royal Navy demonstrated the contrary. The German fleet commanders recognised that, given their numerical inferiority, their best strategy was one of attrition, to try to catch fragments of the British Grand Fleet and destroy them and thus gradually reduce the Royal Navy's numerical superiority.

The Royal Navy had every reason to avoid playing to their opponent's strengths. The technical skill of the German navy could not cancel out the massive advantage dealt to the British by geography. The British Isles blocked Germany's access to the wider oceans. As long as the Royal Navy could deny the English Channel and the Atlantic Ocean to the German fleet, it was achieving strategic success. For the British, Jutland was a tactical shock but a strategic victory. Like the German army on the Somme, the Kaiser's fleet had acquitted itself well but had no desire to repeat the experience. Admiral Scheer, the commander of the German fleet, drew the conclusion from Jutland that the only hope of a German victory in the foreseeable future lay not in another major fleet action but in the 'crushing of English economic life' through the resumption of unrestricted U-boat warfare.[26] This path was to prove ultimately disastrous for Germany. An American newspaper caught the significance of the battle when it wrote: 'The German Fleet has assaulted its jailor; but it is still in jail.'[27] Put simply, the British did not need to defeat the Germans in battle. Even to give battle was to incur a huge risk. Bottled up in ports at home, the German navy was helpless to prevent the destruction of its extra-European commerce and warships, and most of its colonies being mopped up by Britain and her allies.

More importantly, simply by remaining unbeaten, the Royal Navy guaranteed British security. This was the foundation upon which rested the Allied victory in the First World War. From the very beginning of the war, when the Royal Navy enabled the BEF to be transported to France without being hindered by the Germans, its command of the Channel was essential for the Allied war effort. Haig's army on the Western Front was dependent on the Royal Navy for its supplies, just as Wellington's forces in the Iberian peninsula had been a century earlier. Similarly, the fighting and winning of the (First) Battle of the Atlantic against the U-boat threat by the Royal Navy, supplemented by part of the US fleet, was an essential precondition for victory on land. If the Atlantic had been closed to Allied and neutral shipping, merchant vessels could not have carried the foodstuffs and munitions that kept Britain in the war, nor could American troops have been transported to Europe.

Nevertheless, as in previous conflicts, an enemy in possession of the Low Countries posed a major threat to the Royal Navy's ability to protect the homeland and Sea Lines of Communications (SLOCs) across the Channel. One of the bloodiest battles of the war — Passchendaele — was motivated in part by the hope of clearing the Channel coast of U-boat bases. The Admiralty retained grave worries about the German naval threat. As a leading naval historian has recently written, the operations of German submarines, aircraft, destroyers and smaller craft 'were significant, not so much for the damage they actually inflicted, but as a warning of what might happen if the Germans were ever able to concentrate more resources in that vital area. Britain would lose the war, if it lost the Channel.'[28] In the spring and summer of 1917, the German submarine campaign seemed to be on the verge of cutting the link across the Atlantic and thus forcing Britain out of the war. On 18 June 1917 Jellicoe, the First Sea Lord, wrote a memorandum to the War Policy Committee in which he painted a gloomy picture of the options open to the Germans, should they choose to exploit their position in the Channel. Contending that the Belgian coast had to be recaptured to forestall any possibility of Germany holding on to it as the result of a compromise peace, Jellicoe argued for

> the absolute necessity of turning the Germans out of northern Belgium at the earliest possible moment. It must be done during the present summer: every day that we wait the difficulties will increase, and every day that we wait the threat from both sea and air becomes greater.

Jellicoe explicitly recognised that the Royal Navy needed the support of ground troops to eject the Germans from Belgium: 'The operation cannot be carried out by the navy alone, but it can be carried out as a joint business.'[29]

Naval concern with the Belgian coast did not end in 1917. On St. George's Day, 23 April 1918, the aggressive commander of the Dover Patrol, Admiral Roger Keyes, raided the port of Zeebrugge in an attempt to deny it to German U-boats by sinking blockships and destroying port facilities. Neither this operation, nor a subsequent raid on Ostend (10 May) was particularly successful, but they had great value as propaganda and boosted British morale during the difficult days of the German spring offensive. These actions were satisfyingly Nelsonic, and did wonders for the self-esteem of the Royal Navy. As a recent authoritative history has concluded, 'German bases in Flanders, despite their strategic location in the "cockpit of Europe" ... did not really fulfil their potential.'[30]

This is not to say that British fears about the Belgian coast were misplaced; still less that entering the war in the first place was a mistake. The circumstances of a long land war meant that the Germans were never able to capitalise on the conquest of the Belgian coast by developing their naval threat to Britain; their priorities lay elsewhere. However, a genuine threat it remained. One solid achievement of the British and Allied land forces in September–October 1918 was to compel the Germans to abandon their naval bases in Belgium. With the Flanders coast once again in friendly hands, the British had fulfilled one of their principal objectives in going to war. In 1918, as in 1583, Flanders was the counterscarp of British security.

Writing in the 1930s Basil Liddell Hart asserted that the Allied naval blockade 'ranks first' in the reasons for the defeat of Germany.[31] He provided little in the way of analysis to substantiate this claim, which formed part of his crusade against British strategy in the Great War. Nonetheless, the blockade clearly was important. A recent and more sober assessment argues that while the blockade had little direct impact on the ability of the German armed forces to fight, it had 'a social and psychological and, therefore, a political impact on Germany ... that helped undermine ... [its] ability to wage total war'. The blockade was instrumental in reducing the food available to the German population. In 1918 293,000 German civilians died as a result of the blockade. Food riots broke out, and sharp divisions opened between the 'haves' and 'have nots': it was easier to obtain food in the country than in the cities, and the rations of workers in munitions factories were superior to those of other workers.[32] Arguably, eventually the blockade did in fact have a direct impact on the battlefield, as worries about how families at home were faring contributed to the weakening of German military morale.

The recent use of sanctions against Iraq and Yugoslavia has demonstrated all too clearly that an economic blockade is a weapon for the long run. In the Great War, blockade complemented the defeat of the Central Powers on the battlefield but it could not have replaced it. Had Britain relied on the Royal Navy to win the war by blockade while sending a token force to France, the most likely result would have been a German military victory over the outnumbered Allies long before the blockade had any significant effect. This is not to underestimate the importance of the Allied blockade – which was fundamental – but rather to recognise that it could only succeed as part of a wider strategy.

The end of the war at sea, when it came, was a disappointment to many British sailors. They had waited in vain for a new Trafalgar. 'I did not see the surrender of the German Fleet at Scapa Flow, and I was glad of it,' wrote one officer; such 'humiliation ... was no fitting end for such men and such ships'.[33] The debate on the performance of British admirals in the Great War was never as fierce as that on British generalship, but some naval commanders stood condemned for their lacklustre performance, particularly for their failure to win a 'decisive' victory at Jutland, the one major fleet action of the war.[34] In reality, between the years 1914 and 1918 the British fleet achieved a success as decisive as any in its history. British and latterly American maritime power laid the foundations for eventual victory. For the Royal Navy, as for the British army, the Great War remains a largely forgotten victory.

'Side-shows' and Strategy

The one major attempt to use British sea power to outflank the Western Front came in 1915. In March–April of that year the Allies attempted to seize the Turkish Straits. This would have allowed them to pass a fleet through the narrow waters that separate Europe from Asia, and thus threaten Constantinople, the capital of the Ottoman Empire. The idea behind the Dardanelles or 'Gallipoli' campaign, which originally came from Winston Churchill, earns high marks from the point of view of modern military doctrine.[35] It was expeditionary, making use of Britain's naval assets in combination with land power, and 'manoeuvrist', seeking to avoid enemy strengths (on the Western Front) and land a heavy blow that would shatter the cohesion of the Central Powers alliance by knocking Turkey (which entered the war in October 1914) out of the war. It was even, in best manoeuvrist fashion, aimed at Turkey's centre of gravity: the seizure of Constantinople would have made it difficult, if not impossible, for Turkey to continue to fight. It is not surprising that Gallipoli is still studied in staff colleges across the world.

Fifteen years after the campaign, a senior officer who participated in its latter stages commented that 'Mr. Winston Churchill's conception was magnificent'. However, the same officer also stated that 'it was the most damnable folly that ever amateurs were enticed into.'[36] Brilliant as the conception might have been, its execution left much to be desired. A carefully planned joint military/naval assault might have succeeded, although the odds against it were formidable. Lord Kitchener originally refused to commit troops to the venture, so the Royal Navy attempted the operation without the support of ground forces. Lacking troops to attack shore batteries from the land and losing warships to mines, the initial attempt on 18 March to force ships through the Straits was a failure. Even if the fleet had got through this would not have guaranteed a victory, for it is far from clear how a naval force that lacked a substantial body of soldiers could capture the city of Constantinople. It seems that the best hope of success was, as Sir Edward Grey admitted, for the arrival of the Anglo-French fleet to trigger a *coup d'état* in the city.[37] The 'ships alone' gambit having failed, troops were sent to carry out the fully fledged joint operation that should have been launched in the first place.

An opposed amphibious landing is one of the most difficult acts that any force can be asked to undertake. The action of 18 March sacrificed any hope of the attackers achieving strategic surprise, and lengthened the odds against the landings being successful. It would be more accurate to say that it *further* lengthened the odds. It was bad enough that the assault of 25 April 1915 was 'the first time that men had ever attacked a coastline defended by the weapons of warfare of the industrial age'.[38] Worse, General Sir Ian Hamilton, the commander of the assault force, was already labouring under enormous handicaps that included insufficient numbers of troops, poor command and control arrangements, a lack of specialised landing craft, and chaotic logistic arrangements. All of these difficulties were in addition to the communications problems that beset all commanders in the First World War. Once you add to this some inept command performances, brave defenders and bad luck, it is not surprisingly that the British and Anzac troops could do little more than get ashore. There, they faced the tactical conditions of the Western Front: a stalemate, but in harsher terrain and under a Mediterranean sun.

One factor that had a decidedly important influence on the fate of the Gallipoli campaign, but is rarely mentioned, is that it took place in 1915, at the very beginning of the British army's tactical learning curve. This very obvious point came to me several years ago, while standing on Scimitar Hill where the British launched a particularly inept attack in September 1915. This objective was similar to many captured by carefully planned Western Front offensives in 1917–18. At Gallipoli in 1915, the British troops lacked experience, artillery, ammunition, scientific gunnery, aircraft, Lewis guns, Stokes mortars, technical and tactical know-how – everything, in short, that contributed towards the success of the 1917–18 offensives. The exception was courage, which the British and Anzac troops had in abundance; but courage by itself was not enough.

The fate of the Gallipoli expedition is depressingly familiar to anyone who has studied British military history. Like the expeditions to Walcheren in 1809, Norway in 1940 and a host of others stretching back to the sixteenth century, Gallipoli was 'brilliant in conception' but 'lamentable in execution'.[39] Even if the 1809 and 1940 expeditions had been successful they would have made at best a marginal impact on the outcome of the Napoleonic and Second World Wars. The balance of probability is that even if Turkey had been knocked out of the war in 1915, its loss would have contributed little to defeating Germany, at least in the short term. The seizure of Constantinople *might* have led to a pro-Allied Balkan confederacy, which *might* have opened up a viable new front against the Central Powers. But politics, geography and logistics would have made it immensely difficult to press home the advantage accrued from a victory on the periphery of the Central Powers by a direct advance into Austria-Hungary. The fate of the Allied expedition to the Greek port of Salonika – which was bottled up by a Central Powers force from 1915 to 1918 – offers little encouragement to the idea of a decisive Balkan campaign. Similarly, the opening of the Black Sea would certainly have relieved some pressure on the hard-pressed Russians, but it is highly unlikely that this, as some have argued, would have averted the revolutions of 1917, which grew from a combination of military defeat and deep-seated political and social problems.

If a direct attack on the capital offered at least a sporting chance of knocking the Ottoman Empire out of the war, the same was emphatically not true of the various campaigns in the outlying Turkish provinces. Clearly, the loss of the Levant in October 1918 did not help the Turkish cause, but as a recent study of Allenby's campaign in Palestine in 1918 has argued, the loss of Palestine did not in itself threaten the survival of the Turkish Empire. Nor was Palestine and Syria a realistic springboard for an assault on the Turkish heartland. Hundreds of miles of difficult ground lay between the Levant and the Turkish core territories of Asia Minor and Constantinople, terrain that would have been a logistician's nightmare and greatly favoured the defender.[40] Indeed, when considering 'Eastern' options, it is worth reflecting on the time and effort expended in building up an efficient logistic system in France, an area close to the home base with an existing modern infrastructure. How much more difficult would it have been to create a comparable system in the Balkans or the Levant?[41] Much the same was true of the British campaign in Mesopotamia (modern day Iraq), which started in November 1914. The key objectives − Basra, the head of the Persian Gulf and the oilfields − were captured within six months, but the rest of the campaign, which encompassed an embarrassing defeat at Kut in 1916 and subsequent successful operations to restore British prestige, contributed little to enhancing the security of the British Empire, and even less to the defeat of Germany.

British Strategy, 1916–18[42]

By the end of 1915 Britain's difficult financial and economic position was contributing to the undermining of Kitchener's strategy. He was not alive to see its collapse. Lord Kitchener died in May 1916 when an enemy mine sank HMS *Hampshire*, a cruiser taking him to a meeting in Russia. The events of 1916 and 1917 weakened the ability of the armies of France and Russia to bear the burden of the fighting against Germany. Seven months later the man who had appointed Kitchener as Secretary of State for War was out of office. Herbert Asquith was by no means a complete failure as a wartime Prime Minister. He deserves some credit for mobilising Britain's economy and society to fight a major war and for dealing with immense and almost entirely unforeseen challenges with a large measure of success. Many of the developments in creating effective governmental machinery for waging war that have customarily been associated with the Lloyd George coalition had their origins in the Asquith administrations. Asquith's achievement is all the more striking given that he could not concentrate solely on waging war but had to devote a substantial proportion of his time to holding together first his Liberal government and then a coalition administration. Nevertheless, by December 1916 Asquith had largely forfeited his credibility as a national leader.[43]

Asquith's replacement as Prime Minister was another Liberal, David Lloyd George. Lloyd George's style was very different to that of his predecessor. The patrician Asquith conciliated and facilitated, while the populist Lloyd George drove and led. Lloyd George's dynamism and charisma were ideally suited to leadership in what was increasingly becoming a 'people's war'; in that sense his performance is comparable to that of his friend and rival Winston Churchill in the Second World War. When a contemporary proclaimed that 'Mr. Lloyd George was the man who won the war',[44] his hyperbole contained a strong element of truth. Lloyd George's leadership and organisational skills were indeed important elements in the British victory. He introduced a small executive body which was a little more efficient than its larger precursor, and was well served by the secretary of this War Cabinet, Maurice Hankey.[45] Yet he never attained the grip on British strategy that Churchill achieved between 1940 and 1945, for Lloyd George's position as Prime Minister was a difficult and paradoxical one. Lloyd George had made his reputation in peace as a Radical and people's champion, yet by supplanting Asquith he split his own party and was sustained in office by the Conservatives, who recognised his ability to wage total war. His Conservative allies limited Lloyd George's room for manoeuvre in dealing with the generals, especially Haig, who enjoyed Conservative support.

A further paradox was that Lloyd George was both a total warrior and an instinctive 'Easterner' who was genuinely horrified by the carnage on the Western Front. This brought him into direct conflict with senior soldiers, especially Haig and Robertson, who shared the Prime Minister's belief in waging total war but saw the Western Front as the decisive theatre. Lloyd George 'does not agree with Robertson's strategy, & he thinks the Somme offensive is a ghastly failure: but he has made no secret of it; he tells them his views openly', the Secretary of State for War's personal secretary noted on 31 October 1916. 'Robertson thinks that D [i.e. Lloyd George] ought to back him up in everything: D. does not think so.'[46] One historian has suggested that Lloyd George viewed the generals much as he had seen the upper classes and industrialists before the war, as oppressors of the common people, in this case the ordinary soldier.[47] His campaign against Haig and Robertson is thus of a piece with his introduction of Old Age Pensions in 1908 and his 1909 budget, which brought about a clash of the 'peers against the people'. Lloyd George was also well aware of the need to feed the war-weary British people on a diet of victory. He saw no prospect of triumphs occurring in France and Flanders, but on other fronts it was a different matter. General Allenby's capture on 9 December 1917 of Jerusalem, with its associations of the Bible and the mysterious East, was a 'Christmas present to the British nation' which, if nothing else, boosted morale on the home front.

Lloyd George was unable to bend the military to his will. In January 1917, and again in the summer, he floated the idea of transferring the main Allied effort to the Italian Front, but the generals remained stubbornly wedded to the Western Front. Frustrated, the Prime Minister turned to subterfuge. At the Calais conference in February 1917 he conspired to place the BEF under the control of the French commander in chief, General Robert Nivelle, for the forthcoming campaign. This would have had the effect of marginalising Haig, who was at that stage effectively unsackable. Not surprisingly, this further poisoned the already uneasy relations between the Prime Minister and his senior generals. Lloyd George and his Cabinet later acquiesced in Haig's Passchendaele offensive, despite severe reservations. The Welshman would carry the guilt for not having intervened to prevent it to the end of his days.[48]

Haig wished to renew the offensive in 1918 but in January of that year Lloyd George outflanked him by winning over the Supreme War Council to his plan to postpone the next major effort on the Western Front until 1919. In the meantime the Allies would invest heavily in tanks, aeroplanes and guns, and the British would take the offensive in Palestine, thus further improving Britain's geo-political situation and gathering up useful bargaining chips for the post-war peace conference. The firepower that this advanced military technology would supply would be used, in combination with the American manpower which would by then have been added to the Allied order of battle, to defeat the Germans in France and Belgium. This was an unashamed Western strategy, but one that would minimise the expenditure of British lives. Lloyd George capitalised on his strategic success by forcing Robertson's resignation as Chief of the Imperial General Staff (CIGS) in February.

However, in both cases, the Prime Minister's triumphs proved transitory. The new CIGS, the hyper-political Sir Henry Wilson, was a very different character from 'Wully' but his relationship with Lloyd George was by no means easy. More serious were the series of German offensives that began in March 1918. These ensured that the BEF became involved in fighting so heavy that the 'butcher's bill' dwarfed that of Passchendaele. Troops that had been held back in Britain, in the erroneous belief that Haig had enough men to repel a German attack, flooded into France and divisions were sent from Palestine to the Western Front. Like Kitchener before him, Lloyd George could only stand by and watch a carefully crafted and logical strategy destroyed by a combination of enemy action and the demands of coalition warfare. He, too, learned the bitter lesson that it was a case of making 'war as we must, and not as we should like to'.

For better or worse, the British main effort in 1918 was made on the Western Front. The German attacks were defeated by the end of July, and the Allies passed on to the offensive. The subsequent successes of the BEF and other Allied armies during the 'Hundred Days' took Lloyd George and Wilson, and even to some extent Haig, by surprise. London and GHQ do not appear to have grasped either the weakness of the German state and army or the military effectiveness of the BEF. The German capitulation on 11 November 1918 rendered plans for campaigns in 1919 and 1920 redundant.

British Strategy: Right or Wrong? A Conclusion

The Allies won the war in November 1918, but could the British, as Liddell Hart argued, have employed a quicker, less bloody, and more cost-effective strategy to achieve this end? The most obvious alternative strategy was to seek a compromise peace, but such a thing would only have been possible if Germany had been prepared to abandon its conquests in the West. A peace concluded on any other terms would have amounted to a German victory, with unacceptable and highly dangerous consequences for the Allies. Given the degree of political and popular will to fight on both sides, and the fact that the Entente and the Central Powers were roughly evenly matched in their ability to make war, a protracted total war was inevitable once the Germans failed to win a quick victory.

The superficially attractive idea that Britain's war effort should have consisted of sea power, peripheral campaigns and financial support to her Allies falls foul of events in the real world. Such a strategy of limited commitment rather than total war would almost certainly have resulted in a German victory: the Entente needed total British commitment just to stave off defeat. In 1915–17 the French and Russian armies came under enormous pressure, forcing Britain to commit her mass army to battle, and Britain became increasingly economically beholden to the United States. The support of American industry and finance, more so than American troops, was of critical importance in deciding the war in the Allies' favour. In the long term, the strategy of total war did much to undermine British power, a process that was accelerated and completed by the Second World War. The alternative, acquiescing in a German victory in either war, was even less palatable. The adoption of a strategy of total war was undoubtedly the correct decision.

Strategy is a complex matter, never more so than in 1914–18. An 'Eastern' strategy had to exist alongside a 'Western' strategy, as Robertson, allegedly the Westerner *par excellence*, fully recognised.

War after all is a political instrument, and the British government saw it in the national interest to expand the Empire in the Middle East,[49] to support the French – the prime movers behind the Salonika campaign – in the interests of coalition solidarity, and to send divisions to prop up their Italian ally after the military disaster at Caporetto (November 1917).[50] But these operations made a minimal contribution to defeating the main enemy, Germany. As a student of the war commented in the 1930s:

> To the contention that our true strategy would have been to find a way round, it is replied that there was no way round, or, if there was, it was not in fact the shortest way home.[51]

In 1942, Britain was pursuing a strategy akin to Liddell Hart's ideal of a 'British Way in Warfare'. Excluded from the continent after their defeat in France and the Low Countries in May–June 1940, British forces had occupied vast tracts of Italian colonial territory, and were conducting small scale operations in the Mediterranean, combined with a naval blockade, raids launched from the sea on enemy-occupied Europe, and a logical extension of a traditional strategy – a strategic bombing campaign. In that month George Orwell, the socialist political commentator and novelist – and a perceptive military critic – pointed out the fatal flaw in Liddell Hart's strategy: that it assumed an essentially limited war, fought against an opponent who also operated within the same basic parameters.[52] These conditions did not pertain to either of the twentieth century struggles against Germany. Both of these conflicts were decidedly unlimited. In both wars British seapower was absolutely vital, but was not sufficient in itself to bring about victory. Such wars demanded a major commitment of ground forces to grind down the enemy armies, as had the wars against Napoleon a century before. Against Napoleonic France, Britain's allies – Russia, Prussia, and Austria – had provided the bulk of the armies to do the fighting, killing and dying. Between 1941–5 the Soviet Red Army was to fulfil the same role. In the years 1914–17, the anti-German coalition was not strong enough to let the

British off the hook of putting a large army in the field, although their allies bore the burden of the fighting on land for the first two and a half years, giving them time to raise a mass army. Moreover, the BEF was unable to pursue a strategy completely independent of her allies.

To have withheld forces from the Western Front would have risked, at worst, France being defeated and the BEF being forced into a Dunkirk-style evacuation twenty-five years early, with the grim prospect of fighting on alone. One can certainly debate whether the best use was made of the BEF, whether battles could have been conducted more competently and whether the 'butcher's bill' could have been held down. That is a separate issue from the stark reality that Britain had no alternative to committing a large force to the Western Front.

British strategy in the First World War must ultimately be judged a success. Seapower laid the groundwork for eventual victory. Campaigns outside Europe enlarged and to some extent increased the security of the British Empire.[53] The BEF played a pivotal role in defeating the main enemy in the decisive theatre of operations. British strategy was successful in another sense as well; it waged a total war without damaging the essentially liberal and democratic nature of the British state. There were clashes between soldiers and politicians, some apparently serious. Lloyd George professed to believe in the dangers of a military dictatorship, and there was indeed some politicking by soldiers.[54] But ultimately civilian politicians controlled strategy, in partnership, however uneasy, with soldiers. The most visible intervention of a soldier into politics came in May 1918, when Major General Sir Frederick Maurice published a letter accusing Lloyd George of lying to parliament over the numbers of troops available to Haig at the beginning of 1918. Maurice's motivation was his concern for the wellbeing of the army, not an attempt to undermine Lloyd George's government; and his peers, including Haig and the highly 'political' Henry Wilson, frowned upon his actions. British soldiers came from a different military tradition from Hindenburg and Ludendorff, who effectively took control of the German government, usurping the authority of civilian politicians and reducing the Kaiser to impotence.[55]

Clausewitz wisely observed that 'everything in strategy is very simple, but that does not mean that everything is very easy'. The elements of British strategy were essentially uncomplicated, but gaining agreement on strategy and then putting it into practice was anything but straightforward. To take but one example, the gains made by capturing Turkish territory in the Middle East had to be balanced against a possible weakening of the effort against Germany. British and Allied strategy in the First World War was on occasion wasteful and even incompetent, but ultimately proved less wasteful and incompetent than that of Germany and the Central Powers. In the end, this was what mattered. As a modern writer has recently pointed out: 'To succeed in strategy ... all that is required is performing well enough to beat an enemy. You do not have to win elegantly; you just have to win.'[56]

CHAPTER 5

THE EMERGENCE OF TRENCH WARFARE, 1914–15

The armies of Germany, France and Britain went to war in August 1914 believing that the coming conflict would be bloody but swift and decisive. Instead, within three months the offensive strategies of all three armies had failed, and the Western Front was deadlocked. Why did it take so long, and cost so many lives, for this 'trenchlock' to be broken?

The answer often given is the sheer stupidity of the generals. A.J.P. Taylor wrote that Allied and German commanders 'stared' at the trenches 'impotently and without understanding. They went on staring for nearly four years.'[1] In his acclaimed study, *On the Psychology of Military Incompetence*, Professor Norman Dixon quoted Taylor's view approvingly and added:

> Only the most blinkered could deny that the First World War exemplified every aspect of high-level military incompetence. For sheer lack of imaginative leadership, inept decisions, ignoring of military intelligence, underestimation of the enemy, delusional optimism and monumental wastage of human resources it has surely never had its equal.[2]

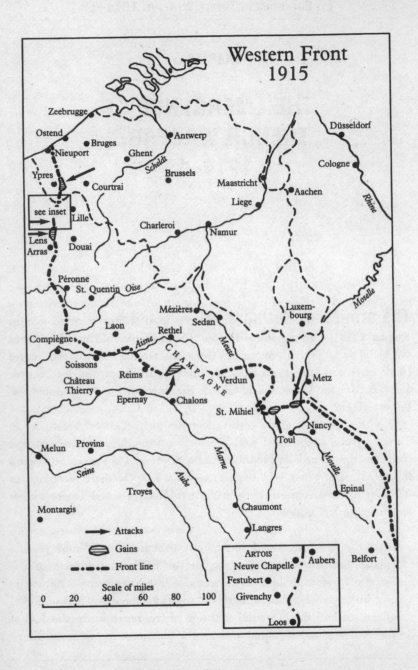

Western Front
1915

Zeebrugge
Ostend
Nieuport
Bruges
Antwerp
Düsseldorf
Ghent
Ypres
Scheldt
Cologne
Courtrai
Brussels
Maastricht
Aachen
Liege
Rhine
see inset
Lille
Charleroi
Namur
Lens
Douai
Arras
Péronne
St. Quentin *Oise*
Mézières
Luxembourg
Moselle
Compiègne
Laon
Rethel
Sedan
Aisne
C H A M P A G N E
Meuse
Soissons
Reims
Verdun
Metz
Château
Thierry
Epernay
Chalons
St. Mihiel
Melun
Provins
Toul
Nancy
Seine
Marne
Moselle
Troyes
Aube
Epinal
Montargis
Chaumont
Langres

→ Attacks
⬭ Gains
▪–▪–▪ Front line

Scale of miles
0   20   40   60   80   100

ARTOIS
Neuve Chapelle
Aubers
Festubert ●
Givenchy ●
Belfort
Loos ●

The generals are condemned not only for their conduct of the war, for failing to adapt to new conditions, but also for failing to anticipate, before 1914, the nature of future war. The social background and political affiliations of senior officers, according to a common view, rendered them incapable of understanding the revolutionary changes that advanced technology in the shape of the machine gun and modern artillery had brought to the battlefield. Before examining the fairness of these deeply held views, we need to discuss the brief phase of open warfare in 1914.

Mons and Le Cateau

Within days of the BEF concentrating on the left of the French Fifth Army in August 1914, the British soldiers discovered the hard way that this placed them directly in the path of von Kluck's advancing German First Army. The Schlieffen Plan had launched seven armies against France. The operation took the form of a *Kesselschlacht*, or battle of encirclement, with the Germans attempting to loop round Paris, surround the French forces, and crush them. On 23 August 1914 British II Corps, under Smith-Dorrien, won a clear defensive victory. Holding the line of the Mons-Condé Canal, the accuracy of their rifle fire halted the German attackers for the loss of 1,600 British soldiers. These casualties, shocking at the time, were to be dwarfed by what was to come. That night the BEF slipped away and joined in the general Allied retreat in this sector. The Germans close on his heels, Smith-Dorrien turned and fought another defensive action at Le Cateau on 26 August.

Le Cateau was also a British defensive success, although the casualties were much heavier: over 7,000 men. Nevertheless, the blow to the Germans was severe enough to give the BEF a head start in the retreat that followed. Le Cateau was the last Napoleonic-style battle fought by the British army. For the last time the guns of the Royal Artillery were pushed up among the infantry, resulting in the loss of 38 pieces when the Germans overran the positions. In future, artillery would be held further back, relying on forward observers to direct fire. The inadequacy of communications, a constant feature of Great War battles, led to unnecessary losses. At the village of Audencourt the Gordon Highlanders failed to see the visual signal to retire, leaving them holding the line until they were overwhelmed, long after the rest of the British army had fallen back. The Germans, too, suffered heavy losses from attacking in dense formations that made easy targets for British artillery, rifle and machine gun fire. Similarly, on other sectors of the Front, the French armies were counting the horrific consequences of their 'Plan XVII' based on the all-out offensive. Thus by the end of the first month of the Great War, both sides were having to rethink their tactical methods in the light of combat experience.

The Beginnings of Trench Warfare

The apparently remorseless German advance and Allied retreat ended on 5–6 September 1914. Kluck, enveloped in the fog of war, believed that the BEF and French Fifth Army were beaten and decided to wheel and pass to the east rather than the west of Paris, thus exposing his flank to a counterstroke from the city. The subsequent Battle of the Marne disrupted the German advance, forcing a retirement to the River Aisne. It was a major victory for the Allies, who now held the initiative. The BEF's advance after the Marne took them across the River Aisne in the area of Soissons. An officer of the South Staffordshire Regiment recalled that while advancing

up the wooded slopes on the far side of the river we came under heavy artillery fire and it was soon clear that this was going to be more than a rear-guard action. The advance soon came to a standstill and we were left to cling rather precariously to positions which were seldom more than a mile from the river.

The village that had been the South Staffords' objective 'remained in German hands for the next four years'. Trench warfare had begun, but at this stage 'the lines were by no means continuous and one could get a lot of fun patrolling; the country was well wooded and it was easy to penetrate behind the enemy's lines either by day or night'.[3]

On 15 September Joffre recognised that the campaign was 'no longer a question of pursuit, but of methodical attack'.[4] On the following day, after 48 hours of fruitless attacks, the British began to dig in. Thus, for the British army, the trench warfare phase of the First World War began on 16 September 1914. It was not to end until 21 March 1918.

The war of movement was not entirely dead. The Germans and French began what is misleadingly known as the 'race to the sea' as each side attempted to turn each other's northern flank. Having been transported north from the Aisne, the BEF played a major role in the First Battle of Ypres, the climax of mobile warfare in the West. The Belgian city of Ypres was a key communications centre, dangerously close to the coast from the British perspective. If it fell to the Germans, they could roll up the Allied line and cut off the BEF from the sea. Bad as the fighting on the Retreat and the Aisne had been, First Ypres was worse, an attritional struggle dominated by artillery. The Allies weathered two major crises, on 31 October and 11 November, and the line held, but only just. Many generals had anticipated a decisive war of movement, but at the end of 1914 commanders were faced with a trenchbound Western Front and the prospect of a protracted war of attrition.

The Firepower Revolution, 1815–1914

This tactical deadlock was not an aberration but the inevitable product of military and technological developments over the previous century. Ninety-nine years before the outbreak of the First World War, the armies of Napoleon, Wellington and Blücher clashed at the joint battles of Waterloo and Wavre. At this time the infantry were armed with muskets with a maximum range of 200 yards and an effective range of just 50. Smoothbore, muzzle-loading artillery fired solid cannonballs a maximum of about one mile. Infantry manoeuvred and often assaulted in dense columns. For defensive action against other infantry, foot soldiers would deploy into a two- or three-deep line to maximise firepower. Faced with charging cavalry, infantry would adopt a 'square' formation that had no vulnerable flanks. For infantry to be caught in line by sword- or lance-armed cavalry was almost invariably disastrous.

In the decades that followed Waterloo firearms underwent a revolution. The principle of rifling – putting grooves into the barrel of the musket or cannon to make the projectile spin in flight, thus increasing both the range and accuracy – had been known for many years. Various technological developments made it possible to produce weapons that were able to supplant their smoothbore predecessors. The invention of breachloading weapons speeded up the rate of fire – the extra time previously taken to ram the ball down the muzzle of the rifle had been a major disadvantage. In addition, the development of various explosive shells dramatically increased the effectiveness of weapons. They were now able to kill more accurately at greater ranges than ever before.

Three examples may serve to illustrate this point. In 1854, during the Battle of Balaklava, the 93rd Highlanders halted an attack by Russian cavalry by the firepower of their rifles. Significantly, this action became known as the 'Thin Red Line'; had it occurred thirty years earlier, the 93rd would have formed square. Nine years later, on 3 July 1863, the Army of Northern Virginia's assault on the Federal centre at Gettysburg – immortalised as Pickett's Charge – was bloodily repulsed, and at Gravelotte-St. Privat in 1870 the Prussian Guard Corps met a similar fate at the hands of the French. Heroism availed little in the face of determined defenders armed with modern weapons, especially if the attacker assaulted frontally in dense formations.[5]

By 1914 weapons were significantly more powerful than those used in the Crimea and the American Civil War. Artillery had enormously improved destructive power, range, and accuracy. Rates of fire were enhanced by the adoption of a hydraulic system, which absorbed the recoil of the gun, ensuring that it did not have to be re-laid (i.e. pointed accurately towards the target), after every shell was fired.

The Royal Artillery's order of battle included the 18-pounder (pdr) field gun, with a range of 6,525 yards and a 4.5-inch howitzer, which fired high-trajectory shots out to 7,300 yards. The 60-pdr heavy gun had a range of 12,300 yards. Above the 60-pdr was a series of siege howitzers and guns of various calibres, the heaviest mounted on railway flatcars. The standard British rifle, the .303-inch Short Magazine Lee-Enfield (SMLE), was a bolt-action repeater with an effective range of approximately 600 yards and a maximum of 2,500 yards. In the hands of a well-trained soldier, the SMLE could produce fifteen aimed shots in a 'mad minute'; otherwise five rounds was more normal. The standard machine gun was the .303 Vickers, with a range of 2,000 yards and a rate of fire of 250 rounds per minute. From December 1914 onwards, an automatic rifle or light machine gun, the Lewis gun (named after its American inventor), was used by the BEF, although it only became available in large numbers during the course of 1915.[6] The German and French armies had broadly comparable weapons.

The artillery piece, not the machine gun, was the most dangerous weapon in the Great War. The German 77mm shell, the equivalent of the 18-pounder, shattered into 500 splinters, each a potentially lethal projectile. Some 59 per cent of all wounds inflicted on British soldiers came from shellfire, including trench mortars; machine gun and rifle bullets accounted for about 39 per cent. The lethality of artillery can be judged by the fact that in France and Flanders, a wounded man was 'three times as likely to die as a result of a shell wound to the chest as of a bullet wound'.[7]

Did the events of 1914 demonstrate that the generals of Europe had been blind to the lessons of recent wars, and thus had failed to anticipate the conditions at the beginning of the First World War? At first sight the answer would appear to be 'yes', especially given the seemingly prescient observations of a civilian, a Polish-Jewish banker, I.S. Bloch. In a five-volume work, of which the first volume was translated into English under the title *Is War Impossible?* (1899) Bloch argued that the power of modern weapons made deadlock inevitable. Some generals shared Bloch's views. One such was Lord Kitchener. In a letter of

1908 he predicted that a major clash between France and Germany would result in stalemated trench warfare, and that the war would be decided by the 'last million' men that Britain put into the field.[8]

But the majority of military men had drawn a rather different conclusion from conflicts such as the Boer War (1899–1902) and Russo-Japanese War (1904–5). In the latter the Japanese attackers succeeded, at the cost of huge losses, in defeating entrenched Russians by using what amounted to siege warfare methods to bring them to grips with the defenders. The lesson seemed to be that if a force won the firepower battle and suppressed the enemy's fire, troops could then go in with the bayonet. It was accepted that the losses would be heavy and to counter this military thinkers stressed the importance of the exceptionally high morale that soldiers would need to cross the zone of death, to stay the course until the final mêlée. French soldiers such as Foch and de Grandmaison are the most famous proponents of these theories, but senior officers in most armies, including the German and the British, held similar views.

Such theories meshed with developments on the home front. Western societies became imbued with the notion of sacrifice, with dying for one's country. The Latin tag *Dulce et decorum est pro patria mori* – 'it is sweet and right to die for one's country' – is now remembered mainly through Wilfred Owen's bitter poem. Before the Great War, such sentiments were commonly held in much of Europe. Willingness to sacrifice was a mark of national virility and an indication of the likelihood of success in war, leading to some official trepidation over the possible resilience of working class morale in time of war.[9] Thus the doctrine of the offensive was not as irrational as it seems at first sight. Soldiers had to plan to fight and win wars – that was what states employed them for – and that involved offensive operations, even if a generally defensive stance was adopted. The emphasis on morale seemed a 'logical ... counter-balance to firepower' that was 'apparently solidly based in the psychological and racial sciences of the day'.[10]

In the event, Bloch's prediction of trench deadlock was, in the short term, more right than wrong. However, many French and German tactical failures of 1914 resulted not from the faults of the offensive doctrine, but from mistakes in putting that doctrine into practice on the battlefield.[11] The battles of 1915–18 were to confirm the original lesson of the Russo-Japanese War: that if attackers could deploy their firepower to suppress enemy artillery, machine guns and infantry, assaults could succeed, albeit at heavy cost. The Western Front thus also demonstrated that the pre-war emphasis on morale was not entirely misplaced. Soldiers of all armies, most of whom were not long-service professionals, proved to be far more resilient than many pre-war commentators had believed – as were the societies from which they were drawn.

The Short War Illusion

If the case for the prosecution of the generals of 1914 rests firstly on their allegedly irrational belief in the offensive, the second charge on the sheet is the widespread prediction that a future war between major European powers would be short. Quite why this was believed is a matter of debate among historians. The most recent wars in Western Europe, the Austro-Prussian clash of 1866 and Franco-Prussian War of 1870–1, had, indeed, been relatively short. The American Civil War and Second Boer War had not, but European soldiers tended to interpret the 'lessons' of recent wars in light of their existing doctrines.

This tendency may be related to conservatism among officers, who feared the social changes that a more technologically based approach might bring. Another more prosaic reason was that various 'lessons' seemed contradictory. The bayonet, singularly useless in South Africa, was perceived as an important factor in the Russo-Japanese War, and this was reflected in the changed emphasis in the British Field Service Regulations between the editions of 1902 and 1909.[12] Above all, a long, total war seemed inconceivable. The most recent clash between major powers – Russia and Japan – had produced a war that closely resembled the Western Front of ten years later. Yet the Russo-Japanese War was relatively short, the fighting on land occupying a little over twelve months. By the end Russia was in the throes of a revolution and even the victor, Japan, was having difficulty funding the war. One obvious lesson to be drawn was that even Great Powers could not sustain such conflicts for any length of time.

A war waged between states of approximately equal fighting power (political, economic and military strength, doctrine, skill, technology and morale) is inevitably going to be protracted. Only if one side has a distinct advantage in fighting power, as the Germans had over the French in 1940, or the Coalition had over the Iraqis in 1991, is a swift victory possible. With some notable exceptions, there was a fundamental failure by European general staffs to appreciate this before the First World War.

The State of the British Army in 1914

In a particularly stressful moment Lord Kitchener was once heard to say: 'Did they remember, when they went headlong into a war like this, that they were without an army, and without any preparation to equip one?'[13] As wartime Secretary of State for War, Kitchener was grappling with the paucity of peacetime preparation for a major war. It is impossible to understand what happened to the British army on the Western Front between 1914–18 without first examining the state of the army before the war.

One writer has suggested that a large peacetime British army would have acted as a deterrent to German aggression.[14] While the Royal Navy did have such a role, the British army of 1914 was far too small to appear as a threat to a potential aggressor. The Regular army fielded 247,432 men, with an additional 268,777 in the Territorial Force, a part-time body of volunteers intended for home defence. Even counting various categories of reserve forces, the total climbs to no more than 733,514. In addition there was the possibility of reinforcement from the Indian army, although not too many troops could be taken from India for reasons of both internal and external security. The BEF initially sent four infantry divisions and a cavalry

The public face of Anglo-French friendship: King Edward VII in Paris, May 1903. Although falling well short of a formal alliance, the *entente cordiale* of 1904 laid the foundations for military and political co-operation in the face of the growing German threat. IWM Q 81788

Archduke Franz Ferdinand and his wife Sophie in Sarajevo, 28 June 1914. The assassination of the heir to the Austro-Hungarian throne was to trigger the series of events that led eventually to the outbreak of war between the major European powers. IWM Q 81831

Kaiser Wilhelm II (centre) with Hindenburg and Ludendorff. An autocratic monarch in peacetime, Wilhelm's power was increasingly usurped by his senior generals after the war began. IWM Q 23964

The ship that heralded a naval revolution and arms race: HMS *Dreadnought*. Germany's challenge to British naval supremacy was a primary reason for the emergence of tensions between the two states. IWM 38705

The far-flung battle line: the 13th Hussars near Kirkuk, in Mesopotamia. Such campaigns extended the influence of the British Empire but did little to hasten the end of the war with Germany. IWM Q 24707

Haig with Joffre (left) and Foch (right), 12 August 1916. In the absence of an overall Allied commander until 1918, personal relationships between military leaders assumed greater importance than ever. Here, the three men emerge after lunch with King George V. IWM Q 951

Lloyd George visits Fricourt, on the Somme battlefield, 12 September 1916. Although a key figure in Britain's mobilisation for total war, he opposed a logical extension – Haig's attritional strategy. IWM Q 1179

Lord Kitchener inspects 10th Division at Basingstoke, 1 June 1915. 'K of K's' strategic vision in creating a British mass army was a vital factor in the eventual victory of the Allies. IWM Q 27688

Members of No. 5 Officer Cadet Battalion in the dining hall of Trinity College, Cambridge. Between 1914 and 1918 the British officer corps became a rough meritocracy, as potential subalterns, regardless of social background, were trained in pre-war values of leadership and paternalism. IWM Q 30322

President Woodrow Wilson meets the Mayor of Dover, December 1918. Wilson's radical views on international relations, his support for democracy and self-determination expressed in his Fourteen Points, helped to shape the ideological battleground for the rest of the twentieth century. IWM Q 58364

American troops leaving Winchester Cathedral on 11 November 1918. At 11 a.m., to mark the moment when the Armistice came into force, the organist had played the British and US national anthems. If the war had continued into 1919, men such as these would have borne the main burden of the fighting on the Western Front. IWM Q 31201

British industry was unable to meet the demands of total war until the middle of the conflict, and only then by a thorough mobilisation of the economy. Here, women are stoking furnaces in a gas works on the Home Front. IWM Q 109991

The RE 8, a two-seater reconnaissance biplane, was one of the workhorses of the Royal Flying Corps. Aircraft such as the 'Harry Tate' were a vital part of the weapons system that evolved on the Western Front. IWM Q 67552

A hasty battlefield burial, marked by an inverted rifle. This man was a casualty of the battle of Morval, fought during the later stages of the Somme campaign in 1916. IWM Q 4316

Indian cavalry near Mory, March 1917. In the conditions of semi-open warfare that existed during the German withdrawal to the Hindenburg Line, mounted troops still had a place on the battlefield. IWM Q 5062

Canadian troops advance on Vimy Ridge, 9 April 1917. Note the German prisoners. The success of the initial stage of the Arras campaign demonstrated that by the beginning of 1917 the BEF as a whole was capable of conducting highly effective set-piece offensives. IWM CO 1155

division to France, with another two infantry divisions following on shortly. The French started the war with 62 infantry and 10 cavalry divisions, and the Germans 87 and 11, both armies relying on conscripts. In sum, the standing military forces of the British Empire in 1914 were to prove hopelessly inadequate for the type and scale of war that was to unfold on the Western Front.

Edwardian British military leaders did not emulate Oliver Twist and ask for more although a retired general, Lord Roberts, vigorously but unsuccessfully campaigned for the introduction of conscription. Some undoubtedly believed a future war would be short; all were aware that 'the General Staff ... [was] under political pressure for caution and economy ...'[15] Political realities pointed away from Britain spending more on its army, let alone raising a conscript force. In a democracy, the military are the servants of the politicians. Should senior officers disagree with government policy, they can put forward their views to the politicians, ask, beg, cajole, and politick. Ultimately, they must accept the decisions of the politicians or resign, in the full knowledge that their successor will carry out whatever policy was the point at issue.

The responsibility for the lack of preparation of the British army for modern war must be set against this background. The Liberal government elected in 1906 was a radical, reforming administration which laid the foundations of the modern Welfare State, in Lloyd George's words to fight 'poverty and squalidness'.[16] This programme enhanced social and political stability and thus actually buttressed British security, but a corollary was restraint in spending on the army. Not that the Liberals neglected defence. Their response to the German-initiated naval race was to ensure that the Royal Navy retained its margin of superiority.[17] A factor here was that the Royal Navy, the world's most powerful fleet, was inexpensive, relatively speaking. This was in sharp contrast to the high cost of the army, even though it was a mere colonial gendarmerie of modest size. In 1910 the navy cost £40.4 million, the army 27.6; in 1914 the respective figures were 47.4 and 29.4.[18]

Nevertheless, if spending remained relatively low, there was substantial modernisation of the army. Setbacks in the Boer War came as a profound shock to the British and spurred a series of military reforms in the first decade of the twentieth century.[19] The post of Commander in Chief of the army, held for thirty-nine years by the reactionary Duke of Cambridge until he was prised out in 1895, was abolished and replaced by an Inspector General of the Forces with a seat on a newly created body, the Army Council. The Committee of Imperial Defence was strengthened and a General Staff formed in broad imitation of the German model. The holder of the post of Chief of the Imperial General Staff became the professional head of the army. These changes at the top of the army, while far from flawless, were sensible enough, although under the circumstances of war the relationship of the various positions changed. Kitchener, the Secretary of State for War, was the *de facto* commander in chief in 1914–15, while in 1916–17 Haig, the major field commander, emerged as a more powerful figure than Robertson, the CIGS.

The Liberal landslide election victory of 1906 brought R.B. Haldane to the War Office. A lawyer with a fondness for German philosophy (a hobby that was to make him extremely unpopular during the First World War), Haldane ranks among the greatest politicians ever to have had dealings with the British armed forces. Haldane created an 'Expeditionary Force' of six divisions, ready to be deployed to the continent or to the empire, as the need arose; and he rationalised the part-time auxiliary forces by creating the Territorial Force, effectively bringing them under the control of the Regular army. Mindful of the pitfalls of conscription, he hoped that he could create a 'nation in arms' based on the voluntary principle, but clearly failed in this aim, as the TF remained understrength.

Haldane may have had one eye on using the Expeditionary Force on the continent alongside the French, but in the early days it seemed just as likely to be used against the Russians in Asia. He certainly would not have won support had he announced it as a down payment on a continental commitment. Nevertheless, the importance of Haldane's creation of the Expeditionary Force, and indeed the Territorials, was to be amply demonstrated on the battlefields of France and Belgium in 1914. In the oft-quoted words of Sir James Edmonds, the British official historian, 'In every respect the Expeditionary Force of 1914 was incomparably the best trained, best organised, and best equipped British Army which ever went forth to war.'[20] However, as another official historian later commented, 'small armies feel losses more sharply than big. *Armées d'élite* would be invincible if wars were fought without casualties. Things being what they are, *armées d'élite* are unlikely to remain so long.'[21]

As effective as Haldane's Expeditionary Force undoubtedly was, it was the right army for a different sort of war than the one it actually came to fight. Virtually no one in the higher echelons of government or army foresaw involvement in a long attritional war, or at any rate no one asked for the funds to buy the equipment to fight one. Perhaps worse, there were no plans for providing a mass force in the *future*; there was no blueprint for national economic mobilisation, nor one to expand the army or provide the munitions, weapons, and equipment for a continental-scale army.[22] This failure was to have serious consequences on the battlefield in 1914–16.

The decade before the Great War is a classic illustration of the 'guns or butter' conundrum. Restraint on defence spending by a progressive government undoubtedly contributed to Britain becoming a better place to live for the majority of its citizens. But looking at it with the cold eye of logic one is forced to admit the justice of Kitchener's outburst quoted above. The Liberal government's foreign and defence policies were out of synchronisation. Carried to their logical end, the increasingly close relations (and the informal military arrangements) between Britain and France should have led to the realisation that there was a possibility, to put it no more strongly, that Britain would get involved in a large scale continental war of long duration. To admit this, let alone make visible preparations for it, would have been politically impossible, as both soldiers and politicians well knew. However, that does not mean that it was impossible to undertake some contingency planning, and Haldane, while rightly praised for what he did achieve, also deserves censure for not going this extra mile. The failure to plan for a protracted conflict before 1914 was not merely a product of military myopia. A large part of the blame also rests with democratic politicians and the British electorate. The British citizen army paid the price. Anthony Eden, who served as a junior officer in the First World War and a senior politician in the Second, once commented that it was unwise to hold 'a high military command in the first two years of any war in the British Army. Far better to wait until the stuff begins to come along. Which, I am afraid, in the last two experiences was after the third year or later.'[23]

Why was Breaking the Trench Line so Difficult?

Trench warfare was not invented in 1914. Trench fighting had played a prominent role in the campaigns in Manchuria in 1904–5, and throughout the ages trench warfare has been an integral part of siege warfare and occasionally appeared on the battlefield. What was new was the 'force to space ratio'. In plain English this means that vast armies armed with powerful weapons were crammed into a relatively small part of Belgium and eastern France. This allowed the creation of a defensive barrier that stretched some 400 miles from the North Sea to the Swiss frontier. The armies on the Eastern Front were also huge, but they had much more space in which to deploy and therefore the fighting was always of a more fluid character.

It is commonly believed that the incompetence of the generals contributed to the murderous deadlock. Brigadier General Sir James Edmonds went so far as to claim in the official history (a series which is commonly supposed to whitewash British high command) that faced with 'siege-warfare ... an "engineer and artillery war"', the Allies renamed it 'trench warfare' and

> the old lessons of siege-warfare were not applied ... instead of the gun and mine preparing a way for the infantry, it was the infantry which was expected to open a door for an inroad of horsemen against the enemy's rear.[24]

Edmonds, it is important to note, was a Royal Engineer officer, and a disgruntled one at that. At the same time, when siege methods such as mining were applied, they certainly achieved spectacular successes on occasions, most notably the Battle of Messines in June 1917. His claims, therefore, have some validity if applied to 1915; much less if applied to 1916–18. In some ways, though, trench warfare was different to siege conditions. A primary purpose of surrounding a city with trenches was to prevent supplies and reinforcements from reaching the garrison, but on the Western Front the defenders were able to reinforce more-or-less at will. Moreover, the Germans, since they were sitting on someone else's territory, were willing to abandon land and fall back to a more defensible position. It is fairer to describe the Western Front as having siege-*like* characteristics rather than being a siege as such.

We must now lower our sights from high command to the battlefield. The basic tactical problem on the Western Front was that the defender had a built-in advantage over the attacker: by placing their soldiers in trenches, they offered a small target to the enemy, difficult to accurately locate and even more difficult to hit with bullet or shell. Conversely, attackers had to expose their whole bodies to enemy fire as they crossed No Man's Land.

The way around this conundrum was to suppress enemy fire – either by destroying artillery pieces and machine guns with shellfire, or, more likely, by killing or driving off the soldiers who operated these lethal machines. To do this was far from easy. First, the target had to be located; then fire had to be accurately delivered on to the target. Much of the story of the Western Front can be summed up as an attempt to develop the means to do this. It was not simply a matter of acquiring the appropriate technology (which in 1915 the BEF did not have); it was also a matter of developing appropriate methods (or tactics) of using the technology in an effective fashion, which was achieved by 1918. In the meantime, the massive and prolonged bombardments that characterised the battles of 1915–17, while sometimes effective, also precluded the achievement of surprise, as well as churning up the ground and thus making it more difficult for the infantry to advance. Not until the end of 1917 did advances in artillery techniques allow surprise to return to the battlefield.

The Problem of Communications

Wellington was able to control his army in person during his battles, which were fought in relatively compact areas. The Iron Duke had been able to rely on a staff of little more than a dozen and had on many occasions been able to ride to danger points to give orders in person, most famously at Waterloo. Even at the time of the American Civil War, generals had been able to exercise a degree of 'voice control'. By the time of the First World War this was no longer possible. Technological developments after 1918 in the form of radios, light aircraft and helicopters were to restore a measure of voice control to commanders. The era of the First World War stands as the only period in history in which high commanders were mute.

In 1915, when the attacking troops clambered over the trench parapet and advanced into the open, the means of commanders communicating with their men were severely limited. Radio (or 'wireless') sets existed but were too bulky to be of much use on the battlefield. Visual signals, using semaphore flags and the like, were available in theory but in practice were not very effective, besides endangering the signaller. Aircraft flew patrols seeking to locate the positions of friendly troops, and it was possible for advancing soldiers to pay out telephone line across open ground, but wire was highly vulnerable to being cut by shellfire. Many signallers earned well-deserved decorations for repairing telephone line under enemy fire. One was Lieutenant Christopher Stone of 22nd Royal Fusiliers, who during the Somme fighting 'was out under a heavy artillery fire ... careering about the Devil's Wood with a coil of wire on his back amongst corpses'. Stone was awarded the Military Cross.[25]

The only semi-reliable method of communication was by runner. A runner was a soldier given a message to deliver who would have to physically carry that message to the recipient. It takes little imagination to envisage the problems involved in this system. The experience of one runner must stand for that of many. By 12.30 p.m. on 1 July 1916, 55

Brigade (18th Division) captured all its objectives on the first day of the Somme offensive, and a runner, Lance Corporal G. Bilson, was ordered to carry a message to brigade HQ. Bilson did not arrive back at his battalion until the morning of 2 July, and 'his clothes and equipment were in tatters, and ... his eyes were crossed in an extraordinary way'. On the way back from brigade HQ Bilson had been concussed by a shell, and had lain unconscious for many hours.[26]

The consequences of these communication problems were profound. Once they had committed their troops to battle, higher commanders, from the commander in chief of the BEF down to humble lieutenant colonels commanding infantry battalions, could do very little to influence the fighting. After infantry had gone over the top, the commanders who mattered were junior officers, NCOs or even privates, and the radius of their ability to command was limited to the distance that they could shout. The one way that higher commanders could affect the battle was by committing reserves at the right time and in the right place to exploit success. Commanders had to make these decisions based on the fragmentary snippets of information available. Thanks to the 'fog of war', reserves tended to be committed too late, or in the wrong place, or not at all.

The defenders' communications tended to be much superior. Their telephone lines, buried deep beneath the ground, were far more likely to survive a bombardment. That meant it was much easier for the defender to get messages back to higher HQs and rush reserves to threatened sectors. Reserves did not have to be held directly behind the front. They could be held centrally and moved by rail, although they then had to move on foot from the railhead to the front line. This built-in advantage to the defender partly explains why, in September 1915, the French with 35 divisions were unable to break through a mere 12 German divisions in Champagne.

It follows that the only sensible place for a higher commander to be was at the end of a telephone line. Ease of connection to an extensive network of telephone lines was one of the rationales of generals being based behind the front line, in a town or a convenient building such as a château. In essence, the closer a general was located to the front line, the fewer troops he could actually command. Even if by some stroke of good fortune a message from the fighting troops reached higher headquarters in good time, the commander still had to analyse the information it contained, make a decision based on this information and then act on it. Today, this process is known as the OODA loop, the acronym deriving from 'Observe, Orientate, Decide and Act'. The commander who goes through this process the fastest is likely to have a significant advantage over his slower opponent, and the receipt of timely and accurate information is all-important. In the OODA battle on the Western Front, the defender had the upper hand.

This fundamental point is illustrated by the Battle of Neuve Chapelle on 10 March 1915. The British massed guns and troops on a weakly held German sector. Following a 35-minute artillery bombardment, the infantry attacked and made good progress, rapidly capturing parts of the German front line. Once the carefully planned 'set-piece' phase was over, things became more difficult. Communication problems meant that it was difficult for the infantry to let their gunners know the location of German positions and wire which needed to be bombarded. In contrast, German gunners had a much easier task, shelling ground that was well known to them. On the front of 25 Brigade, the British infantry could not get forward, hemmed in as they were by friendly artillery fire. These and other factors retarded the British advance and bought time – five hours in all – for the Germans to rush up reinforcements. By the time the British advance was renewed, the opportunity had passed. Some of the frustration felt by the troops can be gauged from a contemporary letter written by an officer of 2nd Rifle Brigade:

We simply boosted through the village [of Neuve Chapelle] capturing about 200 Deutchers ... We then arrived the other side of the village and joined up with the Indians on our right, and our job was finished since we had broken a gap in the line and we could have gone to Berlin at least if there had been anyone behind, but as you know our brilliant staff had two men and a boy behind ...[27]

Although the battle went on for a further two days, the BEF was unable to build on the gains made in the first three hours.[28]

While human errors were in plentiful supply at Neuve Chapelle, the fundamental problem in this battle and all the others in the trench warfare period was how to convert a break-*in* into a break*through* in a situation in which the attacker was unlikely to be able to get inside the defender's OODA loop. Initially successful attacks that were not reinforced quickly enough tended merely to create untenable salients, in which the attackers were surrounded on three sides.

Between Cavalry and Tanks

Not only were the armies of the era of the Great War virtually unique in history in lacking effective voice communications, they also lacked an instrument of exploitation. Throughout history, most armies (there are some exceptions) have been composed of a triad of three arms: infantry, whether Roman legionaries carrying short swords and javelins or modern troops carrying assault rifles; artillery, which has ranged from stone-throwing *ballistae* to the Multi-Launched Rocket Systems of the Gulf War; and a mobile arm. In 1914, the armies of Europe still fielded masses of horsemen. They were intended to carry out reconnaissance and scouting duties, and to act as the instrument of exploitation, to race through a gap in the enemy line to convert a break-in into a breakthrough. They would then turn the enemy's retreat into a rout by advancing faster than the enemy could fall back, and by getting among his forces and dispersing them. Perhaps they would even be able to cut off their retreat altogether. This had been the role of cavalry for hundreds of years. The events of 1914–18 were to demonstrate that under the conditions usually pertaining to trench warfare, a combination of barbed wire and modern weapons rendered cavalry obsolete.[29]

As we shall see, the tank introduced in 1916 was incapable of taking up traditional cavalry roles, thus there was a leg missing from the stool. Even if the artillery and infantry did succeed in forcing a way through the enemy trenches, they could only pursue at the same rate as the enemy fell back. Problems of keeping up the momentum of the advance as the pursuers grew exhausted and ran out of supplies normally led to the enemy line stabilising someway to the rear of the original position. By 1917 the techniques of breaking-in had been mastered by the belligerents. In 1918 it was a question of finding a way to prevent the ruptured front from solidifying. As we will see, the Allies succeeded in this quest but the Germans failed. With this background in place, we can go on to consider the fighting on the Western Front in 1915.

1915: The Failure to Break Through

The story of the Western Front in 1915 is essentially one of repeated attempts to achieve a breakthrough that failed and degenerated into attrition. In December 1914 the French began a series of attacks in Artois and Champagne, the BEF playing a minor role in the former. These offensives failed to break through the German lines, as did a small British offensive at Neuve Chapelle in March. On 22 April, the Second Battle of Ypres began with the Germans launching a surprise attack heralded by a cloud of poisonous gas – the first major use of this weapon in history. While the 33-day struggle forced the Allies back, the Germans seemed to have been surprised by the extent of their initial success and failed to exploit it. In May Joffre planned to snip off the great bulge in the German line by again attacking in Artois and Champagne. Conceptually sound, the plan was a failure. The BEF's part in Second Artois was in the battles of Aubers Ridge (9 May) and Festubert (15–27 May). The first was a bloody failure; the second gained some ground but failed to secure a breakthrough.

From late May until September 1915 the main focus of operations was in Italy and the Balkans. In addition, the Central Powers pushed the Russians out of Poland and the Allies landed on 25 April at Gallipoli, but were unable to push inland from their beachheads. The lull, in relative terms, on the Western Front ended with the commencement of the Third Battle of Artois and Second Battle of Champagne on 25 September. The BEF also attacked that day at Loos, in the largest action the British had yet attempted. In all three offensives some modest gains were made, but the German line remained stubbornly intact. Loos continued until 4 November but was a failure. The British Expeditionary Force had suffered 273,098 battle casualties in 1915.[30]

At the beginning of 1915, Allied generals had every reason to suppose that trench deadlock would soon be broken and mobile warfare would recommence. After all, trench warfare had been a temporary phase in Manchuria in 1904–5. Furthermore, Allied strategy in the West in 1915 was shaped by a number of other factors. First and foremost was the inescapable fact that the German army had occupied most of Belgium and some of the most important industrial areas of France, and the German government showed no credible sign that they were prepared to relinquish their conquests voluntarily. Unless the Allies were prepared to acquiesce in these German conquests, attacking to expel the invader was the only option. Second was the coalition nature of the war. Simply holding their trenches and waiting – for the Kitchener Armies to arrive in strength, or the naval blockade to bite – was not an option for the British junior partner. It would have been unacceptable to the French government. Thus Neuve Chapelle was fought in part to prove to the French that the BEF was pulling its weight; at Loos the BEF attacked over difficult terrain chosen by the French high command rather than the British. Moreover, in 1915 Russia's armies absorbed the bulk of Germany's offensive efforts and suffered heavy defeats in the process. To have simply stood back and let Russia be defeated would have been suicidal, as it would have given Germany the opportunity subsequently to concentrate its resources on the campaign in the West. In 1918, France and Britain only narrowly survived Russia's exit from the war with American help, and three years earlier the United States would not have been there to step into Russia's shoes.

As the armies adjusted to the realities of trench warfare, the BEF was at a significant disadvantage. While the Germans had some stocks of essential trench weapons, the British, suffering from pre-war governmental parsimony, had next to none. The problem was that the BEF was critically short of shells, grenades and a host of other essential weapons of trench warfare. In the jaundiced view of the 1st Glosters in a front line position early in 1915, German 'ammunition seemed inexhaustible, whereas our supply of rather indifferent rifle grenades soon ran out, and we were reduced to the expedient of continually moving the men according to what part of the trench was being bombarded'.[31] Hand grenades and trench mortars had to be improvised from jam tins and water pipes. Such things could not be mass-produced overnight; the British economy would take time in mobilising for total war. Not until 1916, when the economy was gearing up to fulfil the needs of an attritional war, would supply begin to approach demand. Even so, in the summer of 1916 economy of shells had to be practised in some sectors to allow the feeding of the voracious appetites of the guns on the Somme.[32]

In spring 1915 British tactics were in some ways simpler than those of the previous autumn. Assaulting troops would advance by 'alternate rushes' without opening fire, to a point about 50 yards from their objective. Then, in the words of some contemporary instructions, on the commander's signal, 'the assault must be launched in one rush, this is essential if it is to succeed. The energy and courage of the troops will do the rest.' Artillery bombarded enemy trenches while the infantry was going in and would then shell the area behind the trench, to prevent the enemy from bringing up reserves.[33] These tactics were crude in comparison to those used in later years, and training was often rudimentary. Units tended to be trained at home in the tactics of open warfare, and only underwent training in trench warfare on arrival in France.[34] A contemporary account of an exercise by 1st Black Watch in February 1915, in which the battalion 'advanced over 1000 yards odd of perfectly flat ground with not the slightest cover' struck the men carrying it out as unrealistic.[35]

The first action of a Territorial unit, 1st/23rd Battalion The London Regiment, admirably demonstrates the tactical problems experienced in the spring of 1915. 1st/23rd Londons attacked at Givenchy on 26 May 1915 and duly captured its allotted portion of German trench, but took heavy casualties in holding it. The Regimental history highlighted the tactical shortcomings of the time:

> The word 'barrage', if it had been invented, had not percolated to the infantry. The roles of bayonet men, bombers and moppers-up were not imagined, and the general spirit of an attack could, Colonel Streatfield [who commanded the battalion in this attack] suggests, be summarised in the words: 'We will give you as much artillery support as we can; for the rest, here are your objectives, get there as quickly as possible, and take the best measures you can to hold on.'

Each battalion had only two machine guns, and there were no light Lewis guns at this stage. A captured trench had thus to be crammed with riflemen to hold it against counterattack. 1st/23rd Londons suffered nearly 500 casualties, split fairly evenly between killed and wounded. The 'vast majority' were incurred after the trench was captured. The British artillery, which at first 'did wonders' in defending the captured positions, soon ran out of ammunition. For most of the day the luckless Londoners were shot to pieces 'without any chance of retaliation'.[36] As this passage demonstrates, most of the key elements of the victorious tactics of 1918 – heavy and accurate artillery barrages, scientifically calculated to deliver the requisite number of shells (available in unlimited quantities) to neutralise enemy defences; specialised roles within the infantry; and massive infantry firepower – were completely absent in 1915.

The BEF did not simply gape at the trenches with incomprehension in the winter of 1914–15. Instead, British soldiers at all levels began a process of innovation and experimentation as the BEF rapidly began to adjust to the new conditions of warfare.

> If a unit bethought itself of some useful improvisation, such as a new method of firing rifle grenades, carrying rations or making ingenious loopholes combining a better field of fire

with greater safety, details were collected and circulated by Army Headquarters. There was need of ingenuity to balance the great inferiority from which the British troops suffered in the matter of trench stores and munitions.[37]

Tangible evidence of adaptation to the new conditions was the replacement of the officer's sword by a rifle in January 1915. In March, 4th Division ordered that brigades form companies armed with hand grenades, and in June the Army Council authorised the formation of a detachment of one officer, two NCOs and 56 other ranks of 'grenadiers' in each battalion in the army. The use of this title was completely logical and had long historical precedent. However, a vigorous bureaucratic campaign by the Guards succeeded in reserving the coveted name for the Grenadier Guards, and so the term 'bomber' entered the lexicon of the British army.[38] This piece of recidivism notwithstanding, the Guards were as active as any unit in tactical experimentation and improvisation.

Some of the most important developments were in the field of gunnery, which were closely related to the birth of air warfare. Although it is the glamour of the fighter aces of the Royal Flying Corps (RFC) which captured the public imagination at the time and subsequently, it should never be forgotten that one of the primary reasons for the struggle to control the air was to allow friendly reconnaissance aircraft to operate over enemy lines, while preventing the enemy's machines from doing the same job. The RFC, by carrying out an extensive photo-reconnaissance of the German lines, provided the raw material for accurate trench maps. The 'clock code', an efficient but simple system to allow aerial observation of artillery fire, was developed as early as December 1914. Fall of shot was radioed from an aircraft, and artillerymen could make the necessary adjustments to their guns.[39]

At Neuve Chapelle, 354 guns were massed on a frontage of 1,200 yards and gradually registered – fired to find the range of the target – over a period of three weeks before the attack, to try to attain the element of surprise.[40] Before the infantry attacked, the guns fired a

35-minute bombardment. Although the 18-pounders cut the German wire, the howitzers and heavy guns firing at targets up to 5,000 yards distant had less success. The lesson drawn from the battle was that a 'hurricane' bombardment was too short to destroy enemy positions. Unfortunately, in this case, this led tactical thought down a blind alley. The approach adopted after Neuve Chapelle was prolonged bombardments aimed at destruction rather than neutralisation. In fact the complete destruction of enemy trenches and strong-points was a chimera, but effective hurricane bombardments could neutralise the enemy in the trenches, by killing or wounding them or just forcing them to keep their heads down.

One of the key lessons that emerged by the summer of 1915 was the need to increase the co-operation between the artillery and other arms.[41] Problems of communication could make it exceptionally difficult to provide artillery support for the infantry, but at the most basic level steps were taken to enhance co-operation. In February 1915 1st Irish Guards acquired both a telephone link to an artillery battery and a gunner officer attached to battalion headquarters.[42] The personal element – infantry and artillery learning to work with each other – was, in its way, as significant as the introduction of communications technology.

At Loos on 25 September the Royal Artillery was called upon to support an attack altogether bigger than the battles of the spring.[43] The attack frontage was eight times as long as that at Neuve Chapelle, but the quantity of available artillery did not match this bigger job. The concentration of one gun or howitzer every 23 yards was only one fifth of that at the earlier battle. The use of poison gas did not compensate for this weakness in guns, the continuing shortage of ammunition, the surprise sacrificed by a four-day bombardment or the problems faced by the infantry in trying to negotiate a shell-shattered landscape.[44]

Yet in spite of these self-imposed handicaps, the artillery enjoyed some success. New command and control arrangements worked reasonably well, although there was much room for improvement. On the right, the guns played a major role in getting the infantry onto the German first position and maintaining them there. A Kitchener formation, 9th (Scottish) Division even reached the German second position. The term 'barrage', a barrier or curtain of shells, entered British military vocabulary in 1915. In retrospect

> The most significant development in tactics was the use of the 'lifting barrage'. Rather than fire advancing at arbitrary intervals – the 'straight barrage' – the 'lifting barrage' moved in parallel lines but from trench to trench, concentrating fire on the lines of greatest resistance.[45]

As the Somme was to demonstrate, the lifting barrage had its disadvantages, but it was a step in the right direction.

The use of poison gas at Loos was a disappointment. Perhaps mindful of the German failure to take advantage of the surprise obtained by their use of gas at Second Ypres, Haig's First Army ordered that, 'in the intervals between the attack', skirmishers and machine guns were to be sent forward to identify any signs of 'weakening' by the enemy, and also to mislead him.[46] Gas was reliant on the wind blowing in the right direction, and in the event it actually blew back into the faces of some of the British attackers. Rather than underlining the reactionary conservatism of British high command, the story of gas at Loos shows that too much faith was placed in a single unreliable and untried weapon. Subsequent years were to demonstrate that chemical warfare had its place on the battlefield, but as an auxiliary to artillery and infantry, not as a primary weapon.[47]

The Generals in 1915

The BEF of 1915 was an *ad hoc* army. Regular battalions were now Regular in name only, containing few pre-war professional officers or men. By the end of 1914 Territorial units came out to take their place in the front line, to be followed in 1915 by the first divisions of Kitchener's Army. With vast numbers of volunteers thronging the recruiting stations, it was not difficult to fill the ranks of this improvised force. Finding competent staff officers and senior commanders was much more difficult.

As John Bourne has pointed out, the much-maligned 'generals' of the First World War constituted a very large group indeed. Between 1914 and 1918 ten army commanders, 43 corps commanders, 147 infantry divisional commanders and over 700 infantry brigade commanders served with the BEF. Given that pre-war planning had envisaged a BEF of only six infantry divisions and a cavalry division, two things become immediately apparent. First, the army had to reach far beyond the small group of men holding senior positions in August 1914 to command the formations of the bloated BEF of 1915–18. Second, senior commanders would need to think on a much larger scale than that for which their training at Staff College and experience of colonial war had prepared them. Commanders and staff officers needed to lift their sights to think in terms of armies and corps, rather than divisions and brigades. Sir Charles ('Tim') Harington recalled that at Staff College before the war they had never 'even in theory' contemplated dealing with a body larger than the six-division Expeditionary Force. As the chief staff officer of Second Army, he had to deal on occasions with over thirty divisions.[48] Pre-war Regular officers had excelled at 'leadership', in the sense of maintaining morale, looking after the men in a paternal fashion, and setting a courageous example on the battlefield.[49] Command − that is the direction, co-ordination and effective use of military force − of a body as huge as the BEF was a different matter. No one in the British army in 1914 had any experience of that.

Field Marshal Sir John French, a successful cavalry leader in the Boer War, was out of his depth as commander of the BEF in 1914–15. His performance in 1914 was less than impressive. At Le Cateau, the actions of Smith-Dorrien, commander of II Corps, saved the BEF. At one stage on the retreat from Mons, Kitchener had to come out to France to order French to desist from pulling the BEF out of the fighting to refit. Part of the problem was that French remained wedded to the regimental commander model. At the Battle of Loos in September 1915 he 'fought it in his old style, riding round behind the lines'. An observer saw him 'riding quite alone through the shattered villages behind the line and thanking all he met' and visiting the wounded.[50] Such an approach might have boosted morale but that was not the function of the commander in chief; such 'disappearances ... [created] a vacuum in command'.[51] Sir John French's problems in trying to apply the regimental commander model were repeated further down the command chain. Officers promoted to command formations larger than they had dreamed of before the war discovered that familiar techniques worked well enough at brigade level, less so at higher levels.

Loos effectively ended Sir John French's career as commander in chief. He mishandled the reserves, using two unblooded divisions and holding them back too far behind the lines, so subjecting them to a gruelling approach march and virtually guaranteeing the failure of their attack. After the battle a number of senior commanders intrigued with politicians and the King to have French replaced. One of French's leading critics, Douglas Haig, who was by no means blameless in respect of the Loos fiasco, took his place in command of the BEF on 19 December.

The records of other senior commanders in 1915 were mixed. Smith-Dorrien was removed from command of Second Army in May 1915, the victim of French's jealousy and hatred. His replacement was Sir Herbert Plumer, who was to emerge as one of the most successful British generals of the war. Henry Rawlinson made an uncertain start to his career as commander of IV Corps. During the preparations for Neuve Chapelle, he did not seem to understand what was required of him in terms of planning. Only after he had been prodded and rebuked by Haig, the First Army commander, did Rawlinson produce a plan. Haig himself was instrumental in producing an over-ambitious plan at Loos.[52] If judged purely on the evidence of 1915, there is a strong case against British generals. However, many of the generals of 1915 were the same men who led the BEF to victory three years later.

Conclusions: 1915 in Retrospect

If any year in the Great War comes close to fulfilling the stereotype promoted by *Oh! What a Lovely War*, it is 1915. Infantry, when they weren't using improvised weapons that were dangerous to friend and foe alike, were sent against enemy trenches armed with little more than a rifle and bayonet. Often insufficiently trained, the infantry lacked the weapons that were to transform battles over the next two years. They received inadequate support from an artillery force suffering from a chronic lack of shells. Moreover, gunners themselves were grappling with the demands of a task that was rapidly turning from a rule-of-thumb affair into a science. One of the major mistakes of 1915 was the failure to perceive correctly the true lessons of Neuve Chapelle: that hurricane artillery bombardments followed by limited attacks were the way of the future.

Yet at the end of 1915 there was scope for cautious optimism. The BEF was absorbing the perceived lessons of the fighting, and there was a healthy interest in innovation and experimentation at all levels. The Battle of Loos had been mishandled, but the performance of the infantry and artillery had given some cause for satisfaction. The divisions of Kitchener's New Armies were arriving in large numbers and a thoroughly professional officer, Sir Douglas Haig, had now replaced Sir John French. In retrospect, we can see that many of the developments that were to bring about the birth of modern warfare in 1917–18 – scientific gunnery, use of aircraft, modern infantry tactics – had their origins in 1915, the first year of trench warfare.

CHAPTER 6

THE MAN AND HIS ARMY: DOUGLAS HAIG AND THE BRITISH EXPEDITIONARY FORCE

It is difficult to think of a British general with a worse popular reputation than Douglas Haig. He seems to epitomise everything that was wrong with the generalship of the First World War. The popular view sees him as stubborn, stupid, callous, uncaring; a man who spent his war safe in a comfortable and well-appointed château miles behind the lines while his troops suffered and died in rat-infested trenches. He was a cavalryman, and thus, the theory goes, particularly reactionary and resistant to technology, and, like the generals who sent in the Light Brigade in 1854, prone to order hopeless attacks, this time with infantrymen against machine guns and barbed wire. Haig's soldiers were at best indifferent to him; at worst, they hated him.

Given this view of Haig, firmly entrenched in the popular mind by 1963, it is not difficult to understand the sense of outrage brought about by the publication in that year of John Terraine's *Douglas Haig: The Educated Soldier*.[1] The very title was a provocation — how could the most asinine of the 'Donkeys' be educated? Worse was Terraine's view that Haig was a 'Great Captain', in the mould of Marlborough or Wellington, who, recognising that the conditions on the Western Front meant that there could be no easy victories, wore out the German army in attritional battles before delivering the *coup de grâce* in 1918. Rarely can views on an historical figure have been so polarised.

Anyone who undertakes a little serious reading will soon dismiss the 'popular' view of Haig for the caricature it is, but in the 1980s a respected historian produced a groundbreaking study from which Haig emerges with little credit. According to Tim Travers, Haig was greatly influenced by his time at Staff College. There he learned that 'war was mobile, structured, and decisive'. The commander should strive to beat 'the main enemy army. Battles were inevitably fought in three stages: preparation and the wearing out of enemy reserves; a rapid, decisive offensive; and cavalry exploitation'. All three phases would happen in rapid succession, 'and since both sides were technically much the same, the decisive elements were morale, determination, and the will of the commander'. Haig, having made up his mind long before 1914, did not, according to Travers, alter his views to any great extent during the Great War. His remote and forbidding personality made it difficult for his subordinates to discuss matters with him, Travers contends. All of this led to 'command vacuums' at crucial moments and 'a top-down system of command' that 'made innovation at GHQ or in the army difficult'. Travers concludes that Haig commanded 'in nineteenth-century style' and that he clung to the notion of 'the structured offensive, so that the period from 1916 to 1918 was ... an attrition policy waiting for the right moment for the decisive offensive'. This strategy was ultimately successful, but 'the criticism is that more flexible ideas and a more open command style would have prosecuted the war more effectively and might have saved casualties'.[2]

Any assessment of the performance of the British army in the First World War must grapple with the enigma of Douglas Haig. My view is that while he certainly made mistakes that had bloody and tragic consequences, Haig also deserves some of the credit for the steady improvement in the BEF's combat performance. It is always difficult to argue a moderate view when dealing with such an emotive topic, for it has rightly been said that people who walk down the middle of the road run the risk of being run down by traffic travelling in both directions.

Douglas Haig was born in Edinburgh in 1861, a member of a branch of the whisky distilling family.[3] Young Douglas attended Brasenose College, Oxford, although through illness he did not complete his degree. He then went to the Royal Military College Sandhurst in 1884, and was commissioned into the 7th Hussars in the following year. He seems to have been a model regimental officer, efficient, paternal, respected by his men, and a good sportsman.

There are some characters from history whom one can imagine making good dinner companions; Douglas Haig is not one of them. His personality was somewhat austere, the apparent coldness of his manner being reinforced by his taciturnity. He was notoriously inarticulate. As a student at Staff College in 1896 Haig was not particularly popular, but already he was respected and recognised as a professional officer who took soldiering seriously – by no means a common attribute in the army of that time. Active service in the Sudan showed that Haig had his fair share of courage. Haig had a good Boer War, as chief of staff to the cavalry commander, Major General Sir John French, and later in a command of his own. Campaigning in the Sudan and South Africa created Haig's reputation and he was appointed major general in 1904, at the age of 42. Haig was well connected, and was no less averse than any other ambitious soldier to climbing the greasy pole. His contact with the Royal family was enhanced by his marriage in 1905 to the Hon. Dorothy Vivian, a maid of honour to Queen Alexandra. However, Haig's association with R.B. Haldane in his far-reaching reforms undermines the idea that Haig's career prospered merely because of his connections. Someone of Haldane's ability was hardly likely to have been impressed by a socially ambitious duffer. But impressed Haldane clearly was. Haig's reputation continued to grow in the decade before the outbreak of the Great War. He commanded I Corps and First Army in France in 1914–15. When French was sacked as CinC in December 1915, in terms of experience and reputation, Haig was the obvious man to succeed him.

On the eve of the Somme offensive Douglas Haig commanded the largest and most technologically complex army that Britain had ever put into the field. Exactly how he was to command this vast force was a moot point. We have already examined some of the problems facing Western Front commanders. Douglas Haig's command style attempted to make the best of his particular situation. Haig's General Headquarters (GHQ) was located at the town of Montreuil, some way behind the lines, with Haig and his closest staff living in a nearby château. For the Somme, Haig set up a much smaller Advanced Headquarters at a château within a few miles of the headquarters of both Reserve Army and Fourth Army. For the mobile battles of autumn 1918 he used a specially adapted railway train.[4] While operations were in progress, Haig made frequent visits to subordinate commanders, sometimes to hold a conference, more often for less formal discussions. Moreover, Haig, like Montgomery in a later war, used junior officers as liaison officers, to go out to act as his 'eyes and ears'. The idea that Haig spent the entire war in Montreuil, isolated from events, is completely wrong.

Haig 'was known [to the BEF] as "Duggy"; but with no enthusiasm. He was too remote – but that was not his fault. The show was too big.'[5] Many generals of the Second World War, junior officers in 1914–18, reacted against this style of leadership and adopted a populist, 'democratic' approach. It is by no means clear that the ordinary soldiers of the Great War, products of a deferential social system, would have been impressed by an informal approach. Haig's method of leadership, to be seen by as many of his troops as possible at formal parades, was appropriate for the soldiers of his army. Montgomery's method, which was applied to an army much smaller than Haig's, smacked of a politician in election mode. This was appropriate for products of a society rather different from that of 1916. We must judge Haig by the standards of his own time, not a later one.

Was Haig uncaring and callous? Winston Churchill compared him to a surgeon in the pre-anaesthetic era: 'entirely removed in his professional capacity from the agony of the patient ... He would operate without excitement ...' If the patient expired under the knife, 'he would not reproach himself'. However, once Surgeon Haig was 'out of the theatre, his heart was as warm as any man's'.[6] Haig did not find it easy to send men to their deaths, but he possessed to a marked degree the 'mask of command': the gift of self-control, especially the ability to keep a calm exterior in time of crisis.[7] Only once in the First World War did Haig lose his composure in public, when his HQ was surprised by a German night attack at Landrecies in August 1914. Significantly, this occurred when he was unwell, suffering from diarrhoea. Ordinarily, Haig was not a man to let his feelings show. The two occasions in which he attempted grand gestures of leadership merely demonstrated how serious the situation had become. The first was on 31 October 1914, when the British line at Ypres had temporarily given way, and he mounted his horse and rode slowly towards the battle-line. The second was during the German offensive in April 1918, when he issued his 'backs to the wall' order (see chapter 9), couched in uncharacteristically dramatic language.

We must be careful to distinguish between 'callousness' and ruthless determination to succeed. While some generals have doubtless been psychopaths, most are normal human beings who have had to come to terms with the human cost of their decisions. Great War generals had friends or even sons fighting in the armies under their command. General Allenby lost his son Michael on the Western Front, and Haig was profoundly affected by the loss of Brigadier General 'Johnnie' Gough VC, his chief of staff, mortally wounded while visiting the front line.[8] Haig's apparent callousness was in reality part of the mental make up of every successful commander, 'the robustness' to withstand 'the shocks of war' to which Field Marshal Wavell referred in his celebrated lectures on generalship.[9]

Attrition in History

History remembers and condemns Haig as an attritional general. Is an attritional strategy ever rational? Attrition is the wearing down of the enemy's physical and moral strength. All warfare involves a degree of attrition. Quick victories do occur, but normally when there is a gross imbalance of fighting power between the protagonists; and the extent to which conditions for success in great mobile campaigns were created by preliminary attrition is a 'chicken or egg' question that is ultimately unanswerable. It is possible that the rapid victory of the Coalition forces over Iraq in 1991 could have been achieved without the preliminary, one-way attrition by missile, bomb and shell. However, the attrition suffered by the Iraqi forces turned the likelihood of the success of the ground war into a near certainty. Attrition therefore is not always associated with static warfare. According to one great attritional general, Ulysses S. Grant, 'The art of war is simple enough. Find out where your enemy is. Get at him as soon as you can. Strike at him as hard as you can and as often as you can, and keep moving on.'[10]

Before the Great War the German military historian Hans Delbrück argued that there were two forms of strategy: *Ermattungsstrategie* (strategy of attrition) and *Niederwerfungsstrategie* (strategy of annihilation).[11] The Holy Grail for generals has been the battle of annihilation or destruction, which delivers rapid and decisive victory. However, in 1927 the Soviet general A.A. Svechin declared, perfectly correctly, that 'evolution of military art since the time of Moltke [the Elder]"has been running from destruction toward attrition"'. Svechin, who coined the term 'operational art', and other similar thinkers believed that in the era of total war, mass armies and huge fronts, the single 'Napoleonic' decisive battle of annihilation was getting more and more difficult to achieve. Instead, modern warfare should consist of a number of engagements within a theatre integrated into a larger operation. A campaign strategy consisted of a sequence of operations conducted according to an overall plan.[12] In Svechin's famous phrase: 'Tactics makes the steps from which operational leaps are assembled. Strategy points out the path.'[13] Success in modern war was achieved not by a single decisive battle, nor even by two or three; rather, by a series of linked and inherently attritional operations that destroyed the enemy physically and shattered his cohesion.

All warfare contains elements, in differing proportions, of attrition and manoeuvre. Rapid and decisive victories leading to peace had been thin on the ground in the years preceding the Great War. More often than not, warfare had been characterised by attrition, and the same was to be true in the latter part of the Second World War. The employment of attritional warfare *per se* is not necessarily a sign of strategic bankruptcy or stupidity on the part of commanders; indeed, in battles fought between evenly matched foes attrition is virtually inevitable.

Haig, the BEF and the New Warfare

One historian has recently suggested that 'Haig's reputation will be finally determined not by studies of the man himself, but of the man in the context of the armies which he commanded,' but unfortunately we are a long way from that day arriving.[14] Commanding the BEF would in any circumstances have been a challenging task, but Haig's problems were compounded by the rapid changes occurring on the battlefield. Since the 1991 Gulf War the question of a 'Revolution in Military Affairs' (RMA) based on new technology has caused fierce debates within the modern defence community. Some pundits believe that the nature of war is currently undergoing fundamental changes, while others are much more sceptical. During the First World War armies had to cope with a series of developments that added up to a transformation in the conduct of war. Since the 1980s scholars have come increasingly to accept that the changes in war fighting were indeed 'revolutionary' in nature. Williamson Murray, for instance, has referred to the 'combined arms revolution' that occurred on the Western Front.[15] There is, however, still something of a tendency to see the German army as the leaders in the field while downplaying the contribution of the BEF. Traditionally, the birth of the tank has been seen as the most revolutionary aspect of the war, but a significant advance in our understanding has come through the work of a serving British army officer, Brigadier Jonathan Bailey.

Bailey argues, persuasively to my mind, that 1914–18 saw the emergence of what he calls the 'Modern Style of Warfare', which was based on artillery, not armour. Initially, in 1914, battlefields were 'linear' in nature, and artillery was used for the most part only to fire at what the gunners could actually see. The scarcity of aircraft and howitzers, primitive communications and rudimentary gunnery techniques meant that 'an enemy in "dead ground" could probably not even be located let alone hit'. But by 1918 the battle was conducted over a vast area and in three dimensions. Targets that might be many miles behind the front line could be located from the air and by a variety of 'high-tech' instruments, and accurately attacked by 'indirect' artillery fire. Placed at the centre of military planning, 'three dimensional', indirect artillery fire 'can break the enemy's cohesion and will with catastrophic consequences'. Every subsequent military development, in Bailey's view, has merely 'complement[ed]' this basic and revolutionary change.[16]

Robin Prior and Trevor Wilson have argued, again in my view persuasively, that by August 1918 the BEF was 'employing a true weapons system', in which various pieces of technology, lethal and non-lethal, different troop types (infantry, cavalry, engineers, gunners and the like) and effective command and control systems, operated in a synergistic fashion.[17] Some of the elements of this weapons system had been in place in 1914, while others had to be developed when the war was in progress, as a response to the revolutionary changes on the battlefield.

The weapons system was the product of the three 'preconditions of an RMA' acting together: 'technological development'; 'doctrinal and operational innovation'; and 'organisational adaptation'.[18] The marriage of science and the army was not always an easy one. Initially at least, soldiers thought that scientists were 'far too visionary and gadgety to be of any help in the field' while the scientists were baffled 'why their brain waves, which seemed to them such war-winners, made no appeal to the military mind'.[19] Yet it was certainly a fruitful union. By the beginning of 1917 such scientific methods of warfighting were routinely used by the BEF.

Unlike the aeroplane, the tank or the U-boat, the 106 model artillery fuse is not remembered as one of the major pieces of military technology to have emerged from the First World War. Yet in its way, the '106' rivalled the tank in its importance. Indeed, it served one of the same purposes. Just as a major use of the tank was to crush enemy barbed wire, the '106', in Haig's words,

> enabled wire entanglements to be easily and quickly destroyed and so modified our method of attacking organised positions. By bursting the shell the instant it touched the ground and before it had become buried, the destructive power of the explosion was greatly increased.

The dismal sight so common on the first day on the Somme, of infantry pinned down in No Man's Land in front of banks of uncut barbed wire, became much rarer from the spring of 1917 onwards. Haig went on to signal other ways in which the '106' would eventually improve the BEF's operations: 'It became possible to cut wire with a [sic] far less expenditure of time and ammunition and *the factor of surprise was given a larger part in operations.*' An important part of the 'weapons system' that was to win the war had slotted into place.[20]

Another part was the arcane work of the 'flash spotters' and 'sound rangers' of the BEF's Field Survey Companies. The first term referred to the spotting of the muzzle flash from enemy artillery, the position of which could then be determined by trigonometry. The second used microphones to detect the report and the subsequent flight of the shell. Both methods were used to pinpoint the position of German batteries, information vital to counter-battery fire – attempts to destroy or at least suppress (for instance by forcing the gunners to take shelter) enemy artillery. Sound ranging has been described, with pardonable exaggeration, as 'the Manhattan Project' of the Great War. Like the building of the atomic bomb in the Second World War, some of the finest scientific minds worked on sound ranging. These included the physicist W.L. (later Sir Lawrence) Bragg, who had won a Nobel Prize before the war and who, as a lowly lieutenant, commanded the BEF's first prototype sound ranging section, established in 1917.[21] Combined with photography and reconnaissance from the air, and accurate mapping of the Western Front (in itself a vast enterprise), field survey was a formidable addition to the BEF's weapons system.

Created after the Somme, the Counter-Battery Staff Office gave the BEF a 'corps-level ... centralised staff of artillery personnel dedicated to the suppression of the enemy's batteries through the analysis and tactical application of intelligence'. This gave the BEF's gunners a decisive edge over their German opponents.[22]

If artillery was at the centre of the weapons system, there are many other areas of innovation that could be discussed in detail, including the development of machine guns, tunnelling and mining operations, communications[23] and staff work. Lack of space unfortunately precludes all but the most cursory glimpses at these vital areas. However, one area that must be examined is the development of air power, which more than any other epitomises the revolutionary changes in the nature of war.

Powered flight was just eleven years old when the First World War began and aircraft were still in the experimental, powered kite stage. Britain's Royal Flying Corps (RFC) had been created in April 1912 and in August 1914 sent 860 personnel and 63 aeroplanes to France, where they were later joined by ten Royal Naval Air Service (RNAS) machines. In comparison, the French deployed 138 aircraft and the Germans 230.[24] At this stage there was little thought of using aeroplanes to shoot down other aeroplanes or to attack targets on the ground. Indeed, many aircraft were unarmed. Some soldiers acknowledged that aircraft would be useful for reconnaissance, supplementing the role of light cavalry. Others had a less enlightened view. Before the war Haig was highly sceptical about the value of aircraft for reconnaissance. In the course of the war Haig's attitudes to aircraft were transformed and he emerged as the RFC's most influential supporter.[25] In the fifty-two months of the First World War, aircraft were to develop most of the roles known to modern air forces and came to play a crucial role in support of ground forces. In terms of sophistication and size the air services of November 1918 were almost unrecognisable from their primitive ancestors of August 1914: the Royal Air Force, formed from the RFC and RNAS on 1 April 1918, deployed 291,748 personnel and 22,171 aircraft across the world.

From the beginning of 1915, aircraft assumed a vital role in the artillery battle, and this was to increase in importance as the war went on. During 1915 air-to-air fighting also began in earnest. An arms race began, as both sides strove to improve their aircraft, introduce more effective weapons, and develop their tactics. Individual aces offered the public at home a welcome shot of glamour, an item conspicuously missing from the struggle on the Western Front. As the sophistication of the land battle increased, so did the role of air forces. Major General H.M. Trenchard, the commander of the RFC from August 1915, pursued an effective, though costly, offensive strategy that complemented Haig's, carrying the war over the German lines. The great battles of 1916, Verdun and the Somme, marked the beginning of a vital aspect of modern warfare, the struggle for air superiority over the battlefield. Without at least parity in the air, ground battles stand very little chance of succeeding, and infantrymen began to look anxiously skyward for the comforting sign of friendly aircraft. That point was underlined by the development in 1917 of the use of aircraft in the ground attack role. During Third Ypres, men of a Canadian infantry brigade were lectured that:

It is the policy of the GHQ to use the RFC for *Offensive* purposes. This entails aeroplane activity far in the enemy's territory beyond the *sight of our own troops,* and explains why our own men in the front line frequently think our aeroplanes are doing nothing, when in reality they are engaged in the most venturesome and dangerous work.[26]

That military aircraft had become a vital adjunct to the land battle was incontestable by 1918. The RFC/RAF played a vital role in repulsing the German spring offensives in 1918, and 'The combining of ... [the RAF's] operations with those of the other arms, and particularly of the artillery,' wrote Haig in his Final Dispatch, 'has been the subject of constant study and experiment, giving results of the very highest value.'[27] In addition to their reconnaissance and artillery co-operation roles, and the battle for air superiority, aircraft were also used in direct support of troops on the ground, for attacking ('interdicting') routes leading to the battlefield, and even, in an embryonic fashion, for transportation. All of these were in addition to strategic bombing and home defence roles. Warfare in August 1914 had been fought in two dimensions, but by November 1918 it was most definitely fought in three. If, in subsequent chapters, the work of the air arm is less visible than perhaps it might be, I must apologise and ask the reader to bear in mind the lecture given in August 1917 to those Canadian infantrymen.

These British military and scientific developments did not, of course, take place in isolation from those of other countries.[28] Independently of the British, the French developed tanks at roughly the same time (although the Germans were late in developing tanks and their models were distinctly inferior). Likewise, German and French artillery developed on parallel lines, although the Germans never adopted a British style counter-battery organisation, and as late as Passchendaele German sound-ranging techniques were inferior to the British. One area where the Germans were clearly ahead of the British was in the pioneering of modern defensive tactics, which is not surprising, given the respective strategic postures in the West. As a result of their experiences in the Somme, the Germans jettisoned purely linear defence, opting for 'elastic' defence-in-depth based on an out-post zone, which served to canalise an attacking force, behind which was a 'battle zone' of mutually supporting strong-points, with further defences to the rear. A key element was the use of counterattack formations to push back enemy attackers, already disorganised by fighting their way through the defences.[29]

Tactical advances such as these have led many writers to portray the German army of 1914–18 as an innovative organisation years ahead of the plodding BEF.[30] The evidence suggests the truth is somewhat different. Haig is usually regarded just as a battlefield commander. But, in fact, he was far more than that; as CinC he controlled a large and highly complex organisation. Judged purely on results, of coping with profound changes in warfare, of evolving an effective weapons system, of actually winning the war, the BEF emerges as an innovative and highly adaptable force. A judgement of the *a priori* variety would suggest that Douglas Haig, as the man in command of this organisation, deserves some of the credit for its success. Posterity has denied him this, although it has been swift to blame him for the setbacks and disasters. For a man much written about, there are surprising gaps in our knowledge about the wider aspects of Haig's command. We do know, however, that he was not a technophobe, as he has often been branded. On the contrary, he encouraged the development and use of tanks, aircraft and various other pieces of technology. Haig's breadth of vision encompassed such matters as the importance to the army of an effective military police force and the construction of a vast and impressive logistic infrastructure. After some initial suspicion, Haig became an enthusiastic supporter of a civilian businessman, Sir Eric Geddes, who carried out a crucial reorganisation of the railways in France, without which the successes of 1917–18 could never have happened. In sum, Haig 'did not fail in ... the duty of ensuring that his troops had the right tools for the job, and, in the end, enough of them'.[31]

The Ordinary Soldier and his War

Ever since I began teaching about the First World War, a decade and a half ago, I have been struck by just how many British people know something about relatives that served in this conflict. Some have meticulously researched the wartime career of a grandfather or a great-grandfather. Many more have just a photograph of a soldier self-consciously posing behind a chair in a studio, or standing alongside a group of mates in a training camp on Salisbury Plain. Others still have a vague folk-memory: 'he was on the Somme, in the artillery, I think'. My knowledge of my own family's wartime history is sketchy. One great-grandfather served in the Labour Corps and later in the Queen's Royal West Surrey Regiment. I suspect from a few scraps of hard evidence combined with stories from my late grandparents that he was one of the older men 'combed out' to serve in the infantry during the manpower crisis of 1918. My family history is little different from those of millions of others except that, as far as I know, all my relatives returned from the war.

The ubiquity of family memories of ancestors who served in the British army of the First World War gives an indication of both the number of men who served in it (over 5.7 million) and its social composition.[32] Generally speaking, before 1914 the army was recruited from the top and bottom of society. For many years, 'respectable' working class families looked down on the type of man who filled the ranks of the army. The officer corps was recruited from a fairly narrow socially elite group, defined by money, education and birth. While it was possible for a working class ranker to be commissioned – famously, 'Wully' Robertson went from private to field marshal – it was difficult. There was little room for the middle classes, although many were to be found in the ranks and officers' messes of the Territorial Force. So Kitchener's expansion of the army in autumn 1914 brought into the ranks many men who in peacetime would never have dreamed of joining the army. In the 16th Manchesters (1st Manchester Pals) 'all classes mingled in the ranks. The packer from the basement and the commissionaire from the door were, as often as not, put in command of their seniors in the warehouse.'[33]

Upper class ex-public schoolboys have come to symbolise the British army in the First World War. In reality the social base of the British officer corps began to broaden from the very beginning of the war, as Kitchener reached far beyond the traditional officer-producing classes to find leaders for his New Armies. By the mid-war period a rough meritocracy had emerged, in which rankers who had demonstrated leadership potential on the battlefield were sent for officer training more or less regardless of social background. From 1916 onwards almost every officer candidate passed through Officer Cadet Battalions, often based in Oxbridge colleges or similar places. Such men were given crash courses in officership, which included passing on the paternalistic ethos of the pre-war officer corps. Only about 2 per cent of those commissioned in 1913 had passed through the ranks, while about 38 per cent of officers demobilised at the end of the war had working class or lower middle class occupations.[34]

In the course of the Great War 22.11 per cent of the United Kingdom's male population served in the British army, yet this did not represent a true 'cross-section' of society. Some geographic areas produced far more recruits than others. A battalion raised in a relatively thinly populated area, 9th Devons, included only about 80 natives of the county and had to be brought up to strength with men from London and Birmingham. Patriotic feeling, fuelled by the militaristic culture of Edwardian Britain, undoubtedly played a role in the rush to enlist in 1914–15.[35] So did a host of factors that ranged from economic conditions in a particular industry to the age and personal circumstances of individuals. Unemployed men and casual labourers formed a ready source of recruits in the early days of the expansion of the army, while white-collar workers with steady jobs might well have needed some time to settle their affairs. The demands of an economy gearing up for total war also distorted the pattern of recruitment. Workers in industries such as agriculture, manufacturing and transport were less easily spared for the army than those in white-collar occupations, both during the voluntary phase and after the introduction of conscription in 1916. Men who served in the army in the years 1914 to 1918 'were as likely to have been clerks or shop assistants in civilian life as to have been miners or engineers'.[36] However, one should never lose sight of the fact that the army was to a very large extent recruited from the urban working classes: 'the British soldier was essentially the British working-man in uniform'.[37]

Trench Life

It is surprisingly difficult to generalise about what faced the men of the British citizen army when they arrived on the Western Front. A 'front line' soldier like an infantryman or a field gunner would have a different experience from that of a soldier on the lines of communication; an 'other rank' from that of an officer; a man who served in 1914 from that of one who served three years later. Yet it is possible to make some general points. Life in the trenches was always difficult, but in the winter of 1914–15 it was particularly grim.[38] A writer recalled

> the agonies of those seemingly endless days and nights spent, standing feet deep in water ... men so benumbed with cold that they had often to be lifted from their positions or dragged from the depths of mud by means of ropes passed round their waists ... hideous sights of dead men in all the contortions of a violent death, lying about in every direction, crying silently for burial.[39]

The 'trenches' in this period were rudimentary in the extreme, sometimes little more than shell holes joined together with a few strands of barbed wire out in front. Over the next twelve months the trench system was to evolve considerably, making conditions a little easier for the soldier. Sandbags provided an extra measure of protection, 'duckboards' lined the trench floor and the front and rear walls of the trench were bolstered with timber or similar material. Men settled in 'dugouts': in early 1916, an infantry private wrote home describing his

> sand-bag abode [which was] feebly illuminated by a candle dimly burning. My neighbour, who is yet more uncomfortably cramped up, is falling off to sleep, and his muddy, unshaven and jam-smeared face is resting on my shoulder ... The bread has all been devoured, but a few broken pieces of hard tack biscuits lie scattered on the ground beneath this living, semi-sleeping entanglement of men. A bayonet thrust into the wall serves as a candlestick ...[40]

The scene he describes was scarcely luxurious, but conditions on the Givenchy front at this period were considerably better than those experienced by the BEF in the very early days of trench warfare. Officers' dugouts were somewhat better, but best of all were German dugouts, the opulence of which amazed British troops when they captured them.

By the end of 1915 both sides commonly employed a front line trench, a support trench and a reserve trench, connected by lateral communication trenches. At periodic intervals inverted V-shapes jutted out; the object of such 'traverses' was to prevent an enemy entering the trench from firing straight down it, catching the defenders in *enfilade* [in the flank], and also to reduce the impact of an exploding shell or mortar bomb to a minimum. Dense barbed wire belts, sometimes many yards wide, had replaced the meagre obstacles of 1914. Initially, armies crowded the front line trench with soldiers, who would stand on the firestep (the trench could be dug to a depth of some ten feet) to blaze away at intruders. By 1917–18 there had been a general move towards defence-in-depth, which meant thinning out the front line trench, holding it with a small number of men, and making the main line of resistance somewhat further back. In some areas, where water lay just below the surface, conventional trenches were replaced by breastworks. The width of No Man's Land, the strip between the opposing trenches, varied from about 30 yards on Vimy Ridge to half a mile or more elsewhere.

It is a common fallacy that soldiers were in the trenches all the time. Charles Carrington, a subaltern (junior officer) in 48th Division, analysed his diary for 1916 and discovered that he spent 101 days of the year 'under fire', 65 of which were in 'front-line trenches, and 36 more in supporting positions close at hand'. A further 120 days were spent in reserve, and 73 in rest. Of the remaining 72 days, 17 were spent at home on furlough or 'leave' (as he commented, ordinary rankers were far less fortunate in this regard) and 21 at various instructional schools. The remaining time was spent travelling or in a depot camp. Carrington's battalion carried out 16 'tours' in the trenches, varying in length from one to thirteen days. Carrington was present during twelve tours, during which the battalion were involved in fighting on four occasions:

Once I took part in a direct attack, twice in bombing actions, and once we held the front line from which other troops advanced. I also took part in an unsuccessful trench-raid. On six other occasions I had to go up the line either for working parties or to reconnoitre.[41]

Carrington's experience was fairly typical of infantry subalterns in 1916. Being in the trenches occupied only a part of an infantryman's time, while fighting in a battle was a rare event.

Another fallacy is that, while in the trenches, men spent all their time fighting for their lives. In fact there were active and 'cushy' sectors of the front:

Trench life in the [Ypres] Salient was always strenuous. An anomaly was that the nearer the combatants were to each other the less they saw of each other. Firing was carried on by snipers from prepared places of concealment, and observation was carried on by periscope. To show one's head above the parapet was to court death ... artillery fire never ceased day or night – it was only a matter of degree. At night the whole semi-circle of the Salient was brilliantly lighted up with flares ... Sometimes, on calm nights, the opposing lines hurled abuse at each other in between the bursts of fire. The winter was, of course the worse time on account of the mud, cold and wet.[42]

Ypres was always bad, but the activity in other sectors varied according to time and circumstances. The Somme, for instance, was a reasonably quiet area before July 1916. Trench life was made more bearable by informal truces and tacit agreements that developed between opposing sides. The most famous example of this occurred on Christmas Day 1914, when some British and German troops fraternised in No Man's Land. Truces were usually far less spectacular, typically taking the form of refraining to bombard the enemy positions when hot food was being brought up – if you prevented him from eating his breakfast in peace, he would do the same to you, and no one would gain. In March 1916, the 22nd Royal Fusiliers relieved a French unit near Souchez:

> We were confronted by a difficult situation, because the front line was totally cut off from the support line in daylight, and was enfiladed from the German trenches on the Vimy Ridge on our right. The German front line opposite us was only thirty or forty yards away; No Man's Land was a mass of wire entanglements, and a mutual understanding between the French and Germans had reduced offensive warfare to a farce. We were obliged to conform to this arrangement till we could improve the trenches and repair the C.[ommunication] T.[renches]; and there was little or no firing, even at night. By day German officers might be seen sitting on the parapet, laughing, shouting, gesticulating; and a certain degree of fraternisation between sentries in saps only a few yards apart was inevitable. [One German sentry was heard to shout] 'Good morning, you no fire, we no fire.'[43]

In 1915 trench life developed a rhythm of its own. For the British soldier the day began before dawn with 'Stand To', short for 'stand to arms', when the infantry manned the parapet (the front lip of the trench: the equivalent in the rear was the parados) to meet a possible attack in the half light. After breakfast and inspection by an officer, the business of keeping the trench in order – shoring up trench walls and the like – began. The night was the busiest time on the Western Front, as both sides took advantage of the cloak of darkness to relieve men from the front line, or to leave the relative safety of the trench and venture into No Man's Land to carry out sundry tasks. Nervous sentries would peer into the gloom. That object seen by the light of a flare – was it a tree stump or was it an enemy sniper? Recommended practice if caught out in No Man's Land and illuminated by a flare was to stand stock still, for a sudden movement was a sure giveaway.

In all sectors, active or cushy, danger was ever present. A shell, mortar bomb or sniper's bullet could snuff out a life in a 'quiet' period just as effectively as in a major battle. In one such 'quiet' stretch, from 3 to

23 November 1914, the two-division Indian Corps suffered an average loss of 90 men per day. In the space of a ten-minute bombardment on 7 November, 9th Bhopals sustained 55 casualties, with another 15 men hit a little later.[44] In the six-month run-up to the Battle of the Somme, January to June 1916, the BEF lost 107,776 men in minor actions and the usual run of trench warfare. This was in a period in which the BEF fought no battles that would count as 'major' by the standards of the Western Front.[45]

A contributing factor to the steady loss of men was the BEF's policy of maintaining an active front to keep up the offensive spirit of their own men and grind down enemy morale. This led to division-sized 'minor' actions such as 3rd Division's attack at St. Eloi, near Ypres in March 1916. On a much smaller scale was the release of gas, or a sudden artillery bombardment of enemy trenches, which inevitably drew German retribution from which the British infantry usually suffered.

Patrolling and raiding also took its toll. A patrol was a small-scale operation, usually of about four men under an NCO or officer who would venture out at night into No Man's Land with the aim of reconnoitring the enemy positions. Such patrols were essentially stealthy affairs, for the 'object ... was to get information and not to fight'.[46] Patrols were also used for a more aggressive purpose. In late 1917, on the Givenchy front, 25th Division carried out no major operations; 'the work of the units in the line consisted in denying "No Man's Land" to the enemy by means of active patrolling every night', backed by frequent bombardment of the enemy trenches by trench mortars.[47] Such a policy was not untypical.

Raiding was part of the policy that the BEF should achieve domination of No Man's Land and give the enemy no rest, and was intended to enhance the BEF's morale. The first raids, carried out in late 1914, were improvised affairs organised at a local level and conducted on a shoestring budget. Some units – the Canadians, the 2nd Royal Welch Fusiliers – earned reputations as enthusiastic raiders. Like so much else on the Western Front, in the course of 1915 raiding became far more organised, indeed bureaucratised, and became part of the general policy of attrition.[48] Even at the time, some queried it, feeling that the casualties of the raiders and the toll it took on British troops' morale made it counterproductive. An officer wrote in early 1917 that 'raiding is a pretty rotten business, popular with nobody, because of its great risks'.[49] The post-war Kirke report on the lessons of the Great War decided that the raiding policy had not enhanced British morale.[50] Yet this active policy did have its place. Raiding helped the BEF to develop its assault techniques and the steady attrition of the German army undoubtedly contributed to its ultimate failure. In 1916, the raids and bombardments carried out by Second Army at Ypres were intended to pin enemy divisions and to prevent them from reinforcing the Somme. In 1918 small-scale attritional operations played an important role, alongside the big set-piece battles, in the Allied victory in the Hundred Days. But how many raids were enough? Between 15 September and 16 November 1916, while holding a relatively inactive sector, 36th (Ulster) Division launched ten raids, of which six were at least partially successful. The Division's historian, Cyril Falls, a veteran infantryman and one of the wisest of all writers on the war, concluded that 'Raids were frequently useful, and sometimes imperatively necessary; but the British raided too often.'[51]

Morale

There are no straightforward answers as to how the morale of British soldiers, their willingness to endure and fight, was maintained in and out of battle. Some historians have emphasised the importance of patriotism, belief in the cause, and loyalty to the regiment. Others stress the importance of working class values of solidarity and community, and of the creation of familiar patterns of leisure – football matches and concert parties – on the Western Front.[52] My own work has stressed the paternalism of the British officer corps in ensuring that men were well cared for.[53] Correlli Barnett has pointed to the vast infrastructure of baths, canteens and welfare support provided by the army.[54] Work on other armies in other wars emphasises the importance of the primary group, the small clique of three or four men who, cut off from normal sources of affection, formed a substitute family. In battle, men would fight for their mates; to protect them, and to avoid appearing cowardly.[55] This also appears to be valid for the BEF. Niall Ferguson has recently highlighted the fact that some soldiers undoubtedly enjoyed combat and even the act of killing.[56] For some men religion was a solace; for others, cigarettes and rum or, if an officer, whisky. In truth, morale was maintained by a combination of these factors, and others, the precise mixture depending on the individual.

One thing that can be stated with some certainty is that coercion played a relatively minor role in British soldiers' combat motivation. On some very rare occasions officers did shoot, or threaten to shoot, men, but only in moments of extreme crisis. Second Lieutenant G.D.R. Moor was awarded the VC at Gallipoli for stemming a rout, apparently by shooting four soldiers.[57] But it cannot be over-emphasised that this was a highly atypical event. Discipline was certainly important in maintaining unit cohesion – collective morale is of course as important as that of individuals – but discipline is not merely something that is imposed. Although many of the citizen soldiers of the BEF found 'Regular', boot-bulling discipline to be burdensome and unhelpful, arguably, in combat self-discipline became as important as formal discipline. A relationship based on trust and mutual respect between officers and rankers was central to this 'battle discipline'. If the ordinary soldier had lived in constant fear of the officer's revolver, this relationship would have been destroyed, and the evidence overwhelmingly points in the opposite direction. Indeed, the role of regimental officers in protecting their men against the military 'system' helped to cement the bonds of the relationship.

There is a common belief that officially sanctioned battle police were routinely lined up behind infantry to shoot those who refused to go over the top. The role of military police on the Western Front is encrusted with myths, and this is one of them. Such men carried out important tasks, including traffic control, rounding up stragglers and arresting deserters, but summary executions did not fall within their ambit. Executions were intended in part *pour encourager les autres*, to maintain discipline, and thus the British army made a considerable effort to publicise them, reading out the findings of courts martial on parade and the like. Doing away with a malefactor in a hole-and-corner fashion would have defeated a primary object of capital sentences. It would also have been illegal. Some of the men executed for military offences certainly seem to have been the victims of 'rough justice', receiving trials that even by the standards of the time were unfair. Certain men seem to have been suffering from shellshock (or more correctly, were psychiatric casualties). However, the army at least insisted on a formal trial and death sentences had to be confirmed by commanders right up to the level of CinC. In May 1918, during the crisis of the German offensive on the Aisne, a divisional commander asked for permission to short-circuit the system by carrying out death sentences on stragglers to deter others. GHQ turned down the request.[58]

British soldiers of the First World War are commonly regarded as helpless, passive victims of their own commanders. In reality rankers were perfectly capable of making their views known if they thought that they were being treated unfairly. Noncommissioned Officers (NCOs) had a vital role in keeping the officers informed of feelings in the ranks, and a quiet word with a sympathetic sergeant was one way of registering a complaint. Other strategies included unofficial negotiation about orders on the battlefield, yelling abuse from the comforting anonymity of the ranks, or sit-down strikes. At the most serious end of the graph were full-scale mutiny and murder of officers, although these were extremely rare. The Étaples mutiny of 1917 was caused by mundane issues that added up to a sense of unfairness among the soldiers at a base and training camp. However, it was the only major event of its type that occurred in the BEF on the Western Front while the war was in progress. The 'combat refusals' suffered by some Australian units in autumn 1918 were very different in nature; they sprang from exhaustion from continuous and very heavy (albeit successful) fighting. After the war had ended, there was an upsurge of resistance to military authority, ranging from refusals to put up a battalion football team to the burning down of Luton town hall. Some interpreted this as the beginnings of the British revolution but the reality was more prosaic. The British army remained a citizen force of civilians, largely working men, in uniform. Many took the attitude that they had joined up to carry out the task of beating the German army. With that job completed they were no longer prepared to put up with military discipline and demanded that demobilisation should occur as rapidly as possible.[59]

In fact, British soldiers showed remarkable resilience during the gruelling attritional campaigns on the Western Front. Unlike the French, German, Russian and Italian armies, the BEF did not suffer a large-scale collapse in morale or discipline. British military morale certainly experienced peaks and troughs. Morale among the troops caused military authorities some concern over the winters of 1914–15 and 1915–16, while Passchendaele marked the low point of the BEF's morale during the war. The vexed question of the BEF's morale in spring 1918 is considered in some detail in chapter 9. For all that, spirits recovered after each bout of depression. Indeed a significant factor in the Allied victories in the second half of 1918 was the decline in the willingness of German soldiers to fight, while the morale of their British counterparts remained steady and even increased.

What, then, of the 'disillusionment' or 'disenchantment' that so many soldiers are supposed to have experienced? Literary specialists and cultural historians are apt to make sweeping statements about this particular phenomenon, often based on the experiences of a small handful of officer-poets.[60] As a number of scholars have demonstrated, men such as Siegfried Sassoon were completely untypical of the men of the BEF as a whole, in terms of their social class, literary bent, and attitudes to the war.[61] If by 'disillusionment' one means coming to reject the reason why Britain fought the war, as Sassoon did, it may be said that the vast bulk of British soldiers did not become disillusioned. Certainly, some middle class men who joined the army found that their idealism crumpled when brought into contact with the reality of bullying NCOs and the squalor of army life – most famously the high-minded journalist C.E. Montague, author of the eloquently entitled memoir *Disenchantment*.[62] Working class civilians in uniform, for whom life in the army may well have actually brought about an improvement in their standard of living, tended not to share these views. Rather than generalising from a tiny group of atypical officers with literary inclinations, one needs to examine the circumstances and thinking of each individual. After the war, when ex-soldiers discovered that Britain was not a land fit for heroes, some disillusionment certainly set in. Such feelings were fuelled, although not created, by the publication of 'disillusioned' war books, as we have seen.[63] However, this is very different from arguing that they became disillusioned with Britain's cause while the war was in progress – or indeed after it had ended.

'Disillusionment' is capable of such wide interpretation as to become almost meaningless as a concept. What, for instance, is to be made of men disenchanted with post-war life who looked back at the war years through a rosy glow, as the pinnacle of their life? 'Once you have lain in her arms,' Guy Chapman wrote of war, 'you can admit no other mistress.'[64] Such beliefs united men of extreme right-wing militarist views with individuals such as Chapman, who was certainly not of this persuasion. Alternatively, into what category should one place C.E. Jacomb, who hated the army but found compensations in the fellowship of his fellow soldiers?[65] Unless tightly (and rather pedantically) defined, the concept of disillusionment hinders rather than aids understanding of the British soldier in the Great War. It would be as well to discard it altogether.

CHAPTER 7

THE YEAR OF THE SOMME

The *modus operandi* of Sherlock Holmes, the greatest of fictional detectives, was to examine evidence in minute detail and to arrive at apparently miraculously accurate conclusions by the application of ruthlessly logical deduction. A modern day Holmes, knowing nothing of the Battle of the Somme, could deduce much from a visit to the area between the French towns of Albert, which was behind the British lines, and German-held Bapaume. From evidence such as the location of ridges, valleys and woods, war memorials and cemeteries, the dates of death and names of regiments inscribed on headstones, our detective would conclude that the Somme was no swift campaign. Rather, it was an attritional affair in which one side used shells, bullets and soldiers' bodies to grind down the enemy's forces and expel him from his trenches, while the other tenaciously held on to his positions, launching frequent counterattacks.

All battles are shaped by the terrain over which they are fought, and the travellers who head out northeast along the old, straight Roman road from the small town of Albert soon find themselves progressing uphill. Before long, they will reach a low ridge with a village – La Boisselle – nestling on the forward slope. In July 1916, this was the

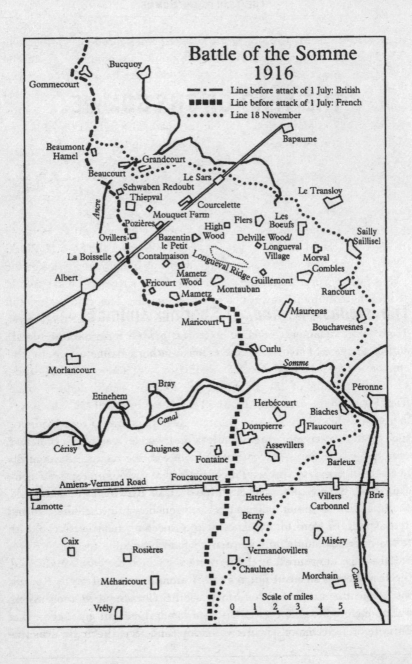

area where the British and German front lines faced each other. No Man's Land was quite narrow at this point, although owing to the lie of the land it widened considerably on either flank. This area was heavily fought over in the early days of July 1916. On the ridge, just under two miles further on up the D929 is another village, Pozières, which straggles along either side of the road. The fighting in this area dates from the latter part of July and early August.

At the far end of Pozières village is a clump of grass-covered mounds, the highest point on the Somme battlefield. These are the remains of a windmill, captured and held after great exertions by the Australian forces that are commemorated on the site. Just across the road is a handsome memorial to the Tank Corps, featuring finely detailed models of period tanks. One bears a bullet hole from the Second World War – a reminder that this area of France was fought over twice in the twentieth century. Standing on the windmill site, one looks beyond the tank monument toward a series of woods. The cemeteries and memorials stand in mute testimony to the fact that Delville Wood, High Wood, Mametz Wood, and the rest proved formidable obstacles to the advance of British troops on the southern flank.

The Plans

The Allies' strategic design for 1916, thrashed out in a series of conferences at the end of the previous year, was fundamentally sound. Germany, in the centre of Europe, was to be attacked in all fronts. The newly enlarged BEF was to take part in an attack in the Somme area as junior partner to the French, while the Russian and Italian armies were to attack in their respective theatres. Faced with a concerted onslaught, the Germans would be unable to switch forces to face each new threat.

On the other side of the lines the Germans were also making plans. In a document known to history as the Christmas Memorandum, Falkenhayn, the senior German commander, set out his belief that Britain was Germany's primary enemy, and that the most effective way of striking at her was to attack 'England's best sword': the French army. If France could be sufficiently weakened so that she settled for a compromise peace with Germany, the threat from Britain would be neutralised. Thus Germany would launch a major attack on France. Eventually, Falkenhayn settled on an assault on Verdun. What he actually intended to achieve is disputed by historians, but it is most likely that the version he set out in his book, written shortly after the war, was the essential truth. Falkenhayn intended to bleed France white and bring about the collapse of the French government, which in turn would lead to peace. He had no faith in a breakthrough battle, but rather sought to exhaust the enemy through attrition before the British were able to do the same to Germany.[1]

On 21 February 1916 Falkenhayn launched Operation *Gericht*, or 'Law Court'. Verdun was an area in which France had invested a huge amount of emotional capital, a little like Ypres for the British. The French battled fiercely for the position, which was as important symbolically as it was a place of real military worth. One historian has denounced Falkenhayn's attritional concept as 'the degeneration of the art of war'. Others have argued he really did intend to seize Verdun, and after the war excused his failure by claiming that he had only intended attrition all along. Paradoxically, Falkenhayn was using total methods to achieve a limited aim; he was a rare example of a Great War general willing to contemplate something less than total victory. *Gericht* achieved two things. In the long term, it dealt a heavy blow to French military morale, although the full fruits of this were not to become apparent until the spring of 1917. In the short term, Falkenhayn seized the initiative from the Allies, which in turn had an important impact on the preparations for the Somme.

The Battle of the Somme had originally been a French conception. Haig would have preferred to fight around Ypres, where there were some genuine strategic objectives, but as junior partner bowed to French wishes. The unforeseen crisis at Verdun sucked increasing numbers of French troops into 'the mill on the Meuse', and by default the British became the leading player in the Somme offensive. Whether the battle would have been better conducted if the experienced French army had remained the senior partner is impossible to say.

The First Day on the Somme

The outline story of the First Day on the Somme is easily told. Haig planned to penetrate the German positions with a mass infantry attack and then feed in mobile reserves to exploit the success. On 1 July 1916, after a seven-day bombardment, 14 divisions attacked on a 27,000-yard front. It was a 'race to the parapet' with the attacking infantry aiming to reach the enemy positions before the defenders succeeded in scrambling up from their dugouts to man their weapons. In most cases, the attackers, who were often hampered by uncut belts of barbed wire, lost the race. In the north, at Gommecourt a diversionary attack failed. The main attack north of the Albert–Bapaume road also failed, although local gains were made in some places. South of the road, XV Corps was more successful, capturing the village of Mametz. At the extreme south of the British line, the picture was radically different. XIII Corps captured all of its objectives, and on their right Fayolle's French Sixth Army had a striking success in their attack both north and south of the River Somme. We shall presently return to this forgotten part of the First Day on the Somme.

The problems faced by British infantry in the northern sector of the Somme battlefield on 1 July are graphically illustrated by the attack of the 36th (Ulster) Division. The Ulsters' initial assault fared very differently from those of many other divisions on that terrible day. The division was aided by effective artillery fire, in which British gunners had the assistance of French batteries. Stokes mortars fired smoke shells that helped to screen the infantry from German view. Sensible infantry tactics, where the men crawled out into No Man's Land before the barrage lifted and thus were able to rush forward quickly were also important. The Ulsters rapidly captured the German first line with only light casualties and pushed on. Here their troubles began.

On their right, 32nd Division's assault on the German stronghold of

Thiepval had been only partially successful, which exposed the flank of the Ulster Division to heavy fire. Soon the German artillery began to pound No Man's Land, making it exceptionally difficult and dangerous for reserves to attempt to reach the advanced troops. On the left of 36th Division, the attack of 29th Division failed, as did the Ulsters' own left flank, held up by a deep ravine and heavy machine gun fire. This allowed the Germans in this sector to concentrate their fire on the left flank of 36th Division. Thus this division, which had pushed ahead and captured the formidable Schwaben Redoubt while the attacks of its neighbours had failed, was as a consequence being raked by enemy fire from the front and both sides, as well as being sealed off from the British lines by a wall of high explosive.

According to the plan, 107 Brigade, the divisional reserve, was to have passed through the assault troops and attack the German second position. Major General Nugent, the commander of 36th Division, queried whether this move ought to be cancelled, given the fact that both their flanks were 'in the air'. At this point the problem of communications came into play. There were delays in getting a response from the higher formation, X Corps. By the time approval of the halt order was received, at 9.16 a.m., it was too late. The field telephone lines carried forward by the signallers were all cut; by the time a runner arrived with the message, 107 Brigade, already savagely reduced by the ordeal of crossing No Man's Land, had begun to advance to the next objective.

'Of that last wild and desperate venture across a thousand yards of open country, few returned to tell the tale.'[2] The remnants of 107 Brigade got to within 100 yards of their objective, where they were held up by the British artillery barrage and suffered heavy casualties. Firing according to a strict timetable, the British gunners were not due to lift their sights until 10.10 a.m. and, thanks to poor communications, there was no way of informing the artillery of the changed situation. The Germans made good use of the enforced delay, reinforcing their trenches and bringing a heavy fire to bear on the Ulstermen lying prone in the open. When the curtain of British shells moved on to its next target, the surviving infantry assaulted the German second position. Pitifully weak by this stage, they could not hold the ground they captured.

The story of the rest of the day was of the Ulsters being forced back from position to position as increasingly violent German counterattacks were thrown in. By the evening of 1 July, most of the survivors of 36th Division were back in the original British lines. A handful of die-hards, reinforced by elements of 49th Division, were clinging on in the German front line and even in the Schwaben Redoubt. The Ulsters had done everything that could possibly have been asked of them. They had paid the penalty of mistakes aplenty, the products of an inexperienced army fighting a major battle for the first time. But they also suffered from the near impossibility of reinforcing success, which was a product of the inadequacy of 1916-vintage communications.

Breakthrough or Bite-and-hold?

The key to British failure on 1 July 1916 was the use of artillery. General Sir Henry Rawlinson, Fourth Army commander, originally wanted to carry out fairly limited infantry attacks, to capture the front line and a few objectives beyond it, which could have been supported by the available guns. Haig changed the plan to increase the depth of positions the infantry were to capture, without increasing the number of guns. Thus the British artillery was spread too thinly for the task it had been set. This mismatch of guns and objectives was to bedevil the BEF throughout the Somme campaign.[3]

This problem was exacerbated by the inadequacies of the ammunition. Of the approximately 1.5 million shells fired in the preliminary bombardment (originally scheduled for five days, it was increased to seven), about a million were shrapnel. This was a type of shell that threw out steel balls when it exploded. Lethal against soldiers standing in the open, they were ineffective against men sheltering in 'dugouts' many feet underground. For this High Explosive (HE) shells were needed, but there were simply too few of these available. Furthermore, many of the British shells were duds. Making the shells and fuses was a delicate art and the massive expansion of the munitions industry in Britain and the USA had led to a dilution of quality.[4]

Finally, the BEF's artillery tactics, based on the idea that 'artillery conquers, infantry occupies', were defective. The British official history states that 'British High Command had relied on the bombardment destroying ... [German] defences and ... morale ... their plan was framed, its tactics settled, and the troops trained in the sure and certain hope that the infantry would only have to walk over No Man's Land and take possession.'[5] This approach both overestimated the effectiveness of the artillery in July 1916 and underestimated the effectiveness of infantry; it has often been said that British high command did not think that the citizen soldiers of Kitchener's Army were capable of doing anything more complicated than advance in a series of 'waves'. The experience of 1917–18 was to demonstrate that artillery was a war-winning weapon, but in July 1916 co-operation between arms was in its infancy. The rigid artillery timetable, in which a barrage would 'lift' from objective to objective, is evidence of this. Too often on 1 July the 'lifts' would race ahead of the infantry, who were supposed to keep pace with it; for it was nearly impossible to recall the barrage. The BEF of 1918 had a finely tuned weapons system. In July 1916 some of the weapons existed but there was scarcely a 'system' at all.

The Unknown First Day on the Somme

In recent years, research has suggested that the tactical picture of the First Day on the Somme was not as clear-cut as had previously been thought. The traditional interpretation has Rawlinson laying down, via *Fourth Army Tactical Notes*, that the infantry should advance in a long, slow-moving line, which resulted in the German machine gunners being presented with perfect targets. Modern 'infiltration' tactics, using small groups to find weak spots in the enemy position were, apparently, years away.

In reality the speed at which battalions crossed No Man's Land was decided at corps or divisional level, or, when the bullets were actually flying, by brigades and battalions. *Fourth Army Tactical Notes* is ambiguous on this point, and is less prescriptive on the matter of tactical formations than the official history implies. At one point it seems to suggest, sensibly enough, the use of small mobile columns for the initial advance, deploying into 'waves' for the assault. Nick Perry's work has recently reinforced this point. He has shown that divisions, and especially brigades, *did* attempt to take advantage of local tactical factors, 'even at the outset of the battle when the dead hand of Fourth Army centralisation was at its worst.' Of the five divisions in the northern sector of Fourth Army, none configured their attacking battalions in precisely the same fashion. Similarly, Tony Cowan's work on 34th Division emphasises that it did not attack in a straightforward wave formation. Taking it right down to company and platoon level, 34th Division attacked in a mixture of column and line. None of this of course changes the fact that many of the attacks on 1 July 1916 resulted in bloody failures. It does suggest, though, that the reasons for those failures were more complicated than is widely believed, and that they cannot simply be laid at the door of battalions blindly following incompetent tactical advice handed down from on high.[6]

As we have seen, in 1915 the BEF had undertaken a good deal of tactical experimentation and this was reflected in the official pamphlets issued prior to the Somme offensive. Paddy Griffith has gone as far as to argue that 'the BEF had already discovered most of the key points of modern assault tactics even before the first day of the Somme'. He contends that the dichotomy that Edmonds identified – followed by 'future generations of Somme-mockers'[7] – between 'infiltration tactics' (using the small group, known as the 'worm' or 'blob' to the British) and the 'wave' or linear approach was a false one. In reality, the concepts were complementary: 'the BEF's 1916 doctrine [called for] ... an aggressive front line to push forward wherever possible [i.e. "infiltrate"] and rearward lines to mop up and consolidate ...' As Griffith argues, this was very similar to the celebrated German 'stormtroop' methods. Failures of execution, not doctrinal weakness, lay at the root of the disaster of 1 July 1916.[8]

The use of the word 'disaster' must immediately be qualified. The achievements of XV and XIII Corps on the southern flank demonstrate that, given the right conditions, the tactics of early July 1916 could be effective. These formations enjoyed several advantages denied to their unluckier neighbours to the north. The German positions in this sector were much weaker in terms of guns and men, and' the British were aided by a large number of highly effective French guns. Moreover, 30th and 18th Divisions employed the 'creeping barrage'. This consisted of a curtain of shells moving ahead of the infantry at a rate of perhaps 100 yards in three to five minutes.[9] The infantry pushed up as close as they could to the barrage, 'leaning' on it: to hang back was to risk German machine gunners popping up from shell holes and shooting the attackers in the rear. By lunchtime XIII Corps was on its final objective, but its units were too weak and exhausted to do more than send out patrols.[10]

We now know that this was a missed opportunity. The defenders in this sector, weak to start with, had been reduced to little more than a few scattered parties defending the woods to XIII Corps' front. Unfortunately, there were no operational reserves to exploit this opportunity. Rawlinson's initial belief that the battle should be a step-by-step affair, graphically vindicated on much of the front, was tragically wrong in this sector. 9th Division, in reserve behind XIII Corps front, was not even concentrated for a rapid advance. The cavalry, poised to exploit a breakthrough, were held further to the north, along the axis of the Bapaume road. In any case, Rawlinson, perhaps disbelieving the messages of success he was receiving, and worried about problems of congestion and co-ordination on the boundary between his Army and the French, refused to deploy the cavalry to the southern sector. Even on 3 July the door was still open. On that day Lieutenant Colonel Frank Maxwell, who had won the VC during the Boer War, carried out a reconnaissance that took his party about two miles in front of the captured positions.[11]

On the British right flank Fayolle's French Sixth Army had done remarkably well on 1 July. French XX Corps attacked on the immediate British flank, with I Colonial Corps assaulting south of the River

Somme, and XXXV Corps on the extreme right. Beginning on 24 June, the French bombardment was highly effective, XX Corps fielding 32, I Colonial Corps 65 and XXXV Corps 20 batteries of heavy artillery respectively. By the end of the day Fayolle's men had captured all of their objectives and taken 4,000 prisoners, for light loss.

By First World War standards, then, the achievements of French Sixth Army and British XIII and XV Corps were considerable.[12] Yet overall, the First Day on the Somme was a failure. The BEF had attempted to run before it could properly walk, and had paid a horrific price in human life as a result. The popular image of British military ineptitude in the First World War is very largely drawn from that day, but the notoriety of the 'First Day on the Somme' should not be allowed to overshadow the fact that it represented an important point on a learning curve, which, at this moment, was very steep indeed.

The Somme: the Next Phases

There was no question of shutting the offensive down after 1 July. For one thing, it would have been politically impossible, given that the French were still under heavy pressure at Verdun. Anglo-French tensions were never far below the surface. As a result of the argument between Haig and Joffre on 3 July over the direction of future British attacks, the Allies fought what amounted to two separate and unco-ordinated battles side by side for the next couple of months.[13] The killing went on, with the British aiming to secure a line from which to launch an attack on the German Second Position. The BEF inched forward in some places – Fricourt fell on 2 July, La Boisselle the next day – but made little progress in others, notably in front of the citadel of Thiepval. Fourth Army's problems were partly related to the effectiveness and tenacity of the defenders, and partly to British tactical failings; but above all the first few weeks of fighting on the Somme cruelly exposed the failure of British commanders at the operational level.

Between 3 and 13 July Fourth Army was constantly in action,

mounting 46 attacks resulting in 25,000 British casualties. These assaults were typical of British actions on the Somme, in that they were piecemeal, poorly prepared, hastily arranged and troops were used in 'penny-packets'. More British soldiers were killed and wounded in these actions than in the two large-scale set-piece operations of 14 July and 15 September put together. Moreover, the formations that were used often did not employ their resources to the best effect. During the fighting for Intermediate Trench in August, infantry were thrown into the assault in too few numbers to be effective.[14] This was an all-too-common occurrence. Moreover, frequently the guns of a corps would remain silent instead of aiding a neighbour's operation. Rawlinson, and ultimately Haig, bear responsibility for failing to co-ordinate the formations under their command.[15]

Contalmaison, a tiny village in the rear of the German front line of 1 July, was the scene of successive attacks by British divisions. Visiting the area today, one can walk along a farm track more or less on the line of the German trenches. After a short trek, one is suddenly faced by a dip in a field that forms a natural amphitheatre. In July 1916 it was a killing ground. One can see with dreadful clarity how infantry, advancing down the slopes of the grassy bowl, would be exposed to enemy machine gun fire from the front, and from Contalmaison and Mametz Wood on the flanks. If held by a determined enemy, this position was *never* going to be taken by a frontal assault. Yet 17th Division unsuccessfully assaulted this position three times, on 7, 8, and 9 July. Only on 10 July, when neighbouring divisions captured Mametz Wood and Contalmaison, was this position unlocked and 17th Division was able to move forward. Ironically, this entire area had been there for the taking on 3 July, being virtually undefended.[16]

Things were no better on Reserve Army's front. This formation, under General Sir Hubert Gough, had taken over operations north of the Bapaume road in early July. There, at Pozières beginning on 23 July, 1st Australian Division, fresh from the Middle East, was committed to its first action on the Western Front, being thrown into a series of attacks on narrow fronts. In six weeks of fighting the Australians sustained 23,000 casualties, which was roughly equal to the losses they had suffered in eight months at Gallipoli. Ten months later Charles Bean, the Australian official war correspondent, noted in his diary that:

> Pozières is one vast Australian cemetery but ... [the bodies] have been shattered & buried too often by shells for much to remain. Thousands of men can go and very few graves remain.[17]

The Dawn Assault

Reserve and Fourth Armies, however bloodily and clumsily, clawed their way through the outlying German defences in the early days of July. A fortnight after the beginning of the battle Rawlinson was at last ready for an attack on the German Second Position. Four divisions, 21st, 7th, 3rd and 9th, with 18th Division guarding the right flank, assembled at night opposite Longueval Ridge. Following an intensive artillery bombardment of five minutes the British attack went in at dawn – 3.25 a.m. – on 14 July. Unlike on 1 July, the initial assault was a stunning success. The Germans were caught unprepared and bewildered by the British shelling. The infantry, mostly Kitchener volunteers, swept onto the ridge and captured it by mid-morning.

Haig had needed to be persuaded before he had agreed to an assault at dawn. An assembly during the night was a difficult operation, involving movement in the dark and lying out in No Man's Land before the attack. The fact that both the assembly and the assault were successful speaks volumes about the capabilities of the Kitchener infantrymen. 'Compared to 1 July the attack was, in several respects, a more accurate reflection of the capabilities of the New Army formations, given imaginative operational planning.'[18] Yet the fact that the attack took place at dawn was less important than the way that the artillery was handled. This was no penny-packet attack.

On 1 July, the Royal Artillery shelled 22,000 yards of front, and no less than 300,000 yards of trench lying in support of the front line.

For the 14 July attack the comparative figures were 6,000 and 12,000 yards. Thus while on the first day of the battle the fire of the British guns had been spread too thinly to be effective, a fortnight later there was a formidable concentration of firepower. Rawlinson's gunners had two-thirds of the guns they had had on 1 July, but on 14 July they only had to bombard just over five per cent of the ground. Fourth Army used 1,000 artillery tubes, 311 of which were heavy guns or howitzers, in the preliminary bombardment which began early on 11 July. Every yard of German trench was subjected to 660lb of shell, 'an intensity of fire twice that of Neuve Chapelle [in March 1915] and five times that achieved before the 1 July attack.'[19] Fourth Army was reaping the rewards of the move towards a total war economy, which made prodigious quantities of shells available to the gunners.

When visiting the Somme, I often take parties to Longueval Ridge. From the misleadingly named Caterpillar Valley cemetery there is a magnificent view across much of the southern battlefield. Facing south, in the distance one can see the position of the old German line captured by XIII Corps on 1 July. It was in this area that Captain Billie Nevill's men of the 8th East Surreys went into action on that day kicking footballs – an act of public school bravado or a shrewd psychological trick of leadership, depending on one's viewpoint. On 14 July the British infantry attacked over the ground to one's front. Turning around and walking over to the other side of the cemetery brings a different view into sight. Now, one can see High Wood, well named because of its commanding position, to the north-west. High Wood is separated by some apparently open ground from the village of Longueval, just over a mile away, adjacent to Delville Wood. On 14 July 1916, on the southern side of the ridge the story was one of major success. On this side, the tale was one of a missed opportunity.

Cavalry in Action

Rawlinson's plan for 14 July envisaged the 2nd Indian Cavalry Division passing through the successful infantry assault to exploit the initial gains. There is a strong suspicion that Rawlinson was aware of Haig's displeasure at the way he had watered down the initial 'breakthrough' plan on 1 July, and no doubt out of a sense of self-preservation, he was determined to let the cavalry have its day. Thus the infantry was held back from going forward to occupy High Wood, which was lightly defended. But *where* exactly to hold cavalry reserves was a matter of fine judgement. Held too far back and they would be robbed of the ability to seize fleeting opportunities. Push them too far forward and they would be highly vulnerable to enemy artillery fire. In the event, bringing the cavalry forward over trenches and shell-pocked No Man's Land on 14 July was difficult and time consuming. They did not arrive on the scene until the early evening, and then only in the strength of two regiments. The 7th Dragoon Guards and an Indian unit, the 2nd Deccan Horse, names redolent of a past era, formed up and attacked. According to the received wisdom this should have been a scene of futile, poetic irony, of horsemen being mown down by machine guns. In reality, the attack was a considerable success.

British cavalry of the First World War were far from an anachronism. The trooper was capable of both mounted action and also of acting as an infantryman, being armed with a rifle and having the support of machine guns. Stephen Badsey has memorably compared their role to that of short-range paratroops. At Arnhem in the Second World War lightly equipped airborne forces were dropped miles ahead of the main body of the army to seize and hold key terrain until relief arrived. On the Western Front, in the right circumstances, the mobility of cavalry allowed them to advance a thousand or so yards ahead of the infantry. The cavalry would then dismount and go into action defending the captured position until the infantry caught up and reinforced the *coup de main* force.

Barbed wire and trenches were the principal enemies of cavalry in the First World War. But the ground before High Wood was relatively clear. The 7th Dragoon Guards, opposed by infantry and machine gunners hiding in crops, charged them, got among the Germans, 'killed a number with the lance', and took 32 prisoners. The cavalry's machine guns 'silenced' a German machine gun. Two infantry battalions simultaneously assaulted High Wood and secured the southernmost corner. The cavalry dismounted and entrenched, but when the support from the infantry did not arrive, they fell back. The horseman had lost about 100 men. As Stephen Badsey has commented, 'if two regiments could charge successfully for 1,000 yards into unprepared German defences, a further two brigades arriving early enough in the day could have continued the charge by a further 1,500 yards to the east, so taking the German positions at Longueval and Delville Wood in the rear ...'[20] The absence of a substantial force of cavalry possibly condemned the BEF to months of heavy fighting before Delville and High Woods passed into their hands.

If nothing else, the dawn assault of 14 July would appear to show that British high command had learned how to conduct a successful 'bite-and-hold' operation. On 27 July the trick was repeated. Two British brigades (one each from 2nd and 5th Divisions) attacked Delville Wood on a narrow frontage supported by no less than two corps's worth of artillery: 369 guns and howitzers, with additional weapons in a counter-battery role. Most of the wood was seized and held. Unfortunately, subsequent operations in the area, some by other brigades of 2nd Division, ignored the lesson of 27 July and allowed the artillery to split its fire between various targets rather than concentrating it. For reasons which still have historians arguing, operational lessons were being imperfectly learned by the BEF, and certainly imperfectly applied.

The story of the two months from 15 July to 14 September is one of struggles of awesome ferocity for individual objectives. The Germans continued to fight for Delville Wood after most of it was captured on 27 July, and it was not finally cleared (by 14th Division) for another month. Elsewhere division after division attacked, painfully advancing the British line a few hundred yards. Not only was artillery mishandled but infantry also continued to attack in penny-packets on narrow fronts. 'Divisional' attacks were often carried out by handfuls of companies. The attacks on Guillemont began in mid-July, but not until 3 September did the ruins of the village fall to the British. Well might the British official historian refer to the 'slow and costly advance throughout July and August'.[21] The result was a loss in this period of 100,000 men for gains of approximately 5.5 square miles. The proportion of casualties to ground gained was similar to that of 1 July.[22]

Enter the Tanks

On 15 September Haig launched another major co-ordinated attack on a ten-mile front. This stretched from Thiepval, in Reserve Army's sector, across to a point near the boundary with the French. This time Haig was pinning his faith on a new weapon: the tank. The concentration of guns was respectable — one heavy piece every 29 yards; the creeping barrage was used to good effect; and five corps attacking side by side gave mutual support, which made it difficult for the defenders to concentrate their fire. The objectives were kept sensibly limited. In the event, the Battle of Flers–Courcelette (as it became known) was a substantial victory for the BEF, but it did not meet Haig's expectations. Overall, the British line advanced by some 2,500 yards. At one sector, around Flers, 41st Division, assisted by tanks, pushed forward some 3,500 yards. Yet the German position, although battered, was not broken. Despite the mighty efforts, despite the tanks, despite the moderate success, the BEF was still a long way from breaking through the German defences on the Somme.

No one individual can be said to have 'invented' the tank, but a number of people, including the author H.G. Wells, Winston Churchill, and Major General Ernest Swinton contributed in some way to its development in various forms. Another was Douglas Haig. On becoming CinC of the BEF in December 1915 Haig was made aware of the 'landships' being developed in Britain. This was through a paper written by Churchill, who at that time was out of political office and serving in the army on the Western Front. Intrigued, Haig, through his staff, found out more information. The result was that this supposedly technophobe cavalryman asked for 150 tanks to be made available for the start of the Somme offensive. The tanks were not ready by that time, but were available for the attack of 15 September. Haig, it is clear, placed considerable faith in the new weapon, writing on 22 August that 'I hope and think they will add very greatly to the prospects of success and to the extent of it.'[23]

The plan for 15 September 1916 featured 'tank lanes' – areas that were not bombarded for fear of churning up the ground. This was probably a mistake. 122 Brigade (41st Division), attacking at Flers, suffered heavy casualties in the advance from machine guns sited in the tank lanes. On 47th (London) Division's sector, the Corps commander, Pulteney, took a particularly inept decision in decreeing that High Wood should be placed in a tank lane. Not only did this decision deprive the infantry of artillery support, but also the difficult terrain put paid to three out of the four tanks supporting this advance. Nonetheless, 141 Brigade took High Wood, aided by a belated bombardment and a trench mortar barrage. On the Western Front tanks were no substitute for an accurate and heavy artillery barrage.[24]

Subsequently, critics had a number of field days attacking Haig's use of tanks at Flers–Courcelette. Lloyd George denounced the 'foolish blunder' of revealing the 'great secret' of the tank before sufficient numbers were available to use them 'on a grand scale'.[25] Before the battle Haig, perhaps anticipating future criticism, had not unreasonably argued that it would be 'folly' 'not to use every means at my disposal in what is likely to be the crowning effort of this year'.[26] Moreover, it would have been difficult to keep the secret for very much longer because of the sheer unreliability of the vehicles; as one historian has noted, the front and the roads leading to it 'would have been choked by broken-down tanks'.[27]

In the 1920s Lloyd George's fellow war leader Winston Churchill, in one of the most emotive passages ever written about the Western Front, accused 'the Generals' of 1915–17 of fighting 'needless and wrongly conceived operations of infinite cost', of being 'content to fight machine gun bullets with the breasts of gallant men, and think that that was waging war'. Churchill proprietarily pointed to the mass use of tanks at the Battle of Cambrai in November 1917 as an alternative, arguing that a similar battle could have been fought in the previous year (that is, at the time of the Somme).[28] An entire book could be spent deconstructing this remarkable passage, which gives a fascinating insight into the mind of a man who gave Britain inspiring but decidedly erratic leadership in two world wars. It combines a blithe disregard for what was possible in 1916 with an astonishing lack of understanding of the realities of combat on the Western Front. Moreover, as will be discussed in the next chapter, the success at Cambrai was as much due to successful use of artillery – which gets only a fleeting reference from Churchill – as it was to tanks.

The machine that Churchill, years after the event, suggested should have been the centrepiece of the BEF's offensive in 1916 was effectively a one-shot weapon. Tanks were mechanically unreliable and prone to breakdown, quite apart from their vulnerability to enemy fire and bad terrain. Of the 60 tanks in France by September 1916, mechanical failure took a heavy toll. Only about 30 were able to cross the start line on 15 September of which 'perhaps 21 did real fighting'; this small number was further whittled away by the morning of 16 September.[29]

The 1916-vintage tank was far removed from the instrument of *Blitzkrieg* of 1940. With an average speed of only 2mph, it is best thought of as a mobile pillbox, which with luck could crush barbed wire, cross trenches and bring much needed fire support to the infantry. It was incapable of sustained pursuit of an enemy, not least because of the conditions in which the unfortunate tank crew had to work. The temperature inside the rhomboidal beast was an average of 125 degrees Fahrenheit; the noise was such that conversation was nearly impossible and orders had to be passed by a series of signs; and the crew breathed an unwholesome mix of carbon monoxide, cordite and petrol fumes.[30] In addition, in 1916 tank production was in its infancy and, even had large numbers of tanks existed, the BEF's logistic system would have been incapable of handling them. In short, Churchill's suggestion of a 'Cambrai' in 1916 was pure fantasy.

Although mishandled in some sectors, at Flers tanks performed about as well as one could have expected. Many have criticised the BEF for failing to use tanks *en masse* (all 21 of them!) in one large blow on 15 September. In reality, 'penny-packeting' of tanks to allow them to give maximum support to the infantry was a sensible way to use the small number of technically unreliable machines available.[31] The simple truth was that Haig expected too much of the new machine on 15 September. At that time the tank was not a war-winning weapon. Nonetheless, Haig thought the tanks did well enough. Shortly after the battle he placed an order for a further 1,000 tanks, a decision that was to have considerable consequences for the future.

The Somme: Final Battles

A breakthrough might have been out of the question, but limited operations were still achieving success. On 25 September eight divisions were involved in the Battle of Morval. This time, efforts were centred on a single German trench system, one that, moreover, was much weaker than those attacked on 15 September. It was, in artillery terms at least, 14 July all over again: a massive weight of shells was delivered onto a restricted area, and the British infantry captured most of the German Third Position on the front of XV and XIV Corps. This was a triumph of the infantry/artillery combination in which tanks were sidelined.[32] The following day, north of the Bapaume road, Thiepval, an objective on 1 July, fell to a carefully planned and well-executed assault by 18th Division.

Haig believed that the Germans were on the point of cracking and, instead of building on the success of limited operations, he returned to grandiose objectives. But the first attack, on 7 October, was hindered by bad weather. This reduced the ground to a quagmire and limited the spotting that the RFC could carry out, which consequently severely reduced the effectiveness of the British artillery bombardment. There were also improvements in the quality of the defenders, both in terms of morale and tactics, and the operation was a failure. Haig renewed the attack on five subsequent occasions, without any appreciable success. The campaign ended with a moderately successful assault by Gough's Fifth Army (as Reserve Army had been renamed). Founded on the virtues of careful planning and massed artillery, the Battle of the Ancre (13–18 November 1916) encompassed the capture of another 1 July objective, Beaumont-Hamel, and the seizure of Beaucourt by 63rd (Royal Naval) Division.

Tactics

As early as 2 July, new tactics were applied to capture a position that had proved impregnable on the first day of the offensive. Faced with the task of capturing La Boisselle, the object of 34th Division's ill-fated attack on 1 July, 19th Division organised a 'Chinese' [i.e., diversionary] bombardment of the village of Ovillers to the north, complete with smoke. When two battalions raced across No Man's Land in light fighting order, that is without being weighed down with masses of heavy kit, they took the defenders by surprise and got into the German front line trench. They then had a gruelling fight to take and hold La Boisselle, but their initial tactics worked extremely well.[33]

This seems to be a case of tactical improvisation at divisional level, and as such was typical of local activity that summer and autumn of 1916 as the raw troops of the BEF learned how to fight a modern war. Before the attack of 23 July at Pozières, an Australian staff officer wisely elicited a number of tips from successful British divisions, including the hard-learned lesson that attacks should not be mounted from further than 200 yards from their objective.[34]

One of the key problems was learning how to use new weapons (or weapons that were becoming available in quantity for the first time) effectively. A basic tactical conundrum lies in learn[ing] how to combine the effect of a number of weapons, of different types, together with the movement of men who are using or serving these weapons. The effective combination of fire and movement ... is the essential problem of tactics ... separated from tactics [weapons] ... become heavy and knobbly things for tired men to drag or carry.[35]

At Delville Wood on 27 July, in their first battle, the advance of a company of 23rd Royal Fusiliers was checked by a German strongpoint. After several failures they captured the position by sending bombers and two Lewis guns (sent up from battalion headquarters) to feel their way around its flanks. Delville thus offers a graphic example of an inexperienced unit literally learning on the job, groping their way towards effective tactics while actually in contact with the enemy.[36] Similar experiences took place in units throughout Fourth and Reserve/Fifth Armies. The net result was impressive. As one historian has recently noted:

The integration of Lewis gun, rifle grenade and trench mortar fire with the advances carried out by riflemen and bombers, all blended with an increasing confidence on the gunners' ability to lay down effective creeping barrages, transformed the British battle performance.[37]

Another lesson learned that summer was the importance of having plenty of 'moppers up' who advanced behind the leading waves and dealt with German troops who had survived the initial bombardment and assault. Equally important was the consolidation of captured positions against the inevitable German counterattacks. This involved deploying sufficient numbers of carrying parties to bring up supplies of barbed wire, sandbags and the like, as well as extra rations of bombs. Doing it this way ensured that the assault troops were not too laden down with kit, a problem that some troops had encountered on 1 July. Other lessons included the importance of careful reconnaissance of ground about to be attacked over; and the crucial need for careful training and rehearsal of battles. Gunners improved their ability to carry out counter-battery work, and creeping barrages became standard throughout the army, and increasingly sophisticated. The problem of communications, although far from 'solved', was addressed as liaison between arms improved.

These lessons were underpinned by training. As the historian of the Welsh Guards noted, 'Training never ceased during the war. The hardened veteran, out of the line for a rest, joined the young recruit, who had just arrived in France for the first time, and trained.'[38] The learning process was still far from complete. Not every division ended the Somme as tactically advanced as the best formations, and there was some debate on the right interpretation to be placed on some experiences. Nevertheless, by the end of the Somme campaign the BEF resembled a coherent weapons system much more closely than it had on 1 July.

As in 1915, 'lessons learned' from operations emanated from all levels of the BEF. At one level were 'Notes from Recent Operations' issued by 55th (West Lancashire) Division following their unsuccessful attack at Guillemont on 8–9 August, which was to be read by all officers and NCOs. This contained a host of practical instructions ranging from salvage to the necessity of infantry following within 50 yards of the creeping barrage.[39] This division applied these lessons learned with great success in their next two battles, on 25 and 27 September.

At the other end of the scale came notes from GHQ. A typical one was issued on 13 August 1916 in which Haig directed that his army commanders should draw the attention of brigade and battalion commanders to his views on the use of local reserves.[40] In addition, there were more formal publications such as SS119 *Preliminary Notes of the Tactical Lessons*, issued in July 1916, while the battle was still in progress. High command's views were informed by information actively garnered from lower formations. During the Somme Major General A.A. Montgomery, chief of staff of Rawlinson's Fourth Army, had a fruitful correspondence on 'lessons learned' with divisions and corps, and Reserve Army likewise gathered a great deal of evidence from lower formations and units.[41]

The tactical fruits of the Somme were two official pamphlets that appeared after the campaign had concluded. SS143 *Instructions for the Training of Platoons for Offensive Action* and SS144 *The Normal Formation for the Attack* represented a significant step forward from the tactical doctrine that existed before the battle. One important advance was 'the reorganisation of the platoon into semi-specialised sections of riflemen, Lewis gunners, bombers, and rifle bombers'.[42] This was a recognition that the platoon of thirty-odd men, rather than a larger body, was the major tactical unit, and gave the platoon commander much more flexibility as well as greater firepower. This was a consequence of the type of problem encountered and overcome by the 23rd Royal Fusiliers at Delville Wood. The British manuals of February 1917 covered essentially the same ground as *Der Angriff in Stellungskrieg* ('The Attack in Position Warfare') issued by the German army eleven months later. Some historians have revered the German pamphlet as a stormtrooper's manual, yet the BEF has received little credit for its tactical sophistication.[43]

It is one thing to produce doctrine; quite another to see it transformed into tactics on the ground. Yet it is clear that British units did train in the new tactics, and, as we will see in the next chapter, the battles of 1917 were to offer conclusive evidence that the lessons of the Somme were absorbed and applied, to great effect, on the battlefield.

Attrition on the Somme

The suffering of British troops on the Somme is so deeply ingrained in Anglophone culture that the impact of the battle on the German defenders is rarely considered. The initial attack by Haig's men can be likened to a strong but inexperienced and only partially trained boxer landing a body blow that causes his opponent to stagger and thus lose the initiative. Of course, the BEF cannot take all the credit for this, for the importance of the successful French attacks south of the Somme must not be underrated. Nevertheless, the operations of the BEF were highly significant.

For the German defenders, the Battle of the Somme began not on 1 July 1916 but seven days earlier, with the beginning of the Allied preliminary bombardment. Ineffective as the British artillery was in achieving the goals that had been set for it, its sheer power, the consequence of the beginning of the mobilisation of British and American industries for war, forced the defenders to endure an appalling ordeal. General Fritz von Below, the commander of Second Army, reported on 28 June that 'our infantry are suffering heavier losses every day, while the enemy is for the time being spared loss of men.' Neither, thanks to the revolution in depth-artillery fire, did things improve after the British infantry attack began. The history of a good class formation, 27th (Württemberg) Division, recorded that:

What we experienced surpassed all previous conception. The enemy's fire never ceased for an hour. It fell night and day on the front line and tore fearful gaps in the ranks of the defenders. It fell on the approaches to the front line and made all movement to the front hell. It fell on the rearward trenches and battery positions and smashed men and material in a manner never seen before or since. It repeatedly reached even the resting battalions behind the front and occasioned there terrible losses. Our artillery was powerless against it ...[44]

The effect of British artillery fire was undoubtedly exacerbated by the policy of *Halten, was zu halten ist* or 'Hold on to whatever can be held'.[45] This involved defending forward, even if this exposed the Germans to enemy artillery fire. When General von Pannewitz, commanding XVII Corps south of the River Somme ordered his troops to pull back on 2 July and prepare to counterattack, he incurred Falkenhayn's displeasure. Not only did this threaten to uncover the flank of the troops north of the Somme, it ran counter to Falkenhayn's order that 'it must be a principle in trench warfare not to abandon a foot of ground and, if a foot is lost, to put in the last man to recover it by an immediate counterattack'. This led, by one calculation, to 330 German counterattacks during the battle. John Terraine has referred to this as the 'true texture of the Somme'; not merely British attacks, but German counterattacks to retake ground that was lost. This rigid German insistence on holding ground for ground's sake played to the strengths of the British, and undermines the view that the German army of the Great War was the epitome of military excellence.[46]

Seen from the German side of the hill, the results of 1 July gave little comfort. The ability of the French to mount a successful attack on the Somme came as a nasty shock in view of their commitment at Verdun, and led, as we have seen, to Pannewitz shortening his line south of the Somme. North of the river, the Germans had lost 109 guns, and to the south, the Germans lost the artillery of 121 Division. These losses, out of 598 field and 246 heavy pieces available to German Second Army on 1 July, had serious consequences. Below complained on 4 July that he could deploy just one battery every 800 metres to lay down a barrage. Only five days earlier he had reported that he had one battery every 350 and 400 metres north and south of the Somme respectively, and this was insufficient; the experience of Verdun had indicated that one battery every 200 metres was required. Below was pessimistic about the chance of major counterattacks, but the Germans made good use of the relative respite after the attack of 1 July to reorganise their line. Even so, German defences in the key sector from Longueval to Ovillers, where the British had made substantial advances, consisted of a thin field-grey line cobbled together from a number of different formations.

The Allied attack of 1 July 1916 had one positive result. If nothing else, it wrested the strategic initiative on the Western Front back from the Germans, who had held it since they attacked at Verdun in February. In reply to Below's cries for reinforcements in the immediate aftermath of the attack, he was sent three divisions, 16 heavy batteries and a number of aircraft. In all, during July and August, an additional 42 German divisions were committed to the Somme front, of which 35 were sent to face the British. This substantial shift of forces led, on 11 July, to Falkenhayn suspending attacks on Verdun – a substantial success for which the BEF deserves a large slice of the credit. At the end of August the Hindenburg–Ludendorff team replaced

Falkenhayn, who was now tainted by German failures at Verdun and on the Somme.

When General Grant explained his strategy for the 1864 campaign, President Abraham Lincoln quickly grasped the purpose of launching main and subsidiary offensives: 'Those not skinning can hold a leg.'[47] While in tactical and operational terms the BEF might have improved its performance on the Somme, in strategic terms they were not only holding a leg, they were skinning it, too. We have seen how by the end of 1915 Kitchener's original scheme to hold back his armies until the French and Germans had exhausted themselves lay in ruins. To maintain the cohesion of the alliance, it was politically imperative that the British take major offensive action. The opening of the German offensive at Verdun simply increased the pressure for Haig to attack.

But the Somme was more than simply a political necessity. It achieved important operational and even strategic results, and might easily have achieved more. Germany was placed under severe pressure by the Allied offensives in France, on the Eastern Front and in the Balkans. Falkenhayn was in the position of a man surrounded by assailants, just about able to ward off their blows but worried that he would be overwhelmed if yet another joined in the fight. The Russian 'Brusilov' offensive, which began on 4 June, initially achieved startling results against the Austrians, forcing the Germans to mount a counter-offensive from 16 to 23 June. We have seen that, with a little more luck, the British could have made some modest but important gains on the Somme by the end of July, which would, at the very least, have made the German position lengthier and more difficult to maintain. In late August Falkenhayn argued in a report to the Kaiser against seeking a decision against Russia, stating that 'Any transfer of our forces in one direction would mean a dangerous weakening somewhere else.'[48] This was equally true of responding to a new threat. Arguably, if Rumania had entered the war in late June rather than on 27 August, the Central Powers' armies would have been stretched so thinly that somewhere their perimeter defences would have given way. Conceivably, the Anglo-French armies could have reaped the rewards on the Somme. As it was, by late August the moment had gone: the Germans had somewhat recovered their equilibrium, and the Somme offensive had clearly passed what Clausewitz would have called its 'culminating point'. Consequently, the Germans were able to defeat Rumania and the window of opportunity for a major Allied victory was firmly closed.

Since the 1920s, there have been attempts to prove the success or otherwise of the Somme by the grisly process of comparing casualty statistics. But to compare losses on a death-by-death basis is to miss the point. The Somme balance sheet for the Germans was almost wholly negative; for the British rather less so. While they prevented an Allied breakthrough, the Germans, having a smaller manpower pool than the British and French empires, were less able to sustain such casualties. Worse, large numbers of experienced German soldiers, NCOs and officers were killed. The Germans could ill afford to lose these men. The British, by contrast, lost mostly green soldiers while those who survived the holocaust benefited greatly, in strictly military terms, by gaining experience. The Somme taught the BEF how to fight, while it degraded the quality of the German army. By the end of 1916 the two armies were much more evenly matched than had been the case six months earlier. Moreover, while British morale remained high, German morale suffered.

There is plenty of evidence from the German side to suggest that the Somme had a profound and detrimental impact on the German army. An official German monograph commented that the casualties had a greater impact on Germany than on the Allies. Troops had to be left in the fighting zone 'until they had expended the last atom of their strength', and German commanders were forced 'to throw divisions time after time into the same battle'. Captain von Hentig, of the Guard Reserve Division, described the Somme in a famous phrase as 'the muddy grave of the German army'.[49]

The Somme in Retrospect

In one sense the Somme was an unavoidable battle. Operating within a coalition severely restricted Haig's freedom of action, and the BEF simply had to attack somewhere. Since in 1916 the BEF was probably incapable of fighting anything but an attritional battle, an action fought elsewhere is likely to have followed a similar pattern. Inexperience was the hallmark of the BEF in mid-1916. None of the three major British commanders, Rawlinson, Gough and Haig, emerge particularly well from this battle, their first attempts to conduct operations on this scale. All three men made a number of mistakes that had bloody consequences for the ordinary soldiers under their command, and brought misery and bereavement to grand country houses and working class terraces alike across Britain and the Empire. They have rightly been criticised for their failure to learn the correct lessons more rapidly and apply them consistently.

But the Somme should not be dismissed simply as a bloody disaster. Douglas Haig's *Final Despatch*, written in 1919, was a well-argued defence of his generalship in which he contended that the victory of 1918 was made possible by the attritional battles of 1915–17. The Western Front, in Haig's words, was 'one great and continuous engagement', which conformed to the pre-war idea of a phased battle, and the Somme was part of the process of 'wearing-out' the enemy.[50] The Final Despatch contains some *ex post facto* rationalisation, but that is not to argue that his case was entirely wrong. The cumulative effects of the attrition of the Somme and the 1917 battles on the physical strength and will to fight of the German army, at all levels and in every sense, played a major role in weakening it sufficiently to make possible the knockout blow in 1918. A cold-blooded analysis of the results of the Somme leads to the conclusion that the battle was, if not a strategic victory, certainly a strategic success.

Given slightly better fortune the success could have been more substantial, although it would still have fallen well short of a decisive victory. At various times in July and early August 1916 it looked as if the Germans might be forced to abandon their positions on the Somme. If they had done so, it is highly unlikely that mobile warfare would have been fully restored and that the war would have been brought to a swift and victorious conclusion. In 1916 the BEF's logistic system was incapable of supporting a major, sustained advance and the cavalry probably incapable of converting a German retirement into a rout. Therefore, with the advantage of hindsight, the best that Haig could have achieved was to push the German line back and fight a new attritional campaign perhaps twenty miles in the rear. However, such a move by the Germans would have represented an Allied political and propaganda victory in that it would have contributed to the Allied strategic objective by liberating some miles of French soil. Moreover, the Germans would have been seen to have been forced to retire at a time not of their own choosing. At this stage the Hindenburg Line position (to which the Germans did retire in the spring of 1917) was not yet constructed; the Allies would have had a chance of inflicting further damage on the retreating enemy. A German withdrawal would have given a tremendous boost to Allied morale and shored up the solidarity of the coalition, as the French were given concrete proof that at long last the British were pulling their weight.

Haig's initial attempt to achieve a breakthrough on 1 July 1916 was a failure. The battle that developed was nonetheless a success for the British army. In February and March 1917, the Germans abandoned their positions on the old Somme battlefield, methodically carrying out a scorched earth policy as they did so. This was in part an acknowledgement of British success on the Somme; the German army was not prepared to endure another such defensive battle on that ground. The German troops fell back to the newly built and formidable fortifications that the British christened the Hindenburg Line. The German decision to attempt to knock Britain out of the war by using unrestricted submarine warfare was also in some measure a consequence of the Somme, in that they recognised that they could not win the war on the Western Front.

While the Somme weakened the German army, the BEF gained

experience and improved its tactics. Commanders at all levels could certainly have conducted the battle more effectively and thus saved lives. Yet unpalatable as it may seem, it is difficult to avoid the conclusion that the Somme was an essential precondition to success in the last two years of the war.

CHAPTER 8

1917: THE TRIUMPH
OF THE SET-PIECE

Arras is a little-known battle, despite featuring passages that matched for horror any on the Somme or at Passchendaele. Even within the circle of those interested in British military history, 'the Battle of Arras' is more likely to conjure up visions of May 1940, when there was one day of small scale fighting by British infantry and tanks against Rommel's 7th Panzer Division. This is another curious example of the historical amnesia that is applied to the Great War, for the fighting at the 'first' Battle of Arras was, in fact, the second of the three great attritional offensives waged by the British army in 1916–17. The BEF's daily loss rate of 4,076 at Arras was greater than the Somme (2,943), Passchendaele (2,323), or the Hundred Days battles of 1918 (3,645).[1] For all that, on the first day of the Battle of Arras, the BEF achieved its greatest success since the beginning of trench warfare. The BEF could now carry out a set-piece attack with great skill, although subsequent days were to demonstrate that capitalising on initial success still presented considerable problems.

At the end of 1916, the Allies were preparing to renew the battle on the Somme, and in January Fifth Army began a series of minor operations that were surprisingly effective. But two events were to alter the Allies' plans for 1917. The first was the German withdrawal to the Hindenburg Line already discussed. The second was the fall from power of 'Papa' Joffre, the imperturbable general who had done more than any other individual to prevent France from being defeated in 1914. His campaigns of 1915–16, which resulted in heavy losses for paltry gains, had exhausted his political credit. In December 1916 he was replaced by General Robert Nivelle, who had won a series of striking minor victories at Verdun by employing the technique of the set-piece attack – infantry supported by massed artillery assaulting limited objectives. Nivelle proclaimed that these methods, which worked well enough on a small scale in the peculiar circumstances of Verdun, could be applied on a much wider front to produce a war-winning offensive. He boldly proclaimed that he would capture the city of 'Laon in twenty-four hours and then break out'.[2] Nivelle, who was half-English and spoke the language perfectly, impressed the new British Prime Minister, David Lloyd George. Between them they engineered Haig, who favoured an attack in the Ypres area, into agreeing to launch a subsidiary attack at Arras.

The Easter Victory

In many respects the first day of the Somme and the first day of Arras are comparable battles. Both began with a prolonged bombardment followed by an assault by 14 British divisions, although the attack frontage at Arras was a little shorter, 25,000 yards to 27,000 on the Somme. Turning to artillery, the picture in April 1917 was a lot brighter for the BEF than it had been in the previous July. One important difference was that the increasingly sophisticated creeping barrage had become a standard tactic. Another was the density of heavy guns, which was about three times greater on 9 April 1917 than on 1 July 1916: 963 guns, or one per 21 yards, as opposed to 455, or one per 57 yards. Moreover, there was more ammunition available than at the beginning of the Somme (although the supply was far from unlimited) and the shells were generally of higher quality, with fewer duds. For

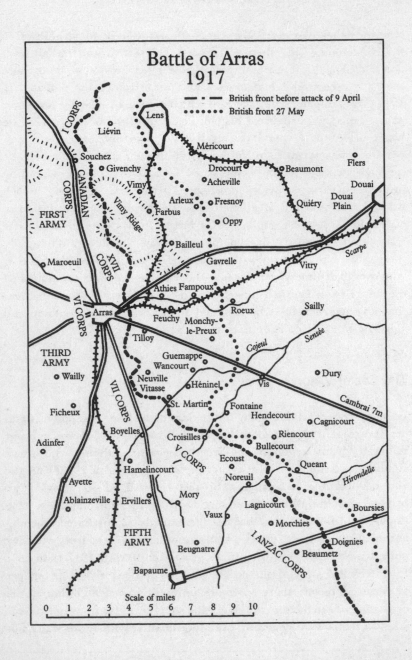

Battle of Arras
1917

— · — · — British front before attack of 9 April

· · · · · · · · · British front 27 May

I CORPS

CANADIAN CORPS

FIRST ARMY

XVII CORPS

VI CORPS

THIRD ARMY

VII CORPS

V CORPS

FIFTH ARMY

I ANZAC CORPS

Lens

Liévin

Souchez

Givenchy

Vimy

Vimy Ridge

Maroeuil

Arras

Méricourt

Drocourt

Acheville

Arleux

Farbus

Fresnoy

Oppy

Bailleul

Gavrelle

Athies Fampoux

Feuchy

Tilloy

Monchy-
le-Preux

Roeux

Beaumont

Flers

Douai

Quiéry

Douai
Plain

Vitry

Scarpe

Sailly

Cojeul

Sensée

Guemappe

Wancourt

Neuville
Vitasse

Héninel

St. Martin

Vis

Dury

Fontaine

Hendecourt

Cagnicourt

Cambrai 7m

Wailly

Ficheux

Boyelles

Croisilles

Riencourt

Bullecourt

Queant

Hirondelle

Adinfer

Hamelincourt

Ecoust

Noreuil

Ayette

Ablainzeville Ervillers

Mory

Vaux

Lagnicourt

Morchies

Boursies

Doignies

Beaumetz

Beugnatre

Bapaume

Scale of miles

0   1   2   3   4   5   6   7   8   9   10

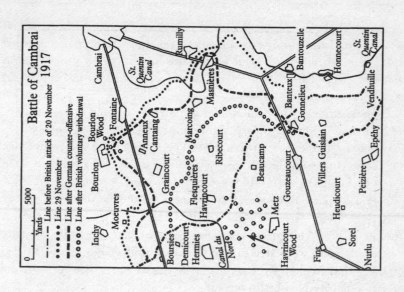

Battle of Cambrai 1917

0   5000
Yards

– – – Line before British attack of 20 November
••••• Line 29 November
Line after German counter-offensive
○○○○ Line after British voluntary withdrawal

Inchy · Moeuvres · Bourlon · Bourlon Wood · Fontaine · Cambrai · St. Quentin Canal · Rumilly · Masnières · Beaurevoir · Bantouzelle · St. Quentin Canal · Honnecourt · Vendhuille

Boursies · Demicourt · Hermies · Graincourt · Anneux · Cantaing · Marcoing · Banteux · Gonnelieu · Villers Guislain · Epéhy · Peizière

Canal du Nord · Flesquières · Havrincourt · Ribecourt · Beaucamp · Gouzeaucourt · Heudicourt · Sorel

Havrincourt Wood · Metz · Fins · Nurlu

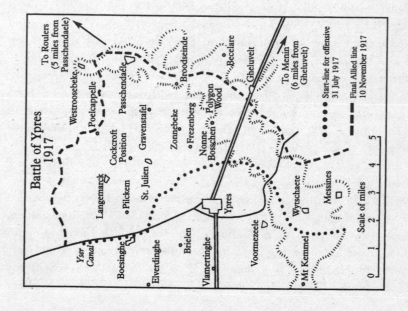

Battle of Ypres 1917

To Roulers (5 miles from Passchendaele)

Westroosebeke · Poelcappelle · Passchendaele · Broodseinde · Becelare · Gheluvelt · To Menin (6 miles from Gheluvelt)

Langemarck · Cockcroft Position · Gravenstafel · Zonnebeke · Frezenberg · Polygon Wood · Nonne Bosschen

Boesinghe · Pilckem · St. Julien · Yser Canal · Elverdinghe · Brielen · Vlamertinghe · Ypres · Voormezeele · Wytschaete · Messines · Mt Kemmel

•••• Start-line for offensive 31 July 1917
– – – Final Allied line 10 November 1917

Scale of miles
0   1   2   3   4   5

all that, BEF divisions each deployed 20 pieces of heavy artillery, which was only half the number available to French divisions. Even in April 1917, after Britain had been at war for nearly three years, British industry, backed by that of North America, could still not supply all the army's needs.[3]

General Allenby, the commander of Third Army, had wanted a short, 48-hour bombardment before his men attacked, but Haig successfully demanded a longer one of five days. The results were impressive just the same. Opposite Vimy Ridge, which was attacked by the Canadian Corps of First Army, the flash spotters and sound rangers of 1st Field Survey Company discovered 86 per cent of the locations of enemy batteries. There was a similar success rate on Third Army's front further south. While relatively few German batteries were actually destroyed, most were neutralised in the initial stages of the British attack — that is, they were unable to bring effective fire to bear, the crews being disabled or driven off.[4]

The careful preparation of the artillery was matched by other staff work. Most famous was the use of tunnels. For the attack on Vimy Ridge, the Canadian Corps constructed twelve tunnels, the longest stretching 1,883 yards, which allowed troops to shelter below ground and emerge close to the front line. The city of Arras has long been a key feature in what Charles de Gaulle called the 'fatal avenue' — that much-contested strip of territory between France and Germany.[5] Caves and tunnels used by inhabitants in times past to shelter from many armies over many centuries were enlarged and improved. In 1917 some 25,000 men could take refuge in this labyrinth, and move in safety to the trenches through tunnels 3,000 yards long.

At 5.30 a.m. on Easter Monday, 9 April 1917, the British and Canadian infantry 'hopped the bags' and advanced through a snow-storm. Fifteen minutes earlier German batteries had been bombarded with poison gas. Like artillery, machine gun tactics had increased in sophistication since the beginning of the war.[6] Massed machine guns fired a barrage over the heads of the attacking infantry, while forty tanks rumbled into action alongside. The first day of Arras was highly successful. At Vimy Ridge, with the support of nine Heavy Artillery

Groups (seven of them British) the Canadians captured most of this formidable position with relatively little difficulty, although at the cost of 11,000 casualties. This was a major achievement, and is rightly celebrated as a landmark in the birth of the Canadian nation. In purely military terms it was highly significant in giving the British good observation over the Douai plain. During the German offensives in the first half of 1918, Vimy Ridge would prove to be a defensive asset of incalculable value.

The triumph of the Canadians at Vimy has tended to overshadow the achievements of Third Army to the south. Here, 4th Division and 9th (Scottish) Division of XVII Corps achieved the longest single advance since trench warfare began – some three and a half miles. VI Corps' advance was of the order of two miles, which included the capture of Battery Valley, where 12th and 15th (Scottish) Divisions overran a mass of German guns. A battery of 77mm guns was still in action when a unit of Scottish infantry reached its position; it 'continued firing at pointblank range until charged by the leading wave and all the gunners bayoneted'.[7] A more modest advance was the 2,000 yards achieved by VII Corps, which nonetheless captured Neuville Vitasse, a strongly held village, and established itself in the front trench of the Hindenburg Line. On the first day of the attack Third Army took 5,600 prisoners, the Canadians a further 3,400, plus 36 guns.

German mistakes undoubtedly aided the BEF's success. On Vimy Ridge Falkenhausen's German Sixth Army seem to have misunderstood the principles of flexible defence-in-depth that had emerged from the Somme. As a result, defenders were crowded onto the ridge, where the Canadians quickly overran them, and the counterattack divisions were held too far back to be able to intervene in a timely fashion. But defensive errors alone cannot explain the success of 9 April 1917. Captain Cyril Falls, the official historian of the battle, was undoubtedly correct to claim that 'Easter Monday of the year 1917 must be accounted from the British point of view one of the great days of the War ... [it was] among the heaviest blows struck by British arms in the Western theatre of war.'[8] As subsequent battles in 1917 were to demonstrate, given time, careful staff work, a sufficient concentration of artillery, and aggressive infantry with high morale, even the strongest position could be captured by a set-piece attack.

The events of the days following the triumph of Easter Monday were to show that as steep as the learning curve since July 1916 had been, the BEF still had major problems in capitalising on initial success, in moving from static and semi-mobile warfare into battles of manoeuvre. Like a child's top running down, the fighting on 10 and 11 April saw the British advance grow more sluggish as the troops tired and as German reserves began to reach the battlefield. Allenby, deprived of his eyes in the sky by the poor weather, did not understand this. On 11 April he gave the most controversial order of his career, declaring that 'Third Army is now pursuing a defeated enemy and risks must be freely taken.'[9] While 9 April had been a defeat for the Germans, by 11 April the German formations arriving on the Arras front amounted to a fresh force that had to be defeated all over again. 37th Division captured the village of Monchy-le-Preux, and Allenby sent forward the lead elements of the Cavalry Corps. But German artillery put paid to his hopes of achieving a breakthrough.

There was further disappointment on Fifth Army's front where, on 10–11 April, Gough's troops had entered the battle. Here, at Bullecourt, there was a reversion to the worst days of the Somme. The attack was imaginative but poorly planned. Tanks and guns were mishandled and the Australian infantry, who did remarkably well in the circumstances, were the victims, taking heavy casualties for scant gains.[10]

At Arras the BEF had initially won a substantial victory, but it had failed, like every other effort on the Western Front up to that time, to turn a 'break-in' into a 'breakthrough'. Allenby's misinterpretation of the situation on 11 April must be attributed in large part to ignorance of the position on the battlefield, which in turn was largely due to the familiar problem with communications. As late as 14 April Allenby was resolved to push on, but in a high level 'mutiny', some of his senior commanders protested and Haig ordered a suspension of operations to allow further preparations.

Artillery had been a crucial element in the success of 9 April, but its very success inevitably led to the ground becoming shattered. Given time, engineers and pioneers would build roads and tracks which would enable the guns to move to new positions, to begin the process of hammering at enemy strongpoints as a preliminary to another major attack. Time, however, was one item that was in short supply. Thus on 11 April the British infantry found themselves up against uncut wire, with the 18-pounder guns that should have been cutting that wire still struggling forward to get in range.

The Unwanted Battle

With hindsight, it is easy to say that Haig should have closed down the battle on 12 April. But the realities of coalition warfare meant that this option, however attractive from a narrow British perspective, was simply not available. Haig had to keep attacking to pin down German forces which would otherwise have been available to face the French offensive that was to begin on 16 April on the Chemin des Dames. History remembers the 'Nivelle Offensive' as a failure, but in reality it was a limited success along the lines of the Vimy/Arras operations, with French forces capturing 29,000 enemy prisoners and a salient four miles deep and sixteen miles wide. But Nivelle had promised much, much more. For sections of the French army, the disappointment of the Chemin des Dames was more than they could bear, coming on top of the massive losses in 1914–15 and at Verdun. Altogether 68 divisions were affected by mutiny. Nivelle fell, to be replaced by Pétain, who in time was to rebuild the French army's offensive spirit. For the rest of the war, however, the BEF was to take the lead in attempting to drive the Germans from occupied soil.

On 23 April the BEF launched its second major offensive of the Battle of Arras. In comparison with 9 April the results were disappointing, but the gain of about a mile across Third Army's front was, judged by the standards of the Somme, impressive enough. Individual actions, notably the capture of Gavrelle by 63rd (Royal Naval) Division, further indicated the tactical proficiency of some units of the BEF. Against this must be placed evidence of poor staff work and less than effective barrages. Conditions of semi-open warfare called for a greater degree of extemporisation than the pure 'set-piece' battle, and it seems that the BEF at all levels was struggling to cope with this more advanced form of combat.[11] On top of this, the arrival on the Arras front of the German defensive specialist Colonel Fritz von Lossberg led to the Germans adopting a more fluid form of defence, which further increased the difficulties of the British infantry and artillery.[12]

The experience of the Grimsby Chums, more formally known as the 10th Battalion of the Lincolnshire Regiment, epitomises the mixed fortunes of British troops during the Battle of Arras. On 9 April the Chums, as part of 34th Division, had benefited from an impressively effective creeping barrage, and had captured their objectives with the comparatively light loss of 110 men. Just a couple of weeks later, though, attacking the village of Roeux, the artillery barrage was a failure and the result was 'the most disastrous action ever fought by the 10th Lincolnshires'. On 1 July 1916 this battalion had been involved in one of the bloodiest actions of the day, suffering 59 per cent losses, yet the 67 per cent loss rate at Roeux exceeded even that.[13]

The final major push of the Battle of Arras began on 3 May 1917, partly to encourage the French to continue operations. Haig wisely limited the objectives. It was, in Falls's blunt words, 'a ghastly failure, some thought the blackest day of the war'.[14] The companion piece to this disaster was another attritional struggle, Second Bullecourt (3–17 May), a battle of which the major result was to further poison Anglo-Australian relations, although Australian staff work and the poor performance of an Australian brigade contributed to the failure.

Arras was a battle fought largely at the behest of the French that the BEF could well have done without. Nevertheless, it was a victory of sorts. General Otto von Moser, commander of German XIV Corps at Bullecourt, later pointed out that 'in 1917, it was the British who were militarily the most obstinate and most dangerous of Germany's enemies'. Coalitions are always vulnerable to internal dissension: if nothing else, at Arras the British Empire visibly pulled its weight. Moreover, as von Moser admitted, Arras had a damaging impact on the German army. As on the Somme in the previous year, the Germans were less able to bear the impact of attrition than could the British.[15] Finally, Arras was another vital if painful point on the tactical learning curve and over the coming months the lessons of Arras were garnered, codified and disseminated. Haig's army was a much more effective force than it had been twelve months previously, but it still had much to learn, particularly about semi-mobile warfare.

Messines

Ypres has been familiar to generations of British soldiers who have fought and died in the area, from the Hundred Years War down to the Second World War. For all that, at no time has the name Ypres — rendered by the British soldier, with a fine disregard for the niceties of pronunciation, as 'Wipers', or 'E-priss' — been more deeply etched on the British psyche than in 1914—18. At the First Battle of Ypres in 1914 the old BEF had virtually been destroyed in the defence of the city, and in the following spring in the Second Battle of Ypres the Germans had unleashed poison gas and pushed the BEF back to hold a precarious position in front of the town. Douglas Haig had long favoured an offensive in this area. He would have liked to attack around Ypres in 1916, which might have been a good option, because at that time the German defences in the area were not as powerful as they were to be a year later.

While a successful offensive around Ypres would have been satisfying emotionally, there were also compelling strategic reasons to attack in this area. The Germans held the high ground that curved around the town, and a relatively modest advance of about seven miles would drive them off it. This would also threaten the key communications junction of Roulers, twelve miles from Ypres. If the Allies captured this town, it would place German logistics in Flanders in jeopardy, and might even force them to withdraw from the area. This would have been of enormous strategic importance to Britain, where, as we have seen, the Admiralty was becoming increasingly nervous at the growing German naval threat based on the Channel coast.

Messines Ridge is a spine of high ground that in 1917 dominated the southern flank of the Ypres Salient. British planners quickly decided that its capture was an essential precondition to the main offensive, and the operation was entrusted to General Sir Herbert Plumer's Second Army. The plan to take the Ridge was to be a variation on the Vimy/Arras theme: another set-piece offensive in which the infantry would advance under a massive artillery barrage to strictly limited objectives. Plumer may have physically resembled Colonel Blimp but he had already established a reputation as a careful general who took good care not to throw away his men's lives. Officers and men appreciated serving under Plumer and his chief of staff, 'Tim' Harington, as much as they disliked serving in Gough's Fifth Army. Harington described the secret of Plumer's success as being down to three Ts: 'Trust, Training and Thoroughness'.[16] Harington's comments were fair on all three counts. Second Army was a cohesive team, not a one-man band, and Plumer's successes were indeed founded on training – not that this formation was unique within the BEF in this respect. Preparations for this offensive, as for all his others, were meticulous. A snapshot reveals that water pipes were laid to supply up to 600,000 gallons per day, while the construction of light railways enabled the 144,000 tons of ammunition stockpiled in Second Army's sector to be fed forward to the Army's 2,266 guns. Such levels of preparation were becoming standard practice for an assault, but there was one unique feature of the planning for Messines: the attack would be heralded by the use of mines.

Beginning as far back as 1915, twenty-four long tunnels were dug under the German positions and packed with explosive. In mining, as in so many things, the BEF had experienced a learning curve since the Somme. At Messines, each mine contained 'an *average* of 48,000 lbs (21 tons)' of explosive, which was double the charge of nearly all of the major mines detonated on 1 July 1916. The most powerful charge was the 95,600 lbs of ammonal laid by 1st Canadian Tunnelling Company at the end of a 1,650-foot tunnel, 125 feet beneath St. Eloi.[17]

Even before the mines were blown, the British won the preliminary artillery battle. Plumer's forces deployed 756 heavy pieces. Between

26 May and the end of 6 June, these guns and their smaller brethren pumped 3,500,000 shells onto the German positions according to a sophisticated fire-plan, designed to take account of the various features of the German defences. The German response was, by comparison, feeble; they were seriously outnumbered by a factor of 2 to 1 in heavy guns, and 5 to 1 in lighter pieces. Thus about half of the defenders' guns were lost before the attack went in on 7 June. A German machine-gunner wrote of the cumulative effect on German morale of the British winning the artillery battle:

> This is far worse than the Battle of Arras. Our artillery is left sitting and is scarcely able to fire a round ... the sole object of every arm that enters the battle is to play itself out, in order to be withdrawn as quickly as possible.

German high command considered withdrawing from Messines Ridge. General von Laffert, commander of XIX Corps, firmly rejected this idea, grossly underestimating the British threat. This was to prove a terrible mistake.[18]

At 3.10 a.m. on 7 June 1917, the attack began with the detonation of the mines. Norman Gladden, a young infantryman of 11th Northumberland Fusiliers (23rd Division) was near Hill 60:

> With a sharp report a rocket began to mount into the daylit sky. A voice behind me cried, 'Now'. It was the hour, and that enemy light never burst upon the day. The ground began to rock. My body was carried up and down as though by the waves of the sea. In front the earth opened and a large black mass mounted on pillars of fire to the sky, where it seemed to remain suspended for some seconds while the awful red glow lit up the surrounding desolation. No sound came. My nerves had been keyed to sustain a noise from the mine so tremendous as to be unbearable. For a brief spell all was silent, as though we were so close that the sound itself had leapt over us like some

immense wave. Almost simultaneously a line of men rose from the ground a short distance in front and advanced away towards the upheaval, their helmets silhouetted and bayonets glinting in the unearthly redness.[19]

This area had been plagued by mine warfare since early 1915 – the visitor to Hill 60 can see the evidence to this very day – but the mines blown here were of a different order to anything that had gone before. The force of the nineteen explosions was experienced in England. It was decided not to detonate three of the mines for tactical reasons, while a fourth had been lost to German countermining in August 1916. Of the mines that were not blown, one exploded as the result of a thunderstorm in 1955. The others, as I have often cheerfully pointed out to visitors to the battlefield, remain beneath these particular Flanders Fields. On the day before the battle Harington had announced that: 'I do not know whether we shall change history tomorrow, but we shall certainly alter the geography.'[20] He was as good as his word.

Hard on the heels of the explosions, nine divisions advanced and swept through the outer German defences and rapidly recaptured Messines Ridge, last held by the British in October 1914. On 7 June 1917 the 36th (Ulster) Division attacked over precisely the same ground, benefiting from a highly effective and thoroughly scientific use of artillery. On this occasion the Germans were deployed on the modern principle of defence-in-depth, concrete pillboxes buttressing their positions. When faced with opposition at the Pick House strong point, the Ulsters carried out a by now standard method of attack, using rifle grenades, and bringing machine gun fire to bear from a flank. Close by, another group of infantry dealt with a machine gun with the help of one of the 72 tanks in support of Second Army, an NCO attracting the attention of the tank commander by the risky but effective method of rapping on its side with a Mills Bomb.[21] Standing on the crest of the ridge, at the memorial to the action of the London Scottish on Halloween 1914, I have often compared 36th Division's sophisticated tactics with the Territorials' desperate fight three years before. In October 1914 amateur, barely trained soldiers armed with little more than rifles (defective rifles at that; they could only be used as single-shot weapons) fought from shallow trenches against German infantry who attacked with bands playing, in densely packed columns of men. The conduct of the war had changed dramatically in the 31 months that separated the two actions on Messines Ridge.

The Battle of Messines was a fine example of the methodical, set-piece, artillery-dominated battle. When Second Army's commander was ennobled after the war, he took as his title 'Plumer of Messines'. Not surprisingly, the army of the United States – which had entered the war in March 1917 – took a keen interest in this state-of-the-art offensive, issuing an edition of a British pamphlet on the battle.[22] Although the struggle was good as won during the first day, fighting, some of it very fierce, continued until 14 June. Moreover, German shelling caused heavy casualties among the British infantry crowded on the Ridge. British losses amounted to 25,000.

Critics have pointed out that the circumstances of the battle, in which mines which had taken months and years to dig played such a prominent role, made Messines a freak, 'one-off' action. This is, of course, correct, although as the action at Vimy in April and battles in the Ypres Salient in the autumn demonstrated, the basic artillery-dominated, set-piece battle was not dependent on mines for success. But Messines, successful as it was, could only be the first step towards breaking out of the Ypres Salient and seizing Roulers. On the second day of the battle Plumer, not unreasonably, told Haig that he could not get his artillery into position for a follow-up attack on the Gheluvelt plateau in less than three days. Haig chose to give the job to Gough, commander of Fifth Army, who spent more time than that just thinking about his options. Gough argued for a broad front attack, as he feared that otherwise success would simply result in a salient jutting out into German territory that would be difficult to hold. While this made a pleasant change from Gough's *modus operandi* at Pozières and Bullecourt, it gave the Germans a breathing space at a time when they were highly vulnerable to an attack following immediately on the heels of the first. Thus most historians have judged that Haig's failure to give Plumer his three days to prepare another operation was a mistake.

However, a recent book by a Canadian historian, Ian Malcolm Brown, has placed the debate in a new light. The study of supply and transportation, collectively known as logistics, has been deeply unfashionable among military historians. Many, myself included, have been guilty of making airy generalisations about the conduct of military operations without considering how troops were to be transported from point A to point B, and how they would be fed and supplied once they got there. Brown has pointed out that the preparations for Messines had been underway since late 1916, and that the attack took place only after three weeks of exhaustive efforts to get all the arrangements in place. His argument, based on a close study of the administrative records, is that the suspension of major operations 'was dictated by the need both to consolidate Messines's success and prepare a new battlefield, admittedly an adjacent one'.[23] That is not to say that Plumer should not have been given time to mount a *limited* attack on the Gheluvelt plateau. Given the clear state of crisis in the German forces immediately after 7 June, it might have achieved some success, although this approach would not have been free of risk. Ideally, a major, multi-divisional assault on a broad front should have been launched straight after the Battle of Messines; but for good logistic reasons, this was an impossibility.

The Third Battle of Ypres

Haig made two major mistakes in the planning for the Third Battle of Ypres. The first was to give the responsibility for the main attack to Gough and his Fifth Army rather than to Plumer's Second. This decision has been exhaustively debated. Haig's reasoning was probably that he thought that a breakthrough was achievable and thus the right man for the job was Gough, the thrusting cavalryman, rather than Plumer, the methodical infantryman. His second error was to send Gough confused signals about the task ahead. A cardinal principle of military command is that subordinates should understand the commander's intent. In Andrew Wiest's words, Haig 'hoped for a breakthrough but also understood the worth of a step-by-step attack to contribute to the wearing down of the German Army'.

Unfortunately, the commander of Fifth Army 'was not subtle enough to understand the dual nature of the offensive'. Haig offered Gough advice on the nature of the German defences and hinted that there should be a preliminary attack against the key ground on the right. He did not, true to his 'hands-off' conception of the role of commander in chief, give Gough a direct order. In the event, Gough chose to ignore the sensible advice he received from GHQ.[24] For the first day of the offensive Gough set ambitious objectives of 6,000 yards, which would carry the attackers to the German Third Position. In subsequent phases over succeeding days, he intended Fifth Army to break out of the Salient altogether.

If all had gone well with the operation, the breakout from the Ypres Salient would have been accompanied by an amphibious landing on the Belgian coast near Middelkirke. British 1st Division had been trained for this role and equipped with specially designed landing craft, and even special ramps to allow tanks to climb over the sea wall. This operation was certainly imaginative and ambitious, and was much better prepared than the Gallipoli landings two years before. Whether it would have worked in the face of opposition is debatable. What is clear is that the operation was an integral part of Haig's campaign plan for Third Ypres, not an optional extra. Not until the failure of the First Battle of Passchendaele on 12 October did Haig finally abandon his scheme for an amphibious landing.[25]

The Third Battle of Ypres, familiarly known from its last phase as 'Passchendaele', began on 31 July 1917. Nine divisions of Fifth Army mounted the central punch, with five divisions of Second Army on their right flank, and two French divisions on their left. Gough's left-hand formation was the Guards Division, which assaulted in the Boesinghe sector, with 1st French Division on their flank. The Guards faced an unusually difficult task, since the Yser Canal ran through No Man's Land to their front. Before the battle the Division had to find a way of crossing this waterway, which 'had a surface of about 70 feet of soft and tenacious mud into which a man sank like a stone, and a narrow shallow stream of water flowing down the middle'. In the event, the Guards devised an ingenious solution: canvas mats, fitted to wire netting and wooden slatted frames. The mats were wisely supplemented by light bridges built out of 'wooden piers with a foundation of petrol tins'. Two entire companies of the divisional pioneer battalion, 4th Coldstream Guards, were trained to lay the mats and bridges. In the event the Guards crossed the Yser Canal on 27 July, four days ahead of the main assault, and then built fourteen bridges across the waterway, allowing the Division to commence the battle on the 'German' bank. This attention to detail was the hallmark of the BEF's successful set-piece operations, circa 1917.

When the main attack began on 31 July, the infantry of the Guards Division was supported by a formidable creeping barrage, with a further standing barrage provided by heavy artillery, which 'lifted' to the east in conformity with the advance of the creeper and the infantry. The men of the Guards Division advanced two and a half miles on a frontage of just under a mile. Lieutenant Colonel Headlam, the division's historian, admitted that given the power of the German guns and the enemy's 'almost uninterrupted observation' over the battlefield, without comprehensive support from the Royal Artillery 'the task of the attacking troops might be too onerous a one – even for the Guards' – an admission indeed. This problem was common across the Ypres Salient where the Germans held the high ground. Significantly, both the divisional and corps commanders in their congratulatory messages to the Guards Division stressed that success was thanks to teamwork. Naturally, the infantry and artillery were praised, but so were the Royal Engineers, pioneers, Labour Companies, carrying parties, and transport drivers. The days of 1916, when infantry and artillery all too often attempted to fight battles more or less independently, were gone. By July 1917 it was clearly recognised that success depended on all the elements of the weapons system, which included the apparently humble 'humpers and dumpers', working together.[26]

Across most of the front, the Guards Division's tactical success was repeated to a greater or lesser degree, and for the same reasons: good artillery support, effective infantry tactics and all-arms co-operation.

But there were three significant problems that overshadowed the success of the day. The assault on the vital ground of the Gheluvelt plateau – the very area where Haig had advised preliminary attacks – resulted in gains of only 500 yards. Elsewhere, the attackers made good progress for the first mile or so because the Germans had chosen to defend their front line lightly, according to the principles of defence-in-depth. The *Eingreif* (counterattack) divisions had then struck the British troops, who were caught off balance. As Harington put it, 'The further we penetrate his line, the stronger and more organised we find him ... [while] the weaker and more disorganised we are liable to become.'[27] The advance halted, and in some sectors the British were even forced back. Fifth Army had been intended to advance some 6,000 yards on 31 July but even the relatively successful divisions, such as the Guards, had managed only half that distance. Gough's drive for objectives deep in the enemy positions had clearly failed. To cap it all, it began to rain and the ground turned to mud.

Mud will always be associated with Passchendaele, 'the campaign of the mud' as Lloyd George famously called it. The immediate effect of the deluge was to force operations to be halted on 2 August; the next major attack did not get underway until the sixteenth of the month, after some minor operations four days earlier. This action, the Battle of Langemarck (16–18 August), simply underlined that Gough's tactics were inappropriate for the circumstances. Gough failed to concentrate his artillery, and operations soon petered out into piecemeal line-straightening affairs. It was harking back to the dark era of the Somme. Fifth Army made a few gains at horrendous cost. In the terrible conditions of rain and mud, the BEF seemed to have lost the formula of Arras and Messines.

One area where the weapons system did work was near St. Julien (not far from the present day site of the memorial of the 'Brooding Canadian' at Vancouver Corner). Here, on 16 September, a combined infantry-armour attack captured some important German pillboxes, largely because the lumbering tanks were able to move along a road, rather than get bogged down lurching across fields. One tank did get stuck in the mud when it attempted to go off-*piste*. Fortunately, it bogged down with a six-pounder gun pointing in the direction of the door of the Maison de Hibou pillbox, with predictable effects. At another strong point, Cockcroft, at the appearance of a tank the garrison simply abandoned their post.[28] Yet this action contrasted strongly with the disappointing performance of Fifth Army as a whole.

It was not as if the methods of Messines had suddenly stopped working. While Fifth Army were floundering, in more senses than one, at Langemarck, some miles to the south the Canadian Corps demonstrated the importance of careful preparation and limited objectives. On 15 August the Canadians seized Hill 70 near Lens and held it after a fierce fight, tying down five German divisions in the process. On the last day of the Hill 70 battle Haig turned the assault at Ypres over to Plumer. Even after the battle had begun, Haig gave Gough hints and advice.[29] In turning to Plumer, Haig implicitly acknowledged the failure of Gough's ambitious but impractical methods, and returned to a tried and tested formula. By this stage the British had suffered nearly 70,000 casualties for meagre returns.

Second Army did not disappoint the commander in chief. Plumer asked for and was granted three weeks to prepare for the next battle. He used his time wisely. When he launched the Battle of Menin Road Ridge on 20 September, the infantry had rehearsed their attacks over and again. The artillery had devised an effective fire-plan; the engineers and logisticians had prepared a firm base for the offensive; and Second Army had a counter to the German tactics of flexible defence, which had been so successful on the first day of the campaign.

At 5.40 a.m. on 20 September 1917 the infantry went over the top protected by a ferocious barrage, 1,000 yards deep. Four divisions – 41st, 23rd, and 1st and 2nd Australian – were in the van, supported by seven divisions (five from Fifth Army) as flank-guards. The Germans were taken by surprise, and the British and Australian infantry, led by skirmishers with specialist teams of bomb throwers, Lewis gunners and rifle grenadiers behind, methodically dealt with German defensive positions.

The effectiveness of the flexible British infantry tactics was, from the German perspective, bad enough. Still more alarming was to discover that their *Eingreif* counterattack formations were neutralised by Plumer's new tactics. By limiting the advance of each British division to a mere 1,600 yards or so, the attackers would stay within range of their own artillery and machine guns. On reaching their objectives, they would halt, consolidate the captured positions, wait for the inevitable German counterattacks, and use firepower to break them up. This was bite-and-hold with a vengeance. The attackers bit a chunk out of the enemy position, held it against counterattacks, and then repeated the process. The German official history bemoaned that the *Eingreif* formations, ready to intervene in the battle at 8.00 a.m., could not get into action 'until the late afternoon; for the tremendous British barrage fire caused most serious loss of time and crippled the thrust power of the reserves'.[30] Moreover, one brigade in every British assaulting division was held back as a reserve and used to defeat counterattacks.

By the end of 20 September the attack had succeeded almost everywhere. It was, in the view of John Lee, who has made an in-depth study of the battle, 'a crushing victory in the main'. The BEF's morale, which had perhaps reached its nadir after Langemarck, 'soared after such a clear cut victory against an over-confident enemy'.[31] How can we account for the victory? Good weather was an example, for once in this campaign, of the bread landing butter-side up, but Plumer's meticulous preparations owed nothing to chance. Opposed by 750 German guns, the Royal Artillery once again proved to be a battle winner.

British guns at Menin Road Ridge, 20 September 1917

	Second Army	Fifth Army
Field guns	720	600*
Heavy guns	575	300*
Concentration of shells compared to 31 July	three times as great	twice as great

*Approximately

Source: Robin Prior and Trevor Wilson, *Passchendaele: The untold story* (New Haven: Yale UP, 1996) p.115.

Both Gough and Plumer deployed a formidable concentration of guns for an attack frontage of 5,000 yards each. However, mere possession of large numbers of guns and shells did not automatically translate into victory on the battlefield, any more than a group of talented club sportsmen automatically make a successful international team. At Menin Road the BEF used their artillery exceptionally effectively – an effectiveness matched by all the other elements of the all-arms team, not least the Poor Bloody Infantry.

The victory of 20 September 1917 was not bought cheaply. In many places, it was far from a walkover. As Robin Prior and Trevor Wilson have recently pointed out, the engagement cost the BEF 21,000 casualties for the gain of 5½ square miles, each square mile costing losses of 3,800 men. Gough's attack on 31 July had cost some 6,000 more men but gained more ground (18 square miles) at a cost of 1,500 casualties per square mile. Prior and Wilson's conclusion is that the success of Menin Road has been exaggerated and that the praise heaped on Plumer was the product of 'the diminishing expectations accompanying the campaign'. Gough had promised much but failed to deliver, while Plumer's more modest endeavour lived up to lower expectations.[32] This is an astute insight. However, although Menin Road gained less ground at proportionately higher cost, it had a more profound impact on the Germans than the operations of 31 July. On that day German defence-in-depth tactics worked successfully. At Menin Road, they did not.

Furthermore, the Battle of Menin Road was not an end in itself. Rather, it was the beginning of a remarkable series of offensives that brought the Germans close to defeat. Plumer delivered another hammer blow at the Battle of Polygon Wood (26 September) and then a third at Broodseinde (4 October). In both battles Plumer repeated the basic formula of Menin Ridge, with similar results. 'The advance up the slowly rising ridge to Passchendaele, once started, had to go on' recalled a corporal of 55th Division,

A fatigue party of the Guards Division crossing the Yser Canal on an improvised bridge, 31 July 1917. Careful engineering and logistic preparations helped to ensure that the first day of the Third Battle of Ypres was far more successful than the first day of the Somme had been, thirteen months earlier. IWM Q 5714

The field of Passchendaele in November 1917. In spite of the appalling conditions, the Canadian Corps demonstrated that, given careful preparation, it was still possible to capture ground. Historians, however, continue to debate the strategic wisdom of seeking to capture Passchendaele Ridge. IWM CO 2265

German troops in St. Quentin on 19 March 1918, two days before the beginning of Ludendorff's spring offensive, Operation Michael. Intended to win the war, Michael's failure actually hastened Germany's defeat. IWM Q 55479

The HQ of 1st Battalion Middlesex Regiment, April 1918. At this stage, the BEF was hastily relearning the techniques of mobile warfare, which called for different approaches from those that had evolved in the years of trench stalemate. IWM Q 6564

Generals Currie (left) and Pershing at Canadian Corps Headquarters. These two North American soldiers were, in rather different ways, among the most significant figures of the Hundred Days campaign of 1918. IWM CO 2601

A field dressing station at Quesnel, during the battle of Amiens, 11 August 1918. Even successful operations such as Amiens invariably took a heavy toll of 'friendly' casualties. IWM Q 7299

An Australian infantry platoon during the Hundred Days, 1918: the figure third from the left is carrying a Lewis gun. This photograph has come to symbolise the Australian military effort in the First World War. IWM E (AUS) 2790

American officers being trained in bombing and rifle grenade techniques at British XI Corps School. The BEF had an important role in training US troops on their arrival on the Western Front. IWM Q 222

Pershing's army in action: US 108th Field Artillery in the Argonne, 3 October 1918. The arrival of large numbers of American troops on the Western Front boosted British and French morale while having the opposite effect on that of the Germans. IWM Q 70711

Advanced Headquarters of Third Army, 28 September 1918. Like infantry battalions and artillery batteries, higher commanders and staffs rapidly adjusted to the conditions of mobile warfare in 1918. Here, Byng's HQ is located in a railway train near Bapaume. Note the camouflage netting. IWM Q 9813

Brigadier General J.C. Campbell VC addresses the men of 37 Brigade, 46th (North Midland) Division, on the Riqueval bridge, 2 October 1918. Three days earlier these men had successfully stormed this position, thus breaking the Hindenburg Line. IWM Q 9534

A motor convoy moving ammunition to Fourth Army troops near Bellicourt, 5 October 1918. This photograph gives some idea of the scale of the logistic effort needed to keep the BEF in supply during the mobile warfare of the Hundred Days. IWM Q 70709

The weapons system reaches maturity: artillery, New Zealand infantry and a Mark V tank near Bapaume, 25 August 1918. Bovington Tank Museum, 883/A5

Britain paid a terrible price for its victory in the First World War. Here, a woman and child, perhaps mourning the loss of a husband and father, examine one of the war memorials that permanently altered the landscape of post-war Britain. IWM Q 48871A

but troops were not going over every day, as on the Somme. Periodical thrusts of greater compass had come to pass, and the creeping barrage. No longer could Jerry lie low in his dugouts, or in this case his pill-boxes, and know that the lifting barrage was an almost infallible signal of our attack. You followed the creeping shells now, and pounced on him still dazed and bewildered. The Somme had not been without its lessons.[33]

The Germans responded by altering their tactics, ordering that the front line of defence be held more strongly. This gambit was unsuccessful and was soon reversed. Plumer's bite-and-hold operations were far from perfect, but they were successful. On 4 October the British had another slice of luck in that their attack began just as the Germans were preparing an attack of their own. British guns slaughtered German infantry crowded into forward trenches. Not surprisingly, a German official history described 4 October as 'the black day', while a German regimental history called it the most terrible day of the war so far.[34]

Modern German historians offer support for these contemporary judgements. One recently wrote that: 'Against the new British approach to the battle, the Germans could find no remedy; the recapturing of ground lost was impossible.' Another writes that the British attacks of 9 and 12 October, usually judged by British historians to be failures, 'produced a crisis in command'. Faced by mounting casualties – 159,000 men by this stage – and a precipitous decline in morale, one faction in German high command advocated limited withdrawal to force Haig to redeploy his artillery. Crown Prince Rupprecht, the local Army Group commander, even began to prepare for 'a comprehensive withdrawal' that would have entailed giving up the Channel ports, which, of course, would have fulfilled one of the major British objectives of the campaign at a stroke.[35] At this time German forces were still badly overstretched in fighting a war on more than one front. No sooner had the threat of the Russian 'Kerensky' offensives, launched on 1 July, been contained than Haig's offensive opened in Flanders. By the autumn of 1917 the German strategic position was not as grim as it had been in July–August 1916, but there was little margin for error.[36]

> For the first time in years, at noon on 4 October on the heights east of Ypres, British troops on the Western Front stood face to face with the possibility of decisive success ... Let the student ... ask himself 'In view of the results of three step-by-step blows [the battles of Menin Road, Polygon Wood and Broodseinde] all successful, what will be the result of three more in the next fortnight?'[37]

The author of these words was no apologist for high command; he was none other than Charles Bean, the Australian journalist and official historian, and scourge of British generals. Of course, we know that the Germans slid back from the abyss of defeat. The British campaign reached its highpoint at midday on 4 October 1917. A number of factors, including the return of bad weather, ensured that further stages of the campaign suffered from the law of diminishing returns. While we have perfect hindsight, Haig did not. Had he halted the entire offensive on the afternoon of Broodseinde, Haig would undoubtedly have been roundly damned by historians for failing to take advantage of the opportunities that presented themselves. In the event, he did decide to push on, with fatal consequences for his reputation.

Third Ypres is remembered as, in A.J.P. Taylor's graphic phrase, 'the blindest slaughter of a blind war'.[38] As a blanket condemnation of the campaign this is a travesty of the truth. Plumer's trio of victories brought the Germans to the verge of a serious defeat; 'near to certain destruction', as one German source put it.[39] As it was, the campaign inflicted appalling damage on the German army. German sources claim that fear of another Passchendaele – which, of course, was the third attritional battering the German army had endured at the hands of the BEF in eighteen months, with the British growing in military skill from action to action – added to the effects of the Allied blockade, prompted the Germans to launch their disastrous last-gasp offensive in spring 1918. While such claims may contain an element of special pleading, they have the ring of truth.

After 4 October Plumer became the victim of his own success in bite-and-hold operations as the problems of Arras resurfaced. Extensive engineering work was needed to get the guns forward over the lunar landscape created by the very bombardment that made success possible in the first place. In battle what is now called operational tempo is all-important. As historian Rob Thompson has commented, 'The timing of successive operations was crucial: too slow and the enemy recovers; too fast and the assault out-ranges its own artillery support.' The next action, the Battle of Poelcappelle, was launched on 9 October when preparations were far from complete. In appalling conditions produced by heavy rain, inadequate numbers of engineers and pioneers struggled to build and maintain wooden plank roads under shellfire. Infantry reached the start line for the attack only after an exhausting journey along duckboard tracks 'which eventually petered-out into waist-deep mud'. Among their many tasks, the sappers had to build gun platforms; otherwise artillery pieces (those that were not 'stuck uselessly on the blocked single-track roads further to the rear') sank into the mud. The result was that on 9 October the already exhausted infantry attacked with the support of a feeble barrage. Even before the Broodseinde battle of 4 October, forward communications in the Salient were showing strain. At the Battles of Poelcappelle and First Passchendaele (12 October) they disintegrated.[40]

Even after these failures, bite-and-hold was made to work. The Canadian Corps was now commanded by Arthur Currie, a Canadian-born pre-war amateur soldier, who was brought up to Ypres and tasked with capturing Passchendaele Ridge. Currie was unhappy at being given the job, but agreed that the task would be achievable, but only with careful preparation; and to achieve this he needed time and manpower. Granted both, Major General W.B. Lindsay, the chief engineer of the Corps, was able to create a workable communications system under the most difficult circumstances. Canadian sappers and pioneers built a plank road close to the front line, enabling ammunition and other vital supplies to be brought forward. 'The road was continually subjected to heavy shell fire' noted an after-action report, 'several direct hits being made on it and the work of the troops engaged on its construction is worthy of great praise.'[41] The Canadians made four attacks, on 26 and 30 October, and 6 and 10 November, securing Passchendaele Ridge at the cost of 16,346 casualties; Currie had predicted a loss of 16,000 men. Haig then halted the battle.

The objective of the last phase gave its name to the entire Third Battle of Ypres. In modern day Belgium, Passchendaele is famous principally for a type of cheese. In Britain, Australia, New Zealand and Canada, Passchendaele has become a symbol for all that is most awful about war in general, and the First World War in particular. The very name offers a grim pun − 'Passion Dale', the Calvary on which the flower of youth of the British Empire was nailed. 'I died in hell − (they called it Passchendaele)' runs a line of one of the most famous poems of the war.[42] Given that the name Passchendaele is loaded with so much emotional baggage, it is difficult, even after 80 years, for a British historian to examine the battle with detachment. Yet that is exactly what a number of historians have done. As a result, some myths about the battle can be laid to rest.

The first myth is that the battle consisted of 'mere blind bashing'. On the contrary, as Cyril Falls commented, 'Tactics were seldom more skilful'. In summarising Third Ypres as 'good tactics, bad ground' historian Andy Simpson introduces the other side of the problem.[43] Even here one can argue that if the weather had not been so wet, the peculiar geology of the Ypres area, which led to the rain producing mud of such spectacularly glutinous quality, would not have been a problem. Recent research has firmly debunked the idea that heavy rainfall could be expected in the area in August. On the contrary, British commanders, informed by the BEF's Meteorological Section (under Ernest Gold, a prominent meteorologist − another example of the appliance of science to warfare) 'could reasonably expect weather in Flanders which would be generally favourable to British plans'. However, the rainfall in the autumn and early winter of 1917 was abnormally heavy.[44] There is a famous story that Kiggell, Haig's chief of staff, on seeing the battlefield for the first time tearfully cried out: 'Good God, did we send men to fight in that?' This unsubstantiated anecdote poses all manner of problems if it is to be accepted at face value. The underlying implication, that Haig and GHQ were unaware of the state of conditions at the front, is simply untrue.[45] That is not to argue, however, that Haig was justified in continuing the offensive after the clear failure of the Battle of Poelcappelle.

Today, Passchendaele is a quiet backwater. Standing just outside the village, among the graves in Passchendaele New British Cemetery, one's eyes travel across the ground the Canadians attacked over in November 1917. A mere seven or so miles in the distance the town of Ypres is clearly visible. The juxtaposition of death and short distances is stark. For me, this place, more than any other on the Western Front, poses the question: was it worth it? Standing on the ground where so many lives were ended and so many dreams destroyed it is difficult to make a judgement unclouded by emotion. But the objective answer is surely 'yes'; at least, this is true of the period from 7 June until 9 October 1917. During this time there was a real possibility of gaining important strategic objectives. That is the true justification for the campaign. To defend the campaign by arguing that the BEF was obliged to attack to divert German attention from the mutinous French armies is less convincing; senior French commanders were not enthusiastic about the bold nature of Haig's plan for a breakthrough.

After Poelcappelle, the continuation of operations becomes much more difficult to justify. The capture of Passchendaele Ridge only made sense if it was used as the jumping-off point for a renewed attack, but there was no enthusiasm for carrying out a major, fresh offensive until the new year. By the spring of 1918, however, the Allies had been forced onto the defensive. The exposed British positions on Passchendaele Ridge were indefensible and, in the face of a major German assault in Flanders, Plumer took the sensible and morally courageous decision to abandon much of the ground captured the previous autumn.

Finally, it comes down to a question of attrition. The question of which side suffered the higher casualties remains deeply controversial, but Richard Holmes's recent suggestion of a compromise figure of 260,000 for each side seems about right.[46] Given the smaller population base of Germany compared to the Allies (who were about to lose the Russians but had gained the United States), in crude terms this figure worked in the favour of the Entente. The other factor to be considered was the impact of attrition on morale. In the short term the fighting spirit of both the German and British armies recovered from Third Ypres. In the longer term Passchendaele probably had a greater impact on German morale than that of the British. In this sense, the full fruits of Haig's 1917 Flanders campaign did not become clear until the victorious autumn of 1918.

Cambrai: The Return of Mobility

Second Passchendaele demonstrated the BEF's mastery of the set-piece, bite-and-hold offensive. It also demonstrated its limitations. But just as the BEF appeared to have reached a tactical dead end, several more elements were added to the weapons system. These were to allow the British army not merely to break *in* to the enemy positions, but then to break *out* into the countryside beyond. Mobility, in short, returned to the battlefield. The first test of this newly improved weapons system came at the Battle of Cambrai, just ten days after the Canadian Corps launched the last of its attacks on Passchendaele Ridge. On the surface, it must have seemed that the British and German armies were exhausted, incapable of making another major effort. If nothing else, the operations at Cambrai demonstrated the amazing resilience and powers of recuperation of the armies on the Western Front. Even more significantly, Cambrai demonstrated that the scales of tactical advantage, for so long weighted in the defender's favour, were now at last tipping towards the attacker.

General Sir Julian Byng's Third Army carried out the attack. The initial plan had evolved since it was first mooted. Brigadier General Hugh Elles, commander of the Tank Corps, saw the Cambrai sector as an area where armoured operations would be possible. The terrain was not ideal, as it contained many water-obstacles, but it was far better suited to tanks than the Ypres Salient. Preliminary ideas that the offensive should take the form of a large-scale tank raid, to 'put the wind up the Boche', as Byng phrased it,[47] were pushed to one side as the plans grew steadily more ambitious. Haig saw the Cambrai operation as an opportunity to salvage something from his 1917 campaigns. From the perspective of London, the BEF's efforts that year had resulted in gains that were as meagre as they were Pyrrhic. A success in this sector brought up the possibility of penetrating the Hindenburg Line and even capturing the key rail junction of Cambrai itself. In the event III and IV Corps attacked, with the Cavalry Corps in reserve.

The Battle of Cambrai is remembered as the first action in which tanks were used *en masse* to launch a powerful, concentrated punch. Third Army fielded 476 tanks, including 98 support tanks loaded with supplies. Cambrai 'heralded the new era of mechanical warfare' wrote a soldier-author in 1942, 'the scope of which is only becoming apparent in the present war'.[48] While such a claim is not entirely unjustified, the attention given to the success of the tank has masked another, and arguably more significant innovation used for the first time at Cambrai. This was a 'predicted' bombardment. Previously the artillery's preparations for an offensive had sacrificed surprise. Guns had been pre-registered by firing preliminary or 'ranging' shots at targets to get the range. As Andy Simpson explains, previously gunners had

lacked the accuracy to set [the] range, direction and trajectory [of shells] by assessing the target's position on the map relative to theirs and making allowances for the idiosyncrasies of the gun or howitzer and its ammunition and for the effect of other factors, such as wind speed and direction. By November 1917, it had been realised that each artillery piece varied slightly, and so they were calibrated against a standard before issue. By the same token, batches of ammunition also had variations, and these too could be allowed for. This meant that no ranging shots were required and so the number and positions of the guns could be hidden from the enemy far more easily. And improvements in mapping meant that the relative positions of gun and target on the map were now accurate.[49]

These developments meant that a long 'Somme'-style pounding of the enemy positions was unnecessary. No longer was the artillery seeking to destroy the enemy positions; its goal now was merely to cut the barbed wire and force the German infantry to keep their heads down while the attackers crossed No Man's Land. These objectives were less ambitious than those of 1916 but more achievable. The days of believing that 'artillery conquers, infantry occupies' had gone. Artillery was now functioning as an effective part of an all-arms team.

'Artillery and secrecy do not seem to go hand in hand,' Byng reflected while lecturing to the officers of the Canadian Corps. Third Army took steps to hide the gun positions. 'We learned more about camouflaging in that fortnight before the battle than we ever thought of before,' Byng admitted later. He went further, dispensing with a preliminary bombardment altogether: the guns only opened up when the infantry and tanks crossed the start-line. The new artillery tactics, along with security measures such as moving troops and tanks by night, enabled surprise to return to the battlefield.[50]

The first phase of the Battle of Cambrai was a spectacular success. At 6.20 a.m. on 20 November 1917, 1,003 guns opened up on the German positions and British infantry and tanks began their advance. On reaching their objectives, the tanks crushed barbed wire obstacles beneath their tracks and crossed trenches with the aid of wooden bundles (fascines). The Germans were heavily outgunned – they had only 150 artillery pieces on this sector – and by nightfall the British had pushed forward up to five miles on a frontage of about six miles. Once again, careful training paid off in the form of effective co-operation between the tanks and infantry. One major check was experienced on the front of 51st (Highland) Division, not, as often alleged, because of poor tactics adopted by its commander, Major General Harper, but because of the peculiarly tough defences, which included an anti-tank battery, at Flesquières village.[51] The Germans held Flesquières as a bastion of resistance, which prevented the British from securing the vital objective of Bourlon Wood.

Thus far, Cambrai was an example of another mostly successful bite-and-hold operation. Like the mines at Messines, the massed tank assault had introduced another novel element into a successful formula. But the offensive had more ambitious aims than Messines or Menin Road. The cavalry were supposed to attack through the gap created by the initial assault. By the time the attackers reached the St. Quentin Canal it was getting dark, and the cavalry operations were limited in scale and achieved little. Yet cavalry remained the only viable instrument of exploitation. Of the 476 tanks that began the operation, only 297 were still 'runners' at the end of the day. The majority of the mechanical casualties had broken down rather than been disabled by enemy fire.

Bourlon Wood was the scene of fierce fighting in subsequent days, but the battle had now degenerated into an attritional struggle. Worse, on 30 November the Germans launched a counter-offensive that prefigured the methods that were to be used with great effect in their 1918 spring attacks: surprise, a short artillery bombardment, stormtroops, low-flying aircraft. The British were pushed back, losing much of the ground captured in the initial assault. Byng and other generals, in assessing the reasons for the debacle, were critical of defensive tactics and the discipline and training of their troops.[52] There was undoubtedly something in this, although Third Army was also at fault for failing to pick up the signals of an imminent counterattack. The Battle of Cambrai, in sum, achieved little of lasting value, but it clearly demonstrated that warfare was changing. Both the British and German armies had developed a weapons system that under the right conditions was capable of breaking the tactical deadlock.

In some respects the situation of the British army at the end of 1917 was remarkably healthy. Building on the experiences of the Battle of the Somme, the BEF had developed an assault technique that could be highly effective, although at a prodigious price in British lives. Technology had been harnessed to tactics, and a robust and increasingly flexible infrastructure had been created to sustain Haig's armies in battle. Morale had taken a battering but had recovered. Command was still presenting some problems, but even here there were signs of improvement. Tactics, however, can no more be divorced from their strategic context than war can from politics, and the growing sophistication on the battlefield must be set against the background of a wider crisis. It was to be the Germans, not the British, who took the offensive early in 1918.

CHAPTER 9

1918: VICTORY ON
THE WESTERN FRONT

The 'March Retreat' of 1918 is remembered as one of the worst defeats in the history of the British army. After four years of deadlock, in their spring offensive the Germans used innovative new artillery and infantry tactics to break through the trenches of the British Fifth Army and reopen mobile warfare. Fifth Army lost large numbers of men and guns captured, and was forced into headlong retreat. Fuelled by inaccurate newspaper reports, the rumours of disasters on the battlefield were given credibility by the Prime Minister, David Lloyd George. In a speech to parliament on 9 April 1918, Lloyd George cast some aspersions on the performance of Fifth Army and its commander, General Sir Hubert Gough, who had been sacked on the eighth day of the battle. In Gough's bitter words, 'All were ... clear that the real cause of the retreat was the inefficiency of myself as a general, and the poor and cowardly spirit of the officers and men.'[1] But this traditional picture is deeply flawed. Fifth Army was not defeated as badly as some have claimed. Overall, the German spring offensives failed, and their failure represents a British defensive victory.

At the end of 1917 the Germans were presented with a rare window of opportunity to win the First World War. Russia, beaten on the field

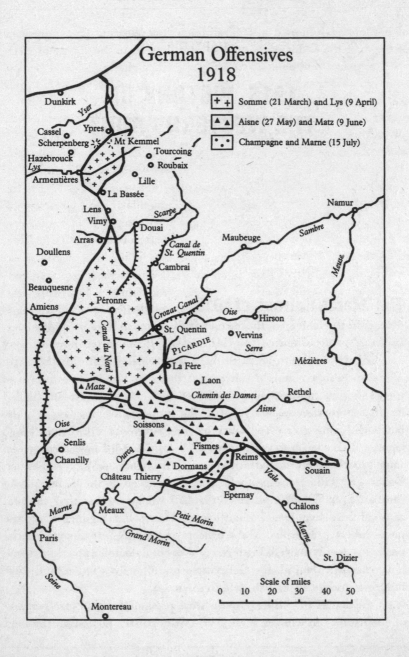

of battle, had collapsed into revolution, thus releasing large numbers of German troops for use on the Western Front: in the spring of 1918 the Germans could deploy 192 divisions, while the French and British could only muster 156. The German policy of unrestricted submarine warfare, introduced at the beginning of the year, had backfired disastrously. Not only had it failed to knock Britain out of the war by cutting her vital Atlantic lifeline, it had prompted the United States to enter the war against Germany. As yet, the vast American war machine was still gearing up for action. Substantial numbers of American troops would not reach Europe until the middle of 1918. The German commanders, Hindenburg and Ludendorff, had no desire to sit on the defensive and risk repeating the battering the German army had received at the hands of the British at Passchendaele in 1917. They decided to stake everything on one last gamble: to strike in the West and defeat the British Expeditionary Force and French army before the Americans could intervene with decisive numbers. Ironically, the fateful decision was taken at a meeting held at Mons on 11 November 1917. Exactly twelve months later the war ended, in great part as a consequence of the decision taken on that day.

On 21 January the plans were finalised. Operation *Michael* was an attack on the British, whom the Germans correctly identified as the most dangerous of the Allied forces, in the Somme–Arras sector. Three German armies were to be employed either side of St. Quentin. Opposite Byng's British Third Army in the Arras area was von Below's Seventeenth Army, while to their south, covering the Flesquières Salient (created as a result of the Cambrai battles at the end of 1917) and the northern portion of Gough's British Fifth Army, was von der Marwitz's Second Army. Both German formations belonged to Crown Prince Rupprecht's Army Group. Facing Gough's southern sector was von Hutier's Eighteenth Army, of the German Crown Prince's Army Group. Broadly, the plan was to crack open the British defences and push through into open countryside, then wheel to the north and strike the BEF's flank. Then further attacks could be launched. In the initial stages of the offensive, von Below and von der Marwitz were to capture the old 1916 Somme battlefield before turning north to envelop Arras, while von Hutier was to act as a flank-guard, dealing with any French forces that emerged from the south, and offering support to von der Marwitz's forces.

The attackers had several advantages over the British. First, numbers. In spite of having greater reserves than the Germans, the British were now suffering from a manpower crisis that had forced divisions to be reduced from twelve infantry battalions to only nine. Haig was forced to make hard choices about where to deploy his divisions. Miscalculating the weight and axis of the German offensive and misled by German deception operations, Haig deliberately left his southernmost Army, Gough's Fifth, weak.[2] Haig correctly calculated that he could afford to give ground in the Somme area, while to yield territory further north would have been catastrophic. A short advance in the Ypres area, for instance, would have brought the Germans to within striking distance of the coast, which would have imperilled the entire British position. Thus Gough had only 12 divisions to defend 42 miles of front, although he faced 43 German divisions. Byng by contrast had 14 divisions on a 28-mile frontage against 19 German divisions. In the *Michael* area, the Germans had 2,508 heavy guns against only 976 – a 5 to 2 advantage. Haig gambled on Fifth Army holding out against heavy odds. 'Never before had the British line been held with so few men and so few guns to the mile; and the reserves were wholly insufficient.'[3]

The second German advantage was in 'fighting power'. For most of the war, the morale, tactics, and weapons of the two sides were roughly equal. But in March 1918, in terms of tactics, they were not. In the previous two years of almost constant offensives, the BEF had become highly effective in the art of attack. While much play has been made of German 'stormtroop' infantry tactics and 'hurricane' artillery bombardments used on 21 March 1918, in truth there was little for the BEF to learn from their enemy in this respect. Fighting on the defensive, however, *was* a novelty, especially because the British had introduced a new concept of defence-in-depth, modelled on the German pattern. In place of linear trenches, defensive positions consisted of Forward, Battle and Rear Zones, utilising machine gun posts and redoubts. But in many cases, lack of time and labour meant that the Rear Zone was never constructed. Also the concept was misunderstood at various levels. Although the Forward Zone was intended to be lightly held, to do little more than delay the attacker and force him to channel his attack where it could be more easily broken up in the Battle Zone by artillery, machine gun fire and local counterattacks, as many as one third of British infantry were pushed into the Forward Zone. 'It don't suit us,' opined a grizzled veteran NCO. 'The British Army fights in line and won't do any good in these bird cages.'[4]

At 4.20 a.m. on 21 March the 'Devil's Orchestra', conducted by Hutier's innovative head gunner, Colonel Bruchmüller, began the overture to the offensive.

It was still dark on the morning of March 21st [1918] when a terrific German bombardment began – 'the most terrific roar of guns we have ever heard' ... The great push had started and along the whole of our front gas and high-explosive shells from every variety of gun and trench mortars were being hurled over. Everyone [in 54th Brigade] realized that the great ordeal for which they had been training and planning for weeks was upon them.[5]

Bruchmüller's gunners hammered the British defenders to the full depth of their positions. Five hours later, assisted by a dense fog, the infantry assault broke on the battered and disoriented British defenders. By the evening, the situation was critical. The BEF had lost 500 guns and suffered 38,000 casualties, and the Germans had captured the Forward Zone almost everywhere. Worse, in the extreme south Hutier had broken through Gough's Battle Zone, forcing British III Corps to retreat to the Crozat Canal. Yet even on the first day of the *Kaiserschlact*, the 'Imperial battle', the British had achieved a modest, but nonetheless important success: they had denied the Germans their first day objectives.

German Seventeenth Army's attack on Byng's relatively strong and well-dug-in Third Army achieved far less than had been intended.

Similarly, German Second Army had failed to achieve the break-through they had sought. All this was at the cost of 40,000 German casualties. These were caused partly by clumsy tactics and relentless attacking, but also by the British seizing the initiative at a local level. These acts of resistance ranged from 18th Division's counterattack at Baboeuf on 24–25 March, to the action of a Lewis gun team of 24th Royal Fusiliers, led by two NCOs, who went forward to delay the enemy advance on their sector.

22 March saw the renewal of the offensive. British XVIII and XIX Corps fell back, in part as a result of confusion among the British commanders. Third Army was still holding its Battle Zone but was now being outflanked as Fifth Army was pushed back. To the south, von Hutier's Eighteenth Army had advanced more than twelve miles, and this led Ludendorff to make an important error. He was painfully aware that the offensive was not going according to plan. He complained of the lack of progress of von Below's army on 22 March, which had a knock-on effect on Second Army. Ever the opportunist, on 23 March – the day that saw the Germans capture the Crozat Canal – Ludendorff decided to make Hutier's army the point of main effort. Hutier's Eighteenth Army had originally been given the role of flank-guard, but now, accompanied by Second Army, it was to attack west and southwest to drive a wedge between the BEF and the French. Von Below's Seventeenth Army and German forces further north were to push back the British. Any Staff College would criticise this plan as breaking two of the fundamental principles of war: to select and maintain the aim and to concentrate force. The resistance of the British defenders had led Ludendorff – whose grasp of strategy and operational art was tenuous at best – to change his plan on the hoof. Now, the Germans were dispersing their force rather than concentrating it, with disastrous effects.

Nevertheless, the next few days were grim ones for the BEF as the Germans continued to advance. A British soldier wrote on 23 March that 'we had to make a hasty retreat with all our worldly possessions – every road out of the village was crowded with rushing traffic – lorries, limbers ... wagons, great caterpillar-tractors with immense guns behind them, all were dashing along in an uninterrupted stream ...' He could even look back with affection on normal army rations: 'I never thought in the days when we looked with disdain on "bully" and biscuits I should ever long for them and cherish a bit of hard, dry biscuit as a hungry tramp cherishes a crust of bread.'[6] On 27 March Gough was removed from command of Fifth Army. He probably deserved this treatment for the way he handled his offensives of 1916 and 1917; it was Gough's bad luck to be sacked for a defensive battle that he conducted with some skill.

Even at this stage there were glimmerings of light for the Allies. On 26 March the crisis led to the appointment of the French general Foch as Allied Generalissimo, to co-ordinate the activities of the Allied forces. This averted the threat of the French concentrating on defending Paris while the British watched their lines of communications. Moreover, Byng's Third Army decisively defeated the next phase of the German offensive, Operation *Mars*. On 28 March nine German divisions attacked north of the Scarpe river. The attackers used much the same methods as had proved so successful on 21 March. But this time they were attacking well-constructed positions without the benefit of fog. The British forces were numerically stronger and conducted a model defensive battle.

In the light of the completeness of the German failure Ludendorff ordered the assaults against Third Army to halt – he had no taste for an attritional battle. His appreciation was shared by an officer of German 26th Division, who wrote in his diary on 28 March of his hope that if German 'operations north and south of us succeed the enemy will also have to give way here': having seen the British defences he feared heavy casualties if ordered to attack.[7] *Michael* was not, however, quite dead, and a few spasms of offensive action remained. Ludendorff now scaled down his objective to that of taking Amiens. But even this was beyond the German troops. They were halted ten miles short of their goal on 4–5 April at Villers Bretonneux, by Australian and British forces. On the same day Byng was again attacked, and again the Germans were thrown back. By this stage Ludendorff the gambler was prepared to throw in his hand. On 5

April he called off the *Michael* offensive and prepared to renew the attack further north.

What had Ludendorff achieved? At the cost of 250,000 casualties, including many of his stormtroops, the sixteen days of battle had captured a large salient some forty miles deep, which as the events of the summer were to show, was extremely vulnerable and difficult to defend. The BEF, especially Fifth Army, was badly battered, but was far from defeated. The French and British armies had not been driven apart. Had the Germans succeeded in converting their operational 'break-in' to the BEF's positions into a 'breakthrough', they could well have won the war.

Fighting returned to Flanders on 9 April. In Operation *Georgette*, German Sixth Army struck out for the key British-held rail junction of Hazebrouck. Just as the *Michael* offensive had taken place in part on the old 1916 battlefield of the Somme, *Georgette* was fought over the battlefields of spring 1915. Today, a splendidly maintained Commonwealth War Graves Commission cemetery containing the remains of many Indian soldiers killed at Neuve Chapelle lies a few hundred yards from a Portuguese cemetery. On 9 April 2nd Portuguese Division was directly in the path of the German offensive. A century earlier Wellington had described the Portuguese as the 'Fighting Cocks' of his army, but in April 1918, poorly trained and officered, low in morale and under strength, their successors did not stand a chance. Today, the Portuguese graves, neglected and overgrown, stand in sad testimony to an unequal fight. The Portuguese were pushed aside and the Germans advanced some 3½ miles.

Thereafter what the British called the 'Battle of the Lys' reverted to the pattern familiar from the earlier fighting further south: furious German attacks and stubborn British resistance. The vital defensive action of 55th (West Lancashire) Division south of the initial German break-in is a case in point. As on 21 March, fog enabled the German attackers to get close to the British without being seen. But the commander of this division, Major General Jeudwine, had trained it in new methods of defence, and his efforts paid off handsomely. The garrisons of outposts fought on even when surrounded, 'and local counterattacks, conducted with splendid initiative and energy by Company, Platoon and Section Commanders on the spot, soon resulted in the re-capture of all the ground occupied, together with a large number of prisoners and machine guns'. Between 9 and 13 April, 55th Division fought a tenacious battle, at one point losing a key position, Route A Keep, only to recapture it, and then hold it. This was 'a stiff fight', to adopt the understated language of the divisional history, which succeeded in sealing off the southern flank of the German advance: the attackers ploughed on ahead, but could not fan out to the south.[8] 40th Division carried out a similar role on the northern flank of the Germans, while reserves moved to bar the path of the attackers.

On 9 April 1918 the 230 heavy guns of German Sixth Army had been opposed by only 200 of British First Army. On the following day, German Fourth Army enjoyed an even greater advantage when it attacked slightly to the north, against British Second Army: 240 guns to 105. Both sides were suffering from the strain of the fighting of the previous weeks. Three British divisions in the front line had already taken a battering in the fighting in Picardy, and Haig was critically short of reserves. The Germans, in turn, were forced to attack using a high percentage of non-elite 'trench holding' divisions. The attackers seized Armentières and gained about three miles. Subsequent attacks forced Plumer to abandon Messines and Wytschaete, taken at such cost in 1917. The situation seemed so grave that on 11 April Haig issued an Order of the Day:

Many of us are now tired. To those I would say that victory will belong to the side which holds out the longest ... There is no course open to us but to fight it out. Every position must be held to the last man: there must be no retirement. With our backs to the wall and believing in the justice of our cause each one of us must fight on to the end. The safety of our Homes and the Freedom of mankind alike depend upon the conduct of each one of us at this critical moment.[9]

This is a remarkable document. For Haig, of all men, to make such an emotionally charged appeal is a clear demonstration of the appalling strain he was experiencing, facing the brutal reality of defeat in the near future.

Three inter-related factors saved the British Expeditionary Force on the Lys: the fundamental flaws in German military methods and operations; the tenacity of the defenders; and the arrival of Allied reserves. Essentially similar factors had contributed to the failure of the *Michael* offensive. The German assault infantry suffered heavy casualties as they advanced, and some units used extraordinarily clumsy tactics. On 30 March Ludendorff ordered that 'the idea of compelling success by the *employment of masses of troops* must be absolutely eradicated. This merely leads to unnecessary losses. It is fire effect which is decisive, and not numbers.'[10] Unfortunately the German artillery, so successful in the initial stages, became progressively less effective as the infantry moved forward. As the British had discovered at Ypres in 1917, moving the guns forward over shell-cratered ground was a difficult and laborious task. This problem was compounded by the fact that Ludendorff rejected the careful bite-and-hold approach. Attacks, he ordered in January 1918, must not follow the pattern of previous British assaults, which trusted to 'the efficacy of their skilfully worked out but rigid artillery barrage' that 'carr[ied] forward the infantry attack, which advanced without any impetus of its own'. Instead, German divisions must 'by skilful tactical leading, preserve its fighting strength, so that divisions are capable of carrying out offensive battles of several days duration and entailing a considerable advance'.[11] Moreover, it took much time and effort to shift the 'battering train' of artillery from one sector to another, slowing the tempo of operations and granting the Allies valuable time to recover between German offensives.

Previous battles on the Western Front had offered ample testimony to the problems of exploiting initial success. Nevertheless, the German high command gambled on succeeding where all previous efforts had failed, and left on the Eastern Front a mass of cavalry which would certainly have been useful in the West, once the zone of barbed wire and trenches had been overcome. Although Ludendorff recognised (at least in principle) the importance of getting artillery forward, what this approach meant in practice was that the German infantry in the second and subsequent days of an advance had to rely on their own resources, not concentrated artillery fire, to get forward against defenders who could call on massive firepower. German stormtroop tactics had merely shifted the advantage enjoyed by the defender from the initial phase of the assault, the break-*in* battle, to the subsequent break-*out* phases. As we will see, when the BEF went on to the offensive later in the year they did not make the same mistakes.[12]

Haig's 'Backs to the Wall' order had hit upon the key to victory: standing firm. The German tactics would succeed only if the initial blow shattered the cohesion of the defenders so comprehensively that the stormtroopers had little to do but mop up what was left. By fighting stubbornly, the British bought time for reserves to arrive. Foch, the new Allied generalissimo, took a calculated gamble on the staying power of the British, keeping divisions in hand should the Germans launch another offensive. Foch had been impressed by the stamina of British Regulars at First Ypres in 1914; his faith that the British citizen soldier of 1918 would prove as resilient was justified. For all that, the Battle of the Lys was a critical moment which could easily have ended in a disastrous defeat for the BEF.

Even while the spring battles were in progress, fingers were being pointed at the state of morale of Fifth Army. Military morale was to be a significant factor in deciding the outcome of the war in 1918, so it is worth examining this question in some detail.[13] The heavy losses of 21 March, and the circumstances in which they occurred, which included large-scale surrenders of British troops, cannot be brushed aside. There is much evidence that morale was low in some cases – the question is, how low? The nineteenth-century Prussian military thinker Karl von Clausewitz differentiated between soldiers' mood and soldiers' spirit.[14] Mood was transient, and could change from day to day or even minute by minute, depending on whether an individual was wet or dry, warm or cold, hungry or fed. Spirit was something very different. It was quite possible for a unit to have good military spirit yet be full of grumbling, whingeing men. In March 1918 British soldiers had much to moan about. Only four months had passed since the gruelling attritional struggle around Passchendaele had ended. The army was short of men, which meant more work for everyone. A number of battalions had just been disbanded, leaving groups of disgruntled men to be absorbed into remaining units. The need to work on the defensive lines meant that the 'rest' periods of the infantry were too often spent on hard manual labour.

On his return from the Western Front in January 1918 General Smuts produced a report for the War Cabinet which categorically affirmed that the morale of the BEF was sound. This view was confirmed by a report based on the censoring of 84,000 soldiers' letters, covering the April–July 1918 period. The report frankly stated that the units of Fourth Army (as Fifth Army had been renamed) could not be described as 'happy': they were war weary, and cynical about politicians and senior officers. But Clausewitz would have approved of their morale. Fourth Army's 'combative spirit' was still 'very high'; the ordinary soldiers were determined 'to stick it to the end'.[15]

Not every soldier fought to the last round. Many stragglers headed for the rear at the beginning of the battle, but they seem to have been mostly non-combatants. By mid-March no fewer than 68,000 men were working on the defensive positions, including 12,000 Italians, 5,000 Chinese, 10,000 POW and 4,500 Indians. The Fifth Army's Deputy Provost Marshal reported that on 21–22 March few fighting troops became stragglers, and they 'were chiefly those who were genuinely lost and anxious to rejoin their Units'. Surviving statistics indicate that the worst period for stragglers came in the period 27–30 March, at least six days after the initial German assault, when sheer exhaustion would have been a major factor.[16]

The numbers of British soldiers taken prisoner, some without putting up much of a fight, is strongest evidence for a collapse of morale on 21 March 1918. The total of 38,000 British casualties sustained on that day included no less than 21,000 prisoners — one of the largest mass surrenders in British military history. Perhaps even more significant was the loss of about 500 guns to the Germans, because when an army loses its artillery, it is generally a sign it is on the verge of collapse. But as Martin Middlebrook has commented, poor British defensive tactics distort the picture. By cramming 27 battalions into the Forward Zone, Fifth Army effectively offered them up as sacrifices. Once the German infantry had got behind their positions, the defenders, seeing no point in useless sacrifice, chose self-preservation. Some men fought on until an inspirational commander was killed, and then they surrendered. This happened to the 16th Manchesters, who defended Manchester Hill until the death of Lieutenant Colonel W. Elstob, who was awarded a posthumous Victoria Cross for his part in the action. Other officers surrendered their commands. One, Lieutenant Colonel Lord Farnham of 2nd Royal Irish Rifles, satisfied his honour by obtaining a note from his German captors which said that his unit had put up stiff resistance before surrendering.[17]

The importance of the surrenders of 21 March must not be exaggerated. If Fifth Army's morale had been uniformly poor, the Germans would have taken all their objectives on the day – which they failed to do. If the morale of Fifth Army had indeed collapsed, the Germans would probably have won the First World War.

After his failure to break through on the Lys, Ludendorff, continuing his theme of strategic opportunism, once again turned his attention to the south. Attacks towards Amiens (24 April), on the Aisne (27 May) and the Matz (9 June) followed the now familiar pattern: initial success, which diminished as the attackers advanced and resistance stiffened, ending in the restoration of stalemate. In all cases the Germans gained some ground but they signally failed to achieve a decisive victory against the defenders. In many ways their limited successes left them worse off than they had been before. They had multiplied their supply problems and their new positions were vulnerable to counterattack. And, of course, the casualties increased alarmingly. The German army was becoming an increasingly fragile instrument. There had been some worrying signs of indiscipline as Germans captured vast British supply dumps and stopped to loot, 'according to taste' wrote one German officer on 28 March, 'the coloured picture-postcard, the silk curtain, the bottle of wine, the chicken or the cow, but in most cases the wine'.[18] For

German soldiers, who had suffered so many years of shortages, to see with their own eyes the abundance of British supplies did nothing to maintain morale.

The immense casualties suffered by the German army in the spring offensive undoubtedly contributed mightily to its eventual defeat in the autumn of 1918. This has led historian Tim Travers to argue that 'to a considerable extent the German army defeated itself through its own offensives from March to July [1918], because these offensives led to excessive casualties due to poor tactics, and because ... [German high command] employed an unwise strategy that did not maintain its objectives'.[19] There is much to be said for this view, but armies do not really defeat themselves. In spring 1918 stubborn resistance by Allied soldiers inflicted those enormous losses on the attackers; the French army took on their share of the hard fighting, especially opposing the Aisne offensive which carried the Germans to within forty miles of Paris. The Germans, by attacking in so reckless a fashion, improved the Allies' chances of defeating their offensives. For all that, the failure of Ludendorff's spring 1918 offensives was not preordained. In terms of sheer scale these battles rate as the greatest British defensive victories in history, for victories they were. Winston Churchill was by no means an uncritical admirer of British generalship in the First World War, yet he argued that 'contrary to the generally accepted verdict [on *Michael*], I hold that the Germans, judged by the hard test of gains and losses, were decisively defeated.'[20] Churchill wrote these words in the 1920s, but at the beginning of the twenty-first century the defeat of the 1918 German offensives remains a forgotten victory.

For a month, from the end of the Matz offensive in mid-June 1918, an uneasy stalemate fell over the Western Front until on 15 July the Germans tried yet again, this time launching a major attack on the Marne. The previous German offensives had failed because they ran out of steam. On this occasion, the Allies counterattacked and inflicted a heavy defeat on the Germans. The counterblow was launched on 18 July by General Mangin's French Tenth Army, which included 1st and 2nd US Divisions, who acquitted themselves well. British and Italian forces also participated in this truly Allied victory. The French employed tanks *en masse*, in the style of Cambrai. As a German source admitted, the Second Battle of the Marne was 'a great strategic success for Marshal Foch'.[21]

Thus at the end of July 1918 the strategic situation was radically different from that of the early spring. The Germans had launched offensive after offensive which had damaged the Allied armies but failed to destroy them. They had gained great swathes of territory in the form of untenable salients with large, vulnerable flanks, and taken enormous losses in the process. After the failure of the Marne offensive, the strategic initiative had clearly passed to the Allies. The best the German high command could hope for was a renewal of the stalemate that had existed before 21 March.

For the Allies the picture was altogether brighter. They had weathered the storm, resisted the worst that the Germans could throw at them. The BEF was battered but far from broken, and its depleted ranks were hurriedly filled by fresh young conscripts who blended with veterans of earlier campaigns to produce a winning combination of enthusiasm and experience. Above all, American troops were flooding across the Atlantic. By the end of September, thirty-nine US divisions had arrived in France, each roughly double the size of its French or British equivalent. At Cantigny on 28 May, 1st US Division had carried out the AEF's first attack of the war. Five weeks later, on Independence Day, American troops were to participate in a small-scale action that nevertheless rates as one of the most significant of the entire war.

It took 4th Australian Division only an hour and a half, on 4 July 1918, to capture the village of Hamel, taking 1,470 prisoners. The attackers, who, despite the reluctance of the American CinC, General Pershing, to sanction their use, included four infantry companies from US 33rd Division, sustained losses of fewer than 1,000. By the end of July, Fourth Army staff had drawn up a study of the battle that was disseminated throughout the BEF – itself testimony to good staff work – which highlighted the reasons for the success. First, the painstaking staff work in planning the operation, not least the maintenance of secrecy that enabled the achievement of surprise. Second, the fine performance of the individual arms: the

Australian and American infantry, the British tanks, and the British and Australian artillerymen. Third, and perhaps most importantly, 'the excellent co-operation between the machine gunners, artillery, tanks, and RAF'.[22]

Lieutenant General Sir John Monash, who since May 1918 had been the commander of the Australian Corps, had devised the plan. Monash was on the face of it an unlikely figure to attain high command in the BEF. He was not a professional soldier − in peacetime he was a civil engineer − and he was Australian-born, of German-Jewish origin. Yet during the course of the Hundred Days he emerged as an outstanding commander who enjoyed the confidence of both Haig and Rawlinson. Monash believed that

a modern battle plan is like nothing so much as a score for a musical composition, where the various arms and units are the instruments, and the tasks they perform are their respective musical phrases. Each individual unit must make its entry precisely at the proper moment, and play its phrase in the general harmony.[23]

Obviously, this is an idealised vision of battle, and what Clausewitz described as 'friction' would get in the way of a note-perfect performance, but British operations in the Hundred Days did tend to follow this pattern. The bad old days of 1915 and 1916, of infantry and artillery fighting what amounted to separate battles, were long past. The BEF's weapons system had reached maturity.

The phrase 'weapons system' should not be taken to mean that the BEF had devised a foolproof 'blueprint' for victory. As we will see, things could and did go wrong. One key element of the weapons system was the use of heavy concentrations of artillery. At Hamel, the Australian Corps could call on 326 field guns and howitzers and 302 heavy pieces, with yet more guns in support on its flanks − firepower took the place of manpower. In some later, more mobile operations, artillery was less important and a greater emphasis was placed on the fighting skills of the infantry. In others, the Hamel pattern of withholding a massive bombardment until the moment of the infantry assault was dropped in favour of longer artillery preparation. In essence, the BEF's weapons system amounted to little more than using all available elements as part of an all-arms team: but that in itself was a considerable achievement. The British army, having initially been confused by the new conditions of warfare, had by July 1918 tamed the new technology and worked out effective ways of harnessing it. The BEF proved highly adaptive and innovative in mastering a Revolution in Military Affairs. Quite how successfully was to be demonstrated at Amiens, a little over a month after Hamel.

Amiens

Amiens marks a true turning point on the Western Front. On 8 August 1918 the Australian and Canadian Corps of Fourth Army attacked German positions east of the city. To the north, British III Corps acted as a flank-guard, while a French corps served a similar function to the south. The attack was planned as an essentially limited operation, a larger scale version of Hamel (although Haig had pushed for more distant objectives during the planning stage), and it achieved complete surprise. The attackers advanced up to eight miles, the longest single advance achieved on the Western Front in one day. Fourth Army's casualties amounted to 9,000 − heavy enough in terms of human misery but amazingly light given the magnitude of the military achievement. The Germans lost about 27,000 men (including 12,000 prisoners) and 450 guns. Impressive as these statistics are, they do not tell the whole story. Amiens was truly a watershed battle, the turning point of the war.

The first clue to the decisiveness of the battle lies in the number and nature of the German losses. These casualties were particularly significant because the loss of substantial numbers of prisoners and, especially, guns is usually the mark of a major defeat. This need not have been immediately terminal for the Germans − it had not proved so for the British on 21 March 1918 − except for one fact. Amiens not

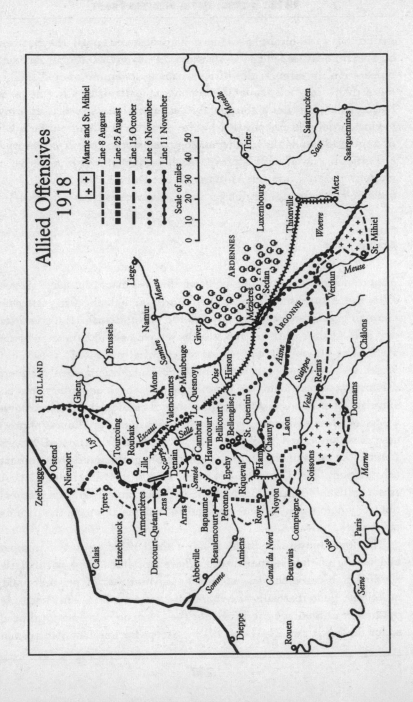

Allied Offensives
1918

Marne and St. Mihiel
Line 8 August
Line 25 August
Line 15 October
Line 6 November
Line 11 November

Scale of miles
0 10 20 30 40 50

Moselle
Saarbrucken
Saarguemines
Trier
Saar
Metz
Thionville
Luxembourg
Woevre
St. Mihiel
ARDENNES
Meuse
Sedan
Verdun
Liege
Meuse
Mézières
ARGONNE
Namur
Givet
Hirson
Aisne
Suippe
Brussels
Sombre
Oise
Reims
Châlons
HOLLAND
Maubeuge
Le Quesnoy
Vesle
Dormans
Ghent
Mons
Valenciennes
Bellenglise
Laon
Marne
Tourcoing
Roubaix
Escaut
Cambrai
Havrincourt
St. Quentin
Chauny
Soissons
Zeebrugge
Lille
Selle
Bellicourt
Ham
Ostend
Lys
Scarpe
Denain
Sensée
Epehy
Riqueval
Noyon
Compiègne
Nieuport
Armentières
Péronne
Roye
Ypres
Lens
Bapaume
Oise
Hazebrouck
Drocourt-Quéant
Arras
Beaulencourt
Canal du Nord
Beauvais
Seine
Calais
Abbeville
Amiens
Somme
Paris
Dieppe
Oise
Rouen

only struck a crushing blow against the troops of German Second and Eighteenth Armies, it had a similar impact on the morale of Erich Ludendorff. Shortly after the war, Ludendorff wrote that:

> August 8th was the black day of the German army in the history of the war. This was the worst experience I had to go through ... August 8th made things clear for both army Commands, both for the German and for that of the enemy.

'Having gambled recklessly and often ineptly with the fortunes of the German empire for two years', Ludendorff decided that 'it was suddenly time to leave the game'. Ludendorff had clearly suffered an enormous psychological shock, perhaps even a nervous breakdown. He offered his resignation to the Kaiser, who rejected it, while agreeing with Ludendorff that 'the war must be terminated'.[24] Ludendorff's collapse contrasts sharply with the ample mental reserves on which Haig and Foch were able to draw at the darkest moments of the German spring offensives. Although pessimism ebbed and flowed in German high command for the remainder of the war, at best they believed that they could hold out for some sort of compromise peace. They recognised that an outright, crushing victory over the Allies was no longer a realistic possibility. Millennia ago, the Chinese strategist Sun Tzu emphasised the importance of deception and psychological aspects in achieving victory.[25] By judiciously combining this approach with a thoroughly Clausewitzian belief in applying overwhelming combat power, in August 1918 Haig achieved what for early twenty-first century military leaders has become the glittering prize: psychological dominance over the enemy commander.

How sophisticated the BEF had become by the middle of 1918 is shown by the odyssey of the Canadian Corps. At this time it was the strongest and freshest formation in the BEF. Based around Arras, its sudden appearance on the Amiens front would be a clear indication to the Germans that a major offensive was about to take place. As a result, an elaborate security and deception plan was put into operation, which included two Canadian battalions being left in the north to simulate the presence of the entire Corps by the use of false radio traffic. Immediately prior to the battle, aircraft flying up and down the front masked the noise of tanks moving up to the start line. By such means, and the advances in artillery techniques first demonstrated at Cambrai, an element of surprise was achieved. The Australian 57th Battalion was certainly taken in. 'A few officers and NCOs went to the front line to view the ground,' reported an Australian infantryman. 'They returned round-eyed with wonder. The woods on the right were full of Canadians. Canadians? We thought they were at Arras.'[26] More importantly, a map prepared for Crown Prince Rupprecht's Army Group, dated 8 a.m. on 8 August, shows that Germans also believed that the Canadian Corps was still concentrated around Arras. Surprise was complete.[27]

This had several important consequences.[28] The German positions about to be attacked were weak, held by understrength divisions of no more than about 4,000 infantry, about 37,000 men in all. With no inkling that they were about to be attacked, there was little enthusiasm for speeding up the desultory strengthening of their positions, let alone the creation of new ones in the rear. Neither did the Germans reinforce this sector. The complacency of the German commanders rendered the psychological impact of the BEF's assault all the more impressive. Above all, surprise denied most of the defenders the opportunity to fight back in an effective fashion. The first they knew about the attack was when, at 4.20 a.m., masses of Canadian, Australian, British and French infantry came into view, supported by 552 tanks, and the world exploded about them.

Out of 1,236 guns and 700,000 shells available to the BEF, 700 artillery pieces fired 350,000 shells during the Amiens battle. Perhaps even more remarkable than the number of guns available was the accuracy of their fire. No fewer than 504 out of 530 German guns had been identified before the attack. The Royal Artillery had 450 heavy guns available for counter-battery work, each with sufficient ammunition to fire four rounds every minute for four hours. The British gunners killed or drove off their German counterparts, leaving the guns to be captured by the advancing infantry. Deprived of artillery support, the German infantry were at a huge disadvantage when faced by tanks and Dominion infantry, largely untouched by enemy artillery fire, debouching from the early morning mist.[29] 'Whenever we found ourselves in trouble,' an Australian infantryman recorded, 'we signalled to the tanks, and they turned towards the obstacle. Then *punk-crash, punk-crash*! ... another German post was blown to pieces.'[30] Some of the defenders stood and fought and were overrun. Many did not.

German problems certainly played a role in the Allied victory. Many positions were weak and formations under strength, and the morale and tactics of many of the defenders were poor. The skill and high morale of the attacking Dominion infantry was another important factor, as was the overwhelming advantage in numbers. Canadian divisions rivalled those of the Americans in size. Whereas British and Australian divisions deployed about 7,000 infantrymen, the four Canadian formations fielded at *least* 12,000 bayonets each, giving Fourth Army an infantry strength of around 100,000 (as against 37,000 German troops). Other factors, such as the efficiency of the BEF's logistic support and the domination of the air by the RAF and the French air arm (albeit at heavy cost), were also important.[31] However, Prior and Wilson are surely correct in emphasising that it was the BEF's weapons system that was the battle winner: 'the Germans, however parlous their circumstances, were defeated by superior firepower tactics, which even their best troops could not withstand.'[32]

It is important to give credit to the BEF, and not just the Canadian and Australian Corps, for the effective use of this weapons system. Until the 1990s, writing on Amiens often emphasised one or other of the Dominion Corps while giving scant credit to other units.[33] This approach is misleading and ignores the nature of a weapons *system*. The infantry were important, but so were the guns, the vast majority of which were operated by British soldiers, as were all of the tanks. The Canadian and Australian infantry were undoubtedly elite, but as we shall see, part of the significance of the BEF's way of battle lay in the fact that it enabled even average infantry to achieve feats that would have seemed miraculous only a year before.

The First Fifty Days

Tactics had unlocked the static front at Amiens and made the possibility of conducting mobile operations a reality. Ever since the onset of trench warfare in late 1914, operations had largely been in abeyance as far as the Allies were concerned. Until the tactical stalemate could be broken, there was little possibility of achieving success on a broader scale. By 1918 both the Germans and the Allies had the means of restoring mobility to the battlefield. The question was how the Allies would respond to this thawing of the Western Front.

In spite of the dramatic nature of the initial advance, the Battle of Amiens in many respects followed the pattern of previous battles. Like the first day of Arras, initial success became more difficult to exploit as impetus ran down on subsequent days and resistance grew stronger. The German offensive of March–June 1918 had exhibited the same characteristics. They had advanced much further, up to forty miles, but were just as unsuccessful in breaking clean through the enemy and destroying them. Even the most successful offensives, Allied and German, had done little more than push back the defending army, battered but essentially intact. For a brief time it looked as if Haig and Foch were going to insist that Rawlinson carry on bashing away at Amiens, an effort which would have undoubtedly suffered the fate of all previous attacks. In the end both men were persuaded otherwise. This time things were different.

Already reeling from Amiens, on 21 August the Germans were faced with a major offensive slightly further north. The Battle of Albert (21–31 August) saw Byng's Third Army attack over the old 1916 Somme battlefield. On 22 August, Fourth Army attacked on Byng's right; four days later First Army assaulted around Arras, on Third Army's left (later this action was designated the Battle of the Scarpe, 22–30 August). On the night of 26/27 August, the Germans began to pull back, abandoning their conquests of the spring in the Somme area, aiming to anchor their position on the Hindenburg Line. In doing so, they uncovered the flank of the German forces in the salient created during the Lys fighting in April. Since 23 August Birdwood's Fifth Army had been carrying out relatively small-scale operations in this area. A combination of British pressure and events further south had by 6 September forced the Germans to abandon the Lys battlefield.

Having caught the defenders off balance, two more blows ensured that the Germans were unable to regain their equilibrium. The River Somme might have been an excellent defensive position for the Germans, but the Australian Corps (Fourth Army) forced their way across the river. On 31 August, 2nd Australian Division stormed and captured the formidable Mont St. Quentin position. This was the key to the city of Péronne, which fell to the Australians on 1 September. Even by the high standards of the Australian Imperial Force, this was an impressive operation. Further north, on 2 September the other major Dominion formation, the Canadian Corps, broke through the Drocourt-Quéant line. With their major forward defensive positions now untenable, the Germans were forced to order another retreat, this time back to the Hindenburg Line. Between 12 and 26 September the British, following up, fought a series of actions in the outer reaches of this formidable defensive position. The battles of Havrincourt and Epéhy, as they became known, were essentially preliminary operations, manoeuvres to gain a favourable start line for a major assault on the Hindenburg system of defences itself. Thus by the end of September the Germans had been forced back to the jumping-off point for the March Offensive. They were back to where they had started.

The BEF were, of course, not the only Allied army to take the offensive in this period. The French had also been attacking, although somewhat sluggishly – understandably enough, given what the French army had been through in previous months and years. In sharp contrast to the battle-weary French troops and commanders, Pershing and his American forces were eager to conduct their first operation as an independent army. This took place on 12 September with a successful assault against the St. Mihiel salient. The Americans were fortunate in that they attacked just as the Germans were pulling out, but it was an important victory. It announced that the ground troops of the United

States were now a force to be reckoned with – a message that brought hope to her Allies, and deepened the gloom in Germany.

In the fifty days from the beginning of the Battle of Amiens until 26 September, Haig's army had advanced about 25 miles on a front of 40 miles. In comparison with the tortuous progress made in offensives in earlier years, this was an impressive achievement. The success had not been easy. As a New Zealand officer wrote of the Somme fighting:

> The enemy had indeed been retiring, but his movements had up till this time been conducted in a great measure deliberately, with marked skill and in good order. His rearguards had offered fight on positions carefully selected to give the greatest scope to well placed machine guns supported by field artillery. The successive lines occupied were independently organised and sufficiently far behind one another to prevent troops who had carried the first from overrunning the second with their initial impetus ... The German rearguards had displayed resolution and had repeatedly sacrificed themselves. Fighting for time, the enemy had in many cases forced from us more of that precious asset than we were disposed to yield, and he had maintained unbroken a screen behind which he had withdrawn his guns and main force.[34]

In the first fifty days of British offensives Haig's army had sustained 180,000 casualties. Judged by the callous arithmetic of battle, in terms of ground gained and victories achieved, these actions were considerably more cost-effective than the Somme or Passchendaele.

Could the BEF have achieved more in the first fifty days in return for the high human cost? Edmonds, the British official historian, while recognising that Haig's lack of operational reserves made it difficult to exploit success, nevertheless criticised the caution shown by many British commanders, particularly their unwillingness to push too deep into enemy positions for fear of presenting a flank vulnerable to counterattack. 'As a whole,' Edmonds wrote, the operations resembled a 'line of advanced guards, which went on until the enemy resistance stiffened.'[35] This criticism, while it contains a grain of truth, is largely unfair. The commanders of 1916 can be condemned for setting their men targets they could not achieve. In 1918 the same men avoided repeating this mistake in the new situation of mobile offensive warfare.[36] The basic circumstances of the Western Front had not undergone a fundamental change. The German line was still intact and continuous, if only just. The 'force-to-space' ratio remained dense – that is, armies continued to be packed into a small area. Newer constraints on the BEF's operations included political pressure to keep down the casualty lists, and also the knowledge that Britain was hard put to keep Haig's divisions up to strength. This was not the time to take unnecessary risks with men's lives. In any case, constant pressure, through small-scale operations up to divisional strength, also played an important role in wearing away German combat power and morale.

The Birth of Operations

Another major factor inhibiting operations in 1918 was the state of available technology, which simply did not allow the type of sustained deep penetration manoeuvres that the *Wehrmacht* and the Red Army were to carry out in the Second World War. The Mark V tanks of 1918 were certainly improvements on those of 1916, but they were still slow and lacked range and reliability. As in 1916, tanks were still essentially one-shot weapons and cavalry was the only credible instrument of exploitation. By the beginning of the Second World War, technological advances were in place that gave tanks and armoured cars greater reliability and enhanced range. Moreover, infantry and artillery could be mechanised to allow them to keep up with the armour. Twenty years of military developments made it possible to convert the semi-mobile warfare of the Hundred Days into the *Blitzkrieg* of Guderian and Rommel and the Deep Battle of Soviet generals Tukhachevsky and Zhukov. Although Soviet theorists of the 1920s and 1930s derided the four months it took the Allies to drive the Germans back sixty miles, in the Hundred Days the BEF used methods not dissimilar to the Soviet principles of operations. The British operational method was based on experience and pragmatism rather than theory: but it was nonetheless highly effective.

In the Hundred Days, then, the BEF, like the Germans in their offensives earlier in the year, could only mount a large-scale and sustained advance at the pace of a marching infantryman or a team of horses dragging a field gun. This meant that the defenders could maintain a more or less continuous front and were simply pushed back, not shattered and dispersed. Unlike the Germans, the BEF came to recognise the limitations imposed on them and operated within them, fighting on a broad front, and 'sequencing' a series of shallow battles rather than persevering with futile attempts to fight deep battles of penetration. What the BEF avoided was the temptation to push too far in one direction. The result was that although there was no single spectacular breakthrough followed by encirclement and destruction of a major German force, continuous pressure kept the front in motion, forcing the Germans back, never giving them time to catch their breath and regroup, all the while inflicting heavy losses in terms of men, materiel and morale. The German army was like a man trying to plug holes in a leaky dam. Every time he patched up one section of the dam, water would burst through somewhere else.

As before Amiens, for the Canadian Corps' (First Army) attack on the Drocourt-Quéant (D-Q) line on 2 September, the BEF deployed the panoply of techniques that would become familiar in the Second World War to deceive the Germans as to the venue of the attack. These, and operations by Third and Fourth Armies further south, diverted German reserves away from the crucial area. The attack itself was carried out on a narrow frontage with the support of no less than 762 guns and howitzers. In these operations 20,500 tons of ammunition was used, more than at Amiens but in a shorter time. As a contemporary report commented, 'the gunners may truthfully be said to have spent almost the entire eight days of August 26 to September 2 firing with one hand and hauling ammunition with the other.'[37] Once the infantry and artillery cracked open the German defences, exploitation forces were pushed through. Because the Canadians were employing the technology of 1918 rather than that of 1945 the exploitation was rather shallow; indeed, an attempt to push armoured cars and cavalry into the enemy rear was not a success. Overall, however, the D-Q operation was, as Niall Barr contends, 'strikingly modern'.[38]

Abundance of artillery was the key to the British victories in the second half of 1918, just as outrunning their artillery support had been a primary reason for the eventual failure of the German offensives of the earlier part of the year. Unlike the Germans in the spring, the BEF was able to maintain the pressure because it was not reliant on a massive artillery battering train that had to be moved up and down the front. Instead, the British had sufficient guns to be able to rely far more on artillery integral to divisions and corps.

Depending so heavily on artillery made tactical sense but placed a huge burden on the BEF's logisticians. During the attack on the Hindenburg Line, in a twenty-four hour period from 28–29 September 1918, British gunners fired 943,947 shells – a record for the Western Front.[39] Sir Eric Geddes' reforms on the lines of communication bore ample fruit in 1918. Not only were the BEF's logistic services able to survive the March Retreat, they then rose to the task of supplying an army on the advance. Two points are particularly worthy of note. Unlike the German offensives, and for that matter some Allied offensives of previous years, the Hundred Days operations were sufficiently limited in scope to be logistically sustainable. That did not mean they were unambitious: rapidly switching the point of attack from one Army sector to another was no light undertaking, and neither was moving the Canadian Corps south for the Battle of Amiens and then returning it north to fight around Arras. The BEF's operations were ambitious but achievable. Challenges that in 1916 would have been beyond the capability of the BEF's logisticians, and in 1917 would have posed huge problems, were managed in autumn 1918 with relative ease. Although by the Armistice its supply lines were badly stretched, the BEF was capable, after a pause for resupply, of continuing operations.[40] In logistics, as in tactics and so much else, during the Hundred Days the British army was at the peak of a learning curve.[41]

The Grand Offensive

As September 1918 neared its end the German army was barely holding its ground. In four days of battle at the end of the month a co-ordinated series of Allied offensives were to bring the Germans to the edge of defeat. Foch and Haig shared the honours in planning the Grand Offensive. Foch's initial vision was fairly limited, but Haig urged a more far-reaching attack and won him over.[42] From then on, Foch's motto was *Tout le monde à la bataille!* ('Everybody into battle!'). Over four days a sequence of blows were to ripple along the German defences, following the by now familiar pattern of the BEF's offensives. The Americans and the French were to attack first, on 26 September, in the Meuse-Argonne area. This caused an inter-Allied dispute, Pershing resisting Foch and Haig's suggestion that he abandon his cherished plan for an attack on the St. Mihiel salient and instead attack to the north-west, which would fit in with Haig's vision of concentric Allied offensives. Eventually, the compromise was for the St. Mihiel operation to go ahead but then for the US forces to redeploy some sixty miles to attack in the Meuse-Argonne area, a decision which presented the AEF's logisticians with an administrative nightmare. British Third and First Armies were to be the next into action, attacking on 27 September in the direction of Cambrai. On the following day a newly created Army Group commanded by King Albert of the Belgians, which included French divisions and Plumer's Second Army, would begin a push in Belgium. The final blow would be that of Rawlinson's Fourth Army and French First Army, due to begin on 29 September.

The Meuse-Argonne offensive was a bludgeoning match reminiscent of the Somme in 1916 (see pages 253–6). The Americans and French ground forward slowly — although this term is relative; they still gained three miles on the first day — 'fixing' and inflicting further losses on the Germans. The British strike on 27 September was more successful. The highlight was the crossing of the Canal du Nord by Currie's Canadians, who once again launched a set-piece attack to devastating effect. Employing a heavy and sophisticated artillery fire plan, the infantry assaulted on a narrow front and on the far bank spread out like the fingers of a hand. Thanks to their foresight in creating a large body of sappers, the Canadians were uniquely well placed to cope with the many engineering tasks, including building bridges over the newly captured canal. Currie's plan was 'audacious', but it worked: 'the Canal du Nord was his operational masterpiece ... [his plan] incorporated risk and maneuver [sic].'[43]

In Flanders, King Albert's Army Group made spectacular progress on the first day of their offensive, breaking out of the Ypres Salient in a single day and driving beyond Passchendaele Ridge. On the following day (29 September) British Second Army recaptured Messines Ridge. This was a psychological as well as a physical barrier: 'It is such a relief,' commented Plumer, sentiments that were no doubt echoed throughout his divisions.[44] Despite the initial success, which carried the Allies forward about nine miles, logistics forced the French and Belgian forces to halt to regroup for two weeks. Nonetheless, the Fifth Battle of Ypres broke the deadlock in Flanders.[45]

Foch and Haig gave the toughest job in the Grand Offensive to Rawlinson's Fourth Army. Building on its successes in the battles of Havrincourt and Epéhy, its objective was the *Siegfried Stellung* in the area of St. Quentin.[46] Its British name, the Hindenburg Line, was misleading because it was not a single position but rather consisted of a belt of six lines of defence, including the St. Quentin Canal, which was up to 35 feet wide and 50 to 60 feet deep. This was impassable to tanks and formed a daunting barrier to an infantry assault. There was one area of potential weakness, relatively speaking, where part of the canal ran through a tunnel for three and a half miles north of Bellicourt. Although the area was strongly defended, this was where the Australian Corps, reinforced by the US 27th and 30th Divisions, was to launch the main attack.

After assessing the strength of the defences, Rawlinson and the Australian commander, Monash, opted for a methodical two-day artillery bombardment, surmising that it was hopeless to achieve surprise because it was so obvious where the attack would take place.

The Australian-American attack on 29 September encountered some difficulties. Monash's plan was complicated and the Germans fought well. The defenders were aided by the strength of their defensive positions, and were particularly effective in anti-tank work. The US 27th Division, fearing that some of its men from a previous attack were still alive in No Man's Land, denied themselves a creeping barrage for the first part of their assault. The results were predictable. An after-action report by a unit of 27th Division concluded that:

> It is agreed by all observers that this great distance [1,000 yards] between troops and barrage was in a large measure responsible for the severe punishment received by our first waves, this because there were many enemy machine gun nests and outposts in the dead space between our troops and barrage. Also because enemy opposition had too much time to reorganize after the passing of the barrage.[47]

The Americans had been set a very difficult task and, like the BEF two years earlier in much the same area, paid the bitter price of inexperience. By the end of the day, the Australian-American assault had achieved only partial success.[48]

It was a very different story further south. The commander of IX Corps, Lieutenant General Sir Walter Braithwaite, carried out in his Bellenglise sector a very different type of operation. He relied on the Amiens method of a surprise bombardment, to be followed by an infantry assault, by 46th (North Midland) Division, straight across the canal. The attack frontage of the infantry was only 3,000 yards, yet 216 heavy guns were concentrated in support, 'more', as Jackson Hughes has recently commented, 'than were used along the entire 13 miles of frontage of the Somme assault of [1 July] 1916'. It was not, however, simply a matter of having more guns, but of using them in a sophisticated fashion. The combination of surprise, good intelligence (thanks in part to captured documents), accurate and heavy bombardment, and effective infantry tactics carried 137 Brigade across the canal. The Staffordshire infantry stormed a bridge at Riqueval before the German pioneers could blow it up. Others crossed the water using life belts from Channel steamers. 137 Brigade's action broke the deadlock on the Australian Corps front by outflanking the German defences.

46th (North Midland) Division was a Territorial formation with a patchy combat record. It had done spectacularly badly on the First Day on the Somme, and even in September 1918 it was not an obviously 'elite' formation. It was, however, a thoroughly competent outfit, which speaks volumes about the quality of even the average divisions of the BEF in 1918. The Territorials' feat of breaking the Hindenburg Line also says a great deal about the effectiveness of the BEF's weapons system against defences far stronger than those at Amiens, and the failure of the Australian-American attack is testimony to what happened when infantry, no matter how brave or skilful, were deprived of artillery support.

The net results of the Grand Offensive were impressive. The sequence of attacks across the Western Front made it impossible for the defenders to respond, as so often had happened in the past, by moving divisions to plug a breach in the line: all were already committed. Instead, Fourth Army's success (the final outwork of the Hindenburg Line fell to Rawlinson on 4 October) triggered a German retreat on almost the entire British front. Third, First and Fifth Armies as well as Fourth benefited from this admission of defeat by the Germans. The BEF had at long last broken free of the battlefields of 1915–17 and had entered open country. As after Amiens, the German defeats had a traumatic effect on Ludendorff. On 28 September (that is, even before Fourth Army's success) he heard that German's ally Bulgaria was suing for peace. This news, added to that from the Western Front, shattered his confidence in victory, and he informed Hindenburg that Germany must ask for an armistice.[49] Like Amiens, the Grand Offensive was a psychological as well as a physical victory.

Enter the Americans

The American and British armies shared a common strategic heritage. Before the First World War, both were essentially colonial gendarmeries. Whereas the British experience was of Africa and India, Americans learned to soldier on the Western frontier and latterly in places such as the Philippines, Cuba and Central America. Just within living memory, the US army had fought in a very large war indeed – the Civil War – but after 1865 the huge armies had been dismantled and the experience of fighting large-scale conventional war had been pretty much forgotten. John J. Pershing was as experienced as any American soldier in 1917, but his background was in small wars and what today would be referred to as counter-insurgency. In the 1890s he had fought against the 'Ghost Dance' uprising, the last major rebellion of Native Americans, and in 1898 he had had a taste of more conventional operations in Cuba during the Spanish-American War. Pershing's last major assignment before being appointed to command the American Expeditionary Force was taking 11,000 men – the largest force he had ever led – in pursuit of Pancho Villa, a Mexican bandit. Like the previous experience of his British counterparts, this was of questionable value as preparation for command of a mass army on the Western Front.

Pershing was unimpressed by the tactical methods of his British and French allies. He believed that they had led to a diminution of their spirit of aggression, with trench fighting leading to the possession of ground becoming the main focus of attacks. 'Black Jack' was convinced that this had caused some commanders to forget that 'the real objective was the enemy's army', and 'to bring about a decision, that army must be driven from the trenches and the fighting carried into the open'. Furthermore, Pershing believed that trench warfare could be broken:

It is here that the infantryman with his rifle, supported by the machine guns, the tanks, the artillery, the airplanes and all auxiliary arms, determines the issue. Through adherence to this principle, the American soldier, taught how to shoot, how to take advantage of the terrain, and how to rely on hasty entrenchment, shall retain the ability to drive the enemy from his trenches and by the same tactics, defeat him in the open.[50]

The order in which Pershing lists the elements of the battle is interesting. Many European commanders of 1914–15 would have agreed with Pershing's views, but they had failed dismally to translate desire into fulfilment. The bloody battles of subsequent years had taught the British and French the severe limitations of the infantryman and they had moved towards the integrated all-arms approach. Pershing's tactical ideas were a throwback to a discredited way of fighting, compounded by a lack of appropriate training. Liddell Hart commented that Pershing 'thought that he was spreading a new gospel of faith when it was actually an old faith exploded . . .'[51]

The results were disastrous for the AEF. The parallels between the American offensives of 1918 and the BEF on the Somme are unmistakable. In both cases enthusiastic citizen soldiers launched clumsy, frontal assaults; in both cases the inexperience of commanders and staffs was all too evident. General von Unruh, the chief of staff of German IV Reserve Corps, noted that at Château Thierry and Belleau Wood in June 1918 he saw 'young regiments coming on in masses, exactly the same as earlier in the war I had seen the Russians advance' – although he was impressed by the 'volume of fire' produced by American artillery.[52] William A. Francis of the 5th US Marines took part in one of those attacks, and left a graphic account of an attack at Château Thierry in June 1918, which could have been written by a member of Kitchener's Army on the Somme two years earlier:

We had a wonderful [creeping] barrage from our artillery, which was falling only a few yards in front of us, all the time we were advancing . . . After we made it to the top of the hill the Germans opened up with their machine guns, hand and rifle grenades and trench mortars. Just then we all seemed to go crazy for we gave a yell like a bunch of wild indians and started down the hill running and cursing in the face of the machine gun fire. Men were falling on every side, but we kept going, yelling and firing as we went. How any of us got through the murderous machine gun fire the Germans were putting up I will never be able to figure out ... On this little hill were at least eight hundred dead men and several hundred wounded.[53]

Some American divisions were of high quality, among them the 2nd, a joint Army-Marine formation, and the 32nd and 42nd (Rainbow) divisions of National Guardsmen.[54] Generally, though, the AEF's allies and enemies were critical of American tactical performance, as indeed were some of the AEF's own reports. A German assessment of the Meuse-Argonne offensive stated bluntly that: 'The American Infantry is very unskilful in the attack. It attacks in thick columns, in numerous waves echeloned in depth, preceded by tanks. This sort of attack offers excellent objectives for the fire of our artillery, infantry and machine guns.'[55] Ironically, given Pershing's obsession with the rifle, German reports indicate that some Americans taken prisoner had only the scantiest of training with their primary weapon, an assessment confirmed by the AEF's own reports.[56]

Many of the AEF's tactical problems can be put down to sheer inexperience. In their attack on the Hindenburg Line while operating as part of British Fourth Army, US 108th Infantry Regiment neglected mopping-up operations, with the result that German machine gunners bypassed by the initial waves were able to fire on American stretcher bearers.[57] This is the sort of mistake that the BEF had learned not to make as a result of the Somme, and no doubt many of AEF's errors would have been corrected in time for the spring campaign of 1919, had it occurred. Likewise, the weakness in battlefield leadership and staff work would have been rectified by experience. Nevertheless, Pershing was culpable in two respects: in his tactical doctrine and in his reluctance to allow comprehensive 'amalgamation'. The latter was the idea of allowing US units and formations to serve under British or French command. Pershing, determined to command an American army in the field, fiercely resisted this proposal, fearing that the AEF would simply be used as piecemeal reinforcements for Pétain and Haig. From the perspective of the long-term national interest of the United States, Pershing was undoubtedly correct, but his reluctance to accept temporary amalgamation, to allow American units to take advantage of the experience of the Allies, was a mistake that may have cost American soldiers their lives. The AEF did not need to work out the details of flash spotting and sound ranging, for instance; the British and Canadians showed them how to do it.[58] Yet Pershing distrusted the advice given by French and British instructors, whom he regarded as peddlers of trench warfare dogma, and refused to accept more help in training from those quarters.[59]

Up to a point, Pershing was justified in wishing to concentrate on open warfare rather than trench fighting. His mistake was ignoring the careful battle techniques that had evolved by 1918. A US Marine Corps report of 1918 suggests that the British espoused 'the system of limited objectives' through weakness; it 'appears', the report concluded, 'to have been due to the inability of the staff to keep pace with advance of their most aggressive troops in the battles of 1916 and 1917'.[60] Even after the war, Pershing remained convinced that limited, 'bite-and-hold' offensives had led to stalemate and that a return to unlimited offensives decided the war.[61] As this book suggests, the opposite was in fact the case.

American historians have been scathing about Pershing's methods. Paul F. Braim goes as far as to say that: 'In the main there weren't any tactics employed. Committing hundreds of thousands of infantrymen in a narrow zone directly against heavily fortified and defended positions guaranteed high casualties and small gains.'[62] James J. Cooke rejects Pershing's criticism of the training of American infantry, instead pointing to the difficulties of frontal assaults against positions held by resolute defenders. These are criticisms familiar to anyone who has studied the British army on the Somme in 1916. By the Armistice in November 1918, the AEF was dangerously close to played out.[63] Its logistic system was groaning under the strain; it had taken 250,000 casualties on the battlefield. At the same time, though, the AEF was beginning to show distinct improvements. The appointment in October of General Hunter Liggett to command US First Army was a key moment. Liggett was a methodical commander, a sort of American Plumer to Pershing's Haig, whose hallmark was careful staff work and attention to detail. In short, he was a general who did not try to make his troops run before they could walk.[64]

Pershing set up a series of training schools in France which, given time, would have produced staff officers in the numbers needed for a mass army. In the short term, this actually handicapped the AEF, as men at the schools were unavailable for their divisions: one course whisked key staff officers away from their formations just before the Meuse-Argonne battle. Nonetheless, if the war had continued into 1919, as nearly everyone expected it would, this scheme would have paid dividends.[65]

The Final Weeks

Although even at this late stage some German units fought well, in the final weeks of the war the Allies kept up their relentless pressure on the German army. Cambrai fell to First and Third Armies on 9 October. On 14 October King Albert's Army Group recommenced operations in Flanders, while many miles to the south the French and Americans renewed the Meuse-Argonne offensive. Fourth Army – now without the Australians, who had been withdrawn from the line after an action on 5 October, but including two US divisions – won a major victory on the River Selle on 17 October. The capture of a landmark of 1914 – the town of Le Cateau, occupied by 66th Division – went virtually unnoticed. In Flanders, Plumer's Second Army crossed the Lys on 19 October, and Fifth and Third Armies were also advancing. Across the BEF's entire front, progress in October was steady rather than spectacular and bought at high cost. Haig's forces advanced about 20 miles, for the loss of 120,000 casualties. For all that, the Germans were incapable of halting the BEF's remorseless advance.

By a quirk of fate, while the campaign of the Hundred Days as a whole is almost totally forgotten by the modern British public, the last major battle on 4 November 1918 is relatively well known. This is entirely due to the death in the action of one particular junior officer, the war poet Lieutenant Wilfred Owen of 2nd Manchesters. Coming so close to the end of the war, Owen's death seems peculiarly tragic. His parents received the telegram that announced his death on 11 November, at the very moment when church bells were ringing to mark the end of the war.[66] It is easy, and understandable, to brand the deaths of Owen and the other men killed in the last week of the war as 'futile', but this view is nonetheless wrong. Even on the morning of 4 November the German leaders were hoping to save something from the chaos around them. As Niall Barr has shown, the British victory at the Battle of the Sambre on that day finally dispelled any remaining illusions the German leadership may have held. They decided that the war had to be terminated immediately: the German army could hold on no longer.[67] In reality, the Germans had lost the war well before the Sambre battle, but in the first week of November bad news came thick and fast. On 1 November, Liggett's American First Army broke the Meuse-Argonne deadlock and two days later was astride the Lille-Metz railway line, heading for Sedan. Valenciennes fell to the Canadians on the following day, and on 3 November Austria-Hungary made peace; the Turks had dropped out of the war at the end of October. For the Battle of the Sambre on 4 November Haig used Third, First and Fourth Armies, which won their final major victories. German morale noticeably deteriorated during the Hundred Days but, to the end, some German units put up fierce resistance. For all that, the outcome was not in doubt. At 11 a.m. on 11 November 1918 the Armistice came into effect. The German army had been defeated on the field of battle and the war was over.

Conclusion

After the breaking of the Hindenburg Line, the analogy of jazz is sometimes more appropriate than Monash's comparison of military operations to a musical score. In its last major attack on 15–18 October, 30th Division crossed the River Lys in a masterpiece of improvisation. It brought pontoons forward under the cover of darkness and built a bridge under enemy fire, getting a battalion across 'on duckboard rafts, Boche "floats", old doors, and anything else that would float'.[68] In the crossing of the Sambre-Oise canal on 4 November, Braithwaite's IX Corps employed similar methods – and endured some very tough fighting. Also on that day the New Zealand Division captured the ancient walled fortress town of Le Quesnoy by a mixture of bluff, diplomacy, and an assault employing an appropriately antiquated method, a scaling ladder.

Keeping in touch with a beaten and retreating enemy presented a major challenge for the BEF. Haig in September asked London for 'yeomanry, cyclists, motor-machine guns. Motor lorries, etc. In fact anything to add to our mobility.' The popular idea that Haig had a mass of cavalry at his disposal was never less true than in the Hundred Days. On 1 September 1918 the Cavalry Corps amounted to 14,000 men, the equivalent to perhaps the bayonet strength of two infantry divisions, of which Haig had about 60. The official history noted that 'the absence of mounted troops was severely felt'. Cavalry units did invaluable work attached by squadrons and troops to infantry formations. Their role was not in boot-to-boot Napoleonic style massed charges, but in reconnaissance and harrying the retreating Germans.[69] Units in France improvised all-arms mobile columns. Brigades in I Corps in early October formed advance guards that included a section of cavalry, some artillery, and a company of machine gunners.[70]

Under these new conditions of warfare the weapons system that had served the BEF so well sometimes became less relevant. Staff officers had less time to develop complicated fire plans, but were able to cope nonetheless: a mark of the improvement in staff work by the last two months of the war. Indeed, the rapid adjustment of all parts of the BEF to offensive open warfare was impressive. The fluid nature of the fighting often did not lend itself to the massive bombardments such as had broken the Hindenburg Line. Given the crumbling of German morale, resistance often consisted of a handful of isolated machine gun posts, which would 'shoot and scoot', or fire and then pull back. In any case, sometimes the battle moved too fast for the heavy artillery to keep up and much depended on the fighting skills of the infantry and field artillery.[71] British infantry tactics in the Hundred Days were simple but effective and the average infantryman was more than capable of carrying them out. On the eve of their participation in the Grand Offensive, the commander of a brigade in 9th (Scottish) Division issued some advice that encapsulated much of the tactical wisdom of the Hundred Days:

Keep as close as you can to 18pdrs (pipsqueak) barrage. Its their [sic], so don't go into it. Never mind your dressing.

Reply at once to any enemy small arm [sic] fire. Fire at once at any enemy you see in range – slowly and accurately from the quickest position, lying, standing or kneeling.

Don't crowd, the loose order will save you casualties if you use your wits.

Watch your flanks and draw them back if necessary.

If held up reply steadily to the fire whilst your comrades get round.

If necessary help your comrades on flank by cross fire.

Surround pill-boxes and Machine Guns. They can only fire one or two ways.

Don't have more than about 100x [yards] between sections. Don't scatter from your sections, file is best for advancing, a few paces interval for firing.

Push steadily forward in your little groups, using slow covering fire where necessary, and stick roughly to your own line of ADVANCE.[72]

Combined with support from other arms, these were battle- and, indeed, war-winning tactics.

One of the clearest statements of the reality of the tactical learning curve comes from the memoirs of D.V. Kelly, a Somme veteran who in 1918 was serving as a captain in 6th Leicesters, a battalion of 21st Division. His comments on the successful assault on Beaulencourt on 1 September 1918 are worth quoting at length:

[This attack] gave a striking proof of the enormous advance made by the new British Army in the technique of warfare, for it was a small masterpiece achieved with one tenth of the casualties it would assuredly have cost us in 1916. The long western-front of the village, which appeared the main line of approach, was defended by numerous well-concealed pits for riflemen and machine guns, and had we been attacking in the 1916 method the course of events would probably have been as follows. A tremendous artillery bombardment, perhaps for two days, would have annihilated the village and churned up the ground, and at zero hour our troops would have advanced in waves across the belt of land commanded by the various posts, who, as our barrage passed on behind them, would have opened a murderous direct fire on them and taken a enormous toll of casualties. Very possibly we should never have reached the village, but consolidated a line of shellholes a few hundred yards beyond the starting-point, from which a fresh attack would have been delivered perhaps several days later.

By September, 1918, however we had acquired an improved technique. The Western side of the village was left severely alone, and the attack was arranged for the northern end of the village, a procedure which involved in itself a movement and assembly by night that would have been difficult for inexperienced officers. The artillery fired numerous periodic 'crashes', and their support at zero was arranged to appear merely a repetition of one of these and did not specially indicate the time or direction of the attack. Under cover of complete darkness the village was rushed and the defences taken in the rear, the whole affair being a complete surprise ... It is very important to remember that the artillery had improved their technique just as had the staffs and the infantry: in 1916 one could hardly have relied on the accuracy and exact synchronization, which one had now learned to expect, required for such an operation.[73]

Kelly's comments can be allowed to speak for themselves.

Co-operation between the various arms was the key to the BEF's victories in 1918, as it has tended to be throughout history. Haig and GHQ have been criticised for returning at the end of August 1918 to 'semi-traditional' methods of warfare, based on infantry and artillery, rather than making the most of the tanks, which while not war-winners in themselves, might have economised on casualties.[74] This view sits uneasily with the enthusiasm evinced by Haig and other senior officers for technologically advanced equipment, including aeroplanes and, crucially, artillery, which in 1918 represented an altogether higher level of military technological sophistication than the tank. It is true that tanks were not again employed on the scale of Amiens, but they were used when they were available, sometimes in large numbers. The key words here are 'when they were available'. The wear and tear on both the machines and their crews militated against their use in sustained operations. After Amiens, Allied strategy rested on constantly pushing against the Germans, giving them no time to rest or regroup. It would have made no sense to slow the tempo of operations to give tanks time to catch up with the advancing infantry and guns.[75] In short, the importance of tanks in 1918 should not be overrated.

How much credit can Douglas Haig and other senior commanders claim for the victory? Was it the case, as the popular interpretation goes, that the BEF won despite its commander in chief? Command was certainly decentralised during the Hundred Days. Travers sees this as the result of the collapse of GHQ's control of the action during the spring battles, with commanders from Army level downwards filling the vacuum.[76] It is true that Haig did take something of a back seat during 1918, but this was in large part because of the emergence of more experienced and capable subordinates; with less to do, he was a more effective commander. Haig was able to fight the type of 'hands-off' battle to which he had aspired in previous years, although on occasions he still interfered unduly.[77] Haig's confidence in the imminence of victory wavered at various times in the Hundred Days between optimism and relative pessimism, but his drive and determination to finish the war before Christmas were of vital importance. This is not to deny the importance of other individuals – especially Foch, the Allied Supreme Commander – but Haig deserves at least some of the victor's laurels. As Peter Simkins has pointed out, if he and other generals deserve the blame for the disasters of earlier years of the war, they also deserve the credit for the victory of 1918.[78]

The role of the AEF in the defeat of the Kaiser's Germany was impressive. To build a huge army from scratch and put it into the field within two years was a significant achievement. The crisis of 1918 forced the US to bring over troops and put them into battle before they were fully trained – just as the circumstances of 1915–16 had compelled the British to commit Kitchener's Armies. In March 1918 the Allies had fewer troops on the Western Front than the Germans, but by the autumn, thanks to the arrival of American forces, the Allies had the numerical advantage, which stood at some 37 per cent in October 1918.[79] The victories at St. Mihiel and Meuse-Argonne fell short of knockout blows but were nonetheless important, as the capture of 43,000 prisoners and 1,421 guns by the AEF indicates.

In the end the most significant contribution of the AEF might have been psychological. Senior German officers remained sceptical about the combat effectiveness of the AEF until the end of the war, but the apparently inexhaustible resources of the Americans, brought into the field earlier than the Germans anticipated, was an important factor in forcing the realisation that the war was lost.[80] These fears were echoed much further down the command chain. The diary of Rudolf Binding, a German officer, gives some clues as to the impact of the arrival of the Americans on the German belief in ultimate victory. On 22 April 1918, while noting that the German offensive was halted, he mentioned that 'the threat of an American Army gathers like a thunder-cloud in the rear of our other enemies'. By 12 July, Binding still saw a chance of victory if the Germans could arrive at the coast 'before the Americans reach land'. A couple of weeks later, on 25 July, his hope had gone: 'The American Army is there – a million strong. That is too much.'[81] Many other ordinary German soldiers felt the same way. America's decisive offensive was won in the minds of its enemies.

On the day the Armistice was signed, 11 November 1918, General Sir Henry Horne, commander of First Army, wrote:

Now the mighty German nation is completely humbled and the great German army, which regarded itself as the most powerful fighting machine in the world, is in retreat to its own frontiers, broken and defeated![82]

The victory of 1918 was a coalition effort, and although this book has concentrated on the efforts of the Anglo-American armies, the contributions of the French and Belgians and other allies should not be forgotten. The burden of fighting the German army fell mainly to the French and Russians in the first two and half years of the war, but in 1918 it was the turn of the BEF. Between them, the French, Americans and Belgians took 196,700 prisoners and 3,775 guns between 18 July and the end of the war. With a smaller army than the French, Haig's forces captured 188,700 prisoners and 2,840 guns in the same period.[83] This was, by far, the greatest military victory in British history.

CHAPTER 10

THE AFTERMATH AND
THE CONSEQUENCES

The First World War was the key event of the twentieth century, from which everything else flowed. The way the war ended and its immediate aftermath is as controversial as the war itself. This final chapter examines the end of the war and the Peace that followed, before looking at the place of the war in the development of modern warfare and the history of the twentieth century.

The End of Imperial Germany

'Britain and France did not defeat us on the battle-field. That was a great lie.'[1] When Adolf Hitler made this claim, in a speech on 8 November 1939, he was returning to a theme that had served the Nazis well since the foundation of the Party. Hitler was not the author of the assertion that the undefeated German army had been stabbed in the back by traitorous elements on the home front. It had its origins in the last days of Imperial Germany. The German generals might have failed dismally in their attempt to defeat the Allies, but they were highly successful in shifting the blame for their defeat away from the army. At the beginning of the Second World War, it was seen as worthwhile for a prominent British military historian to write a pamphlet to counter the myth that the German army had not been defeated in the field in 1918. Even today the notion crops up now and again.

The longevity of the stab-in-the-back myth is testimony to the success of the 'great lie' – not the Anglo-French one to which Hitler referred, which was in fact not a lie at all – but the one that Hitler himself propagated. As Ian Kershaw has stated in his masterly biography of Hitler: 'In reality, of course, there had been no treachery, no stab-in-the-back. This was a pure invention of the Right ... Unrest at home was a consequence, not a cause, of military failure.'[2]

The genesis of the stab-in-the-back myth can perhaps be traced back to 1 October 1918.[3] At a meeting of German army high command Ludendorff candidly admitted that the war was lost, and that 'an unavoidable and conclusive defeat' beckoned. The Chancellor having resigned, Ludendorff had advised the Kaiser to 'bring ... into the government [those Social Democrats and Liberals] whom we can mainly thank that we have come to this ... They should make the peace that must now be made. They made their bed, now they must lie in it!'[4] Ludendorff's instructions came to pass. The liberally inclined Prince Max of Baden became Chancellor on 3 October and two days later asked President Wilson to bring about a peace founded on the Fourteen Points, which in the face of military defeat suddenly possessed virtues that had previously gone unnoticed by the German leadership. On 28 October the Imperial Constitution was altered in such a way that Germany became something close to a constitutional monarchy on the British pattern. But this was building sandcastles to resist a high tide. Hindenburg, having belatedly discovered that Wilson had no intention of dealing with the existing regime in Berlin, tried to sabotage Prince Max's attempt to bring about peace. Ludendorff fled to Sweden on 26 October and was replaced by General Wilhelm Groener, who rapidly and accurately assessed the state of the German army as parlous. Modern historians have referred to soldiers taking a form of 'strike action', which fed into the outbreak of revolution.[5] The Imperial navy, which had contributed so mightily to the tensions that led to war, had one final part to play. Admirals Scheer and von Hipper ordered the High Seas Fleet to carry out one last mission in the North Sea. For the sailors, this was the last straw. Mutiny broke out on 29 October.

German high command was located at Spa, in Belgium. Here, on 9 November 1918, was played out one of the last acts of the reign of Wilhelm II, Kaiser of Germany and King of Prussia. After consultations with generals on the reliability of their troops, Groener was forced to confront Wilhelm with the truth that the 'All Highest' still refused to face:

> Sire, you no longer have an army. The army will march home in peace and order under its leaders and commanding generals, but not under the command of Your Majesty, for it no longer stands behind Your Majesty.[6]

Events in Berlin complemented those in Spa. The same day, with Germany in revolution, Prince Max resigned the Chancellorship in favour of a moderate Social Democrat, Friedrich Ebert. The German Republic, also proclaimed on 9 November 1918, survived the months of revolution with the aid of an alliance between the army and the new political leadership. 'After half a century in opposition to and excluded from all imperial agencies of power, the Social Democrats were asked to pick up the pieces.'[7] It was to prove a difficult legacy.

A Carthaginian Peace?

The Peace that ended the German war of 1914–18 is one of the most vilified treaties in history. It is widely seen as a harsh, 'Carthaginian' peace that simply stored up resentment and made a German bid to reverse it – and hence the Second World War – inevitable.[8] A mirror image of this view is that the Peace was far too lenient, that Germany escaped relatively lightly from the war. I take a middle position: that the Peace was insufficiently harsh to crush Germany and thus ensure that it would no longer be in a position to menace its neighbours, but neither was it moderate enough to conciliate the Germans. The peacemakers of 1919 thus opted for the worst of all worlds. Four hundred years earlier, Machiavelli had wisely advised that defeated enemies 'must be either pampered or crushed'.[9] The treaty of Versailles did neither. It inflicted humiliations on Germany but did not cripple it. Furthermore, by signing an unpopular Peace, the new German republic was tainted almost from its birth and thus the chances of democracy taking root were significantly undermined. Twenty years later Germany re-emerged as a threat, hungry for revenge. It is easy to portray the Allies as having won the war but lost the peace. The victorious Allies did not make the same mistake in 1945, when a defeated, occupied and partitioned Germany had fresh political and social structures imposed upon it.

One of the major problems that faced the peacemakers in Paris was the unwillingness of Germany to accept the reality of military defeat. Fed on a diet of victory in early 1918, and shielded from the events on the front line until the very last minute, many Germans refused to come to terms with what had happened to them. The Allies unwittingly aided this collective self-denial by granting Armistice terms that allowed German troops to march home rather than insisting on their surrender. This seemed to compensate for other tokens of defeat – evacuation of captured territory, surrender of war goods, occupation of the Rhineland by Allied troops. German soldiers returned to streets bedecked with flowers and flags, to be greeted as victors. The new Chancellor, Friedrich Ebert, proclaimed in December 1918 that troops were returning without having been defeated.[10]

Some Allied commanders, Pershing among them, were in favour of fighting on in November 1918 until the Germans agreed to unconditional surrender. Others, including Haig and Henry Wilson and politicians such as Lloyd George, who underestimated the extent of the crisis afflicting the German army and state, favoured more moderate terms. Sir Eric Geddes, by now First Lord of the Admiralty, wrote on 12 November: 'Had we known how bad things were in

Germany, we might have got stiffer terms; however, it is easy to be wise after the event.'[11] Even if 'stiffer terms' had fallen short of unconditional surrender, they might have included occupation of German territory on the east bank of the Rhine. The west bank was occupied, and as a consequence Rhinelanders lived with the visible evidence of defeat − British, French and American troops on German soil. The temporary incarceration of the German army, and Allied victory parades in Berlin, Munich and other major cities would undoubtedly have forced the German people as a whole to face the actuality of defeat. In the absence of such reminders of the Allied victory, the stab-in-the-back myth flourished and Adolf Hitler was the eventual beneficiary.

Given the 'dreamland' inhabited by the German delegates to Versailles and the German people alike, it is not surprising that the eventual terms came as a body blow.[12] In truth, the terms were not unduly severe. After beginning, fighting and losing a total world war Germany was deprived of about 13.5 per cent of its territory, about 27,000 square miles, which went principally to the reconstituted Polish state and to France, in the shape of Alsace-Lorraine. Along with this territory went approximately 7 million people and 13.5 per cent of Germany's economic productivity. In addition Germany had to pay £6,000 million in reparations; her overseas colonies were forfeited; and restrictions were placed on her armed forces − the army was limited to 100,000 men, there were to be no tanks, no submarines, no aircraft.[13] Compared to the treatment that Germany had meted out to defeated Russia in 1918 at the Peace of Brest-Litovsk the terms seem almost moderate. They bear no comparison with what happened to Germany in 1945.

The same self-delusion enabled some Germans to cling to the belief that Wilson's Fourteen Points would spare them from the wrath of the Allies. Some of the new German leadership, Matthias Erzberger of the Centre Party for one, had genuinely supported the Fourteen Points for some time, but the deathbed conversion of the Imperial German elite to Wilsonian idealism had fooled few on the Allied side. Later, Germans were able to claim that Germany had been 'cheated', that it had accepted an armistice on the basis of the Fourteen Points and a lenient peace, but the subsequent settlement had not been moderate.[14] Such claims were disingenuous in the extreme. The Fourteen Points underpinned the policy of the United States but not that of France and Britain. Ever since their announcement the British and French had been sceptical, and bitterness followed when London and Paris were excluded from the bilateral exchanges between Berlin and Washington in October 1918. On 13 October the British CIGS Henry Wilson noted that his American namesake 'must make it clear to the Boches that his 14 points (with which we do not agree) were not a basis for an armistice, which is what the Boches pretend they are ... Everyone angry and contemptuous of Wilson.'[15] In the short term, Britain and France, backed into a corner, were forced to go along with Wilson's view. Nevertheless, Germans were soon to discover that their leaders' belated espousal of the Fourteen Points had not handed them a 'get out of jail free' card that absolved them of any responsibility for the events of the previous four years. The reality, as German historian Klaus Schwabe has recently written, was that Germany had lost the war and thus had to pay the price of a Peace imposed by the victors.[16]

From a distance of eighty years it is possible to make a good case that the 'Big Three' − Lloyd George, Wilson and the French leader Clemenceau − should have willingly granted the mildest of terms to Germany. This would have given the infant German republic the best of all christening presents and would have laid the ground for reconciliation. Regrettably, the circumstances of 1918−19 militated against such an enlightened approach. At the end of a long, bitter war public opinion in the victorious states was crying out for revenge and security. A combination of primal desire for retribution and concerns about future security made a thoroughly high-minded Peace all but impossible to achieve.

That the settlement was not high-minded was a central theme of an immensely influential book, published in December 1919, by the British economist John Maynard Keynes. As a Treasury official, Keynes had been present at the peace discussions, and he asserted that Germany was unable to meet the reparations payments demanded by the Allies, and that French plans to enhance their security by keeping Germany weak were counterproductive. British and French politicians, Keynes claimed, 'run the risk of completing the ruin, which Germany began, by a Peace which . . . must impair yet further . . . the delicate, complicated organisation . . . through which alone the European peoples can employ themselves and live'.[17] Keynes's book *The Economic Consequences of the Peace* helped to undermine the validity of the Versailles settlement almost before the ink on the treaty was dry.

Feelings of guilt among the Anglo-American liberal elite at the way Germany had been treated in 1919 were to contribute significantly towards the undermining of the Versailles settlement in the interwar period. A major source of this remorse was the so-called 'war guilt' clause, discussed in chapter 2, which, ironically, was intended to limit German responsibility to pay reparations. Article 231 stated that the Allies were morally entitled to demand that Germany pay for the war in its entirety, but Article 232 set out that reparations would be confined to sums that Germany could actually pay. Being saddled with the blame for the war outraged the Germans, but it gave their politicians and diplomats a powerful weapon that was wielded with some skill to undermine the moral validity of the Peace, thus hastening Germany's re-admittance into the international community.[18]

So, was the Second World War an inevitable consequence of the Treaty of Versailles? Or should the major origins of the war that broke out in 1939 be located in the peculiar circumstances of the previous decade? In the immediate aftermath of the Second World War, the causes of the conflict seemed straightforward. The First World War and the deeply flawed Versailles settlement between them destroyed the old balance of power and left a host of intractable territorial disputes. The imposition of reparations on Germany, it was pointed out, was damaging to the world economy, and the harshness of the settlement helped Adolf Hitler to power. In his political testimony *Mein Kampf*, written in 1924, Hitler set out a plan for world domination that he began to set in motion shortly after his appointment as German Chancellor nine years later. Western leaders misguidedly attempted to appease Hitler, the interpretation went, thus allowing him to achieve his aims more or less bloodlessly, while whetting his appetite for more. Only when Hitler ripped up the Munich agreement signed only a few months before and occupied the whole of Czechoslovakia in spring 1939, did the scales fall from their eyes. Hitler's next move, against Poland, triggered a war with Britain and France that expanded into a global total war and cost millions of lives. If only the peacemakers of 1919 had had the foresight to be more generous, or if the democracies had taken prompt and resolute action when Hitler began to menace the peace of Europe, this 'unnecessary war', to use Winston Churchill's phrase,[19] could have been avoided.

This consensus was shattered in 1961 by the publication of A.J.P. Taylor's *The Origins of the Second World War*.[20] Taylor caused outrage in some circles by treating Hitler as a 'wicked' but otherwise normal statesman who reacted to events, rather than as a uniquely evil monster coldly executing a master plan for world domination.[21] Worse, in the view of his critics, Taylor refused to join in the ritual denunciation of Neville Chamberlain and appeasement. While this upset many Anglo-American readers, statements such as 'Hitler (like every other German statesman) intended Germany to become the dominant power in Europe' offended many Germans, already reeling from Fritz Fischer's work on the origins of the First World War which, coincidentally, appeared in the same year.[22] By denying the uniqueness of Hitler, by seeing his foreign policy as a continuation of that of Bismarck and Wilhelmine Germany, Taylor helped to challenge the use of the Führer as Germany's alibi for the crimes of the Third Reich. In doing so he reinforced the notion of a new Thirty Years War that began in 1914 and ended in 1945, with a breathing space of twenty years in the middle.

One of the major problems in accepting the Thirty Years War thesis, as Michael Howard has observed, is that twenty years after the Armistice 'the verdict of Versailles had been effectively reversed without a shot being fired'.[23] Most of the grievances that emerged from the Peace of 1919, from reparations to territorial losses, had either been settled in Germany's favour, were in the process of being settled, or at the very least were likely to be resolved. In truth, Versailles was not the Carthaginian Peace that Keynes had feared. His views on reparations were challenged subsequently,[24] and are still the subject of historical debate.[25] In the end Germany and the Allies compromised on reparations, and against the opposition of Britain and the USA the French were unable to force through the more extreme of their demands, for instance that the Rhineland be detached from Germany. Indeed, in relative terms, Germany emerged from the First World War in good shape. The German state, even after its losses, remained fundamentally intact and was the largest and potentially the most powerful entity in central Europe: Austria-Hungary had fragmented into a number of smaller countries and the Soviet Union was a weakened pariah state.

By contrast France's strategic position was weaker than it had been in 1914. In place of the might of Imperial Russia as an ally on Germany's eastern frontier, France now had smaller and weaker states such as Poland. That the wartime alliance had disintegrated was forcibly demonstrated by Britain's refusal in 1923 to support the Franco-Belgian occupation of the Ruhr, mounted to force the continued payment of reparations. France could no longer count on British support even to the limited degree that had existed prior to 1914. Certainly, neither of the Anglo-Saxon powers would join France in a formal alliance guaranteeing her security against future German aggression. Many historians agree that the Versailles settlement could have been enforced, but two of the victors, Britain and the United States, lacked the will to do so.[26] The United States turned its back on Europe and retreated into isolationism while Britain preferred to conciliate Germany. Bereft of the support of their erstwhile allies, the French were unable to implement the Peace as rigorously as they would have liked.

Under Gustav Stresemann, foreign minister from 1923 to the end of the decade, Germany pursued a 'strategy of accommodation' with Britain and France. By signing the Locarno Treaty in 1925 (thus guaranteeing Germany's western frontiers, but not, significantly, the eastern), renegotiating the reparations terms, taking up a seat on the League of Nations, and getting American loans to rebuild its economy, the Weimar government improved both Germany's international status and domestic position.[27] Stresemann certainly wanted to revise the Versailles settlement — Taylor was right about that — but he sought to do so through conciliation with the Western powers. The British and, more reluctantly, the French worked with him to these ends, and continued this policy for the best part of a decade after Stresemann's death in October 1929 — right up to the spring of 1939, in fact. Thus in the 1920s and 1930s, the Versailles Treaty, which was anyway far from being a 'Carthaginian Peace' to begin with, was steadily revised in Germany's favour. This process resulted in Germany's return to a position of dominance in central Europe without war. Why, then, did the Second World War break out?

Ten years after the signature of the Treaty of Versailles many problems remained unresolved. Eastern Europe in particular was an obvious source of political instability, and the Weimar state continued to rest on somewhat rickety foundations. Overall, however, observers could be cautiously optimistic about the outlook for peace and stability in Europe. Then, in October 1929, came the Wall Street Crash. In the USA and Britain democracy survived the subsequent worldwide economic Depression battered, but in reasonable shape. In France, democracy was weakened but tottered on; across the Rhine, the blow was fatal. The sufferings of the masses led to the radicalisation and polarisation of German politics, with both Hitler's Nazi party and the German Communist Party making electoral gains. The German political elite, many of whom had never been reconciled to the Weimar republic, abandoned democracy. Even before Hitler's appointment as Chancellor in January 1933, authoritarian rule had effectively replaced parliamentary democracy.[28]

Hitler was the child of the Depression. But for the Wall Street Crash, it seems unlikely that the circumstances which brought him to power would have ever arisen. Once in power, he set about a policy of expansion, which at first Britain was prepared to tolerate and even encourage. Up to a point, he was indeed, as Taylor suggested, pursuing traditional German foreign policy goals. But Hitler was an altogether different character from Bismarck or even the men who took Germany to war in 1914. His racist ideology, the sheer scale of his ambitions, and the ruthlessness with which he set out to achieve them, set him apart from what had gone before. By September 1939 Hitler's expansionism had reached a stage that the Western democracies, especially Britain, were no longer prepared to accept. At that moment Britain once again returned to its policy of maintaining the balance of power in Europe. For the second time in twenty years, Britain and France went to war against a German regime seeking hegemony.

The war that broke out in September 1939 was *not* the inevitable consequence of the settlement of 1919.[29] To play the game of 'what if', Weimar Germany might well have survived but for the Depression of 1929. Even if it had not, it was not inevitable that Adolf Hitler and the Nazi Party would have come to power. It is entirely plausible to postulate the collapse of democracy in Germany and the emergence of a right-wing, nationalist, possibly military regime that did not embark on a course which led to war with Britain and France. Such a regime could have revised its borders with Poland, even by force, with Britain's acquiescence or even encouragement. There may well have been conflict as the result of Germany flexing its muscles, but not carnage on the scale of that unleashed by Hitler in September 1939. A limited conflict with Poland over the Danzig corridor would have been of a very different order to the genocidal war launched against the Soviet Union by Hitler in June 1941. Imperfect as it undoubtedly was, the Treaty of Versailles was not the direct 'cause' of the Second World War.

The First World War and the Development of Warfare

The Armistice of 11 November 1918 was signed in a French railway carriage. The very same carriage was used for the same purpose on 22 June 1940, although this time it was the Germans who forced the French to agree to a humiliating armistice. In a campaign lasting only six weeks, the German army had smashed the forces of France, Britain, Belgium and the Netherlands; had occupied Paris and the Channel ports; had forced the British into mounting a seaborne evacuation – and all this had been achieved at a cost of only 27,000 German fatalities. The first day of Operation *Michael* in 1918 had alone cost 11,000 German dead. The *Blitzkrieg* (lightning war) of 1940 might seem to point to the emergence of a radically new type of warfare, the antithesis of the attritional fighting of 1918. The truth is somewhat different.

Most of the methods of fighting battles and campaigns in the Second World War built upon First World War prototypes. The effectiveness of the exceptions, such as paratroops and commando-style Special Forces, remains a matter of some controversy. The 'mainstream' weapons, such as artillery, aircraft, tanks, and machine guns were more powerful and reliable than their Great War ancestors, but remained essentially similar and were most effective when used in all-arms teams, just as in 1918. Two new developments were especially significant. The first was the evolution of radio communications, which enabled a measure of voice control to return to the battlefield. The second was a significant increase in the range and reliability of armoured vehicles. These two factors restored the triad of infantry, artillery and 'cavalry'; once again commanders had the ability rapidly to exploit opportunities and vigorously pursue a retreating enemy. To a great extent these developments freed Second World War commanders from the shackles worn by their Great War predecessors.

Better tanks and communications were not the only advantages enjoyed by the German forces in 1940, or even the most important ones. The key factor was a vast gulf in the fighting power of the two sides. The balance of forces and technology was roughly equal between the Allies and the Germans, but in terms of doctrine, tactics and morale the latter had a significant advantage. The same was true of the initial stages of Operation *Barbarossa* in 1941, which came close to defeating the Soviet Union.

Blitzkrieg was an aberration, born of a disparity in fighting power between adversaries. By 1942 Germany's enemies had returned to rough parity as their tactics and doctrine improved. Given the advances in armour and communications, battles were rather more mobile than in 1914–18, but they were no less attritional, and the Second World War had its share of static fighting, such as the battles of Stalingrad, Cassino and Normandy. Just as in the Great War, artillery was a dominant weapon in most theatres in 1939–45. All this resulted in 'butcher's bills' that exceeded those of the earlier war. Soviet military casualties in 1941–45 amounted to some 13 million, which sets the total of British dead of both world wars into sobering context. The lower British figure for the later war reflects the lack of a long-running commitment to a ground campaign on the scale of the Western Front. Nevertheless, casualties in individual units and campaigns exceeded those of the Great War. The loss rate in British and Canadian infantry battalions ran at about 100 per month on the Western Front. In the campaign in north-west Europe from D-Day to V.E. Day in 1944–45, battalions suffered a minimum of 100 casualties per month, but figures of 175 were not uncommon.[30] 1st Battalion Gordon Highlanders sustained losses of 75 officers and 986 soldiers in the ten and a half months that followed their arrival in France. Of the 55 officers who had commanded rifle platoons, 'fifty-three per cent were wounded, twenty-four per cent invalided, and five per cent had survived'. On average, their service with the Gordons amounted to 38 days.[31] In 1945, as in 1918, high intensity warfare took a fearful toll of soldiers' lives.

Conventional wars since 1945 have reinforced the impression that methods of fighting have not changed markedly from the all-arms, air-ground model that emerged in 1917–18. When one side has an overwhelming advantage in combat power, as the Israelis had over the Egyptians in 1967, success is swift. Where two sides are evenly matched, as were the Iranians and the Iraqis in 1980–88, deadlock ensues. The one major attempt to move away from the all-arms concept, when in 1973 the Israelis, misreading the lessons of 1967, tried to fight an armour-heavy battle against strong Egyptian defences on the banks of the Suez Canal, ended in heavy losses for the attackers. The Israelis rapidly revised their tactics, returning to an all-arms approach, and defeated the Egyptians. Currently, some military analysts are predicting that sophisticated new weapons will transform the nature of warfare, while others see new weapons as producing more of the same, with ever-heavier casualties.

> The armies of Europe and the United States still train for essentially the same style of warfare that was developed on the Western Front in 1914–18 . . .[32]

This statement was written in 1987, but at the beginning of the twenty-first century it still holds true.

The First World War and the Short Twentieth Century

Between 1989 and 1991 the Cold War came to an end. The collapse of Communism created in Europe a situation that, as many commentators pointed out, bore a resemblance to the end of the First World War. New states emerged, and instability and conflict replaced the certainties of the bi-polar world of the Cold War. In retrospect, the years 1914 to 1991 can be seen as one discrete period, dubbed by historians the 'Short Twentieth Century'. It was a time of confrontations between ideologies, dominated by war and its aftermath, distinctly different both from the 'Long Nineteenth Century' (1789–1914) that preceded it, and the world at the turn of the twenty-first century.[33] The notion of a Short Twentieth Century is a helpful one, providing that it is not understood as implying that the war that broke out in 1914 inevitably led to a further global conflict. The two World Wars and the Cold War fit into a pattern stretching back to the late fifteenth century. Since 1494, ten or so major wars have occurred in times when the international system was undergoing fundamental change, with power shifting away from some actors and towards others. Indeed, no general (as opposed to smaller scale, local and limited) conflicts have taken place unless there was a major upheaval in the international system.[34] Against this background of the rise of Germany, the USA, Japan, and the USSR, and the decline of Britain and France, conflict in some form, if not the wars that actually occurred, begins to look inevitable.

One charge that can be levelled against Woodrow Wilson is that his policies, the product of naïvety and idealism, helped to create the conditions of instability that succeeded the First World War. His lofty ideals of self-determination clashed head on with the realities of Central and Eastern Europe. Ethnic groups did not live in self-contained areas that could easily be converted into nation states. This led to the situation where, for instance, the new Czechoslovakian state contained 10 million Czechs and Slovaks, 3 million ethnic Germans, 700,000 Hungarians, 500,000 Ukrainians and 60,000 Poles. Moreover, democracy, another of Wilson's cherished ideals, did not take root in Germany nor in most of the newly independent states. Wilson's third ideal, collective security through the newly created League of Nations, proved useless in the face of determined aggression in the 1930s.

But that is not the end of the story. From the perspective of the early twenty-first century Wilson appears as something other than a mere naïve idealist. Behind Wilson's inflated rhetoric and expectations was a shrewd recognition that American security would be improved by establishing democratic regimes around the world. At the beginning of the twentieth century, the future had seemed to belong to large empires. But when Britain and France enlarged their empires at the end of the war, they were walking into a blind alley, with the dead-end already visible to the clear-sighted. Wilson, by contrast, had correctly identified the future, embracing the concept of nationalism at the very moment when empires began to break up, and then attempted to set the agenda for the newly emergent states. In such countries, and for the Anglo-American liberal/left, Wilson became a hero. In the 1930s H.G. Wells wrote that Wilson, for a short period, 'ceased to be a common statesman; he became a Messiah. Millions believed in him as the bringer of untold blessings . . .'[35] In contrast, some have viewed Wilson's liberal internationalism as a cloak for the advancement of American capitalism. They are wrong in seeing this as a prime motive in Wilson's behaviour, although he certainly believed that the free market was the essential partner of democracy.

Wilson's approach was rejected in his own country even while he remained in office. Later, successive American administrations found it expedient to support right-wing, undemocratic regimes with strong anti-Communist credentials, with sometimes unhappy results. Nevertheless, Wilson's stance provided a key element in American foreign policy for much of the twentieth century. Ultimately, Woodrow Wilson achieved a posthumous victory. In the Second World War the democracies — Britain as well as the USA — were a source of hope to peoples under Nazi oppression, and by the end both states had adopted Wilsonian principles to a greater or lesser degree. After 1945 they remoulded West Germany and Japan in their own democratic image. Collective security was reborn in a modified form at the United Nations. The UN proved a little more successful than its predecessor, the League, if only because governments of all ideological stripes felt the need to pay it at least lip service. In the 1970s another Democratic president, Jimmy Carter, insisted on placing human rights on the international agenda. Although Carter was reviled at the time as another naïve idealist, it is now clear that his strategy played a significant role in undermining the legitimacy of Soviet rule.[36] Ronald Reagan, in most respects a most un-Wilsonian president, followed Carter. Reagan fought the Cold War with a relish that would have been alien to Wilson; yet Reagan's broad-fronted attack on Soviet power included a crusade for democracy. With the 'People Power' revolutions of 1989 in Central and Eastern Europe, Wilson, '... the first world leader to respect the power of nationalism and to try to channel its great strength in the direction of democracy and international cooperation ...',[37] was finally vindicated.

In 1989 an American political scientist, Francis Fukuyama, celebrated the conclusion of the Cold War by declaring that history had come to an end — that the triumph of liberal capitalism, having seen off its ideological foes, meant that there were no more big issues to fight about. Ralf Dahrendorf, more cautiously, suggests that 'the great conflicts of the twentieth century have certainly run their course'.[38] While I disagree with the former proposition and am sceptical about the latter, it is certainly the case that since 1914 liberal capitalist democracy has endured the assaults of three powerful foes — autocratic and then Nazi Germany, and Soviet Communism — and emerged victorious.

Moreover, the record of the twentieth century would suggest that democracy plus welfare capitalism is a good, although imperfect, recipe for stability and prosperity.

From this perspective, the victory of 1918 is more important than ever. Looking back from the year 2000, we know that the twentieth century ended more positively than anyone might have dared hope in 1917 or 1941, or during the Great Depression of the early 1930s, or in the two most dangerous years of the Cold War, 1962 and 1983. We can see that the Allied victory in the First World War was a vital element in the relative peace and prosperity enjoyed by the West at the end of the century. To claim that the First World War was 'futile' because it was succeeded within twenty years by an even worse conflict is akin to proclaiming the Second World War futile because dissension among the victors led to the Cold War. In both cases, the victories over Germany produced 'negative gains': in other words, they prevented something from happening. To argue that the world in 1919 would have been a better place if the Great War had not taken place, or more parochially, if Britain had not become involved, misses the point. A German victory in the First World War would have produced a situation significantly worse than the imperfect 'real' world of 1919. The First World War was a just and necessary war fought against a militarist, aggressive autocracy. In Britain and the United States it is a forgotten victory. It has remained forgotten for too long.

NOTES

Introduction

[1]   J. Laffin, *British Butchers and Bunglers of World War One* (Stroud, Sutton, 1988).

[2]   A.A. Gill, *Sunday Times*, 7 July 1996.

[3]   John Keegan, *The First World War* (London, Hutchinson, 1998) p.315.

[4]   Stephen Badsey, unpublished paper, 1998. I am indebted to Dr Badsey for allowing me to consult and quote from this piece, and also for discussing the whole subject with me, over many years.

[5]   For a definition of the scientific method of writing history, see John McManners, 'Introduction' to *The Oxford History of Christianity* (ed. J. McManners) (Oxford, Oxford UP, 1993) p.5.

Chapter 1

[1]   *Guardian:* 'The Season: supporters guide to the 1999–2000 English football season, August 1999' p.4.

2 B.S. Barnes, *This Righteous War* (Huddersfield, R. Netherwood, 1990) p.4.

3 *Guardian*, 30 July 1999.

4 *Daily Express*, 16 March 1994.

5 *Sun*, 8 April 1982, quoted in Robert Harris, *Gotcha! The Media, the Government, and the Falklands Crisis* (London, Faber and Faber, 1983) p.45.

6 B. Bushaway, 'Name upon Name: The Great War and Remembrance' in Roy Porter (ed.), *Myths of the English* (Cambridge, Polity, 1992) p.145. For the evolution of the process of commemoration and attitudes towards the war, see this source and A. Gregory, *The Silence of Memory* (Oxford, Berg, 1994).

7 Hugh Cecil, *The Flower of Battle* (London, Secker and Warburg, 1995) p.3. This book includes five case studies of authors under the collective heading of 'War, the Positive View'.

8 C.E. Jacomb, *Torment* (London, Melrose, 1920).

9 W.G. Bell, *The Great Plague of London* new edition (London, Bracken Books, 1994) p.120.

10 George A.B. Dewar assisted by J.H. Boraston, *Sir Douglas Haig's Command 1915–1918* Vol. I (London, Constable, 1922) pp.160–67.

11 Robert Robinson, *Skip all That* (London, Century, 1996) pp.2–3.

12 Max Plowman, *The Right to Live* (London, Dakers, 1942) p.214. The original article was written in 1939.

13 Modris Eksteins, 'All Quiet on the Western Front', *History Today* (November 1995) pp.29–34; Cecil, *Flower* p.4.

14 Michael Howard, *War and the Liberal Conscience* (Oxford, Oxford UP, 1989) pp.75–8.

15 A.J.P Taylor, *The Trouble Makers* (London, Panther, 1969) p.16.

16 Martin Ceadal, *Thinking About Peace and War* (Oxford, Oxford UP, 1989) pp.5, 118–19.

17 C.L. Mowat, *Britain Between the Wars 1918–1940* (London, Methuen, 1968) pp.422, 538, 541–2.

18 See George Orwell, 'My Country Right or Left', in Sonia Orwell

and Ian Angus, *The Collected Essays, Journalism and Letters of George Orwell* Vol. I (Harmondsworth, Penguin, 1970) pp.589–90; and Evelyn Waugh, 'The War and the Younger Generation' in Donat Gallagher (ed.), *The Essays, Articles and Reviews of Evelyn Waugh* (Harmondsworth, Penguin, 1986) pp.61–3.

[19] Brian Bond, *Chief of Staff: The Diaries of Lieutenant General Sir Henry Pownall* Vol. I (London, Leo Cooper, 1972) p.99.

[20] G.D. Sheffield, 'The Shadow of the Somme: the influence of the First World War on British Soldiers' Perceptions and Behaviour in the Second World War' in Paul Addison and Angus Calder (eds.), *Time to Kill: The Soldier's Experience of War in the West 1939–1945* (London, Pimlico, 1996) p.29.

[21] Brian Bond, 'A victory worse than defeat? British interpretations of the First World War', text of Liddell Hart Centre for Military Archives Annual Lecture, 20 November 1997 p. 7.

[22] Rosa Maria Bracco, *Merchants of Hope: British Middlebrow Writers and the First World War, 1919–1939* (Oxford, Berg, 1993) pp.149–53, 178, 185–6.

[23] Eksteins, 'All Quiet' p.34.

[24] Cecil, *Flower* p.5 and 'British War Novelists' in Hugh Cecil and Peter H. Liddle (eds.), *Facing Armageddon: The First World War Experienced* (London, Leo Cooper, 1996) p.803.

[25] Uri Bialer, *The Shadow of the Bomber* (London, Royal Historical Society, 1980).

[26] Sheffield, 'Shadow' pp.30–32.

[27] Ian F.W. Beckett, *The Judgement of History* (London, Tom Donovan, 1993) pp.xx–xxi.

[28] Jeffrey Richards, *The Age of the Dream Palace: Cinema and Society in Britain 1930–1939* (London, RKP, 1984) pp.257–95.

[29] Richards, *Dream Palace* p.291.

[30] Michael P. Malone and F. Ross Peterson, 'Politics and Protests' in Clyde A. Milner et al, *The Oxford History of the American West* (New York, Oxford UP, 1994) p.511.

[31] David Kennedy, *Over Here* (New York, Oxford UP, 1982) p.205.

32   Mark Meigs, *Optimism at Armageddon: Voices of American Participants in the First World War* (London, Macmillan, 1997) p.218.

33   These surveys, used by Meigs, are held in the US Army Military History Institute at Carlisle Barracks, PA.

34   *US News & World Report*, 19 October 1998.

35   Patrick Quinn, 'The Experience of War in American Patriotic Literature' in Cecil and Liddle, *Facing Armageddon* pp.752–66.

36   Kennedy, *Over Here* pp.217–30.

37   Maldwyn A. Jones, *The Limits of Liberty: American History 1607–1980* (Oxford, Oxford UP, 1983) p.423.

38   F.E. Montgomery to Hon. William Colmer, 23 January 1941, William M. Colmer papers, University of Southern Mississippi. I owe these references to Professor Kenneth G. McCarty.

39   Quoted in Modris Eksteins, 'Memory and the Great War' in Hew Strachan (ed.), *The Oxford Illustrated History of the First World War* (Oxford, Oxford UP, 1998) p.313.

40   Lyric quoted in Steven Mintz and Randy Roberts, *Hollywood's America: United States History Through its Films* (St James, NY, Brandywine Press, 1993) p.86. For the Bonus Marchers, see Richard Severo and Lewis Milford, *The Wages of War* (NY, Touchstone, 1990) p.274.

41   James J. Cooke, *The All-Americans at War: The 82nd Division in the Great War, 1917–1918* (Westport CT, Praeger, 1999) pp.91, 123.

42   Jay Hyams, *War Movies* (New York, Gallery, 1984) pp.60–61.

43   *Life* November 1997; US News and World Report 13 November 1995. I am indebted to my friends Dr Kathy Barbier of Yale University and Professor Andy Wiest of the University of Southern Mississippi for sharing their insights into the attitudes of modern Americans towards the Great War. Also, many thanks to those people who took the trouble to discuss these matters on-line on the UKANS World War I discussion group.

44   See for example D. Clayton James and Anne Sharp Wells, *America and the Great War, 1914–1920* (Wheeling, Harlan

Davidson, 1997); John Lukacs, '1918', in *American Heritage* (November 1993).

[45] Quoted in James S. Olson and Randy Roberts, 'Distorted Images, Missed Opportunities' in Mintz and Roberts, *Hollywood's America* p.290.

[46] George Donelson Moss, *Vietnam: An American Ordeal* (Englewood Cliffs, NJ, Prentice Hall 1994) p.412.

[47] Leon Wolff, *In Flanders Fields* (London, Longman, 1958); Alan Clark, *The Donkeys* (London, Hutchinson, 1961); A.J.P. Taylor, *The First World War* (London, Hamish Hamilton, 1963, quotations from the 1978 Penguin edition). For contemporary criticism of *The Donkeys*, see material in Bond, 'Victory' p.11 and John Terraine, 'Instant History', *JRUSI*, CVII, 1962 pp.140–44; for a scathing modern critique, see the Marquis of Anglesey, *A History of the British Cavalry 1816–1919* Vol.8 (London, Leo Cooper, 1997) p.xxii.

[48] Laffin, *British Butchers*; J.H. Johnson, *Stalemate! The Great Trench Warfare Battles of 1915–17* (London, Arms and Armour, 1995).

[49] A school textbook in current use, for example, does not reflect revisionist thinking on the fighting on the Western Front; C. Shephard, A. Reid, K. Shephard, *The Schools History Project: Discovering the Past Y9 Peace & War* (London, John Murray, 1993). I am indebted to Mr Roger Coombes and his 1995 Year 9 history set at Collingwood College, Camberley, and to Dr Keith Grieves for their guidance on history in the national curriculum. Similar thanks are due to Mrs Gerda Bennett for her advice on the teaching of poetry.

[50] C. Martin, *War Poems* (London, Collins Educational, 1991); M. Marland, The Times Authors No.5: *The War Poets* (London, Times Newspapers, nd). The latter is an information pack aimed at school children, edited by a teacher. However, B. Bergonzi, *Heroes' Twilight* revised edition (London, Macmillan, 1980) and especially A. Rutherford, *The Literature of War* (London, Macmillan, 1978), chapter 4, place the War Poets into historical context.

51   P. Fussell, *The Great War and Modern Memory* (London, Oxford UP, 1975).

52   These comments are taken from reviews of a book influenced by Fussell, Geoff Dyer's *The Missing of the Somme* (London, Hamish Hamilton, 1994); *Sunday Times*, 23 October 1994 (Kate Saunders); *Independent*, undated clipping, 1994 (Mick Imlah).

53   'The Initial Shock ... A conversation with Paul Fussell', p.1 at http://raven.cc.ukans.edu/~kansite/ww_one/comment/fussell. htm

54   See his review in *Newsletter of the Friends of Amherst College*, winter 1976.

55   R. Prior and T. Wilson, 'Paul Fussell at War' *War In History*, 1, 1 (1994), esp. pp.66–72; Paul Fussell, *Wartime: Understanding and Behavior in the Second World War* (Oxford, Oxford UP, 1989).

56   Quoted in John Hill, *Sex, Class and Realism: British Cinema 1956–1963* (London, BFI, 1986) p.24.

57   The following section is indebted to Alex Danchev, '"Bunking" and Debunking: The Controversies of the 1960s' in Brian Bond (ed.), *The First World War and British Military History* (Oxford, Clarendon Press, 1991) pp.281–8 and Joan Littlewood, *Joan's Book* (London, Methuen, 1994).

58   Theatre Workshop, *Oh! What a Lovely War* (London, Methuen Drama, 1998) pp.105–6; Littlewood, p.691.

59   *The Times* 13 September 1999.

60   For this series see Danchev, 'Bunking' pp.79–81 and Kenneth Passingham, *The Guinness Book of TV Facts and Feats* (London, Guinness Superlatives, 1984) pp.89–90.

61   For a concise statement of Terraine's thesis, see his 'Haig' in M. Carver (ed.), *The War Lords* (London, Weidenfeld and Nicolson, 1976). For a critical assessment of Terraine's thesis, and a listing of Terraine's works, see Danchev, 'Bunking and Debunking', pp.273–80 and Keith Simpson, 'The Reputation of Sir Douglas Haig' in Bond, *First World War* pp.151–5, 161–2.

62   John Charmley, *Churchill: The End of Glory* (London, Hodder and Stoughton, 1993); *The Times* 2 January 1993 (review by

Alan Clark); *Sunday Times* 10 January 1993 (review by Anthony Howard).

[63] Jay Winter and Blaine Baggett, *The Great War and the Shaping of the 20th Century* (New York, Penguin Studio, 1996) p.6.

[64] *The Spectator* 18 January 1997 pp.18–19.

[65] Stephen Badsey, 'The Great War since *"The Great War"* (1964)', unpublished paper, 1998.

[66] See letters of praise published in *The Radio Times* 21–27 August, 25 September–1 October 1999.

[67] *The Times* 17 July 1998; *Daily Express* 6 November 1998.

Chapter 2

[1] Or at least that part which involved Germany. Separate treaties were signed with other belligerents.

[2] Harold Nicolson, *Peacemaking 1919* (New York, Grosset & Dunlap, 1971) pp.368–9.

[3] Quoted in Alan Sharp, *The Versailles Settlement: Peacemaking in Paris 1919* (New York, St Martin's Press, 1991) p.87.

[4] David Lloyd George, *War Memoirs* Vol. I new edition (London, Odhams, 1938) pp.32–4. See also Keith Wilson, 'Britain' in Keith Wilson (ed.), *Decisions for War, 1914* (New York, St Martin's Press, 1995) pp.175–6, and chapter 1 above.

[5] Donald Kagan, *On the Origins of War and the Preservation of Peace* (New York, Anchor Books, 1996) p.101.

[6] David Dilkes, 'Introduction' to *Retreat from Power* Vol. I *1906–1939* (London, Macmillan, 1980) p.2.

[7] In Craig Wilcox (ed., assisted by Janice Aldridge), *The Great War: Gains and Losses – ANZAC and Empire* (Canberra, Australian War Memorial and Australian National University, 1995) p.211.

[8] The title of a chapter in Gwyn A. Williams, *When Was Wales?* (London, Penguin, 1991).

[9] Quoted in Donald Read, *Edwardian England 1901–1915* (London, Harrap, 1972) p.72.

10   Among the most accessible texts on Wilhelmine Germany are: David Blackbourn, *The Fontana History of Germany 1780–1918: The Long Nineteenth Century* (London, Fontana, 1997); Holger H. Herwig, *Hammer or Anvil? Modern Germany, 1648–Present* (Lexington, MA, D.C. Heath, 1994); Ian Porter and Ian Armour, *Imperial Germany 1890–1918* (London, Longman, 1991).

11   Herwig, *Hammer or Anvil?* p.32.

12   Blackbourn, *Germany 1780–1918* p.418.

13   John C.G. Röhl, *The Kaiser and His Court: Wilhelm II and the Government of Germany* (Cambridge, Cambridge UP, 1994) pp.3, 158–60.

14   For a critique, see A.J. Nicholls, 'The Myth of the German Sonderweg' in Cyril Buffet and Beatrice Heuser, *Haunted by History: Myths in International Relations* (Oxford, Berghahn, 1998) pp.209–22.

15   Röhl, *Kaiser* p.8.

16   The literature on the subject is truly vast. The best book-length survey is probably James Joll, *The Origins of the First World War* second edition (London, Longman, 1992).

17   This section is based largely on Holger H. Herwig, *Luxury Fleet: The German Imperial Navy, 1888–1918* (London, Allen and Unwin, 1980) and Williamson Murray, 'Naval Power in World War I' in Colin S. Grey and Roger W. Barnett, *Seapower and Strategy* (London, Tri-Service Press, 1989) pp.188–91.

18   Quoted in Paul Kennedy, *The Rise and Fall of British Naval Mastery*, third edition (London, Fontana, 1991) p.255.

19   Quoted in Holger H. Herwig, 'Strategic Uncertainties of a nation-state: Prussia-Germany, 1871–1918'. in Williamson Murray, MacGregor Knox, and Alvin Bernstein, *The Making of Strategy; Rulers, States and War* (Cambridge, Cambridge UP, 1994) p.270.

20   V.R. Berghahn, *Germany and the Approach of War in 1914* second edition (London, Macmillan, 1993) pp.42, 44, 53.

21   Fritz Fischer, 'German war aims 1914–1918 and German Policy before the war' in Barry Hunt and Adrian Preston (eds.), *War*

Aims and Strategic Policy in the Great War (London, Croom Helm, 1977) pp.106–7; Berghahn, *Germany* pp.102–3.

22 For a stimulating discussion of the whole subject, see Paul M. Kennedy, *The Rise of the Anglo-German Antagonism 1860–1914* (London, Ashfield Press, 1987).

23 Quoted in Paul Kennedy, *The Realities Behind Diplomacy* (London, Fontana, 1983) p.129.

24 Hew Strachan, *The Politics of the British Army* (Oxford, Clarendon, 1997) pp.264–5.

25 Joll, *Origins* pp.71–4; Blackbourn, *Germany 1780–1918* pp.374–5.

26 Gerhard Ritter, *The Schlieffen Plan* (Westport, CT, Greenwood, 1979); Arden Bucholz, *Moltke, Schlieffen and Prussian War Planning* (Oxford, Berg, 1991) chapters 3 to 6.

27 e.g. Holger H. Herwig, *The First World War: Germany and Austria-Hungary 1914–1918* (London, Arnold, 1997) p.47; William H. McNeill, *The Pursuit of Power* (Chicago, University of Chicago Press, 1984) p.306.

28 Azar Gat, *The Development of Military Thought: The Nineteenth Century* quoted in Bond, *Pursuit* p.94. Terence Zuber, 'The Schlieffen Plan Reconsidered' in *War in History* 6 (3) 1999 pp.262–305, however, argues that there was no one 'Schlieffen plan', but rather a series of plans, and that German strategy had more flexibility than has been asserted.

29 Röhl, *Kaiser* pp.162–89.

30 Berghahn, *Germany* p.180; H.W. Koch, 'Introduction' in H.W. Koch (ed.), *The Origins of the First World War* second edition (London, Macmillan, 1984) p.12.

31 Röhl, *Kaiser* pp.166, 176.

32 See Samuel R. Williamson, Jr, *Austria and the Origins of the First World War* (New York, St Martin's Press, 1991) and Fritz Fellner, 'Austria-Hungary', in Wilson, *Decisions* pp.9–25.

33 Quoted in Porter and Armour, *Imperial Germany* pp.99–100.

34 Gordon Martel, *The Origins of the First World War* second edition (London, Longman, 1996) p.79.

35 See Berghahn, *Germany* pp.156–74.

36   Egmont Zechlin, 'Cabinet versus Economic Warfare in Germany' in Koch, *Origins* p.198–201.

37   John C.G. Röhl, 'Germany' in Wilson, *Decisions for War* pp.32–4; Harmut Pogge von Strandmann, 'Germany and the Coming of War' in R.J.W. Evans and Harmut Pogge von Strandmann, *The Coming of the First World War* (Oxford, Clarendon, 1990) pp.116–17, 122–3; David E. Kaiser, 'Germany and the Origins of the First World War', *Journal of Modern History* 55 (1983) pp.445, 458, 468.

38   John F.V. Kieger, 'France' in Wilson, *Decisions* p.145.

39   Walter Scott (ed.), *A Collection of scarce and valuable tracts ...* second edition (London, 1809) p.169. I owe this reference to David Trim, who has generously shared the fruits of his as yet unpublished research with me.

40   Winston S. Churchill, *The World Crisis* Vol. II (London, Odhams, nd) p.1015.

41   Christopher D. Hall, *British Strategy in the Napoleonic War 1803–15* second edition (Manchester, Manchester UP, 1999) p.86.

42   Brian Bond, *Liddell Hart: A Study of his Military Thought* (London, Cassell, 1977) p.69.

43   Quoted in Kennedy, *British Naval Mastery* p.33.

44   Niall Ferguson, *The Pity of War* (London, Penguin, 1998) p.67.

45   Winston S. Churchill, *The Gathering Storm* (New York, Bantam, 1961) p.488. See also Eliot A. Cohen, 'Churchill and Coalition Strategy in World War II' in Paul Kennedy (ed.), *Grand Strategies in War and Peace* (New Haven, Yale UP, 1991) pp.60–63.

46   Quoted in C.J. Bartlett in *Defence and Diplomacy: Britain and the Great Powers 1815–1914* (Manchester, Manchester UP, 1993) p.125.

47   Quoted in Gordon Craig, 'The System of Alliances and the Balance of Power' in J.P.T. Bury (ed.), *The New Cambridge Modern History*, Vol. X, *The Zenith of European Power 1830–70* (Cambridge, Cambridge UP, 1967) p.249.

48   Rudyard Kipling, 'Recessional' in Helen Gardner (ed.), *The New Oxford Book of English Verse 1250–1950* (Oxford, Oxford UP, 1984) pp.815–16.

49   Paul Kennedy, *The Rise and Fall of the Great Powers* (London, Fontana, 1988) p.295.

50   P.M.H. Bell, *France and Britain 1900–1940: Entente & Estrangement* (London, Longman, 1996) p.50.

51   For the *Entente Cordiale*, see Bell, *France and Britain* pp.23–59.

52   Zara S. Steiner, *Britain and the Origins of the First World War* (London, Macmillan, 1977) p.77.

53   Berghahn, *Germany* pp.106–8.

54   John Gooch, 'The weary titan: Strategy and policy in Great Britain, 1890–1918' in Murray et al, *Making of Strategy* p.281.

55   Bell, *France and Britain* pp.48–9; Kennedy, *Realities* p.134.

56   Ferguson, *Pity* pp.62–3.

57   H.H. Asquith (Michael and Eleanor Brock eds.), *Letters to Venetia Stanley*, new edition (Oxford, Oxford UP, 1985) p.146.

58   Keith Wilson, 'Britain', in Keith Wilson (ed.), *Decisions for War, 1914* (New York, St Martin's Press, 1995) pp.184–5.

59   Colin S. Gray, *Modern Strategy* (Oxford, Oxford UP, 1999) p.66.

Chapter 3

1   Ken Weller, *Don't be a Soldier! The Radical Anti-War Movement in North London 1914–1918* (London, Journeyman Press, 1985) pp. 37–9.

2   Alexis de Tocqueville (Richard D. Heffner, ed.), *Democracy in America* (New York, Mentor, 1956) pp.278, 282.

3   Neil A. Wynn, *From Progressivism to Prosperity: World War I and American Society* (New York, Holmes & Meier, 1986) p.41.

4   Weller, *Don't be a Soldier* p.29.

5   John Horne, 'Introduction: mobilizing for "total war", 1914–18' in

John Horne (ed.), *State, society and mobilization in Europe during the First World War* (Cambridge, Cambridge UP, 1997) p.3.

6   Ian Beckett, 'The nation in arms, 1914–18' in Ian F.W. Beckett and Keith Simpson, *A Nation in Arms: A social study of the British army in the First World War* (Manchester, Manchester UP, 1985) pp.15–17.

7   On this subject, see Peter Simkins' authoritative *Kitchener's Army* (Manchester, Manchester UP, 1988).

8   On this complicated subject see Keith Grieves, *The Politics of Manpower, 1914–18* (Manchester, Manchester UP, 1988).

9   Simkins, *Kitchener's Army* p.xiv.

10 Figures from Robert Holland, 'The British Empire and the Great War, 1914–1918' in Judith M. Brown and Wm. Roger Louis (eds.), *The Oxford History of the British Empire* Vol. IV, *The Twentieth Century* (Oxford, Oxford UP, 1999) p.117. Regrettably, space precludes any further examination of the Home Fronts of the Empire, but see Jeffrey Grey, *A Military History of Australia* (Cambridge, Cambridge UP, 1990) and Desmond Morton, *A Military History of Canada*, fourth edition (Toronto, McClelland & Stewart, 1999).

11 R.J.Q. Adams, *Arms and the Wizard: Lloyd George and the Ministry of Munitions 1915–16* (London, Cassell, 1978) pp.172–5, 182.

12 Peter Dewey, *War and Progress: Britain 1914–1945* (London, Longman, 1997) p.28.

13 Keith Grieves, *Sir Eric Geddes* (Manchester, Manchester UP, 1989).

14 J.M. Bourne, *Britain and The Great War* (London, Arnold, 1989) p.192.

15 Wynn, *Progressivism* p.30.

16 Paul A.C. Koistinen, *Mobilizing for Modern War: The Political Economy of American Warfare 1865–1919* (Lawrence, KS, University Press of Kansas, 1997) pp.124–6.

17 John Patrick Finnegan, *Against the Spectre of a Dragon* (Westport, CT, Greenwood Press, 1974) pp.190–91.

[18]   Timothy K. Nenninger, 'American Military Effectiveness in the First World War' in Allan R. Millett and Williamson Murray, *Military Effectiveness* Vol. I (London, Unwin-Hyman, 1988) p.121.

[19]   Quoted in Malcolm Brown, *The Imperial War Museum Book of the First World War* (London, Sidgwick and Jackson, 1993) p.226.

[20]   Nicholas Reeves, 'The Power of Film Propaganda – myth or reality? *Historical Journal of Film, Radio and Television* 13: 2 (1993) p.186.

[21]   On this whole question, see the important article by John Horne, 'Remobilizing for "total war": France and Britain, 1917–1918' in Horne, *State, Society and Mobilization* pp.195–211.

[22]   This idea draws upon the 'military participation ration' thesis: see S. Andreski, *Military Organisation and Society* new edition (London, RKP, 1968).

[23]   Horne 'Remobilizing' p. 15; Wilhelm Diest, 'The German army, the authoritarian nation-state and total war' pp.165–72, both in Horne, *State, Society and Mobilization*.

[24]   Richard Bessel, *Germany After the First World War* (Oxford, Oxford UP, 1995) pp.41–2.

[25]   David Stevenson, *The First World War and International Politics* (Oxford, Oxford UP, 1988) p.89.

[26]   Stevenson, 'War Aims and Peace Negotiations' in Strachan, *First World War* p.207.

[27]   Brian Bond, *The Pursuit of Victory* (Oxford, Oxford UP, 1996) p.105; Stevenson, *International Politics* p.95; idem, 'War Aims and Peace Negotiations' in Strachan, *First World War* pp.205–7.

[28]   Michael Howard, 'British Grand Strategy in World War I' in Paul Kennedy (ed.), *Grand Strategies in War and Peace* (New Haven, Yale UP, 1991) p.34; idem, *Studies in War and Peace* (New York, Viking, 1972) p.105.

[29]   In Africa things were different: see Matthew Bennett, 'The German Experience' in Ian F.W. Beckett, *The Roots of Counter-Insurgency* (London, Blandford, 1988) pp.63–6.

30 For the French experience of occupation see Helen McPhail, *The Long Silence* (London, Tauris, 1999).

31 Annette Becker, 'Life in an Occupied Zone: Lille, Roubaix, Tourcoing' in Cecil and Liddle, *Facing Armageddon* pp.633–6, 640.

32 Jacques Willequet, 'Belgium: Life under German Occupation' in *Purnell's History of the First World War* Vol.5 No.3 (1971) pp.1877–9.

33 William Alexander Percy, *Lanterns on the Levee* new edition (Baton Rouge, Louisiana State UP, 1996) p.163.

34 Quoted in Antony Polonsky, 'The German Occupation of Poland During the First and Second World Wars: A Comparison' in Roy A. Prete and A. Hamish Ion (eds.), *Armies of Occupation* (Waterloo, Ontario, Wilfrid Laurier UP, 1984) pp.127–8; see also p.141.

35 Stevenson, 'War Aims' pp.207–8; David French, 'The Strategy of the Entente Powers, 1914–1917' in Strachan, *First World War* pp.56–7.

36 'Preface' to Keith Neilson and Roy A. Prete (eds.), *Coalition Warfare: An Uneasy Accord* (Waterloo, Ontario, Wilfrid Laurier UP, 1981) p.viii.

37 Arthur M. Schlesinger, Jr, *The Cycles of American History* (Harmondsworth, Penguin, 1989) p.53.

38 George W. Baer, *One Hundred Years of Sea Power: The U.S. Navy, 1890–1990* (Stanford, CA, Stanford UP, 1993) pp.35–40.

39 David Reynolds, 'The United States and European Security from Wilson to Kennedy, 1913–1963: A Reappraisal of the '"Isolationist" Tradition', *JRUSI*, Vol.128 No.2 (June 1983) p.20.

40 Comments quoted in Michael H. Hunt, *Crises in U.S. Foreign Policy* (New Haven, Yale UP) p.26.

41 There is a good brief account of America's path to war in Hunt, *Crises* pp.7–55, along with some useful documents.

42 Albert Fried (ed.), *A Day of Dedication: The Essential Writings and Speeches of Woodrow Wilson* (New York, Macmillan, 1965) p.230.

43 Hunt, *Crises* pp.11, 30–31.

44 Fried, *Day of Dedication* p.252.

45 For the text of the House–Grey memorandum see Edward M. House, *The Intimate Papers of Colonel House* Vol. III (London, Benn, 1926) pp.200–202.

46 Hunt, *Crises* p.53.

47 Hunt, *Crises* p.53.

48 Tony Smith, *America's Mission* (Princeton, NJ, Princeton UP, 1994), pp.88–9. My interpretation is indebted to Professor Smith's fine book, as will be obvious to anyone who is familiar with it. See also Thomas J. Knock, *To End All Wars: Woodrow Wilson and the Quest for a New World Order* (New York, Oxford UP, 1992) pp.272–6.

49 James M. McPherson, *Drawn with the Sword* (New York, Oxford UP, 1996) p.209.

50 John Lewis Gaddis, *We Now Know: Rethinking Cold War History* (Oxford, Clarendon, 1998) p.5.

51 Fried, *Day* pp.281–7, 319–20.

52 David French, *The Strategy of the Lloyd George Coalition 1916–18* (Oxford, Clarendon, 1995) p.274; Taylor, *First World War* p.206.

53 Brian Gardner (ed.), *Up the Line to Death: The War Poets 1914–1918* (London, Magnum, 1977) p.49.

54 Robert Saunders' diary, 1 December 1917, in John Ramsden (ed.), *Real Old Tory Politics* (London, The Historians' Press, 1984) p.92.

55 V.H. Rothwell, *British War Aims and Peace Diplomacy 1914–1918* (Oxford, Clarendon Press, 1971) p.65; Stevenson, *First World War* pp.112, 137–8.

56 Lloyd George, *War Memoirs* Vol. II pp.1510–17.

57 French, *Strategy of Lloyd George Coalition* pp.202–5.

58 Trevor Wilson, *The Myriad Faces of War* (Cambridge, Polity, 1988) p.655.

59 Nicholas Reeves, 'The Power of Film Propaganda: myth or reality?' in *Historical Journal of Film, Television and Radio*

Vol.13 No.2 (1993) p.186. For the remobilisation of morale, see the important article by John Horne, 'Remobilizing for "total war": France and Britain, 1917–1918' in Horne, *State, Society and Mobilization* pp.195–211.

60 Bond, *Pursuit* pp.109–11.

Chapter 4

1 B.H. Liddell Hart, *The British Way in Warfare* (London, Faber, 1932) pp.13–17, 37.

2 C.R.M.F. Cruttwell, *The Role of British Strategy in the Great War* (Cambridge, Cambridge UP, 1936) pp.1–4.

3 Christopher D. Hall, *British Strategy in the Napoleonic War 1803–15* (Manchester, Manchester UP/Sandpiper, 1999) pp.76–7. For extended critical analysis of Liddell Hart's *British Way in Warfare* see Brian Bond, *Liddell Hart: A Study of his Military Thought* (London, Cassell, 1977) chapter 3 and Alex Danchev, *Alchemist of War: The Life of Basil Liddell Hart* (London, Weidenfeld & Nicolson, 1998) pp.168–78.

4 John Gooch, 'Maritime Command: Mahan and Corbett' in Colin S. Grey and Roger W. Barnett, *Seapower and Strategy* (London, Tri-Service Press, 1989) pp.41–2.

5 Samuel R. Williamson, Jr, *The Politics of Grand Strategy: Britain and France Prepare for War, 1904–1914* new edition (London, Ashfield, 1990) pp.187–94.

6 Gooch, 'Weary titan' pp.298–9.

7 For Kitchener see George H. Cassar, *Kitchener: Architect of Victory* (London, Kimber, 1977).

8 What follows is largely based on David French, *British Strategy and War Aims 1914–1916* (London, Allen & Unwin, 1986). Professor French provides a convenient summary of his thesis in 'Allies, Rivals and Enemies: British Strategy and War Aims during the First World War' in John Turner (ed.), *Britain and the First World War* (London, Unwin-Hyman, 1988). See also

Michael Howard, 'British Grand Strategy in World War I' in Paul Kennedy (ed.), *Grand Strategies in War and Peace* (New Haven, Yale UP, 1991).

9 Cited in Jehuda Wallach, *Uneasy Coalition: The Entente Experience in World War I* (Westport, CT, Greenwood, 1993) p.21.

10 Paul Kennedy, 'Military Coalitions and Coalition Warfare over the Past Century' in Keith Neilson and Roy A. Prete, *Coalition Warfare: An Uneasy Accord* (Waterloo, Ontario, Wilfrid Laurier UP, 1983) p.3.

11 William Philpott, 'Britain, France and the Belgian Army' in Brian Bond et al *Look to Your Front: Studies in the First World War* (Staplehurst, Spellmount, 1999) pp.121–2.

12 J.E. Edmonds, *Military Operations France and Belgium, 1914* Vol. I, reprint edition (Woking, Shearer, nd) p.499 [the British Official History: in future, volumes will be given an abbreviated title].

13 John J. Pershing, *My Experiences in the First World War* Vol. I (New York, Da Capo, two volumes in one edition, 1995) p.38; Wallach, *Uneasy Coalition* p.5.

14 Ferdinand Foch (trans. by T. Bentley Mott), *The Memoirs of Marshal Foch* (London, Heinemann, 1931) p.272.

15 Diary of Major General G.S. Clive, 18 April 1918, CAB45/210, P[ublic] R[ecord] O[ffice], cited in Gary Sheffield, 'British High Command in the First World War: An Overview' in Gary Sheffield and Geoffrey Till (eds.), *Challenges of High Command in the Twentieth Century* Occasional Paper 38 (Camberley, SCSI, 1999) p.20.

16 G.D. Sheffield, 'How Even Was the Learning Curve? Reflections on the British and Dominion Armies on the Western Front, 1916–18' paper forthcoming in *Proceedings* of 2000 Canadian Military History Conference.

17 Desmond Morton, 'Exerting Control: The Development of Canadian Authority over the Canadian Expeditionary Force, 1914–1919' in Timothy Travers and Christon Archer, *Men at War* (Chicago, Precedent, 1982) p.7.

18 See the notorious meeting between Sir John French and General Lanrezac in August 1914: John Terraine, *Mons: The Retreat to Victory* new edition (London, Leo Cooper, 1991) p.55.

19 Cassar, *Kitchener* p.389.

20 French, *British Strategy* pp.xii–xiv.

21 For Britain's increasing reliance on American financial and material aid see French, *British Strategy* pp.121–4, 248.

22 Peter Dewey, *War and Progress: Britain 1914–1945* (London, Longman, 1997) pp.43–6; Kennedy, *Rise and Fall of the Great Powers* p.314.

23 A.T. Mahan, *The Influence of Sea Power upon History* new edition (London, Methuen, 1965) p.138. For a stimulating account see Jon Tetsuro Sumida, *Inventing Grand Strategy and Teaching Strategy* (Washington, DC, Woodrow Center Press, 1997).

24 I.F. Clarke, *Voices Prophesying War 1763–1984* (London, Panther, 1970) pp.83–5.

25 For an authoritative and very readable study of Jutland, see Andrew Gordon, *Rules of the Game* (London, Constable, 1996).

26 Paul G. Halpern, *A Naval History of World War I* (London, UCL Press, 1994) pp.328–9.

27 Geoffrey Bennett, *Naval Battles of the First World War* (London, Pan, 1983) p.226.

28 Geoffrey Till, 'Passchendaele: The Maritime Dimension' in Peter H. Liddle (ed.), *Passchendaele in Perspective: The Third Battle of Ypres* (London, Pen & Sword, 1997) p.85.

29 Andrew A. Wiest, *Passchendaele and the Royal Navy* (Westport, CT, Greenwood, 1995) p.104.

30 Halpern, *Naval History of World War I* p.416.

31 B.H. Liddell Hart, *History of the First World War* (London, Cassell, 1970 edn.) p.592.

32 B.J.C. McKercher, 'Economic Warfare' in Hew Strachan (ed.), *The Oxford Illustrated History of the First World War* (Oxford, Oxford UP, 1998) pp.125, 133. See also Bessel, *Germany* pp.35–44.

[33]   Surgeon Rear-Admiral John R. Muir, *Years of Endurance* (London, Philip Allan, 1936) p.291.

[34]   Bryan Ranft, 'The Royal Navy and the War at Sea', in Turner, *Britain and the First World War* p.54.

[35]   Geoffrey Till, 'The Gallipoli Campaign, Command Performances' in Sheffield and Till, *Challenges of High Command* pp.26–8.

[36]   Lieutenant General Sir George McMunn, *Behind the Scenes in Many Wars* (London, Murray, 1930) pp.120–21.

[37]   Wilson, *Myriad Faces* p.119.

[38]   John Lee, *A Soldier's Life: General Sir Ian Hamilton 1853–1947* (London, Macmillan, 2000) p.xxvi. For Hamilton's problems, see chapter 9.

[39]   Michael Howard, *The Causes of Wars* (London, Temple Smith, 1983) p.186.

[40]   Matthew Hughes, *Allenby and British Strategy in the Middle East 1917–1919* (London, Cass, 1999) pp.64–6, 157–9.

[41]   I owe this point to Professor Peter Simkins.

[42]   The best study of British strategy in this period is French, *Strategy of Lloyd George Coalition*.

[43]   See George H. Cassar, *Asquith as War Leader* (London, Hambledon, 1994) for a sympathetic but fair assessment.

[44]   Walter Roch, *Mr Lloyd George and the War* (London, Chatto & Windus, 1920) p.218.

[45]   David French, 'A One-Man Show? Civil-Military Relations in Britain during the First World War', in Paul Smith (ed.), *Government and the Armed Forces in Britain 1856–1990* (London, Hambledon, 1996) pp.79–83.

[46]   A.J.P. Taylor (ed.), *Lloyd George: A Diary by Francis Stevenson* (London, Hutchinson, 1971) p.120.

[47]   David R. Woodward, *Lloyd George and the Generals* (Newark, NJ, University of Delaware Press, 1983) pp.334–5.

[48]   Woodward, *Lloyd George* p.186.

[49]   Hughes, *Allenby* p.160, however, persuasively argues that the effort expended in Palestine and Syria to attain security for the Empire was 'excessive'.

50   Arguably, the presence of a relatively small number of British and French troops in Italy helped to tie down Austrian troops that might have been used on the Western Front in 1918 with decisive results. This commitment in support of a major Allied army was, however, of a rather different order to the various campaigns mounted against the Turks. See George H. Cassar, *The Forgotten Front: The British Campaign in Italy, 1917–1918* (London, Hambledon, 1998) p.222.

51   Captain E.W. Sheppard, *Military History for the Staff College Entrance Examination* second edition (Aldershot, Gale & Polden, nd, c. 1936) p.67.

52   Sonia Orwell and Ian Angus, *The Collected Essays, Journalism and Letters of George Orwell* Vol. II (Harmondsworth, Penguin, 1970) pp.284–5.

53   But see the comments on the 'side-shows' above.

54   John Turner, *British Politics and the Great War* (New Haven, Yale UP, 1992) p.297.

55   Hew Strachan, *The Politics of the British Army* (Oxford, Clarendon, 1997) pp.137–43.

56   Colin S. Gray, 'Why Strategy Is Difficult' in *Joint Forces Quarterly* summer 1999 p.12.

Chapter 5

1   Taylor, *First World War* p.34.

2   Norman Dixon, *On the Psychology of Military Incompetence* (London, Futura, 1979) p.80.

3   A.B. Beauman, *Then a Soldier* (London, P.R. Macmillan, 1960) p.31.

4   Quoted in J.E. Edmonds, *A Short History of World War I* (Oxford, Oxford UP, 1951) p.61.

5   See Grady McWhiney and Perry D. Jamieson, *Attack and Die: Civil War Military Tactics and the Southern Heritage* (Tuscaloosa, AL, University of Alabama Press, 1984). See also

Paddy Griffith's important qualifications to the idea of a 'rifle revolution' in the American Civil War in *Forward into Battle* second edition (Swindon, Crowood, 1990) pp.78–82.

6   Paddy Griffith, *Battle Tactics of the Western Front* (London, Yale UP, 1994) pp.115, 130, 136.

7   Geoffrey Noon, 'The Treatment of Casualties in the Great War', in Paddy Griffith (ed.), *British Fighting Methods in the Great War* (London, Cass, 1996) pp.90, 101, 102.

8   Quoted in V.W. Germains, *The Kitchener Armies* (London, Peter Davies, 1930) p.16.

9   Michael Howard, 'Men against Fire: The Doctrine of the Offensive in 1914' in Peter Paret (ed.), *Makers of Modern Strategy from Machiavelli to the Nuclear Age* (Oxford, Clarendon Press, 1986) pp.519, 522; Tim Travers, *The Killing Ground* (London, Unwin-Hyman, 1987) chapter 2.

10   Griffith, *Forward* p.75.

11   Griffith, *Forward*, pp.89–94; Howard, 'Men against Fire' pp.522–4; Bruce I. Gudmundson, *Stormtroop Tactics: Innovation in the German Army, 1914–1918* (Westport, CT, Praeger, 1989) pp.5–13.

12   I.F.W. Beckett, lecture given to the British Commission for Military History, 13 November 1999.

13   Lord Kitchener quoted in John Hussey, 'Without an Army, and Without any Preparation to Equip One: The Financial and Industrial Background to 1914', *British Army Review*, 109, April 1995 p.76.

14   Kagan, *Origins* pp.211–14.

15   Cassar, *Kitchener* p.331.

16   Quoted in Kenneth O. Morgan, 'Lloyd George and the Modern World', in *David Lloyd George: The Llanystumdwy Lectures 1990–1996* (Gwynedd Council, 1997) p.31.

17   Halpern, *Naval History of World War I* p.7.

18   Figures from Hussey, 'Without an Army' p.76.

19   Edward M. Spiers, 'The Late Victorian Army 1868–1914' in David Chandler and Ian Beckett (eds.), *The Oxford Illustrated History of the British Army* (Oxford, Oxford UP, 1994)

pp.205–7, 211–14. See also idem, *Haldane: A Military Reformer* (Edinburgh, Edinburgh UP, 1980).

20 Edmonds, *Military Operations 1914*, Vol. I p.10.

21 Cyril Falls, *The First World War* (London, Longman, 1960) p.16.

22 David French, *British Economic and Strategic Planning 1905–1915* (London, Allen & Unwin, 1982) pp.36, 48.

23 Quoted in Harold E. Raugh, Jr, *Wavell in the Middle East, 1939–41* (London, Brassey's, 1993) p.2.

24 J.E. Edmonds and G.C. Wynne, *Military Operations 1915* Vol. I (London, Macmillan, 1927) p.152.

25 Lieutenant Colonel R. Barnett Barker to Mrs Stone, 2 August 1916 in G.D. Sheffield and G.I.S. Inglis (eds.), *From Vimy Ridge to the Rhine: The Great War Letters of Christopher Stone DSO MC* (Marlborough, Crowood, 1989) p.64.

26 G.H.F. Nichols, *The 18th Division in the Great War* (Edinburgh, Blackwood, 1922) p.42.

27 Lieutenant C. Pennefather to Lieutenant C. Hoskyns, March [?] 1915, quoted in Tom Donovan (compiler), *The Hazy Red Hell* (Staplehurst, Spellmount, 1999) p.25.

28 For Neuve Chapelle, see Edmonds and Wynne, *Military Operations 1915* Vol. I, chapters 5–7.

29 But see chapter 7 below for some important exceptions to this rule.

30 Edmonds, *Military Operations 1915* Vol. II p.393.

31 A.W. Pagan, *Infantry* (Aldershot, Gale & Polden, 1951) p.27.

32 Cyril Falls, *History of the 36th Ulster Division* (Belfast, M'Caw, Stevenson & Orr, 1922) p.68.

33 Bill Rawling, *Surviving Trench Warfare: Technology and the Canadian Corps 1914–1918* (Toronto, University of Toronto Press, 1992) p.23.

34 V.E. Inglefield, *The History of the Twentieth (Light) Division* (London, Nisbet, 1921) p.8.

35 Donald C. Richter (ed.), *Lionel Sotheby's Great War* (Athens, OH, Ohio UP, 1997) p.58.

[36] Anon, *The 23rd London Regiment 1798–1919* (London, The Times, 1936) p.42.

[37] J.C. Latter, *The History of the Lancashire Fusiliers 1914–18* Vol.I (Aldershot, Gale & Polden, 1949) p.35.

[38] Sir Frederick Ponsonby, *The Grenadier Guards in the Great War of 1914–1918* Vol. III (London, Macmillan, 1920) pp.230–33.

[39] John H. Morrow, Jr, *The Great War in the Air* (Shrewsbury, Airlife, 1993) p.115.

[40] 'Report on Action at Neuve Chapelle', appx. 12, March 1915, WO 95/269, PRO.

[41] Rawling, *Surviving* p.46.

[42] Rudyard Kipling, *The Irish Guards in the Great War: The First Battalion* (Staplehurst, Spellmount, 1997) p.83.

[43] Technically, the Royal Regiment of Artillery was at this stage divided into the Royal Horse Artillery (RHA) with light guns, the maids-of-all-work of the Royal Field Artillery and the Royal Garrison Artillery, equipped with the heaviest weapons.

[44] Jonathan Bailey, 'British Artillery in the Great War' in Griffith, *British Fighting Methods* p.29.

[45] Bailey, 'British Artillery' p.29.

[46] First Army 'Plan of Operations', WO 106/390, PRO.

[47] For gas, Edward M. Spiers, *Chemical Warfare* (London, Macmillan, 1988) chapter 2; Tim Cook, *No Place to Run: The Canadian Corps and Gas Warfare in the First World War* (Vancouver, UBC Press, 1999).

[48] Sir Charles Harington, *'Tim' Harington Looks Back* (London, Murray, 1940) p.53.

[49] J.M. Bourne, 'British Generals in the First World War' in G.D. Sheffield (ed.), *Leadership and Command: The Anglo-American Military Experience Since 1861* (London, Brassey's, 1997) pp.93–116.

[50] Richard Holmes, *The Little Field Marshal* (London, Cape, 1981) p.305.

[51] Bourne, 'British Generals' p.109.

52   Robin Prior and Trevor Wilson, *Command on the Western Front* (Oxford, Blackwell, 1992) pp.25–32, 100–7.

Chapter 6

1   John Terraine, *Douglas Haig: The Educated Soldier* (London, Hutchinson, 1963).
2   See Tim Travers, *The Killing Ground* (London, Unwin-Hyman, 1987). For convenience, these quotations are taken from his article in Chandler and Beckett, *Oxford History* pp.218–19.
3   There are numerous studies of Haig. Terraine's *Douglas Haig* has yet to be superseded, but should be supplemented by the essays in Brian Bond and Nigel Cave (eds.), *Haig: A Reappraisal 70 Years On* (London, Leo Cooper, 1999). Denis Winter's *Haig's Command* (London, Viking, 1991) is a deeply flawed book centred on a bizarre conspiracy theory. For a devastating critique by a reputable scholar see Jeffrey Grey's review in *Journal of the Society of Army Historical Research* LXXI, 25 (1993) pp.60–63.
4   John Terraine, *The Smoke and the Fire: Myths and Anti-Myths of War 1861–1945* (London, Sidgwick and Jackson, 1980) pp.174–5.
5   Quoted in Niall Barr and Gary Sheffield, 'Douglas Haig, the Common Soldier, and the British Legion' in Bond and Cave, *Haig* p.226. This comment, apparently by a BEF veteran, is written in the margin of a biography of Haig held in the library of RMA Sandhurst.
6   Winston S. Churchill, *Great Contemporaries* (London, Fontana, 1959) p.184.
7   John Keegan, *The Mask of Command* (London, Cape, 1987) p.11.
8   Ian F.W. Beckett, *Johnnie Gough, V.C.* (London, Tom Donovan, 1989) pp.202–8.
9   Field Marshal Earl Wavell, *The Good Soldier* (London, Macmillan, 1948) p.4.

[10] McWhiney and Jamieson, *Attack & Die* p.70.

[11] Gordon A. Craig, 'Delbrück: the Military Historian' in Peter Paret (ed.), *Makers of Modern Strategy from Machiavelli to the Nuclear Age* (Oxford, Clarendon, 1986) pp.341–3.

[12] Jacob Kipp, 'Two Views of Warsaw: The Russian Civil War and Soviet Operational Art, 1920–1932' in B.J.C. McKercher and Michael A. Hennessy, *The Operational Art: Developments in the Theories of War* (Westport, CT, Praeger, 1996) pp.61–9.

[13] Quoted in Shimon Naveh, *In Pursuit of Military Excellence: The Evolution of Operational Theory* (London, Cass, 1997) p.183.

[14] J.M. Bourne, 'Haig and the Historians' in Bond and Cave, *Haig* p.5

[15] Williamson Murray, 'Thinking about Revolutions in Military Affairs', *Joint Forces Quarterly* summer 1997 p.107.

[16] Jonathan Bailey, *The First World War and the Birth of the Modern Style of Warfare*, Occasional Paper 22 (Camberley, SCSI, 1996). Quotes are from pp.3, 4, 6, 32.

[17] Prior and Wilson, *Command* p.309. I made a similar point in 1988: see G.D. Sheffield, '*Blitzkrieg* and Attrition: Land Operations in Europe 1914–45' in G.D. Sheffield and Colin McInnes, *Warfare in the Twentieth Century: Theory and Practice* (London, Unwin-Hyman, 1988).

[18] James R. Fitzsimonds and Jan M. Van Tol, 'Revolutions in Military Affairs', *Joint Forces Quarterly* spring 1994 pp.25–6.

[19] Sir Lawrence Bragg et al, *Artillery Survey in the First World War* (London, Field Survey Association, 1971) p.31.

[20] Guy Hartcup, *The War of Invention: Scientific Developments, 1914–18* (London, Brassey's, 1988) p.58. Emphasis added by present author.

[21] Peter Chasseaud, 'Field Survey in the Salient, Cartography and Artillery Survey in the Flanders Operations in 1917' in Peter Liddle (ed.), *Passchendaele in Perspective: The Third Battle of Ypres* (London, Pen & Sword, 1997) pp.117–39; idem, *Artillery's Astrologers* (Lewes, Mapbooks, 1999).

[22] Albert P. Palazzo, 'The British Army's Counter-Battery Staff

Office and the Control of the Enemy in World War I', *Journal of Military History* 63 (January 1999) pp.56–7, 73.

23   See R.E. Priestly, *The Signal Service in the European War of 1914 to 1918 (France)* (Chatham, Mackay, 1921).

24   Figures from Peter Simkins, *Air Fighting 1914–18* (London, Imperial War Museum, 1978), which is an excellent brief introduction to the subject. For what follows, see this source and Morrow, *The Great War in the Air*.

25   Sir Frederick Sykes, *From Many Angles: An Autobiography* (London, Harrap, 1942) p.105; D.J. Jordan, 'Army co-operation missions of the Royal Flying Corps/Royal Air Force 1914–1918' Ph D, University of Birmingham, 1997.

26   11 Canadian Brigade order, 13 August 1917, F.R. Phelan papers, MG30 e54 Vol. 1 file 18, N[ational] A[rchives] of C[anada].

27   J.H. Boraston, *Sir Douglas Haig's Despatches* new edition (London, Dent, 1979) p.320.

28   See a Canadian officer's report on French tactics in 1916, which had a distinct family likeness to developments in British tactics: Currie papers, MG 30 E100, Vol.35, file 159, NAC.

29   Timothy T. Lupfer, *The Dynamics of Doctrine* Leavenworth Paper No.4 (Fort Leavenworth, KS, 1981); G.C. Wynne, *If Germany Attacks* (London, Faber and Faber, 1940).

30   e.g. Martin Samuels, *Doctrine and Dogma: German and British Infantry Tactics in the First World War* (Westport, CT, Greenwood, 1992) and *Command or Control?: Command, Training and Tactics in the British and German Armies, 1888–1918* (London, Cass, 1995).

31   Michael Crawshaw, 'The Impact of Technology on the BEF and its Commander' in Bond and Cave, *Haig* p.169.

32   For a good overview, see Peter Simkins, 'The Four Armies 1914–1918' in Chandler and Beckett, *Oxford History*. See also the seminal collection of essays in Ian F.W. Beckett and Keith Simpson (eds.), *A Nation in Arms: A Social Study of the British Army in the Great War* (Manchester, Manchester UP, 1985).

[33] Anon, *Sixteenth, Seventeenth, Eighteenth, Nineteenth Battalions The Manchester Regiment: A Record 1914–1918* (Manchester, Sherrat & Hughes, 1922) p.6.

[34] See G.D. Sheffield, *Leadership in the Trenches: Officer-Man Relations, Morale and Discipline in the British Army in the Era of the Great War* (London, Macmillan, 2000) chapters 3 and 4; *Statistics of the Military Effort of the British Empire during the Great War* (London, HMSO, 1922) p.707; J.M. Winter, *The Great War and the British People* (London, Macmillan, 1985) pp.83–4.

[35] Anne Summers, 'Militarism in Britain before the Great War', *History Workshop* 2, 1976 pp.104–23; for the limitations of militarism see Gerard J. DeGroot, *Blighty: British Society in the Era of the Great War* (London, Longman, 1996) pp.39–42.

[36] P.E. Dewey, 'Military Recruiting and the British Labour Force during the First World War' in *The Historical Journal* 27, 1 (1984) p.221.

[37] John Bourne, 'The British Working Man in Arms' in Hugh Cecil and Peter Liddle (eds.), *Facing Armageddon: The First World War Experienced* (London, Leo Cooper, 1996) p.336.

[38] For good evocations of the trench life, see John Ellis, *Eye Deep in Hell* (London, Croom Helm, 1976) and Denis Winter, *Death's Men* (London, Allen Lane, 1978).

[39] Everard Wyrall, *The History of the Duke of Cornwall's Light Infantry 1914–1919* (London, Methuen, 1932) p.3.

[40] Christopher Stone (ed.), *A History of the 22nd (Service) Battalion Royal Fusiliers (Kensington)* (London, privately published, 1923) pp.30–31.

[41] Charles Edmonds (pseud.), *A Subaltern's War* (London, Peter Davies, 1929) pp.120–21.

[42] A.R. Burrowes, *The 1st Battalion Faugh-A-Ballaghs in the Great War* (Aldershot, Gale & Polden, nd) p.48. He was writing of the first half of 1915.

[43] Stone, *22nd Royal Fusiliers* pp.31–2; WO 95/1289, 4 March 1916, PRO.

44 Gordon Corrigan, *Sepoys in the Trenches* (Staplehurst, Spellmount, 1999) p.100.

45 Edmonds, *Short History* p.160.

46 C. Dudley Ward, *The Welsh Regiment of Foot Guards 1915–1918* (London, Murray, 1936) p.80.

47 M. Kincaid-Smith, *The 25th Division in France and Flanders* (London, Harrison, c. 1919) p.126.

48 Tony Ashworth, *Trench Warfare 1914–1918: The Live and Let Live System* (London, Macmillan, 1980) chapter 8.

49 Terence Denman, *Ireland's Unknown Soldiers* (Blackrock, Co. Dublin, Irish Academic Press, 1992) p.106.

50 WO 32/3116, appx. 1 p.15.

51 Falls, *36th Division* p.71.

52 See for instance John Baynes, *Morale* (London, Cassell, 1967); John Keegan, *The Face of Battle* (Harmondsworth, Penguin, 1978); Richard Holmes, *Firing Line* (London, Cape, 1985); J.G. Fuller, *Troop Morale and Popular Culture in the British and Dominion Armies 1914–1918* (Oxford, Clarendon 1991); Bourne, 'British Working Man'.

53 Sheffield, *Leadership in the Trenches*.

54 Correlli Barnett, *The Collapse of British Power* new edition (Gloucester, Alan Sutton, 1984) p.432.

55 Anthony Kellett, 'The Soldier in Battle: Motivational and Behavioral Aspects of the Combat Experience' in Betty Glad (ed.), *Psychological Dimensions of War* (Newbury Park, CA, SAGE, 1990) pp.224–6. This whole chapter is an admirable concise introduction to the subject.

56 Ferguson, *Pity* pp.357–66.

57 Stephen Snelling, *VCs of the First World War: Gallipoli* (Stroud, Alan Sutton, 1995) p.122.

58 G.D. Sheffield, *The Redcaps: A History of the Royal Military Police from the Middle Ages to the Gulf War* (London, Brassey's, 1994) pp.65–6.

59 Sheffield, *Leadership in the Trenches* pp.150–54, 172–4.

60 e.g. George Mosse, *Fallen Soldiers: Reshaping the Memory of*

the World Wars (New York, Oxford UP, 1990) pp.59, 69; Eric J. Leed, *No Man's Land: Combat and Identity In World War I* (Cambridge, Cambridge UP, 1979) p.94.

[61] e.g. Martin Stephen, *The Price of Pity: Poetry, History and Myth in the Great War* (London, Leo Cooper, 1996) pp.182–93; Barnett, *Collapse* pp.428–35.

[62] Published by Chatto and Windus in London, 1922.

[63] I owe this point to Lloyd Clark, who generously shared with me the fruits of his unpublished work on the subject.

[64] Quoted in Brian Bond, 'British Anti-War Writers and Their Critics' in Cecil and Liddle, *Facing Armageddon* p.826.

[65] C.E. Jacomb, *Torment* (London, Melrose, 1920).

Chapter 7

[1] Erich von Falkenhayn, *General Headquarters and its Critical Decisions* (London, Hutchinson, 1919) pp.209–18; Holger H. Herwig, *The First World War: Germany and Austria-Hungary 1914–1918* (London, Arnold, 1997) pp.179–82; Jehuda L. Wallach, *The Dogma of the Battle of Annihilation* (Westport, CT, Greenwood, 1986) pp.170–82.

[2] Falls, *36th Division* p.56.

[3] Prior and Wilson, *Command* p.148.

[4] Edmonds, *Military Operations 1916* Vol. I pp.121–4.

[5] Edmonds, *Military Operations 1916* Vol. I p.485.

[6] Messrs Perry and Cowan's work is part of the SHLM project assessing the military effectiveness of British divisions, and my thanks are due to them for making it available to me. For details of SHLM, see John Lee's article in Griffith, *British Fighting Methods*.

[7] Edmonds, *Military Operations 1916* Vol. I pp.290, 489.

[8] Paddy Griffith, *Battle Tactics of the Western Front* (New Haven, Yale UP, 1994) pp.56–64.

[9] Sir Martin Farndale, *History of the Royal Regiment of Artillery:*

Western Front 1914–18 (London, Royal Artillery Institution, 1986) pp.146–7.

10   Appx II, July 1916, WO 95/2050, PRO.

11   G.H.F. Nichols, *The 18th Division in the Great War* (Edinburgh, Blackwood, 1922) p.48.

12   Edmonds, *Military Operations 1916* Vol. I pp.342–3.

13   Philpott, *Anglo-French Relations* p.105.

14   C.G.T. Dean, unpublished account, L[iddle] C[ollection], University of Leeds.

15   Prior and Wilson, *Command* pp.187–9.

16   There is a good account of the fighting in this area in Michael Stedman's book in the 'Battleground Europe: Somme' series, *La Boisselle, Ovillers/Contalmaison* (London, Leo Cooper, 1997) pp.80–83, 88–92.

17   Bean diary, 30 May 1917, 3DRL 606 Item 70 [2], quoted in G.D. Sheffield, 'One vast Australian cemetery', *Wartime*, 7 (spring 1999) p.22.

18   Peter Simkins, 'Introduction' to Chris McCarthy, *The Somme: The Day-by-Day Account* (London, Arms and Armour, 1993) p.9.

19   Prior and Wilson, *Command* pp.191–2.

20   This account of the cavalry action is based on W. Miles, *Military Operations 1916* Vol. II pp.83–8 and Stephen Badsey, 'Cavalry and the Development of the Breakthrough Doctrine' in Paddy Griffith, *British Fighting Methods in the Great War* (London, Cass, 1996) pp.156–7. After many shared battlefield tours, Dr Badsey finally converted me to the 'short-range paratroops' thesis!

21   Miles, *Military Operations 1916* Vol. II p.560.

22   Robin Prior and Trevor Wilson, 'Summing up the Somme' in *History Today* November 1991 p.39.

23   J.P. Harris, *Men, ideas and tanks* (Manchester, Manchester UP, 1995) chapters 1 and 2; for Haig see pp.54–7, 62.

24   For the role of tanks in this battle, see Trevor Pidgeon, *The Tanks at Flers* (Cobham, Fairmile Books, 1995). I am indebted

to Michael Piercy and George Karger of the SHLM project for information on 41st and 47th divisions respectively.

25 David Lloyd George, *War Memoirs* Vol. I (London, Odhams, 1938) p.385.

26 Quoted in Harris, *Men, Ideas and Tanks* p.62.

27 Kenneth Macksey, *Tank Warfare* (London, Granada, 1976) p.36.

28 Winston S. Churchill, *The World Crisis 1911–1918*, Vol. II (London, Odhams, nd) pp.1219–20.

29 Harris, *Men, ideas and tanks* pp.65, 67.

30 Frank Mitchell, *Tank Warfare* (Stevenage, Spa/Tom Donovan, 1987) pp.17–20.

31 Griffith, *Battle Tactics* p.169.

32 Prior and Wilson, *Command* pp.246–8.

33 Everard Wyrall, *The History of the 19th Division 1914–1918* (London, Arnold, nd) pp.41–2.

34 Appx. 7 and 9 July 1916, War Diary, 1st Australian Division, WO95/3156, PRO.

35 Tom Wintringham and J.N. Blashford-Snell, *Weapons and Tactics* (Harmondsworth, Penguin, 1973) p.11.

36 Report from commander 99th Brigade, 29 July 1916, WO95/1368, PRO.

37 John Lee, 'Some Lessons of the Somme: The British Infantry in 1917' in Bond, *'Look to your Front'* p.80.

38 C.H. Dudley Ward, *History of the Welsh Guards* (London, John Murray, 1920) p.18.

39 Dated 21 August 1916, WO95/2900, PRO. I owe this reference to Michael Orr.

40 O.B. 1792, 13 August 1916, S[taff] C[ollege] L[ibrary].

41 See 'Notes on Somme', files 47 and 48, Montgomery-Massingberd papers, L[iddell] H[art] C[entre] for M[ilitary] A[rchives], King's College London; Fifth Army tactical reports in WO158/344, PRO.

42 H. Stewart, *The New Zealand Division 1916–1919* (Auckland, Whitcombe and Tombs, 1921) p.159.

43 Lee, 'Some Lessons' pp.79–87.

44   Edmonds, *Military Operations 1916* Vol. I p.494.

45   The following paragraphs are largely based on Miles, *Military Operations 1916* Vol. II pp.26–7 & [G.C. Wynne] 'The German Official History: The First Two Months of the Somme', *Army Quarterly* Vol. XXXV, 1 (October 1937) pp. 28–36.

46   Wynne, *If Germany Attacks* pp.118–31; Miles, *Military Operations 1916* Vol. II p.27; Terraine, *Smoke* p.124.

47   James M. McPherson, *Battle Cry of Freedom* (New York, Oxford UP, 1988) p.722.

48   Wynne, 'German Official History' p.35.

49   Sources in this paragraph quoted in Edmonds, *Military Operations 1916* Vol. I pp.494–5.

50   Boraston, *Haig's Dispatches* pp.319–20.

Chapter 8

1   Jonathan Nicholls, *Cheerful Sacrifice: The Battle of Arras 1917* (London, Leo Cooper, 1990) pp.210–11.

2   Anthony Clayton, 'Robert Nivelle and the French Spring Offensive, 1917' in Brian Bond (ed.), *Fallen Stars* (London, Brassey's, 1991) pp.52–63.

3   Trevor Wilson, *The Myriad Faces of War* (Cambridge, Polity, 1988) pp.449–53; Edmonds, *Short History* p.229.

4   Chasseaud, *Artillery's Astrologers* pp.263, 285.

5   Richard Holmes, *Fatal Avenue* (London, Pimlico, 1993) p.1.

6   Chris McCarthy, 'No Body's Child: A Short History of Machine Gun Tactics', *Imperial War Museum Review* No.8 pp.63–71.

7   Report from 15th Division, circulated by GHQ, 23 April 1917, O.B./1782/A, SCL.

8   Cyril Falls, *Military Operations, 1917* Vol. I (London, Imperial War Museum, 1992) p.201.

9   Falls, *Military Operations 1917* Vol. I p.259.

10   See Jonathan Walker, *The Blood Tub: General Gough and the Battle of Bullecourt, 1917* (Staplehurst, Spellmount, 1998).

11   See the critical reports on recent operations issued by First Army, [No.1227 (G)], 3 and 9 May 1917, SCL.

12   Wynne, *If Germany Attacks* chapters IX and X.

13   Peter Bryant, *Grimsby Chums: The Story of the 10th Lincolnshires in the Great War* (Hull, Humberside Leisure Services, 1990) pp.99, 112–13.

14   Falls, *First World War* p.256.

15   Walker, *Blood Tub* p.196.

16   Sir Charles Harington, *Plumer of Messines* (London, Murray, 1935) p.79.

17   Ian Passingham, *Pillars of Fire: The Battle of Messines Ridge June 1917* (Stroud, Sutton, 1998) pp.66–71. This section on Messines leans heavily on this excellent book.

18   Passingham, *Pillars* pp.82–3, 111.

19   E. Norman Gladden, *Ypres 1917* (London, Kimber, 1967) p.61.

20   Quoted by Passingham in unpaginated section of *Pillars*.

21   Falls, *Ulster Division*, pp.94–5.

22   *The Attack of the British 9th Corps at Messines Ridge* (Washington, Government Printing Office, 1917).

23   Brown, *British Logistics* p.164.

24   Andrew A. Wiest, 'Haig, Gough and Passchendaele' in G.D. Sheffield (ed.), *Leadership and Command: The Anglo-American Military Experience Since 1861* (London, Brassey's, 1997) pp.77–92.

25   Andrew A. Wiest, *Passchendaele and the Royal Navy* (Westport, CT, Greenwood Press, 1995). See also William Philpott, 'The Great Landing: Haig's plan to invade Belgium from the sea in 1917', *Imperial War Museum Review* No. 10, 1995 pp.84–9.

26   C. Headlam, *History of the Guards Division in the Great War 1915–1918*, Vol. I (London, Murray, 1924) pp.225–55.

27   Second Army 'Notes on Training …' 31 August 1917, Monash papers, 3DRL 2316 Item 25, A[ustralian] W[ar] M[emorial].

28   Frank Mitchell, *Tank Warfare* (Stevenage, Spa Books, 1987 edn) pp.106–9.

29   See the advice on tactics in Kiggell to Army commanders, 7 August 1917, Acc. 3155 (116), Haig papers, National Library of Scotland.

[30] J.E. Edmonds, *Military Operations, 1917* Vol. II p.277.

[31] Introduction to Chris McCarthy, *The Third Ypres Passchendaele: The Day-by-Day Account* (London, Arms and Armour, 1995) p.11.

[32] Prior and Wilson, *Passchendaele* p.123.

[33] W.V. Tilsley, *Other Ranks* (London, Cobden-Sanderson, 1931) p.240.

[34] J.E. Edmonds, *Military Operations, 1917* Vol. II p.318

[35] Heinz Hagenlucke, 'The German High Command' in Liddle, *Passchendaele* p.53. See also German Werth, 'Flanders 1917 and the German Soldier', in *ibid.*

[36] Giordan Fong, 'The Movement of German Divisions to the Western Front, Winter 1917–1918', *War in History* Vol.7 (2), 2000, p.226.

[37] C.E.W. Bean, *The AIF in France* Vol. IV, new edition (St. Lucia, University of Queensland Press, 1982) pp.877, 881.

[38] Taylor, *First World War* p.194.

[39] J.E. Edmonds, *Military Operations, 1917* Vol. II p.xiii.

[40] Rob Thompson, 'Mud, Blood and Wood: BEF Operational and Combat Logistico-Engineering during the Battle of Third Ypres, 1917' (unpublished paper, 2000). See also J.E. Edmonds, *Military Operations, 1917* Vol. II pp.323–5.

[41] 'Administrative Report ... 1st Canadian Division at Passchendaele ...' 7 December 1917, MG30 E54 Vol 2 file 15, Phelan papers, NAC.

[42] Written by Siegfried Sassoon, who was not actually present at the battle. 'The Tablet' in *Collected Poems* (London, Faber and Faber, 1961).

[43] Falls, *First World War* p.286; Andy Simpson, *The Evolution of Victory* (London, Tom Donovan, 1995) chapter 6.

[44] John Hussey, 'The Flanders Battleground and the Weather in 1917' in Liddle, *Passchendaele* p.151. See also Peter Doyle, *Geology of the Western Front, 1914–1918* (Geologist's Association, 1998).

[45] Brian Bond, 'Passchendaele: Verdicts, Past and Present' in Liddle, *Passchendaele* pp.482–3.

46 Richard Holmes, *Western Front* (London, BBC, 1999) p.174.

47 'Lecture on Operations at Cambrai by General ... Byng', p.1, 26 February 1918, Phelan Papers, MG30 E54, Vol.1 file 3, NAC.

48 Captain J.R.W. Murland, *The Royal Armoured Corps* (London, Methuen, 1943) p.33.

49 Simpson, *Evolution* pp.105–6.

50 'Lecture on Operations at Cambrai by General ... Byng', pp.1–3, 26 February 1918, Phelan Papers, MG30 E54, Vol.1 file 3, NAC.

51 Bryn Hammond, 'General Harper and the failure of 51st (Highland) Division at Cambrai, 20 November 1917' *Imperial War Museum Review* No.10 (1995) pp.90–99; John Hussey, '"Uncle" Harper at Cambrai: A Reconsideration', *British Army Review* No.117 (December 1997) pp.76–91.

52 Report of Cambrai Enquiry, WO 158/54, PRO.

Chapter 9

1 Hubert Gough, *Soldiering On* (London, Barker, 1954) pp.176–8.

2 David French, 'Failures of Intelligence: The Retreat to the Hindenburg Line and the March 1918 Offensive' in Michael Dockrill and David French (eds.), *British Policy During the First World War* (London, Hambledon, 1996) pp.94–5.

3 Edmonds, *Short History* p.280.

4 J.E. Edmonds, *Military Operations, 1918* Vol.I p.258.

5 Anon, *The 54th Infantry Brigade 1914–1918* (Aldershot, Gale & Polden, nd, but c. 1919) p.127.

6 Signaller C.L. Leeson to 'Will', 29 March 1918, Leeson papers, LC, quoted in G.D. Sheffield, 'The Indispensable Factor: The Performance of British Troops in 1918' in Peter Dennis and Jeffrey Grey, *1918: Defining Victory* (Canberra, Army History Unit, 1999) p.82.

7 'Annex to G.H.Q. Summary of Information of the 10th April, 1918', Ia/48295, SCL.

8 J.O. Coop, *The Story of the 55th (West Lancashire) Division*

(Liverpool, 'Daily Post' Printers, 1919); 'Notes on Recent Fighting – No.7', 24 April 1918, SCL. I am also grateful to my colleague Dr Helen McCartney for sharing her as yet unpublished research with me.

9   Quoted in C.R.M.F. Cruttwell, *A History of the Great War 1914–1918* (Oxford, Clarendon, 1936) pp.518–19.

10   'Translation of a German Document' in 'Notes on Recent Fighting No.6', 19 April 1918, SCL (italics in original).

11   'Notes on the Offensive Battle' [translation of German document] in 'Notes on Recent Fighting March – 1918' (London, HMSO, 1918) pp.5–6.

12   Robin Prior and Trevor Wilson, 'Winning the War' pp.34–6, and Ian M. Brown, 'Feeding Victory: the Logistic Imperative behind the Hundred Days', pp.144–6, both in Dennis and Grey, *1918: Defining Victory*.

13   For a thorough assessment, see G.D. Sheffield, *The Morale of the British Army on the Western Front, 1914–1918* (ISWAS Occasional Paper 2, De Montfort University, Bedford, 1995).

14   Karl von Clausewitz (Michael Howard and Peter Paret, eds.), *On War* (Princeton, NJ, Princeton UP, 1976) pp.187–9.

15   Memo, 3 January 1918, GT 3198, CAB 24/37; Appx. to July 1918, WO 256/33, both PRO.

16   G.D. Sheffield, 'The Operational Role of British Military Police on the Western Front, 1914–18' in Griffith, *British Fighting Methods* pp.80–81.

17   Martin Middlebrook, *The Kaiser's Battle* (London, Allen Lane, 1978) pp.105, 300–18, 341.

18   Rudolf Binding, *A Fatalist at War* (London, Allen & Unwin, 1929) p.211.

19   Tim Travers, *How the War was Won* (London, Routledge, 1992) p.175.

20   Churchill, *World Crisis* Vol. II, p.1289.

21   Quoted in Paul Greenwood, *The Second Battle of the Marne 1918* (Shrewsbury, Airlife, 1998) p.193.

22   SS218, *Operations By the Australian Corps Against Hamel, Bois*

de Hamel, and Bois de Vaire, 4th of July, 1918 p.10. See also P.A. Pedersen, *Monash as Military Commander* (Melbourne, Melbourne UP, 1992) p.232.

23 Sir John Monash, *The Australian Victories in France in 1918* (London, Imperial War Museum, 1993) p.56.

24 Erich Ludendorff, *My War Memoirs* Vol. II (London, Hutchinson, 1919) p.679; Laurence V. Moyer, *Victory Must Be Ours: Germany in the Great War 1914–1918* (New York, Hippocrene, 1995) p.254; Robert B. Asprey, *The German High Command at War* (London, Warner Books, 1994) pp.449–50.

25 See Sun Tzu (Ralph D. Sawyer, translator and editor), *The Art of War* (New York, Barnes and Noble, 1994); Michael I. Handel, *Masters of War: Classical Strategic Thought* second revised edition (London, Cass, 1996).

26 W.H. Downing, *To the Last Ridge* (Sydney, Duffy & Snellgrove, 1998) p.135.

27 S.F. Wise, 'The Black Day of the German Army: Australians and Canadians at Amiens, August 1918' in Dennis and Grey, *Defining Victory* pp.23–4.

28 This account of Amiens is based on Prior and Wilson, *Command*, chapters 26 to 29.

29 Prior and Wilson, *Command* pp.313–15.

30 Downing, *Last Ridge* p.143.

31 S.F. Wise, *Canadian Airmen and the First World War* (Toronto, University of Toronto Press, 1980) pp.518–41.

32 Prior and Wilson, *Command* p.320.

33 As modern Dominion-based historians Prior and Wilson, and Wise, readily acknowledge.

34 Stewart, *NZ Division* p.458.

35 J.E. Edmonds, *Military Operations, 1918* Vol. IV p.514. See also J.E. Edmonds, *Military Operations, 1918* Vol. V pp.575–6.

36 J.P. Harris with Niall Barr, *Amiens to the Armistice* (London, Brassey's, 1998) p.296.

37 Quoted in Shane B. Schreiber, *Shock Army of the British Empire* (Westport, CT, Praeger, 1997) pp.79–80.

38   Niall Barr, 'The Elusive Victory: The B.E.F. and the Operational Level of War, September 1918' in Andrew A. Wiest and Geoffrey Jensen (eds.), *War in the Age of Technology* (New York, New York University Press, 2001). I am grateful to Dr Barr for letting me use this important article ahead of its publication.

39   C.H. Maginniss, 'Heads of Steel: Logistic Support to the BEF's All Arms Battle, July–November 1918', *British Army Review* No. 122 (1999) p.77.

40   Harris, *Amiens* pp.289–91.

41   Brown, *British Logistics* pp.197–204.

42   Haig's diary, 27 and 29 August 1918, in Robert Blake (ed.), *The Private Papers of Douglas Haig 1914–1919* (London, Eyre & Spottiswoode, 1952) p.325.

43   Schreiber, *Shock Army* p.110.

44   Harington, *Plumer* p.181.

45   Counting the German offensives in the area in spring 1918 as the fourth battle.

46   This account of the battle is based largely on Jackson Hughes, 'The Battle for the Hindenburg Line' in *War and Society* Vol.17 No.2 (October 1999) pp.41–57, and Prior and Wilson, *Command* pp.358–78.

47   J.F. Oakleaf, *Notes on Operations of the 108th Infantry Overseas* (Olean Times, 1921) p.12, at http://raven.cc.ukans.edu/~kansite/ww_one/memoir/Oakleaf/108th.htm

48   C.E.W. Bean, *The AIF in France* Vol. VI (St. Lucia, University of Queensland Press, 1983) p.994.

49   Asprey, *German High Command* p.467.

50   John J. Pershing, *My Experiences in the First World War* Vol. I (New York, Da Capo, 1995), p.12. See also Timothy K. Nenninger, 'American Military Effectiveness in the First World War' in Allan R. Millett and Williamson Murray, *Military Effectiveness* Vol. I (London, Unwin-Hyman, 1988) p.143.

51   Quoted in Donald Smythe, 'General of the Armies John J. Pershing' in Michael Carver (ed.), *The War Lords* (London, Weidenfeld & Nicolson, 1976) p.175.

52 Narrative by Unruh in Sidney Rogerson, *The Last of the Ebb* (London, Barker, 1937) p.143.

53 Account by William A Francis, Box WWI 1918–23, 2-A-1, USMC Archives, Quantico, Virginia.

54 James J. Cooke, *The Rainbow Division in the Great War 1917–1919* (Westport, CT, Praeger, 1994) p.239.

55 Quoted in Michael E. Hanlon, 'Shortcomings of the AEF's Tactical Doctrine' at http://www.worldwar1.com/dbc/doctrine.htm

56 Gregory Martin, 'German Strategy and Military Assessments of the American Expeditionary Force (AEF), 1917–18' in *War in History* 1994 1 (2) p.183.

57 Oakleaf, *Notes* p.13.

58 See 'Report … upon observations made on the Western Battle Front and in France' [May?] 1918, Box WWI, 1918–23, 2-A-1, USMC Archives, Quantico, Virginia.

59 James J. Cooke, *Pershing and his Generals* (Westport, CT, Praeger, 1997) p.111.

60 'Confidential report … of observations made … in France, May 13, 1918 to July 1 1918' p.8, Box: WWI 1918–23, 2-A-1, USMC Archives, Quantico, Virginia.

61 William O. Odom, *After the Trenches: The Transformation of U.S. Army Doctrine, 1918–1939* (College Station, TX, Texas A& M UP, 1999) p.39.

62 Paul F. Braim, *The Test of Battle* (Newark, NJ, Associated University Presses, 1987) p.153.

63 Cooke, *Pershing* pp.134–5.

64 David F. Trask, *The AEF and Coalition Warmaking, 1917–18* (Lawrence, KS, University Press of Kansas, 1993) pp.151, 161–2; Edward M. Coffman, *The War to End All Wars: the American Military Experience in World War I* new edition (Lexington, KY; UP of Kentucky) pp.329–33.

65 Cooke, *Pershing* pp.124, 152.

66 Jon Stallworthy, *Wilfred Owen* (Oxford, Oxford UP, 1977) p.286.

67 Niall Barr, paper given to the 2000 annual conference of the Western Front Association.

68 Anon, *A Brief History of the 30th Division from its Reconstitution in July, 1918 to the Armistice* ... (London, War Narratives Publishing Co., 1919) pp.48–57.

69 J.E. Edmonds, *Military Operations, 1918* Vol. V p.535; Marquess of Anglesey, *A History of the British Cavalry* Vol. VIII (London, Leo Cooper, 1997) pp.252–83.

70 Coop, *55th Division* pp.136–8.

71 A.H. Hussey, *Narrative of the 5th Divisional Artillery* (Woolwich, RA Institution, 1919) pp.34–6.

72 Appendix G to September 1918, WO 95/1775, PRO.

73 D.V. Kelly, *39 Months with the 'Tigers', 1915–1918* (London, Ernest Benn, 1930) pp.137–8. See also J.E. Edmonds, *Military Operations, 1918* Vol. IV p.378.

74 Travers, *How the War* chapters. 4–6; idem, 'Could the Tanks of 1918 have been war-winners for the British Expeditionary Force?' *Journal of Contemporary History* Vol. 27 (1992) pp.389–406.

75 My views on this subject have been informed by reading Harris, *Men, ideas and tanks* pp.159, 182–9.

76 Travers, *How the War* p.177.

77 Prior and Wilson, *Command* p.305; Peter Simkins, 'Haig and the Army Commanders' in Brian Bond and Nigel Cave, *Haig: A Reappraisal 70 Years On* (London, Leo Cooper, 1999) pp.95–7.

78 *JRUSI*, December 1998 p.82

79 Martin, 'German Strategy' p.178.

80 Martin, 'German Strategy' p.193; anon, *Why Germany Capitulated on November 1, 1918: A Brief Study based on Documents in the possession of the French General Staff*, SCL p.37.

81 Binding, *Fatalist* pp.220, 233, 238.

82 Horne to wife, 11 November 1918, Horne papers, Imperial War Museum.

83 John Terraine, 'Foreword' to Boraston, *Haig's Dispatches* p.vii.

Chapter 10

1   Cyril Falls, *Was Germany Defeated in 1918?* Oxford Pamphlets on World Affairs No.35 (Oxford, Clarendon, 1940) p.3.

2   Ian Kershaw, *Hitler 1889–1936: Hubris* (London, Allen Lane, 1998) p.97.

3   This account of the last days of Imperial Germany is largely based on Herwig, *First World War* pp.425–46, idem, *Hammer or Anvil* pp.215–18, and Asprey, *German High Command* chapters 43 and 44.

4   Diary notes of Oberst von Thaer, 1 October 1918 at http://www.hcu.ox.ac.uk/mirrors/www.lib./~rdhbyu.edu:80/wwi/1918/thaereng.html. See also Herwig, *First World War* pp.425–6.

5   Wilhelm Diest, 'The Military Collapse of the German Empire: The Reality Behind the Stab-in-the Back Myth', *War in History 3*, No.2 (1996) pp.206–7.

6   John Wheeler-Bennett, *Hindenburg: The Wooden Titan* new edition (London, Macmillan, 1967) p.197.

7   Herwig, *Hammer or Anvil?* p.218.

8   This is the conclusion of *The Economist* 'Millennium special edition January 1st 1000–December 31st 1999' p.38.

9   Niccolo Machiavelli (George Bull, trans.), *The Prince* (Harmondsworth, Penguin, 1975) p.37.

10   Bessel, *Germany After the First World War* pp.84–5.

11   Quoted in David French, '"Had We Known How Bad Things Were in Germany, We Might Have Got Stiffer Terms": Great Britain and the German Armistice' in Manfred F. Boemeke, Gerald D. Feldman and Elisabeth Glaser, *The Treaty of Versailles: A Reassessment after 75 Years* (Cambridge, Cambridge UP, 1998) p.86.

12   Fritz Klein, 'Between Compiègne and Versailles: The Germans on the Way from a Misunderstood Defeat to an Unwanted Peace' in Boemeke et al *Treaty of Versailles* p.205.

13   Alan Sharp, *The Versailles Settlement: Peacemaking in Paris, 1919* (New York, St. Martin's Press, 1991) pp.96, 124–5, 127–8.

14   For a sympathetic treatment of this claim, see J.F.C. Fuller, *The Second World War 1939–45* (London, Eyre and Spottiswoode, 1948) pp.17–23.

15   Quoted in Alan Sharp, 'A Comment', Boemeke et al *Treaty of Versailles* p.136.

16   Klaus Schwabe, 'Germany's Peace Aims and the Domestic and International Constraints' in Boemeke et al *Treaty of Versailles* pp.37–67.

17   J.M. Keynes, *The Economic Consequences of the Peace* (London, Macmillan, 1920) pp.1–2.

18   Sharp, *Versailles* pp.86–7, 100–1; Schwabe, 'Germany's Peace Aims' pp.63–4.

19   Winston S. Churchill, *The Second World War* Vol. I, *The Rising Storm* (London, Cassell, 1949) p.x.

20   First published by Hamish Hamilton in 1961; references are to the 1964 Penguin edition.

21   Gordon Martel, 'The Revisionist as Moralist – A.J.P. Taylor and the Lessons of European History, in Gordon Martel (ed.), *The Origins of the Second World War Reconsidered: The A.J.P. Taylor debate after twenty-five years* (Boston, Allen & Unwin, 1986) pp.1–16.

22   Taylor, *Origins* p.171.

23   Michael Howard, 'A Thirty Years' War? The Two World Wars in Historical Perspective', *Transactions of the Royal Historical Society* 6th Series Vol. III (London, RHS, 1993) p.176.

24   Etienne Mantoux, *The Carthaginian Peace* (Oxford, Oxford UP 1946).

25   Compare the essays of Sally Marks, Gerald D. Feldman and Niall Ferguson in Boemeke et al, *Treaty of Versailles*.

26   Zara Steiner, 'The Peace Settlement' in Strachan, *First World War* p.303.

27   Richard Overy with Andrew Wheatcroft, *The Road to War* (London, Macmillan, 1989) pp.26–7; P.M.H. Bell, *The Origins*

of the Second World War in Europe (London, Longman, 1986) pp.31–6.

28 Kershaw, *Hitler* pp.317–18, 322–5, 333–5, 379–80, 404–12.

29 The views in this paragraph have been informed by reading Howard, 'A Thirty Years' War?' and Bell, *Origins*.

30 Sheffield, 'Shadow of the Somme' p.36.

31 Martin Lindsay, *So Few Got Through* new edition (London, Leo Cooper, 2000) pp.248, 254.

32 Sheffield, '*Blitzkrieg* and Attrition' p.76.

33 Eric Hobsbawm, *The Age of Extremes* (London, Michael Joseph, 1994).

34 F.H. Hinsley, 'The Origins of the First World War' in Wilson, *Decisions* p.1.

35 H.G. Wells, *The Shape of Things to Come*, cited by Knock, *To End All Wars* p.1.

36 Robert M. Gates, *From the Shadows* (New York, Touchstone, 1997) pp.95–6.

37 Smith, *America's Mission* p.7.

38 Francis Fukuyama, 'The End of History?' in *The National Interest*, 16 (1989); Ralf Dahrendorf, 'Towards the Twenty-First Century' in Michael Howard and Wm. Roger Lewis, *The Oxford History of the Twentieth Century* (Oxford, Oxford UP, 1998) p.338.

The First World War as a Global War

This book has concentrated on the Western Front, and on the doings of the British and the Americans. It is important to remember that the Anglo-Americans fought as part of a coalition, and this brief survey of the war as a whole is intended to place their activities in a wider context.

1914

The first Allied forces to engage the Germans in the West were Belgian, when on 5 August the German army attacked the fortress of Liège. Belgian resistance was vital in delaying the Germans from initiating their main thrust through Belgium and into northern France until 18 August. The main Belgian army, commanded by King Albert, fell back on the great fortress-port of Antwerp, where, reinforced by a small British force, it tied down six German divisions and bought yet more time for the Allies. On 6 October the defenders evacuated Antwerp and made a stand on the River Yser, where they played a key role in holding off the German attacks north of Ypres.

The British actions at Mons and Le Cateau were part of a vast series of battles in which the French army bore the brunt of the fighting against the Germans. During the Battle of the Frontiers the French suffered heavy casualties in battles such as Morhange and Sarrebourg (20 August) and the Sambre (21–3 August). However, these actions played a part in disrupting the German advance, and at Guise (29 August) French Fifth Army delivered a stinging blow on the flanks of German Second Army. Space does not permit a detailed discussion of French actions in 1914. Suffice it to say that the French army was the mainstay of the Allied defences – by the end of the first Battle of Ypres, there were more French than British soldiers fighting in Flanders.

At first, French and British hopes and German fears that the Russian army would steamroller through East Prussia seemed well founded. However, between 26 and 29 August German forces inflicted a crushing defeat on the Russian army at Tannenberg. At the Masurian Lakes (6–12 September) the Russians suffered a further defeat and were bundled off German territory. However, the Germans had not won a decisive victory, for the Russians lived to fight another day. Indeed, in Poland, Russian forces won major victories over the Austro-Hungarian armies in the Lemburg campaign (September 1914). By December, the Austrians had suffered further humiliation by being thrown out of Serbia. Further fighting (the Battle of Lodz, 11–25 November) restored the Central Powers' position in Poland. At the end of 1914 the situation on the Eastern Front, as in the West, was deadlocked.

The first British offensive of the war took place in West Africa, when on 7 August a combined British-French expedition invaded the German colony of Togoland. By the end of 1914, the Allies had mopped up large portions of Germany's overseas empire. In Africa, however, the Cameroons held out until the beginning of 1916 and in East Africa, Colonel von Lettow-Vorbeck emerged as one of the greatest guerrilla leaders in history, remaining undefeated until he voluntarily capitulated after Germany had surrendered in Europe. At sea, the Royal Navy lost a squadron of obsolete ships off the South American coast

(Battle of Coronel, 1 November 1914) but gained revenge at the Battle of the Falkland Islands (8 December 1914). The German warships *Goeben* and *Breslau,* trapped in the Mediterranean, eluded the British fleet and sailed to Turkey, where they acted as the catalyst that brought the Ottoman Empire into the war on 29 October 1914.

1915

As in 1914, the French dictated the course of Allied operations on the Western Front during 1915. The BEF's offensive operations in May and September were fought to conform to the large-scale French attacks in Artois and Champagne. In 1915 Germany made its major effort on the Eastern Front. In January to March the Russians enjoyed some success, but in the Gorlice-Tarnow operation (2 May–27 June) German and Austrian forces created a major breakthrough in Poland. By September 1915, the forces of the Central Powers had advanced some 300 miles, capturing most of Poland in the process. However, the Russians succeeded in withdrawing their forces in surprisingly good shape.

The Serbs, who had fended off Austro-Hungarian invasions in 1914, were utterly defeated by a combined German-Austrian-Bulgarian attack launched on 6 October 1915. British and French forces, which had landed at the neutral Greek port of Salonika on 5 October, were unable to aid their Serbian ally. Bulgaria's decision to enter the war was influenced by the Anglo-French failure at Gallipoli. There, an attempt by British and French warships to force the Straits had failed on 18 March 1915. The initial landings at Anzac and Helles took place on 25 April 1915. A subsequent landing on 6 August at Suvla tried but failed to reinvigorate the campaign. Meanwhile, Turkish forces had invaded the Russian-held Caucasus in November 1914; indecisive campaigning was to continue on this front until 1917. A British force landed in Turkish-held Mesopotamia (modern-day Iraq) in late 1914, and in the course of 1915 was drawn further and further inland, aiming for Baghdad.

Italy, which in 1914 had been an ally of Germany and Austria-Hungary, remained neutral on the outbreak of war and in May 1915 actually joined the Entente. The Italians launched four attritional Battles of the Isonzo in 1915, trying and failing to break through Austrian positions towards Trieste and, eventually, Vienna.

In 1915, the main actions in the naval war were confined to the German U-boat campaign. The one major exception was the action of Dogger Bank, a clash between British and German battlecruisers that resulted in a tactical victory for the Royal Navy. In a new departure, the Germans used Zeppelin airships to conduct air raids against civilian targets in Great Britain.

1916

The twin struggles at Verdun (February–December) and on the Somme (July–November), the principal events of 1916 on the Western Front, were paralleled by Russian offensives in the east. The Russians launched an unsuccessful attack at Lake Naroch near Vilna (18 March), in response to French requests to relieve pressure on Verdun. On 4 June a Russian Army Group under Brusilov attacked on a 300-mile front and smashed an Austrian army. Two further pushes, on 28 July and 7 August, brought Brusilov to the Carpathian mountains. The campaign fizzled out in September 1916. The offensive did grievous damage to Austria-Hungary, which had to be propped up with German forces, but the loss of a million men further weakened the Russians. Austria-Hungary's problem was, for the Central Powers, somewhat balanced by the conquest of Rumania, which had entered the war on 27 August 1916. Victorious at the Battle of the Arges River (1–4 December), German forces occupied Bucharest two days later, leaving only a small strip of land under Rumanian control.

On the Italian Front, 1916 saw a continuation of the strategy of the previous year. The Fifth Battle of the Isonzo was fought 11–29 March, but on 15 May the Austrians attacked in the Trentino area (also known as the Asiago offensive), catching the Italians by surprise and gaining ground by the time the campaign wound down in mid-June. This Austrian victory was partially balanced by Sixth Isonzo (6–17 August), in the course of which the Italians took Gorizia. The attritional Seventh, Eighth and Ninth Battles of the Isonzo (September to November 1916) followed.

Turkey enjoyed mixed fortunes in 1916. On 5 June Arab tribes revolted in the Hejaz (now part of Saudi Arabia), beginning a guerrilla campaign that posed a threat to Turkish lines of communications. This campaign was to make the name of T.E. Lawrence ('of Arabia'). In Egypt, Turkish forces under a German commander attacked British forces in the Sinai peninsula and were driven back with heavy losses (Battle of Romani, 4 August). However, in Mesopotamia, a British force was besieged at Kut-al-Amara and capitulated on 29 April. Not until December did the British, now reinforced, once again take the offensive in this theatre.

At sea, 1916 was the year of Jutland (31 May), which was for the Royal Navy a far greater success than many believed at the time. The German High Seas Fleet ventured out into the North Sea on 18 August, but without a major contact resulting. Although the Germans continued to send surface raiders against the British coast, their main effort was now the U-boat campaign. The Battles of Verdun and the Somme marked the first occasions on which the struggle for control of the air was an integral part of a ground campaign.

1917

The two crucial events of 1917 took place away from the battle-field. The first was the entry of the USA into the war on 6 April, the virtually inevitable consequence of the German resumption of unrestricted submarine warfare on 31 January. While some sur-face actions took place, the main focus of the war at sea was the attempt by German U-boats to starve Britain into submission by sinking merchant vessels. The adoption of the convoy system by the British on 10 May was an important step in countering the German campaign.

The second was the Russian Revolution. The 'liberal Revolution' of March overthrew the Czar's regime and briefly seemed to revive the Russian war effort. The Russian army launched a major offensive, named after the War Minister Alexander Kerensky, on 1 July. After initial success the Germans counterattacked on 19 July, and followed this on 1 September with an offensive towards Riga. The failure of the Kerensky Offensive destroyed the credibility of the Provisional Government. With Russia in chaos, on 7 November Lenin's Bolsheviks seized power in Petrograd, triggering a civil war.

On the Western Front, the British Battle of Arras and the French Second Aisne and Third Champagne battles (collectively known as the Nivelle Offensive) were fought in tandem in April–May 1917. At this stage the Germans held the advantage in the air; British pilots remembered this time as 'Bloody April'. The Third Battle of Ypres ('Passchendaele') was fought from late July to early November, and was succeeded by Cambrai (20 November–3 December). The Italians launched the Tenth (May–June) and Eleventh (August–September) Battles of the Isonzo, the latter capturing some important ground. However, at Caporetto (or Twelfth Isonzo, 24 October–12 November 1917) a German-Austrian army inflicted a heavy defeat on the Italians, leading to British and French troops being sent to the aid of their ally.

In the Middle East the British, advancing from Egypt, fought three battles at Gaza, the gateway to Palestine. The first two battles (26 March and 17–19 April) resulted in stalemate. The third, also known as the Battle of Beersheba, on 31 October broke through the Turkish defences. Under the command of General Allenby, the British captured Jerusalem on 9 December. In Mesopotamia, British forces captured Baghdad (11 March) and continued their advance.

1918

Fighting on the Western Front in 1918 falls neatly into two phases. The first began on 21 March with the German attack on British Fifth Army, and concluded with the Second Battle of the Marne (15 July–5 August; the Allied counterattack began on 18 July). Phase two began with the British-Australian-Canadian-French offensive at Amiens on 8 August, and ended with the Armistice of 11 November. The events in France and Belgium decided the outcome of the First World War, but nonetheless occurrences on other fronts were significant.

Russia was lost to the Entente cause, yet inadvertently helped its erstwhile allies by continuing to tie down large numbers of German troops. Initially refusing to sign a peace treaty, Bolshevik recalcitrance prompted German forces on 18 February to renew their advance. This compelled the Bolsheviks to sign the Treaty of Brest-Litovsk (3 March) which brought the Russo-German war to an end. This did not bring peace to a Russia torn by civil war.

In June the Austrians attempted finally to knock the Italians out of the war. The high tide of the Austro-Hungarian advance came at the River Piave (15 June), where the Italians held the attack. In the autumn, the Allied (British and French as well as Italian) forces took the offensive and won a stunning victory at Vittorio Veneto (24 October–4 November). The Austrian army, and indeed the Austro-Hungarian Empire, was in a state of collapse. On 4 November the fighting came to an end, the Italians having finally seized Trieste on the previous day.

By that stage another of Germany's allies, Turkey, had already capitulated. Harassed by Lawrence and his Arab guerrillas, the Turks were struck by a major British offensive. From 19–21 September Allenby's forces smashed the Turks in the Battle of Megiddo (or Armageddon), and then followed up seizing Damascus (1 October) and Aleppo (25 October). In Mesopotamia, in October a British force captured the Mosul oil fields. Turkey dropped out of the war after signing an armistice on 30 October. The Russian town of Baku, taken but subsequently lost to Turkish forces by the British earlier in the year, was recaptured in November.

The Allied troops based at Salonika had fought some actions with German and Bulgarian forces in 1916 and 1917, but in September 1918 at long last the Allies launched a major offensive. Under the command of French general Franchet d'Esperey, the Allies defeated a mainly Bulgarian force at the Battle of the Vardar (15–29 September 1918). The Bulgarians capitulated on 29 September, and the subsequent advance brought Franchet d'Esperey to the Danube by the time of the Armistice with Germany.

German aircraft replaced the Zeppelin as the main means of bombing Britain during 1917, and for a time appeared to pose a serious threat to British cities. By the early summer of 1918 this threat had been mastered, and in turn British aircraft were bombing targets in Germany. These strategic bombing campaigns were mere pinpricks in comparison to those of the Second World War, but nonetheless they were harbingers of things to come. At sea, the most dramatic events of 1918 were the partially successful British raids on Zeebrugge and Ostende (23 April) and again against Zeebrugge (9 May). On 29 October the German High Seas Fleet was ordered to sea. This prompted a mutiny among the German sailors, adding to the crisis that brought the German Empire crashing down. After the Armistice the German Fleet sailed to the British base at Scapa Flow, where on 21 June 1919 German sailors scuttled their ships.

SUGGESTIONS FOR FURTHER READING

General

The best single-volume history remains Cyril Falls, *The First World War* (London, Longman, 1960). For the purely military side of the war, see J.E. Edmonds, *A Short History of World War I* (Oxford, Oxford UP, 1951). For historians, the First World War is a dynamic subject, with new ideas and interpretations being put forward at a bewildering pace. For snapshots of current thinking about not just the military and political history of the war but numerous other aspects, Hew Strachan (ed.), *The Oxford Illustrated History of the First World War* (Oxford, Oxford UP, 1998) is indispensable. For recent research on diverse and specialised topics, see the important collection of essays in Hugh Cecil and Peter Liddle (eds.), *Facing Armageddon: The First World War Experienced* (London, Leo Cooper, 1996). American readers might try Michael J. Lyons, *World War I: A Short History* (Englewood Cliffs, NJ, Prentice Hall, 1994), a superior college textbook that reflects recent research. Niall Ferguson, *The Pity of War* (London, Penguin, 1998) is a challenging and often controversial re-examination of various facets of the war.

Individual Countries

For Britain, see Trevor Wilson, *The Myriad Faces of War* (Cambridge, Polity, 1988) for comprehensive coverage of every aspect of the war. In John Turner (ed.), *Britain and the First World War* (London, Unwin-Hyman, 1988), a number of experts provide concise but authoritative analysis of important facets of the British war effort. Three more specialised books deserve special mention: Peter Simkins, *Kitchener's Army* (Manchester, Manchester UP, 1988), a study of the raising of the British New Armies, and David French's two-volume study of British strategy, *British Strategy and War Aims 1914–1916* (London, Allen & Unwin, 1986) and *The Strategy of the Lloyd George Coalition 1916–18* (Oxford, Clarendon, 1995).

For the United States see David Kennedy, *Over Here* (New York, Oxford UP, 1982), and Neil A. Wynn, *From Progressivism to Prosperity: World War I and American Society* (New York, Holmes & Meier, 1986). An older book, Edward M. Coffman, *The War to End All Wars: the American Military Experience in World War I* new edition (Lexington, KY, UP of Kentucky, 1998), still repays reading. For Woodrow Wilson, see Thomas J. Knock, *To End All Wars: Woodrow Wilson and the Quest for a New World Order* (New York, Oxford UP, 1992). Tony Smith's important book *America's Mission* (Princeton, NJ, Princeton UP, 1994) puts Wilson's ideals into a wider context.

For good coverage of all aspects of Germany's war, see Holger H. Herwig, *The First World War: Germany and Austria-Hungary 1914–1918* (London, Arnold, 1997).

The Origins of the War

For a judicious and accessible full-length introduction to this most contentious of topics, see James Joll, *The Origins of the First World War* second edition (London, Longman, 1992). A short book containing analysis and documents is also very useful: Gordon Martel, *The Origins of the First World War* second edition (London, Longman, 1996). For British foreign policy and strategy over the long term, see C.J. Bartlett, *Defence and Diplomacy: Britain and the Great Powers 1815–1914* (Manchester, Manchester UP, 1993) and Paul Kennedy, *The Realities Behind Diplomacy* (London, Fontana, 1983). Paul Kennedy's *The Rise and Fall of the Great Powers* (London, Fontana, 1989) sets the origins of the war into a broader context. For diplomatic efforts during the war itself, see David Stevenson, *The First World War and International Politics* (Oxford, Oxford UP, 1988).

Haig and Pershing

Haig has been much exposed to authors but John Terraine's admiring biography *Douglas Haig: The Educated Soldier* (London, Hutchinson, 1963) has yet to be superseded. See also, however, Tim Travers' important books *The Killing Ground* (London, Unwin-Hyman, 1987) and *How the War was Won* (London, Routledge, 1992), which are more critical of Haig. A recent collection of essays, Brian Bond and Nigel Cave (eds.), *Haig, A Reappraisal 70 Years On* (London, Leo Cooper, 1999) contains much important material that goes some way towards refurbishing Haig's reputation. John J. Pershing is also controversial, for some of the same reasons as Haig. There are several good biographies, including Donald Smythe, *Pershing: General of the Armies* (Bloomington, Indiana UP, 1986). A recent, more technical study is also very useful: James J. Cooke, *Pershing and his Generals* (Westport, CT, Praeger, 1997).

The Western Front

There are a number of good introductions to the military history of the Western Front. Richard Holmes, *Western Front* (London, BBC, 1999) and Andy Simpson, *The Evolution of Victory* (London, Tom

Donovan, 1995) are both readable and up-to-date introductions to the British experience. A large format 'coffee table' book, Peter Simkins, *World War 1 1914–1918: The Western Front* (Godalming, Colour Library Books, 1991) contains both an excellent text and outstanding photographs. It has subsequently been reprinted under different titles.

The BEF's 'learning curve' is best approached through three seminal books. Robin Prior and Trevor Wilson, *Command on the Western Front* (Oxford, Blackwell, 1992) is a military biography of Rawlinson, which rates as one of the most important books ever written on the campaign. Paddy Griffith, *Battle Tactics of the Western Front* (London, Yale UP, 1994) is just as valuable for the lower, battlefield level, while Bill Rawling provides an important case study in his *Surviving Trench Warfare: Technology and the Canadian Corps 1914–1918* (Toronto, University of Toronto Press, 1992).

The British Official History has many defects, but remains indispensable as a narrative of events. The Western Front is covered in the series edited and largely written by J.E. Edmonds: *Military Operations France and Belgium* (14 volumes, 1922–47). Originally published variously by HMSO and Macmillan, the entire series has recently been jointly republished by the Imperial War Museum and Battery Press.

Individual campaigns and battles of the Great War have received patchy coverage. While some have been examined by scholars using a full range of evidence, most have not. Richard Holmes, *Riding the Retreat* (London, Cape, 1995) is an off-beat and highly entertaining account of the early 1914 campaigns, part history, part travelogue, based on a trip across the battlefields on horseback, which has a serious historical purpose. 1915 remains something of a forgotten year as far as the Western Front is concerned; we lack an adequate modern treatment of Loos, for example. For the period 1916 onwards the picture is somewhat brighter. Martin Middlebrook, *The First Day on the Somme* (London, Allen Lane, 1971) was the first and remains the best of the histories written from the point of view of the ordinary soldier. Jonathan Nicholls, *Cheerful Sacrifice: The Battle of Arras 1917*

(London, Leo Cooper, 1990) does a similar job for Arras. Jonathan Walker, *The Blood Tub: General Gough and the Battle of Bullecourt, 1917* (Staplehurst, Spellmount, 1998) is a model history, well written, well researched, which throws new light on a controversial episode. There are now two major studies of Passchendaele: Robin Prior and Trevor Wilson, *Passchendaele: The Untold Story* (New Haven, Yale UP, 1996) and Peter H. Liddle (ed.), *Passchendaele in Perspective: The Third Battle of Ypres* (London, Pen & Sword, 1997). The latter is an extremely wide-ranging collection of essays which is invaluable in bringing to a wider audience scholarship that would otherwise be buried in the obscurity of academic journals. The curtain-raiser to Passchendaele is well covered in Ian Passingham, *Pillars of Fire: The Battle of Messines Ridge June 1917* (Stroud, Sutton, 1998). For 1918, see Malcolm Brown, *The Imperial War Museum Book of 1918: Year Of Victory* (London, Sidgwick and Jackson, 1998), which draws on the riches of the museum's archival holdings; Martin Middlebrook, *The Kaiser's Battle* (London, Allen Lane, 1978), the author's second treatment of a Great War theme; and J.P. Harris with Niall Barr, *Amiens to the Armistice* (London, Brassey's, 1998), a useful narrative history of the Hundred Days.

Recently, historians have begun to take a comparative approach to the military history of the two world wars. Two books give an excellent example of this approach: Paul Addison and Angus Calder (eds.), *Time to Kill: The Soldier's Experience of War in the West 1939–1945* (London, Pimlico, 1996) and John Bourne, Peter Liddle and Ian Whitehead (eds.), *The Great World War 1914–45* Volume I, *Lightning Strikes Twice* (London, HarperCollins, 2000).

Personal Experience

There are a number of books that attempt to capture the experience of the ordinary soldier on the Western Front. Among the best are: John Ellis, *Eye Deep in Hell* (London, Croom Helm, 1976); Denis

Winter, *Death's Men* (London, Allen Lane, 1978) and Andy Simpson, *Hot Blood & Cold Steel: Life and Death in the Trenches of the First World War* (London, Tom Donovan, 1993). The number of accounts by participants in the war is huge and continues to grow. Two of the finest are John Terraine (ed.), *General Jack's Diary*, republished by Cassell in 2000 (despite its title, for most of the war Jack was a regimental officer) and the memoir of a Regular ranker, John F. Lucy, *There's a Devil in the Drum* (London, The Naval & Military Press, 1992, originally published in 1938). For morale, see G.D. Sheffield, *Leadership in the Trenches: Officer-Man Relations, Morale and Discipline in the British Army in the Era of the Great War* (London, Macmillan, 2000); John Baynes, *Morale* (London, Cassell, 1967); John Keegan, *The Face of Battle* (Harmondsworth, Penguin, 1978); Richard Holmes, *Firing Line* (London, Cape, 1985); J.G. Fuller, *Troop Morale and Popular Culture in the British and Dominion Armies 1914–1918* (Oxford, Clarendon, 1991).

INDEX